V JEAN TYLER

V. Jean Tyler

FOLLOW ME

>>>>>>> → ← <<<<<<<

Edited and Published
d'Arblays Press

ALSO by V Jean Tyler

    FLASHBACK   - December 2002
    GRAINS OF SAND - January 2004
    RELEASE   - January 2005
    SURVIVAL   - March 2008
    GOING IT ALONE   - September 2008

This Edition first published in November 2010 by

d'Arblays Press
23 Brookbank Close
Cheltenham
Gloucestershire GL50 3NL

Printed and Bound in England by

Creeds – *Printers by Design*
Broadoak
Bridport
Dorset DT6 5NL

ISBN: 978-0-9548646-5-1

Front cover: King Penguins, South Georgia

Dedication

to my long-suffering family
who have not yet stopped me travelling

Acknowledgements

to Margot Collingbourn-Beevers of
d'ARBLAY'S PRESS
for her friendship and expertise

and

to the continuing camaraderie and encouragement
from the Torrington First Thursday Writers' Group

CONTENTS

Foreword

As I write this Foreword I'm remembering that it's sixteen years since my first "Going it Alone" venture up Kilimanjaro in 1993. The seven annual holiday diaries contained within the covers of that book, which didn't see the light of day until 2008, had a good reception. Thus encouraged I hope now you will "Follow Me" to share the next eight travel escapes.

I still make the choice, do the planning and leave home on my own, but once the journey starts, with all its anticipation and then the people and places, I am never alone. I can choose who I want to engage in conversation, be it other travellers, local people, staff, the enchanting wildlife – oh yes, I talk to them, and I'm not inhibited by having a close fellow traveller whose interests may be different and whom I would feel bound to consider. This sounds selfish: I suppose it is but it's what I do. It's freedom!

This series started in The Maldives, where I had just one week, and found myself in the happy company of two, younger, lady health service employees, one of whom had an advanced qualification in scuba-diving. She persuaded me to have a go. The underwater colours and movement of fish and weed were dazzling and could be gently touched as well as seen. When I went to Australia the following year because of a family association, I couldn't, at the end of the holiday, resist the scuba-diving off the Barrier Reef. There was a moment of sudden strange darkness down at 13 metres and Zoe, my instructor, pointed to a large Manta Ray hovering silently overhead. I was frustrated at not being able to express my excitement as it happened, but it made a good story afterwards!

The wildlife in Madagascar was magic but there was such a degree of travel mayhem that at times I really did wonder about the wisdom of travelling alone. I was the only member of the 'group'! Two young Malagasey guides, Benoît and Eldorique, together with the wealth of Lemurs of many varieties, may have made it the most special of all, even if I never did see that Aye-aye.

More recently this 'older woman' has fallen for the cruise experience, first to Antarctica where the blinding whiter-than-white everything, the sea life, (no, I didn't scuba dive, but I did swim for all of seven minutes in a thermal pool) and the birds – especially the Penguins which, like so many wild creatures could teach us humans a thing or two about parenting and family life – all added up to a cold but comforting continuity.

The Indian Ocean cruise was, of course, warm and wonderful, with a daunting number of passengers on board, but I managed to join the company of other retired medics. Our young lady guide, Robin, was an incredibly well qualified marine biologist, who dived deeper than any for her research projects, but who had that enviable common touch when it came to not only caring for her somewhat senior passengers, but also being able to impart her knowledge intelligibly and with infectious enthusiasm.

Friends ask, "Why are you going there?". Like most people I'm attracted by a 'good offer', by the prospect of special wildlife opportunities, and by family connections. It was Ruth, a niece working in Vietnam, who enticed me there. I spent time with her, living the real thing, and then joined a group for the 'tourists-must-see' experience: a perfect combination. The 'agent-orange' legacy of human deformity and bare earth is heart-breaking, yet the welcoming, industrious, cheerful population was like a phoenix risen from the ashes.

The visits to India to see my daughter Helen and family provided much-needed time to catch up with the growing family and, in 2002, having gone so far, I then went to Sri Lanka where the company was convivial without being intrusive, and I did so enjoy the elephants! I joined the family again for Christmas and New Year 2007/8, and went with them on their annual holiday to Goa. Here I was at last able to meet 'my' Pooja, at Rainbow House, run by the El Shaddai Street Child Rescue charity. It was her thirteenth birthday. When I have sold sufficient copies of this book to cover the cost of publication any profits will go to El Shaddai.

I've done a preparatory read of these eight travel diaries in quick succession and find I'm smug about my 'light luggage', moan about 'early mornings' and 'gastric turbulence', and buy a lot of earrings: trivia! I am just so thankful to have been able to appreciate all that this travelling about has had to offer. Gin has a celebratory mention from time to time, as do the, totally unrelated, occasional tumbles.

My orthopaedic surgeon icon, Mr Chris Mills, replaced my right hip just a few months before my last trip to India and I am totally mobile and free of pain. The left one is eighteen years old! Thank you.

The homecoming is always special because most of the time I'm very content to be here.

Autumn 2010

The
MALDIVES

with **THE TRAVEL COLLECTION**

MALDIVES MAGIC 2000

Sunday January 2nd

This is the day! The Shuttle Service is collecting me at 2.15 pm to take me to Gatwick for the start of my trip to the Maldives. I am 'in recovery' from flu and have not eaten anything worth mentioning since Tuesday. One of the family went down with it on Christmas Eve so I suppose it was inevitable that some of us would succumb. Yesterday I decided I could not go, and got out the insurance papers which seemed to indicate that, if I had a doctor's certificate, I could claim back everything except the deposit. I really do feel better today and have been longing for this break.

Lydia, of the Shuttle Service, was on time and I emerged with my luggage. I always intend to travel light, mainly because these days I do struggle with a heavy load, but it was weightier than I intended. We stowed it in the boot of her splendid vehicle, together with the hand luggage, which contained the camera, washing things, and a change of clothes just in case … I kept hoping I had done everything. I still feel it's quite a responsibility being solely in charge of leaving an empty house, especially when firing on only one cylinder. Good neighbours keep an eye on the property, and feed the sheep, during my absence.

We were not on the road very long before we were enveloped by fog. I was glad I had opted for the luxury of being driven. I had read in the travel information provided by The Travel Collection, through whom I had booked the holiday, that I should be at the Monarch desk three hours before the time of departure. This seemed a bit over the top, and the plan had been to give me two hours' booking-in time. In the event, the fog, and consequent sporadic traffic hold-ups, set us further and further behind schedule. Every now and then the knowing Lydia left the motorway in an effort to by-pass the problems and travelled along dusky country lanes and through places such as Wilton and Shepton Mallet.

The scheduled take-off time for Monarch flight 2018 was 8 pm and I presented myself at the desk at 7.15 pm, explaining about the fog etc. The smart unsmiling lady said the desk was closing and the boarding time was 7.30 pm, but she did the business and I made my way to the departure lounge, where I discovered the flight had been delayed until 9.15 pm. I suddenly felt hungry for the first time for days and was unexpectedly seduced by Harry Ramsden's fish and chips. The portion was enormous but I managed to put away most of it - much more expensive than Torrington's Taffs, and the batter not as crispy.

I heard someone comment about a flight delay until 10.45 pm and thought poor things, and then read that it was 'my' Monarch flight 2018: I was going to have more than that three hours' checking-in time. By now I had, of course, got shot of my main luggage, and had my hand luggage and person X-rayed. I went shopping for camera batteries at W H Smith and wished I'd got round to buying them at Torrington Lloyds with my discount card. I always find it a fascinating exercise watching the world go by at airports. There were the frail elderly, in wheelchairs, the middle-aged cheerful couples in holiday gear, often matching, middle-aged miseries making a meal out of the flight delays, a few honeymoon'ish-looking couples hardly able to leave each other alone, and lively youngsters with enviable energy and all their lives before them. One little chap of about three suddenly shot off away from his parents like a hand grenade with the pin pulled out.

The flight eventually took off at 10.45 pm, the third scheduled flight time, and I sat comfortably in F18, an aisle seat of a three-seat centre block. Next to me was a pleasant young couple who held hands most of the way. I ordered a gin and two tonics and was surprised to have to pay for the privilege. I picked at the indifferent meal - well, of course, I'd already had fish and chips. Some time now it became ...

Monday January 3rd

I slept for a couple of hours and then dozed on and off in between times. We approached Bahrain when my watch read 5 am and we were instructed to move the time on three hours, so it was suddenly getting-up time. We were required to take all our luggage off the plane. The airport transit lounge was pleasant and airy, and the hole-in-the-floor loo clean and sweet smelling. It was noticeably warmer and I changed into light trousers, and forced my thick black skirt and heavy sweater into my hand luggage. There was a one-and-a half-hour wait for refuelling etc, during which I did my usual people-watching, especially the Muslim ladies, and then continued reading Helen Dunmore's "A Spell of Winter", a beautifully-written tale of strange and powerful emotions, which made me feel sad.

Back in F18 I toyed with the leathery breakfast omelette but enjoyed the fruit and the fruit juice. We were scheduled to arrive at Male' at 5 pm their time, which necessitated another two hours' moving on of the watch, as the Maldives are five hours ahead of the UK. I settled for a sweet and sour vegetarian dish for lunch but by the time the service reached the no-man's-land of F18, there was only lamb. I have plenty of that at home, but it was very tasty.

The airport at Male' was buzzing with tanned, returning holidaymakers and pale, post-'flu arrivals like myself. My luggage was almost the last to arrive but, once outside, the welcoming warmth was like a comforting blanket. A Travel Collection representative directed us to a table under the trees, where we waited until everyone had been assembled and identified. As I had imagined, several of those I'd seen on the flight were to be fellow passengers on the Island Explorer. Our luggage was sitting on the quayside and I watched anxiously as my limp bag hung precariously at the edge, just waiting to be unbalanced and fall into the water. It was handed down safely into the hold and we were all helped aboard the small boat. I sat on top, next to a pleasant, well-rounded lady of around forty who introduced herself as June. She was travelling with a slimmer, possibly younger, lady called Julia.

I felt happy and warm as we made the short trip to the Island Explorer, which gleamed invitingly in the late evening sun. The crew helped us aboard and we were directed to the bar where the Captain gave us a few pointers and general information about the ship. My cabin was 8A - which was wonderfully convenient, being on the same deck as Reception and one deck below the restaurant and swimming pool. It sported a double bed which I am used to, and had the luxury of a porthole through which I could see the Indian Ocean if I looked sideways.

I unpacked and got myself sorted and suddenly felt very weary. I went to the bar and bought a rum and coke, or rather was asked to 'sign for it later', which seemed to be one of the touches of old Empire tradition on board. I deposited myself in a corner of the lounge where June and Julia found me, with their diet cokes. The room was tastefully festooned with hundreds of tiny fairy lights, which reminded me that, although Christmas and New Year were over, Twelfth Night was still to come.

The dining room was large, colourful, and attractively lit, with a vase of orchids on each table. I sat with June and Julia and felt relaxed and comfortable with their company. The long buffet bar gave out delicious and seductive aromas and offered an impressive choice of menu. Having been deprived of my sweet and sour dish on the flight over, I went for the sweet and sour fish for the main course and it was very good. Fresh fish was caught every day from the boat and I intended to go on one of the night fishing trips before the week was over. The sweets ranged from the mousses to dense chocolate sponge with black cherries. We had been advised not to drink the water from the tap, so I bought a bottle. It was all right but no water tastes like Heronslake well water.

I made for bed at 9.30 pm, feeling uncommonly tired even though it was only 4.30 pm UK time. It was about then that I realised the 'flu was still lingering. I was suddenly burning hot, my skin was on fire to the touch of my ice-cold fingertips, and my pulse was 140! I imagined myself being air-lifted to some intensive care unit. I thought the air-conditioning wasn't working, but it was my own system that was on the blink. I drank copiously, took cold showers, and eventually slept at 3 am - until 8 am, when I was relieved to wake and find myself limp but cool.

Tuesday January 4th

I ate a pile of fruit and drank several cups of tea for breakfast, to quench a considerable thirst. Maybe my symptoms had just been of dehydration. June and Julia arrived on the scene with their own individual teapots and fruity tea bags, which they had evidently presented successfully to the stewards on the flight on the way over. Our Island Explorer waiter-steward was a genial, smiling fellow who took it all in his stride, after registering a flicker of discernible surprise. After breakfast we all assembled with life jackets for the mandatory lifeboat drill, conducted by the Captain who made it all very clear, as he paced up and down like a university lecturer. Some of the passengers showed not the slightest bit of interest and talked amongst themselves. It reminded me of airline passengers who do much the same when the safety procedures are being explained. Even if they think they know it all, it seems very rude and ignorant.

This was followed by a snorkelling instruction session by the swimming pool (which was empty, so it was hardly a practical demonstration), given by Dieder, a young Belgian. He was pleasant, spoke charmingly accented English, and generally seemed to command more attention than had the Captain. Following the lifeboat drill, the boat sailed and most of us enjoyed the unaccustomed warmth by the pool, where I sat, or rather lay, on one of the very comfortable reclining seats, and jotted a few notes in the diary. I was glad of this lazy session to continue my 'recovery'.

I studied the other passengers. The boat accommodated something like seventy people, I think, but I reckoned that there was probably less than half that number on board, which meant that we had the undivided attention of the staff and plenty of room for manoeuvre. There were two families of mum, dad, and two daughters apiece. One 'set' looked Jewish and the attractive mum was busy doing paper work as she sat on deck. The daughters of the other family were younger, probably sixteen and fourteen. Dad was something of a better-upholstered version of René of "Allo! Allo!" fame. Mum was comely and caring, and seemed to do everything for the rest.

A couple of German ladies kept very much to themselves and I imagined, mistakenly as it turned out, that they understood little English. One was short and blonde with a pre-holiday tan and designer clothes, the other tall and rangy. I couldn't help surmising that they might be an item. There were two amenable men from London, one in his late forties who had a broad knowledge of literature and music and who had had a variety of fascinating jobs, the other much younger, charming and diffident, who reminded me of an older, titled acquaintance. My psychosexual counselling training led me to wonder about their relationship but, by the end of the week, I knew they were simply sharing a cabin. I couldn't help my mind wandering like that: old habits die hard. A thirty-something couple looked like Glastonbury material. He was tall, unshaven, had very long hair and took giant strides. She was very slim, had spiky blonde hair, round shoulders and a winning smile. The female half of an Italian couple was seriously addicted to sunbathing. She was dark brown, with a wrinkled face, and a mouth that turned down at the corners. Her tolerant man hung about in the shade, responding to her every whim. Like the German lady she wore impressive designer beachwear but of much smaller sizing. Several older couples (probably younger than me!) glanced at the pool, now filled with water, and disappeared, no doubt to sit somewhere else.

Lunch was good and I selected a variety of salads with rice and pasta and very fresh white rolls. It was so long since I had eaten white bread that I'd forgotten how good it could be. The Island Explorer, after passing a selection of tempting distant islands, had now put down its anchor in the South Male' Atoll and a trip to the Laguna Beach resort, an island at the northern end of the Atoll, was scheduled for the afternoon. The first boat which came alongside was for the divers, the second came to the opposite side from where some of us were waiting and it was full by the time we'd moved across, so the third boat was ours.

I had always imagined that pictures I'd seen of these islands had been taken with some colour-enhancing lens but, as we approached Laguna, the turquoise sea, the white sand, the lush green vegetation and the blue sky were breathtakingly beautiful and real. The neat accommodation buildings blended into the landscape and were in no way intrusive. Cheerful Bougainvillea, Hibiscus, Oleander, and other flowering shrubs I could not name, of innumerable shades and hues, lined the winding path which June, Julia and I took, dilatorily, to the beach beyond.

It was many years since I had snorkelled, probably the last time was during a family holiday in Spain, close on thirty years ago. I had managed to find my snorkel but it had perished and gone all sticky, so I'd thrown it out. Son-in-law Trevor had kindly lent me his, so I was about to try it out. June and Julia were very experienced snorkellers, and dear June took great pains to make sure that I spat into the mask and then got all strands of hair from underneath it. I imagined we'd have to swim a long way out but no, the reef was within easy striking distance and in a few minutes I was marvelling at the variety, colours and unexpected numbers of fish. I found myself smiling broadly with delight, which wasn't very sensible for this broke the seal of the snorkel! Blue, green, red, yellow, black, and white fish and various colour combinations swam into view, in and out of the coral on all sides. It was magic: I had got to find a chart to identify some of them.

Afterwards, we sat in the shade and chatted. June and Julia were disappointed with the snorkelling, having had other recent experiences with which to compare it, and sad to see the dead, white coral, reputedly the effect of El Niño. June said, "I knew it wouldn't be all that wonderful. Building such as there is here is not allowed in areas where the diving and snorkelling are really good." Julia went off on a wander while we stayed put until it was time to walk round to the other side of the island to the waiting boat. She returned with fish fridge magnets, cards and a new dress she'd bought at the island shop.

During the brief crossing back, a lone Seagull flew above us. We'd seen just two Parakeets on the island, and one of the London men said he'd seen what he thought was a Dipper of some kind. Where are all the birds? Once back on board the Island Explorer, I bought a fish identification chart and then went to the cabin for a shower and hairwash. I couldn't get the water to flow through the shower and, as I was already stripped off, didn't fancy calling the steward but made do by crouching under the tap, making a mental note to report the matter.

At 7 pm I went up to the sundeck, to the Captain's cocktail party. June and Julia were absent and the steward steered me in the direction of two London gents, Nigel and Daniel, with whom I was happy to sit. I enjoyed a Bucks Fizz, some imaginative snacks and good conversation. June arrived later at dinner alone: Julia was not at all well, bad headache and vomiting. Sounded as if it might be her turn to be dehydrated or something, poor thing. Afterwards I talked to the young blonde girl. She had been diving and it sounded amazing. I went into the lounge to watch the film about scuba-diving - I felt that I must have a go. I eventually went to bed and had a much better night than last night.

Wednesday January 5th

I was still coughing when I was writing this, but I had slept well. The Island Explorer took off at about 4.30 am. I had found the motion soothing, but by 8.30 am there was quite a swell. I indulged in a generous helping of the fresh breakfast pineapple and drank several cups of tea. There was no sign of June and Julia while I was in the dining room.

Suddenly someone jumped up from a neighbouring table and ran over to the picture-porthole window: several of us followed suit and there, only a few yards from the boat, were several Dolphins surfing the water, and every now and then exposing most of their shining bodies to the morning sun - lovely, and such easy viewing.

I went to enquire about the diving but there was no-one at the Diving School on the lower deck, and yesterday's information was still on the locked door. I made for the swimming pool, where the water was sloshing about over the reclining seats with the movement of the boat. I found a comparatively dry patch and watched the seascape, as islands near and far were left behind in their turn. Other passengers emerged to look at the view. One lady in the most enormous sunhat turned tail when the hat almost took off in the wind: there'd be no retrieving it here! Others tested different seats for shelter from the wind, as well as shade from the sun. It was tempting to imagine that one might not get burned in the pleasant breeze. I hadn't used any sun barrier cream yesterday, and had got just a slight redness on my chest and the tops of my feet, although I had worn the recommended T-shirt while snorkelling. I was wearing covering shoes today.

I really needed a book about the Maldives and went to see what they'd got in the shop. I liked the look of Royston Ellis' "Guide to the Maldives" at fifteen dollars and bought it. I understood that books were cheaper at the airport but I hadn't thought about it on the way out and didn't want to wait until the return journey. I had the time and the inclination now. I went to find the Diving Instructor again but still no sign of him at the School. I went to Reception to enquire and was told that he would meet me at the Diving School now. In truth I wasn't really sure I had the bottle for this ... I found myself making excuses such as the 'flu, my age etc.

The young Belgian instructor, Dieder, was charming and encouraging and said he'd "taken down a man of 84." (A cynical friend, to whom I recounted this later, enquired as to whether he'd brought him up again.) It was all booked for the next day, when I was to present myself for the theory session at 9 am. This would be followed by a 'testing session' for safety procedures etc 'not far below the surface', and then, if all went well, a 'proper' dive. We anchored at 1 pm off Ifuru in the lovely Raa Atoll. June and Julia appeared for lunch, Julia pale but recovering. She decided not to opt for the visit to Ifuru in the afternoon but to have a quiet time on board.

June and I went snorkelling and she encouraged me to go much further out than I would have done on my own. I could see the coral was more varied, and very obviously regenerating, with an infinite variety of fish weaving in and out. There were shoals of tiny bright fish, large Parrot fish, Butterfly fish, Angel fish, Gobies, blue-striped Snappers, Pipe fish, Cleaner Shrimps, Wrasse, Moray, an oedematous black Starfish, and a host of others which I could not identify in spite of studying the chart. I snorkelled for about half an hour and then sat under the trees, above which several large Fruit Bats obligingly came into view. There were a few Hooded Crows about and I heard a familiar call, a Coucal perhaps? On the return trip we saw a solitary Grey Heron. There are reputed to be thirteen different species of Heron in the Maldives.

The shower was now working so I had a comfortable clean up. I hoped my hair would not fall out with the shock of being washed so often. At 7.15 pm we returned to Ifuru for a BBQ supper. The little boat had no navigation lights, and the way was lit by a large, hand-wielded, torch. The crew had been busy earlier in the day, draying equipment and ingredients to the island. It was a delicious meal with Barracuda, red Snapper and Emperor fish on offer, together with baked potatoes, rice and plenty of salads. There were several sauces, one a superb garlic sauce that I specially liked.

June asked the chef if it was a trade secret or could he give her the recipe. He said he would but I never did hear whether they pursued the matter. We sat with Nigel and Daniel and shared their bottle of dubious South African wine. They were nice company and I was a little taken back when Julia objected to Nigel smoking an innocent Cheroot. Admittedly he did ask permission which was probably his mistake. Being a gentleman he went on walkabout. There was a moonless sky, full of a million stars which eclipsed the lights of the Island Explorer on the dark water.

Bodu Beru dancers arrived, all male but one dressed as a woman, and presented their energetic display, passing leaves to some of us who were encouraged to join in and then pass the leaf on to another. It was fun and most of the holidaymakers took part. On the short walk back to the boat we watched Hermit Crabs of all sizes as they skittered along the shore.

It was nearly 11 pm by the time we got to the ship. I lay awake for a while, wondering about the wisdom of the morrow's scheduled scuba diving.

Thursday January 6th

This was the day! At 9 am I met up with handsome Dieder and endeavoured to absorb the theory, which he whisked through, no doubt for the n'th time, in his strongly accented English. He fitted me up with goggles and flippers. I'd said size 6 shoe, but after trying on the size 6 flippers he decided they were too small. I questioned his decision, having visions of a larger size falling off somewhere in the hidden depths. However, on removing the size 6 flippers, I could see the tops of my bunions looking unhappily red. Dieder knew best.

At 10 am we departed in the divers' boat for Ifuru. There were racks for the air bottles and resuscitation gear. An unsmiling Maldivian diving assistant sat opposite, eyeing me with undisguised scepticism. We anchored near the shore and I donned flippers, mask, 4 kilograms of weights on a belt around my middle, a depth meter on my left wrist, and then the weighty air-bottle-aqualung strapped into the adjustable buoyancy lifejacket - which seemed to weigh a ton and which ground me down into the sand from whence we were commencing the exercise. Dieder went through all the signs and safety measures which we'd discussed during the theory session but now it was for real. We shared air, filled the mask with water so that I had to use the clearing technique (I wasn't too keen on that), gave a signal of distress - a sort of horizontal oscillation of the right hand - and checked depth, pressure and air levels. We were only about ten feet under. We swam around for about 45 minutes, and I enjoyed even more of the splendid little fish. By this time my jacket was slightly inflated and we surfaced.

I was helped to strip off my apparatus and was told there would be a twenty-minute break before the real thing. I hadn't been sure whether the whole exercise was over but this was just the beginning. I went and sat in the sun in my snorkelling T-shirt and realised that I'd been quite cold. I talked to Petra, a very attractive blonde German girl, reputed to be a trainee travel representative. She was quite charming but incredibly vague, and I wondered whether she'd ever make the grade.

A signal from Dieder indicated that this was action time. He took the boat out into the lagoon and I got togged up again with some assistance on board. I was then requested to "walk off the boat on to the water". It was a strange feeling but Dieder held my hand,

6 January 2000

OFF IFURU - SURGEON FISH

which was very reassuring. Once submerged, we descended after a little deflation and my left ear started to pain quite acutely. I did the right hand thing and pointed to the offending ear. We ascended again and repeated the pressure-levelling exercise of blowing against closed nose and mouth. It seemed OK but, after going a little deeper, the pain returned and we repeated the exercise several times before it felt comfortable. I thought about my recent 'flu and how I'd signed the diving form to say I was fighting fit.

We swam along the reef, going down to 13 metres. It was like being on the slopes of a very high mountain. The fish were everywhere, some in sizeable shoals. One such shoal of Neon Fusiliers, eye-catching in their orange and blue florescence, turned as a body, in and out of the light, like a flock of Lapwings in the early morning sun. It was all so breathtaking (just with the wonderment) and there was so much to see that I just could not recall everything afterwards. A pair of Turtles moved lugubriously over a flat pocket in the wall of the coral. Dieder pointed to two larger fish some distance away and told me afterwards that they were White-tipped Reef Sharks, although I have to admit I didn't get a very good view of them. There were strange Sea Slugs, huge Sea Anemones and coral of every shade. After a while Dieder signalled that it was time to go up. I was amazed to discover that we had been down there for 55 minutes and I suddenly felt very shivery. We surfaced slowly, inflating a little as we went. Dieder removed my heavy gear in the water and then climbed up into the boat with his own gear still in place and carrying mine. Oh, to be so young and fit.

We went back to the Island Explorer, where I had a luxuriously long hot shower and hair wash, then went and sat on deck in the sun, had a coffee and wrote up the day's account. Lunch was very welcome and I chose the beefsteak from Sri Lanka followed by two helpings of yoghurt and honey and plenty to drink. I was still very thirsty, and experienced diver June pointed out that the scuba diving air is very dry. She was one of those who had encouraged me to have a go, and was delighted that I'd been and done it, as it were. She was surprised that I'd stayed down for nearly an hour. I had had that luxury of one-to-one instruction. Petra made timetable announcements over the intercom: she sounded like Gladys Pugh in "Hi-de-Hi", with a different accent.

That afternoon we went further north into the Raa Atoll and at 3 pm we anchored and went ashore on Ungoofaaru, the capital of the Raa Atoll, with 1,100 inhabitants. It was uncomfortably hot. Ramadan was not yet over and there was hardly a soul about. After a brief guided walk round the town, during which we saw the school and the neat, well-ordered-looking little hospital, I retreated to a grove of Coconut Palms, took some pictures and sat in the shade. I was feeling a bit weary after the morning's excitement. Later I joined other overheated passengers in the shade on the little boat, and then realised I'd left my sunglasses by the palms. I retrieved them with all haste, which made me hotter still.

Back on the Island Explorer I had a leisurely swim in the pool, and then changed for dinner before going to the t'ai chi session on the sun deck. Except for the diving man with the long hair, only women joined in although I noticed several men seated around, ostensibly reading their books, but casting frequent glances in our direction. The supper moussaka, was very appetising and I gave myself a large helping, followed by a delicious black cherry mousse.

The Captain, supported by some of the staff, gave a talk on the Maldives and fielded around all sorts of questions about the government, health, education, and religion. He admitted to having two wives. He had little to say in answer to my question about the birds but assured me that there were "plenty somewhere". Julia was none too well again and June persuaded her to see the doctor immediately, before the night got any older. They had called him out at midnight previously and he had been very frosty and given them a selection of pills accompanied by rapid glib instructions in his strong Indian accent, which they had had difficulty in understanding. He had promised to "follow up" the next morning but had made no contact. On this occasion he didn't seem to remember her, but was distinctly more civil. I went to bed at 10.15 pm and couldn't get to sleep for a while. I was re-living the dive: I had done it!

Friday January 7th

I went to the Diving School after breakfast to get my logbook filled in but there was no one about. We went ashore at Kudakurathu, an uninhabited island of white, white sand, surrounded by the deep turquoise water, under a threatening sky. June, Julia and I walked along the beach in the sultry heat, and I found myself longing for some rain. I put on the sun lotion and the insect repellent, wondering whether anyone made

7 January 2000
KUDAKURATHU - Turquoise Water : Grey Skies

a combined preparation. I'd been badly bitten on my bottom at Laguna on the Tuesday and wanted to prevent a repeat performance.

Putting on the mask and snorkel I had another good hour with lots of fish but also more of the sad, dead, bleached coral. I took some pictures with the underwater camera but the best fish always seemed to swim out of view just before I'd got my act together. Julia had recovered and we sat and talked on the beach while June stayed snorkelling.

We had an excellent BBQ lunch of Emperor fish and Jackfish, under the trees. The skies became heavier but we opted not to go back on the 2 pm boat. June and Julia went on an 'explore'. I was idle and lay down on the Travel Collection towel, with grey skies threatening rain rather than sunburn. I dozed a little and then took a walk towards the pick-up point. The heavens opened and I put the towel around me and made for the woods, where I stood with others under an inadequate rush shelter, which soon leaked all over. I had not been so wet since the Okavango trip, this time last year.

At 2.55 pm we walked out through the downpour in the direction of the pick-up boat, anchored off the decrepit landing stage: there was no sign of life but a cacophony of noise from the dripping would-be passengers woke the crew, who donned elaborate waterproofs and brought the boat in. They contrasted incongruously with our attire of bathing costumes, shorts and sodden towels. We were shown inside down below where it was warm and dry, and where there was evidence that the two-man crew had been having a siesta - and why not?

It was a good drip back into cabin 8A, where I unpacked the wet things and had a hot shower (this bit definitely more luxurious than the Okavango experience). It was still grey and threatening outside but the rain had stopped. I ordered a pot of tea and made for the comfortable Neptune lounge and wrote my diary. In the fullness of time, a pot of coffee arrived instead of tea, but I said not to worry. He didn't charge. The rain lashed down again and I suspected that the deep-sea fishing trip at 5.30 pm, for which I'd booked, might well be cancelled. I hadn't brought waterproofs. At 5 pm Petra made the expected announcement - that the trip was off. When I heard the rain and saw the turbulent waters, I wasn't sorry.

After dinner the crew entertained us in the Karaoke lounge with more of the Bodu Beru dancing and got most of us to join in. I sat with Nigel and Daniel. 'Rene' spontaneously took over one of the drums and played like a professional until the perspiration poured down his face. His performance brought a well-earned enthusiastic round of applause from the audience, not least from the crew. June and Julia arrived late and took other people's seats while they were dancing! A short session of Karaoke followed, by which time many of the participants had left.

I joined June and Julia on deck to watch the flying fish - from which spectacle they had dragged themselves away with difficulty earlier. I could see why. Every now and then one would go literally over the top and land on the deck. Their backs were dark blue and streamlined like Swallows, and the 'wings' shone like jewelled lace in the lights of the ship. They brought to mind a cross between a bird and an exotic insect. Julia took a picture while June held one of them.

This was Julia's second exciting picture of the day. During the afternoon's rain, when most of us had left Kudakurathu on the 3 pm boat, they had been still on their 'explore' on the other side of the island, where the shoreline had been more rugged and rocky. They'd come across a White-tipped Reef Shark and a Stingray in the same shallow shore pool. I wished I'd stayed with them, rain or no rain!

We watched the Flying Fish for some time. They swam against the tide, sometimes skimming the water like a flat stone, at other times propelling themselves several feet into the air. It was a stunning display. I think I preferred it to the Bodu Beru dancing! We eventually turned ourselves in at 11.30 pm

Saturday January 8th

The ship set sail again at 6 am. I was vaguely conscious of the throb of the engines and by the time I was properly awake at 8.30 am, we had arrived off Milaidhoo in the Baa

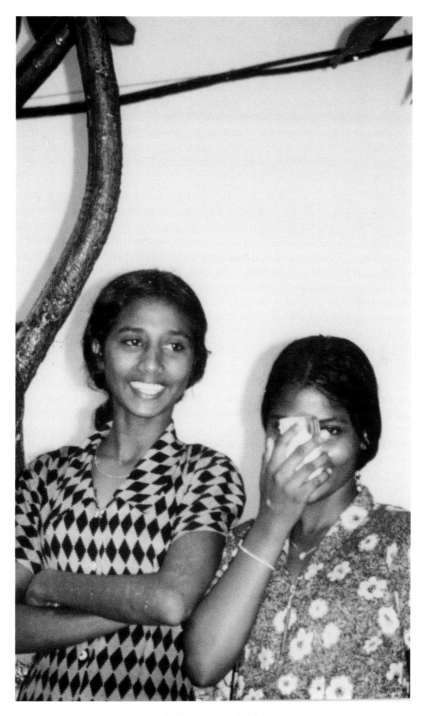

8 January 2000
KAMADHOO FACES
Intrusion!

Atoll, a picture postcard of an island surrounded by that Maldives' white sand and the turquoise sea. The sky however was heavily overcast but somehow this accentuated the intensity of the turquoise and white.

At 10 am we departed for Milaidhoo, and the rain started as soon as we arrived there, which doesn't really matter if you're snorkelling. I don't think I'd ever get bored with these colourful lively fish: I took a whole film of 27 shots. The coral was mostly colourful with its own life, as well as that of the fish, and I enjoyed it for over an hour. I felt free and unencumbered without a covering T-shirt and copious dollops of sun factor – well, it was very grey and I was looking well seasoned and brown.

We had a lunch of good goulash on board and then, just after 3 pm, we were off again, this time to Kamadhoo, a lovely inhabited but unspoiled island. The people were very relaxed and friendly: the fact that Ramadan was just over may have had something to do with their spirit. I bought a Dolphin carved out of coconut wood and three charts of the Maldives fishes. The rain came on heavily again and 'Rene' offered to put the latter under his arm with his wife's charts. I declined and managed to cover most of their length with a plastic bag.

We saw the little school which seemed well ordered: the sides were open all along its length so I couldn't help thinking about the lack of surfaces for posters, but an "owl babies" natural history chart was sandwiched between the blackboard and the ceiling. The blonde German lady asked whether she could go into the Mosque but the guide said no-one could be admitted just now as it was prayer time, and that in any case, women were not allowed inside. Surprisingly to most of us but to the guide in particular I suspect, from the confused expression on his face, she said "But I am a man! ... "

The Fruit Bats were with us again. Unlike other bats, they are not nocturnal. It rained all afternoon and we dripped back on to the Island Explorer. The plan had been another evening BBQ on Milaidhoo but the weather put paid to that. We ate the BBQ in the shelter of the Karaoke lounge. I chatted to Nigel and Daniel. I had imagined Nigel to be in his late fifties but discovered he was only forty-eight.

The evening's entertainment was also brought on board and we watched the lovely lady Bandiya dancers of Kamadhoo perform elegant traditional numbers, sometimes with cooking pots and other workaday props. The movements were accompanied by strange, high-pitched singing.

There were a couple of very thin learners at our end, who watched their mentors closely, smiling at the successes and the slip-ups. They were all dressed in long blue floating garments and matching headoblongs over their dark hair. One of the guests, an American gentleman teaching in Beirut, took a series of polaroid pictures and gave them to the dancers. They seemed delighted.

It had been another great day and although it was only 10.45 pm I felt ready for bed.

8 January 2000

SPACE AND SHELTER

Sunday January 9th

Last day! The rain had stopped. We were off to Kurumba, another island at the southern tip of the North Male' Atoll, where Kurumba Village was the equivalent of the island's Grand Hotel. This was the first resort to open and was still considered the best - large, rambling, luxurious and set tastefully in spacious grounds, with clear pathways and masses of colourful flowers. We took pictures at the entrance to this five-star emporium and then wandered across to the beach on the far side. We dumped our gear and gathered together three reclining chairs as a base. (Julia, our shopaholic, had gone off on her own for a while.)

We were just preparing for a good snorkel when a German gentleman came and informed us that two of the chairs were numbered and belonged to him! The third was pretty decrepit but good enough to hold our possessions. The snorkelling lived up to expectations. I was going to miss this. My left ear ached a bit, so may be it was time to give it a rest. I lay on the towel under a comfortably cloudy sky and tried to imprint the snorkelling scenes on to my mind's inner eye for ever.

The clouds cleared and it became really hot again as we went the long way round back to the boat at 12.30 pm. There was a proper, well-maintained landing stage here. During lunch the hitherto unsociable blonde German lady made some derogatory remark in perfect English about the food on board - something to the effect that the quality dropped a little each day. I really could not agree with her: I thought the food was excellent and suggested that her standards must be higher than or different from mine. She didn't speak to me again and I made a mental note of the fact that she understood English very well.

The afternoon boat for Male' was late and I waited outside with a couple of solicitors from Stow-on-the-Wold. He worked in an ethics department and she was in practice with her father. He was a quietly spoken, calm young man whereas she was anxious to talk, seemed quite opinionated, and struck me as a powerful lady. It was a half-hour ride to Male', and here there was the bustle of people arriving and leaving in numerous boats, and visitors and locals walking up and down the quayside and the roads beyond. It was a week since we had seen so many humans.

Our guide took us to the outside of the Mosque but, as it was prayer time (again), any look inside was destined for later in the afternoon. The public park looked very attractive through the locked gates. It was explained that this was because today was the post-Ramadan public holiday. It seemed strange to lock a public park on a public holiday. The municipal building was draped with patterns of tiny lights, just like every other building of any importance. It must look amazing at night.

We were then taken to the fish market which was something else: fish of all sizes, colours and shapes were set out in rows, heaps, clusters over a wide area of stone floor, and there was plenty of bartering. Equally impressive was the indoor food market, where we sampled (and bought) tiny sweet bananas - quite the best I've ever tasted, "Bounty" - which was like a long roll of compressed, sweetened coconut, tightly contained in a swathe of Palm leaves (also delicious), and pinkish coconut and honey oil.

Shopping was next on the agenda and we were taken up a narrow staircase to a pre-arranged venue, where the array of goods of all kinds was overwhelming. I did much searching and finished up buying a long, wrap-around skirt-trousers (difficult to describe but very clever design) in wonderful colours of jade, scarlet, amber and black, a pair of shell earrings, and some postcards. The proprietors gave us a welcome free drink.

Some of us then returned to the Mosque where we took off our shoes before mounting the elegant marble steps. The building felt uncluttered and airy, and from the broad gallery we viewed the carpeted central area, which holds 5,000, and which, according to the guide, is "often full". The worshippers ranged from very young boys to elderly grey-haired men. There was an area roped off for women. The white lining of the golden dome, the shiny marble floor, the screened shutters, the colourful stained glass windows and the chandeliers all played mesmeric tricks with the filtered sunlight. I stayed for a while.

We were due back at the Landing Stage 1 at 5.30 pm and I was relieved to find it early. I chatted to an elderly lady who'd been keen on the t'ai chi. I had spoken to her husband earlier, a pleasant man with a strong St Helens' accent who thought I'd been a lecturer on some Saga cruise they'd done! June and Julia joined us. They'd been flirting with the locals and Julia, true to form, had spent a small fortune. Petra was leaving us to do a stint of training on the island and gave us all enthusiastic double kisses. There was a lovely fresh breeze on the half-hour return trip to the Island Explorer. Once aboard we demonstrated our purchases to each other, and then I made for 8A, showered, and put on my new skirt and earrings and a vaguely toning top.

It was settling-up time and I collected my bar bill, which included the diving fees. I had some ancient travellers cheques in American dollars, which made the exercise comparatively painless, and I topped it up with cash of the same currency, keeping enough to tip our lovely waiter, the Diving Instructor, and the cabin steward. The German lady was scrutinising all her individual bills and making grunting noises.

Dinner was late tonight and eight lucky people, who had had their cabin numbers pulled out of a hat the previous evening, ate at the Captain's table at 8 pm. Julia studied my 'top' and said "Is that from M and S?" "No, I don't think so" I replied, "I hardly ever shop there. It'll be from some catalogue". I contorted myself to expose the label: it read "Marks and Spencer"! She's not a shopaholic for nothing. A tuneful little band, playing '70s songs (and three of them could really sing), entertained us on the sundeck afterwards. I sat with the solicitors and another pleasant couple and really enjoyed the night, the music and the company. Only about half the guests were taking advantage of all this. It seemed a shame: miserable lot.

Suddenly someone shouted "Dolphins" and we all rushed to look over the side; and there they were, several of them, circling round and leaping out of the water, gloriously visible in the lights of the ship - another magic moment.

Julia appeared later: she and June had been busy packing. I went to my cabin just before midnight and packed most of my stuff.

Monday January 10th

This really was the last day! I got up in good time to have breakfast with June and Julia, who were leaving at 9.30 am with the majority of the passengers, to spend a second week on Full Moon, another island in the south of the North Male' Atoll. I felt envious but it was entirely my own choice to take just the one week. We chatted while they waited for the boat. Nigel was threatening to come and see me in Devon, and I knew June and Julia intended to pay me a visit. We'd exchanged addresses and telephone numbers and the girls had given me cards to post at the airport: I had this feeling I might forget. I waved them all goodbye as the little boat drew away. I returned to the poolside for my last two hours of sun. It was bliss. I didn't mind if I got burned that day!

I talked to the Jewish lady, who was keen to tell me that she was a Magistrate and had also just completed a law degree. I murmured that I had served on the Bench for 25 years, latterly as Chairman. She was London based, with nearly 200 Magistrates. She asked the size of 'my' Bench and said how "sweet" to have only 20 members! We talked about her elder daughter, who had done well to get her PADI diving certificates, ordinary and advanced, during the week. She had got on well, very well, with Dieder who, her mother now told me, had got the sack for 'fraternising' with the guests: this decision was as a consequence for some attachment the previous week. It seemed a bit hard. A little later I heard the diving belle, with the minimally-bikini'd fulsome bosoms, ask her father longingly if it was possible to get the train to Belgium. He looked across at me from the other side of the pool and raised his eyes to heaven! He's obviously quite a guy, this Dieder.

Time was running out. I dragged myself away from the pool, got dressed and finished packing. We sat and waited for the boat to take us to Male' and then the airport. The Jewish lady was again holding court and telling of her legal interests and qualifications and how she was now doing GCSE English and Maths because she was going to teach Law and everyone involved in education had to have them. I volunteered that no-one had asked me about my School Certificate subjects when I took on the sex education slot at the local secondary school. This sparked interest from the blonde-haired diving lady who said she'd worked for the Family Planning Association for seven years but now worked for a vet.

The boat arrived at 12.30 pm promptly, and half an hour later we were off-loading our luggage and looking for trolleys. 'Rene' very kindly gave me one of the extra ones he'd commandeered. We paid our 10 US dollars airport tax and then joined a very long and slow-moving queue for the usual formalities. Flights were arriving and leaving and the airport was crowded. I was hungry and made for the departure restaurant where I devoured a cake and drank Sprite. I sat at the same table as an attractive coloured girl who had spent a week in Male' with her still-white son, who was now costing her a fortune on crisps and other snacks. I saw the young girl I'd sat next to on the way out. She'd had a wonderful time and was well tanned.

I tracked down the Coral Reef Field Guide, which June had recommended, and which proved to be an excellent buy. I also bought three fish fridge magnets and an underwater video.

The plane took off on time and I settled down into my H17 aisle seat and read the Coral Reef book. I sat next to a young couple from Oxford. He'd qualified as a diver before he'd gone to the Maldives - sensible fellow. That's what I intended to do next. There was the usual re-fuelling stop in Bahrain and ultimately we were just half an hour late at Gatwick.

Lydia and I missed each other initially, mainly because one of the exits was under repair, which necessitated going a long way round. The drive back was uneventful and speedy. Once home, I retrieved the envelope and cheque (which I was supposed to have given her on the outward journey but which I'd left on the desk in the living room), and by 5 am I was curled up in my own bed, in my own house. Nothing quite like it.

The next morning, when I had the strength to unpack etc, there were the cards from June and Julia winking at me from my handbag. The local post office confirmed my suspicion that in no way would Maldives stamps qualify for delivery here, so of course I had to add the celebratory British Millenium variety. June rang me after she had returned home following their second week. It had gone well and she was ringing to thank me for posting the cards. They'd arrived very quickly! June was a Community Psychiatric Nurse who I imagine gave her all - she had a special, warm charisma.

Julia was an Occupational Therapist who worked in the community and they had worked together in the same team in various fortunate parts of the country, but lived in different areas now.

I've taken the plunge, just theoretically up to now, to start a scuba-diving course at the end of February at the Barnstaple Leisure Centre ...

A RECONNECTION

AUSTRALIA

with **WEXAS INTERNATIONAL**

AUSTRALIA 2000

Sunday December 17th

The BT wake-up call at 4.30 am found me, uncharacteristically, not only awake, but already up and about, and wondering whether it was really such a good idea to make for the other side of the world at this time of year. Over the last forty-two years, apart from two notable exceptions – one, a Christmas with elder daughter Wendy, a few days after my mother's funeral, and another with on-call veterinary son Richard - I have cheerfully done the family Christmas with all the cooking preparations, decorations, present-opening, and ask-the-neighbours-in for Christmas-morning drinks - not to mention all the seasonal singing commitments - and I've loved it. I've felt well blessed and privileged.

This year Charles and Helen, the two younger siblings and their families, are going to their respective in-laws, Richard is on call again, and Wendy and Trevor have wisely opted for a quiet Christmas (as quiet as it can be with three young children) in their lovely, recently acquired, converted barn home. I am a sun-worshipper, rarely sitting in its rays, you understand, but enjoying outdoor tasks, and an invitation to spend Christmas in Australia from a tenuous family connection (the nature of which will become clear as this diary progresses) prompted me to think that this might be a good year to break the mould.

I've indulged in January sun-seeking adventure holidays since I've been on my own for the last nine years, and this would be, well, just going away a bit earlier. It had been another indifferent summer, and the dreariness of the grey autumn had been intensified by serious flooding - which had, literally, spilled over into early winter. I would go. I made the decision and booked the whole trip before I had time to change my mind.

I booked the Shuttle Service, my indulgence over the last four years. I justify the expense by quoting the cost of parking at Heathrow for nearly three weeks and, depending on check-in time, the added cost of overnight accommodation in some impersonal establishment near the airport, not to mention the hassle of driving there and back on my own. The minibus arrived promptly at 5.15 am, driven by Neil, ex Customs and Excise he told me, and highly energised.

We called at the Durrant House Hotel in Bideford to collect a hung-over honeymoon couple who were off to Lapland to ski, as well as to see Father Christmas, and who had an awful lot of luggage. We changed vehicles in Tesco's car park where we were joined by, dare I say it, an elderly lady who had lived much of her life in Singapore and who was to spend Christmas in California with her daughter and family. Here was I, going just about as far away from my family as it was possible to be. I felt a pang of conscience - guilt, remorse, or some such thing? We drove through the dark dawn into a murky drizzle and I thought of the sun. As ever, I was amazed to see all the vehicles on the road so early in the morning, especially on a Sunday. Not surprisingly, the newly-weds slept for the entire journey.

Our driver David, who emanated calmness and efficiency, made good time and dropped me at Heathrow's Terminal 4 at 9.15 am: take-off time 11.15 am. The Qantas desk was immediately visible, and I joined the queue at the end of the maze of the continuous-roped section. I asked politely for an aisle seat if possible. My legs get stiff if I sit for more than half an hour but I guess with all the recent media high profile given to DVT, others had asked earlier. I should perhaps have taken a lesson from a pink-clad Barbara Cartland look-alike, who persisted hysterically with the same request and succeeded.

We boarded the 744 and I discovered that 30B was the middle seat in a threesome on the port side of the plane. I was there first and put my hand luggage overhead. I was joined by a tired-looking, almost silent, Australian on my left (he just said "my pleasure" when I asked him to unscrew the cap from my red wine) and an attractive young Australian girl called Natasha in the aisle seat on my right. She was homeward bound for Queensland after an unhappy three months of working as a hairdresser for some Norwegian cruise line based in Miami. The itineraries and the idea of cruising had seduced her but she had soon become disenchanted with the twelve-hour day, poor accommodation, food, and pay, not to mention the majority of the well-heeled American passengers with their commanding tones, 'boring hairstyles', upstairs-downstairs culture and "How lucky you are to be doing this job!" She had left before the end of the contract and was looking forward to surprising her parents. I always feel slightly ill at ease with hairdressers, imagining they are studying my unimaginative bun style of fifty years, and yes, they're so right, I never use them!

I studied the in-flight magazine, as one does, and extracted for my sister an article on Kodaikanal International School in India, where one of her daughters had been a pupil. The plane was forty minutes late taking off but I wasn't too bothered. It would knock some time off the unconscionably-long scheduled wait of eleven hours in Singapore. I dozed and kept moving my legs about. It was dark at 2.30 pm and it was only then that I realised that the meal at lunchtime, of stir-fry beef, water chestnuts and mange-tout, had in fact been dinner. We were now embarking on evening and night and the next meal to be mentioned would be breakfast.

I dozed for an hour or so and then started Norman Tattersall's autobiography. Through my singing teacher, Sheila, I have had a couple of masterclass sessions with this extraordinary musician: originally a mechanical engineer, then soldier, then celebrated soloist, and finally international teacher and adjudicator. I became totally immersed and read the whole hundred pages straight off. I tapped on the mini personal TV to discover that Perth is eight hours ahead, so the flight was not as long as it sounded (it'll be longer coming back!). I adjusted my watch accordingly and then sat back and composed an appreciative letter to Norman in my head.

We arrived in Singapore on time. It is an amazing airport: spacious, immaculate, with a minimum of intrusive noise (how do they do that?), artistic motifs, and masses of plants including extensive displays of pink and white Orchids. I now calculated that I had twelve hours to wait there. Natasha had thirteen before her flight to Brisbane. I began to admit to myself that maybe I'd been foolish not to take friends' advice and spend a night or two in Singapore. I'd told myself I hadn't the time. What was I, retired or not?

We walked round the well-appointed shops and Natasha bought some duty-free whisky for her unsuspecting father who would be thinking she was still in Miami. We sat outside in a colourful cactus garden. It was warm and humid and we retreated back into the air-conditioned inside. There was a positive hedge of white Orchids being watered by a caring employee who removed any fading foliage. A collection of purple Orchids was arranged around a waterfall, above which was an imaginative painting of outsize colourful butterflies on the ceiling. Further along, paintings of players' masks and fans reminded me of the Mikado.

However pleasant, it was pretty wearing waiting about as the hours ticked slowly by. I had wholemeal cheese sandwiches at lunchtime, and Natasha went for a chicken pie, which was served with some dreadful chips that she returned and got her money back. By 4.30 pm Singapore time (still only 8.30 am UK time) we were in a state of collapse - Natasha on the floor and me on a chair, with my feet on my hand luggage.

Natasha's blond hair and long elegant body, clad only in a scanty white halter top and khaki miniskirt, atttracted much passing male attention as she lay sleeping. She had a whorly tattoo at the nape of her neck, a bracelet-like tattoo on her left wrist, a pierced tongue, which I'd espied when she laughed, and evidence of various other facial piercings, not currently in use. I felt maternally protective as I kept an eye on her and her luggage. She was twenty- six, so I could well have had her as my daughter when I was a little older than the age at which my daughter Wendy had had her Genevieve. I dozed and fantasised.

Eventually 6.30 pm came and it was time for me to check in at Gate C17. We said our goodbyes and exchanged addresses. I wished her a happy surprise home-coming and Christmas.

I had a window seat 51J and found myself next to a chatty girl, Nicole, from Frankfurt, where she was doing a PhD in Meteorology. She was engaged to an Australian, doing a PhD in Maths in the States, and they were meeting up at his parents' home for Christmas. I felt very sleepy and slept intermittently through the stupid American rubbish on the TV. My pre-dinner request for a gin and ginger ale brought the usual checking query from the steward. The meal was a repeat beef stir fry with inferior vegetables. I slept for a couple of hours and then woke to find it was 12.25 am and we were nearly there.

On going through customs I was asked whether I'd had contact with farm animals and of course I mentioned my sheep, whereupon I was whisked off for further questioning. The unsmiling lady interviewer could only be described as 'crisp', with an accent and overall in keeping. I answered all her questions about my minimalist flock and was allowed into the country.

I had had this nagging anxiety about the possibility of Elizabeth and Ian, my hosts, not being there to meet me for some reason. I had only their Coromandel farm address and no idea of the whereabouts of their house in Perth, and had neither of the telephone numbers. I was mightily relieved to see them standing the other side of the barrier, smiling and waving. My luggage appeared early and we were soon in their car, driving through the pleasant suburbs of Perth and arriving at their home in Cleopatra Street, in the Palmyra district, at around 2 am. I suddenly felt wide awake and we talked and drank tea till 3 am. They could not have been more welcoming. I determined to look at the interesting pictures on the walls tomorrow.

I had arrived!

Tuesday December 19th

Monday had been swallowed up with travelling and time changes. I slept until 5 am and then again until 11.15 am. It was very quiet. I sat outside in their pleasant little courtyard, had coffee and toast and talked to Liz. The air was warm and welcoming and not at all humid. There were interesting bird songs and I saw Common Bronzewing Doves, White-fronted Honeyeaters, Woodswallows, and what I think were Little Crows.

Liz and I went to the other side of the city to collect a couple of folding garden chairs which were to be a Christmas present for Michael (Ian's son) and family. I have never seen such a collection of camping and outdoor equipment as they had at that store. Well, I suppose they do have the weather here! All along the route and back, I was aware of the many coloured Bougainvilleas, the mauve-flowered Jacarandas, Oleanders, Hibiscus, flowering Eucalyptus, and many others yet to be identified! A couple of Pelicans flew gracefully across the sky in front of us on our way home. Ian was waiting when we got back: he wanted to take the car, a Volvo 240 Estate, to get the dashboard light repaired. Liz and I talked again, mostly about the times when she and John's younger brother, Philip, were married. We had not seen each other since both of them had died, Philip ten years ago and John nine years ago.

Ian returned with the repaired vehicle and we did a tour, looking first at the Bell Tower, which housed the bells from St Martin in the Fields, London. They were to have been smelted and recast into something less heavy for the sake of the church tower, which was showing signs of wear - but were saved by Perth in exchange for Australian metal to cast the lighter version. No-one could tell me why Perth had been thus favoured. The modern tower was handsome and quite a tourist attraction.

Perth was a beautiful city with wide views of the River Swan from the highway and a long avenue of Eucalyptus trees in King's Park, each tree named in memory of someone who had been killed in the First World War. The peeling barks created a kaleidoscope of colour to the tall trunks, from deep orange to silver. We went to look at the University where Philip had been a professor. The buildings were impressive, especially Winthrop Hall, and were set in delightful grounds. A lovely open-air theatre, excellent sports facilities and a charming grass quadrangle (with an abundance of Willie Wagtails) all contributed to the very good memories I have of the place.

We toured the suburbs next, and saw the houses where Philip and Elizabeth had lived, the first small and full of character, the second larger and more modern. Elizabeth indicated the area where she'd been to school, the schools where Andrew and Julia (Ian's children) had boarded, and the house where she, Elizabeth, had lived with her parents.

We called at Liz's brother's house to deliver an engagement present but Alphonse was not yet home. Liz spoke to his landlady living next door, an elderly farmer's widow with comfortable carpet slippers and a snow-white bun.

We drove on to the Surf Café, a spacious establishment with a sheltered glass-walled area for eating outside. Clumps of Evening Primrose marked the shoreline and Australian Gannets made impressive high-speed dives into the water. The evening had turned cool (by Australian standards) so we went inside. Ian opted for a steak and Liz and I wallowed in a seafood platter for two, while we watched a golden sunset over the white surf. Good wine and warm talk: these two were great company. I couldn't have had a better first day in Australia. And so to bed, at 11 pm.

Wednesday December 20th

We got up just after 8 am, had breakfast and packed. We were going to the sheep farm but making stops on the way and taking two days about it. We drove south from Perth through a pleasant town called Pinjarra and then on to Dwellingup ("up" means "fresh water", Ian explained.) After Philip and Elizabeth had divorced, Philip had lived somewhere in the vicinity but neither of us could remember the exact address, so Ian asked at the local store. A very helpful lady, who had known and liked him, gave us directions. "He was very happy here", she said. We motored some way following her directions to Hollyoake and eventually came across a house which looked a possibility. We drove up the drive to be greeted by a dog and a little girl. Her father spoke to us. The house we sought was further on.

A young man, Carl, in mining in the north, now owned the property. He was positively charming, welcomed us and gave us coffee. This was his country retreat. He hadn't known Philip but he chatted amiably about the area. I espied his Kilimanjaro certificate, framed and hung on the wall, and dated the year I had been there, so we talked about that. Finally, we took commemorative photographs, thanked him for his hospitality and got back on the road. We were very quiet in the car: I felt we'd laid a ghost. It must have been more disturbing for Elizabeth.

We came to Milltown with its huge sawmills and all the dwellings clustered round them. Carl had told us how the business is now being conducted properly, with good management and replanting. We stopped for lunch and when Ian went to pay the machine would not take his credit card so I tendered mine, which was also rejected! But the proprietor accepted my UK cash, which pleased me as I wanted to pay for something. We passed through a place called Pintard (an alternative for 'pintade', the French for guinea fowl?) of which I remember nothing. I do remember seeing plenty of cattle during the drive afterwards: some looked like Fresians, but others resembled South Devons, which was unlikely I suppose.

At Yarloup it rained heavily, splashing on lakes in the vicinity and plopping off the Karri Trees. Bunbury (reminded me of Oscar Wilde), Bridgetown and Manjimup all took our attention. At Pemberton we bought some wine at a drive-in cellar and then went and located our reserved Wattle Cottage (Mimosa to me) in a holiday park, Pump Hill Farm Cottages: a glorious Bush setting. The rain had stopped and we walked to a very high

Karri Tree with footholds up to 61 metres. We didn't go up: it looked dangerously wet and slippery. A colourful Western Rosella settled on my shoulder and Liz took a picture, but it came out as a rainbow blurr! We identified an Australian Magpie-lark, a Fairy Wren and Black Swans.

We ate at the local restaurant: a good meal of snapper, followed by cheese cake, all enhanced by the Jacobs Creek wine we had bought earlier in the day, the establishment being of the BYO (bring your own) variety. We returned to Wattle Cottage and chatted cosily by the wood-burning stove. The night was quite cool by my standards: I was being broken in gently. It had been a day full of interest and at times charged with emotion. We went to bed well after midnight.

Thursday December 21st

I slept well but was aware of heavy rain during the night. I watched Laughing Kookaburras from the picture window. I hadn't realised until then that Kookaburras are in fact Kingfishers and of course they look just like outsized versions. The massive bill, black above and horn below, makes them less elegant, I thought, than some of their relatives. I remembered that old Girl Guide song:

> The Kookaburra sits in the old gum tree
> Merry, merry king of the bushes he
> Laugh Kookaburra, laugh Kookaburra
> Gay your life must be!

and that's exactly what they did. They raised their tails when they came in to perch and somehow reminded me of Wrens, of all things.

There were various domestic pets on the estate and we saw a trailer load of children (not classed as domestic pets, of course) excitedly feeding very tame cattle and ponies. We left the lovely Wattle Cottage and took the road to Walpole (echoes of writers and a Statesman). The vegetation was lush and the Karri Trees very tall. We stopped mid-morning for coffee but Ian had a 'Devon cream tea'. Pots of thriving, flowering shrubs lined the pavement at the side of the café and in particular I noticed a really beautiful full-blown, full-blooming Abelia. So that was how it was supposed to look! I thought of my scantily-clad, angular version at home and remembered that I had not put it in the greenhouse. For the first time, I wondered what the weather was like in Devon.

We stopped at Normalup and parked by the entrance to Tree Top Walk in the Valley of the Giants: this forms part of the National Park of Western Australia. Ian opted to stay in the car and listen to the cricket. It was a strange experience being so high up near the tops of the Tingle (=Gum=Eucalyptus) Trees with, literally, spectacular bird's eye views. There was a kind of Oak Tree, which looked more like a Tamarisk to me, and plenty of Wattle with the yellow cotton bud flowers. On the ground it was possible to see the very broad base of the Tingles, made up of superficial roots spreadeagled over a wide area and necessary to give sufficient support in the light sand: in fact I found the trees almost more impressive from below. Blue Forget-me-not-like flowers covered either side of the paths, interspersed with delicate pink blooms.

We returned to the car but, when Ian attempted to start it up, it was evident the battery was flat - too much radio? He rang the RAC from the ticket office but then a German trio, who came and parked their people carrier next to the Volvo, offered to help. Ian got out his jump leads and fixed them between the two vehicles for some considerable time, without success. I talked to Connie, the mother, and she told me of their exciting year's trip round Australia, carrying with them most of what they needed: in her 'normal life' she was a teacher of the blind. In the meantime there was the problem of what to do next, as it was likely to be hours, even a day, before the rescue service got to us. "The distances are rather different here", volunteered Elizabeth when I raised my eyebrows. The man of the other party, Eric I think, suggested that his jump leads should be used. Ian admitted that it was years since his had been put to the test. There then followed a complicated unpacking exercise before Eric's jump leads were located. Once put into use, Ian's car started almost immediately and we were all delighted. A pair of Australian Ravens wailed their objection to the associated pollution - or their approval to the fact that we were going - and a Grey Currawong foraged and 'clinked' at the edge of the car park. We motored on through Denmark to Albany.

Albany was a very pleasant town, with large administrative buildings and mechanism for transferring the grain from a vast surrounding region on to boats in the harbour. I wished we had had more time to explore the secluded harbours, the Vancouver Arts Centre and Torndirrop National Park but I did get the flavour of the place, not least from excellent fish and chips which we went for, after finding our chosen hotel closed. We talked to another local farmer's wife while we waited for the feast. She was tall, blonded, and an 'Essex girl' who was going on a visit to England (business class with 'Air Miles') in the New Year.

We drove past, amongst other colourful vegetation, a clump of brilliantly orange-flowered 'Christmas trees' on our way to an attractive new suburb, where we sat in the car and ate our supper in view of a stretch of peaceful coastline. Corrugated roofs are traditional but one or two of the newer houses were tiled.

We were now en route for 'Coromandel', the farm. The forested areas (some of which had been planted - with tax concessions for the owners - in an attempt to restore areas that had previously been cleared) gradually gave way to low, more sparse, vegetation. The Blue Stirling Mountain Range on our left made a dramatic backdrop to the darkening evening sky and crimson-tipped sunset clouds. The route was lined by colourful shrubs, notably the Banksia with its large cylindrical candle-like flowers, ranging from green through vibrant tan to bright yellow. Personalised post-boxes, decorated with kangaroos, birds, and flowers, at farm entrances, reminded me that there were people living in this apparently deserted landscape. We saw a few Aberdeen Angus and some Hereford cattle.

At last, as darkness fell, we turned into Coromandel, or at least into the long red road that led to it. Ian said "Look!" and stopped the car and then backed up a little. He had spotted a Kangaroo lolloping across the landscape. Being aware of us maybe, it 'froze' for a while, making an impressive dark silhouette against the twilight sky. I felt excited and found myself smiling broadly.

On reaching the farm, it was discovered that Michael (Ian's son) and his family had already left for their Christmas break in Perth, so immediate attention was given to the Kelpies - Mate and Choco - and to the large, lovable, but practically useless Tippy, a Huntaway: this breed was not mentioned in my comprehensive dog breed book. Ian and Elizabeth sorted and read some of their Christmas mail. Ian was quite stunned by a very good letter, which he asked me to read. It was from a friend of his, previously 'David', who had changed sex and become a 'Diana'. For my part, I was delighted to read how helpful had been his GP and the two consultants involved in his counselling and treatment. Ian and Elizabeth knew my particular interest and we had a sort of seminar over coffee.

I was feeling comfortably welcomed and settled at this sheep farm in Australia, somewhere I'd fancied being for a long time.

Friday December 22nd

I awoke at 5.30 am and took a picture of an unimpressive dawn (which didn't come out) and then slept again until 8.30 am. After breakfast I went with Ian to see the sheep. He drove the Volvo to the farm buildings where we collected the grain and got into the Nissan. There was this feeling of space, which seemed to go on for ever, as far as the eye could see, but the earth was burned and brown in the extended drought, the worst for thirty years. The sheep, literally in their thousands, were divided up into this year's rams, next year's hogs and so on. They had rounded faces and rounded ears and somehow looked biblical, except for the fact that they had all been docked. (Fancy docking all those). They soon became aware that there was food in the offing and did a great ovine mobbing act as they ran towards Ian: a lovely scene.

One young ram had a dirty behind so Mate, the Kelpie, was summoned to help separate him from his peers. Ian gave the appropriate calls and the obedient little Mate responded with incredible speed and know-how. I was allowed to hold the ram while Ian returned to the Nissan to collect the Jeyes-smelling fluid for its maggot-abused bottom, the areas around which were looking fleeceless and fiery. The wool of the fleece felt so soothingly soft and, I had to admit to myself, softer and finer by far than that of a Devon Longwool, which I had always considered 'the best'.

In the interim, a few of the rams got over-excited and raced through (quoting Ian) "one of Michael's inadequate fences" into the next paddock. Ian lifted up one section and balanced it on a strategically placed loose Mallee root, but once he'd let go of the suspended wires, it slipped off, so then I held it in place while Ian and Mate between them persuaded the escapees to join the rest of the flock.

We moved on to find one of the young ewes stuck in the mud of the dam. I had a sense of déjà-vu. Ian took off his boots and socks and waded bare foot into the pale grey sludge and rescued her. She stumbled a little as she struggled up the bank but then regained her balance in spite of what must have been the considerable increase in weight of her sodden muddy fleece. Shortly afterwards Ian pointed out a Racing Goanna, a large Monitor Lizard, as it lurked absolutely stock still by the side of the track. Then suddenly it lived up to its name and tore off out of sight in a matter of seconds.

We returned to the house where Liz was waiting for us. We drove to see Tony and Margaret Gooch at the next farm and met various members of their family, including grand-daughter Abbie who was a very beautiful three year old, with blue eyes and an extensive vocabulary. She insisted that she was "just three", and "not three and three quarters", even though her birthday was in March. We drank coffee and ate substantial pieces of Christmas cake in their delightful house.

We had lunch at the Bremer Bay Hotel, served by a waitress from Oxford. Ian had fish and chips and I was expecting a 'prime steak', which turned out to be a prime steak burger. We did a little tour and went to look at the bay, where the sea shaded from a deep blue to a rich turquoise as it came over the very white sand. I had a Maldives flashback. It was very beautiful. Oyster Catchers and Terns made their presence heard as well as seen, and an Australian Pelican sailed on the water like a stately galleon. I reminded myself that this was December.

We called at the local baker's on the way back and met Ernie, an educated, well-upholstered, charming, bearded man. I selected one of his home-made chocolate éclairs for my tea. Back at Coromandel Ian collected the post, which was delivered on Tuesdays and Fridays.

I sat outside for a while and did some writing and then went with Liz to water the plants and the dogs, and leave post at Michael's house. Liz and Ian had lived there before they moved to their smaller accommodation. Michael and his wife Gabriel had four children aged, from two to six years, their photographs displayed in both houses. I looked forward to meeting them.

I bird-watched for some time. Galahs in grey and salmon pink flew about in sixes and sevens: green Mulga Parrots hooted softly and Ringnecks did their "twenty-eights" (their call sound), while an Australian Kestrel hovered overhead. I went with Ian to see more sheep. He showed me the White Lupin seed feed, as we went looking for any ewes that had been sire-marked by the ram's blue marker. The ram didn't seem to have had done much business up to date. As before, Ian and Mate, the Kelpie, worked swiftly and efficiently. I was thrilled to have a daylight view of a Kangaroo followed by a young one, hopping along the nearside of a Mallee hedge. Shortly afterwards we saw a Fox, and then a Rabbit which didn't look too well. There was very little vegetation apart from the occasional Thistle and the Mallee scrub. The flock looked to be in remarkably good order and I think Ian said that they had been put on to the crops that had not been worth harvesting.

Ian took me to the lake, a great expanse of water, shining blindingly in the strong sunlight. Paper Bark Trees gleamed around, and in, the lake - the latter reminding me of the pale fossil trees in Lake Kariba. A couple of Black Swans completed the black and white study.

Back in the house, we washed, and then enjoyed a chicken dinner after Ian had finished watching the financial report and the sport. Ian talked of his ancestors: names such as Cumming from Aberdeen who, together with Campbell and Dowling, had become more than competent sheep farmers, and of Second Lieutenant Neil Leslie Campbell, who had been killed at Gallipoli in 1915. These people, as well as many others, featured in the "Biographical Dictionary of the Western District of Victoria", to which Liz and Ian had contributed family information. Another large tome, of over 1000 pages, was devoted entirely to the Merino sheep. It had been a memorably sheepy day.

Saturday December 23rd

I had slept well, apart from a rude awakening by a noisy TV programme at 3.30 am. Liz had been recording something and I imagined the live TV programme returned to the screen when the video time expired. The walls were not very thick.

Today we were to return to Perth by a more direct route. Liz and I went over to Michael's house to see to the dogs and the chickens and check something to do with the dishwasher. Colourful Galahs and Twenty-eights flitted among the trees in their garden. Then we went to Pam's, a short drive away: her family was going to see to the dogs until Michael returned. Pam had a truly English garden and was already watering the lawn and one of the borders. What effort and commitment was needed to establish and maintain such a garden in that climate and especially during the current drought. Water was getting short so soon she might well have to sacrifice this hobby for a while. Locusts had already played havoc with much of the vegetation. It was a lovely plot but somehow artificial, contrived. I shall remind myself of that situation when I'm having a moan about the weather at home.

We set off in earnest at 11 am, dropped some papers into a neigbouring mailbox in Gairdner, and made for Jerramungup, where Liz checked in at the hospital where she worked part-time as a Staff Nurse. It was situated in a pleasant suburb and had a nice set of rooms and included a well-equipped X-ray unit. It dealt with emergencies from a very wide area including, not surprisingly, many injuries from farming accidents. It was under such circumstances that Ian and Liz had first met, when he was being treated for a serious hand injury. They talked of a recent air crash when the pilot, who was crop-spraying, had flown into overhead cables and died. He was a young local farmer, known to them both, and they had been very upset. Liz was called to the scene but was immediately aware that nothing could be done.

Around Ongerup everywhere looked particularly brown and dead, and the dams were completely dry. A full-sized dead Kangaroo lay at the side of the road. Signs warned motorists of their presence on many of the roads but, as Ian said, "Sometimes they just jump right out in front of a vehicle and there's no chance of stopping in time." Rather like the Deer at home, I thought.

It was getting hotter and I was thankful for the air-conditioning in the car as we drove through Gnowangerup. We saw an imaginative Veterinary Practice sign in Katanning, and shortly afterwards drove across a level crossing at Woodaniling to Rosseville Park and a Merino stud - where two of Ian's prize-winning rams, Colin and Gordon, were being nurtured for greater things. The lady caring for them was quite a star and pulled them out gently from among several other good-looking Merinos. Ian spent time holding their heads and studying them, looking at their teeth, feeling their fleeces etc. It was just so obvious that Ian and sheep shared a mutual affinity, no doubt born of a lifetime's work and association. He seemed pleased with what he saw.

23 December 2000

IAN'S PRIZE-WINNING RAMS

COLIN and GORDON - Rosseville Park

The lady carer had an astonishingly complicated piece of stained glass, half completed, around a mirror - all in the cool of the sheep shed.

At Wagin we supplemented our sandwich lunch with goodies from a nearby bakery and then sat and ate alfresco on a shaded seat in a nearby park. A juvenile White-faced Heron stood like a statue, between overhanging plants, on the edge of an island in the small lake.

We drove on long, straight roads with red soil on the hard shoulders and tall trees on either side. The sky was an uninterrupted blue. We were delayed briefly by road works at Yangebup, after which we were soon in the outskirts of Perth where Liz had been hoping to do some shopping, but at 5.40 pm the supermarket was closed. We continued home to Palmyra and Ian went to shop elsewhere and collect another family history book.

Liz and I sat in the cool courtyard and talked and drank tea. I had a bath and changed (I was beginning to feel the heat) and then we had a substantial supper with champagne ("much cheaper here" said Ian) and lots of family history talk, which prompted some light-hearted teasing from Liz.

We went to bed just after 10 pm: very early for me but I was ready.

Sunday December 24th : Christmas Eve

Ian was already washing the car by the time I surfaced at 8 am. Elizabeth and I went to St George's Cathedral, walking past the law courts and colourful gardens. The Cathedral was a very pleasant, lofty, red brick building designed, like St Andrew's Cathedral in Sydney, by Mr Edmund Blacket of Sydney, and consecrated in 1888. There was an immediate welcoming ambience - maybe the temperature had something to do with it. I couldn't help but think of my beloved St Michael and All Angels at home in Torrington, and its associated shiver-my-timbers temperature at this time of the year.

I collected an order of service on the way in and then realised I couldn't read it because my glasses were in Palmyra. Dear Elizabeth trailed back to the car in all the heat and brought me a spare pair.

In her absence the choirmaster, in casual striped shorts and a sloppy cream T-shirt, rehearsed the stand-in choir of eight women and six men. Their rendering of Psalm 98 "O sing unto the Lord a new song" was perfectly chanted and enunciated and most moving. The choirboys were saving themselves for the Christmas Eve Midnight Mass.

"The Angel Gabriel from Heaven came", "Tell out my soul the greatness of the Lord" and "A great and mighty wonder" made for enthusiastic congregation singing, and the mighty organ (one of two in the cathedral, built by Knud Smenge and installed in 1993) thundered forth in concert.

The heat met us at the door as we left the pleasant temperature of the fan-cooled cathedral. We stopped at the supermarket on the way home and I noticed how pale and fraught everyone seemed to look: well, it was Christmas Eve. It was all very well for me: I'd left behind all the hassle and planning and I was enjoying it.

I chatted to Ian before lunch. He was watching a detailed programme about organic farming, from carrots to beef to grain to noodles for the Japanese supermarket. The market was expanding and those who had got in at the beginning were making a steady, but not excessive, profit. When it was over, Ian talked about farming in general. He and Diana (formerly David) were working on a robot shearer mechanism, which could make it possible for (real) women and other less physically strong persons to use. They had got funding from the relevant wool marketing authorities, and Ian intended to pursue this project after he had, more or less, retired from farming next year. He was also planning to try sheep 'coats', so as to improve the quality and cleanliness of the wool. His illustrious ancestors would have been proud of him.

After a sandwich lunch, we set out for Alphonse and Michelle's house, but found we had forgotten the flowers, so had to go back and collect them. The couple were celebrating their engagement and had erected a canopy over the terrace behind the house. Here we sat at the Christmas-set table and got very hot.

Michelle's twin sister Dionne was there with her husband and small boy Jack, as was the twins' younger sister Kim. There were also friends: Marganita, a law graduate, now studying Italian, and Jeanne, a part-time actress, but who also head-hunted for a finance company. Bernadine, mother of Elizabeth and Alphonse, and a brief appearance by the teenage son of Alphonse from a previous marriage, completed the company: all very personable.

Alphonse and Michelle were flying off to Michelle's mother later that night, but they prepared an excellent meal of risotto (very light and creamy), then lamb with an impressive potato salad and an imaginative collection of vegetables. At some time during the course of the meal the table was moved, from its hothouse-effect position by the house, to the bottom of the garden, where it was distinctly cooler. The champagne flowed and there was plenty of good wine. We took photos and opened presents. I was mildly embarrassed to receive gifts of fig jam from Kim, shortbread made in Scotland from Alphonse and Michelle, and a candle from Kim. I had brought gifts only for the family I was expecting to meet on Christmas day. Once the evening cooled we moved the table back to the terrace, where Michelle served up a mouth-watering sweet of fine pastry, caramelised apples and cream, straight from the oven.

Somehow it was all eaten, enjoyed, and cleared away in an apparently unhurried manner, in time for the special couple to leave for their flight at 9.30 pm.

It was a Christmas Eve with a difference that I won't forget: interesting company, exceptional food, and an extraordinary collection of mosquito bites!

Monday December 25th : Christmas Day

I was given a 6.30 am call so as to be in time for the 8 am service at St George's. The church was full of Christmas people in every kind of dress, from a man with dishevelled hair, baggy shorts, and hairy legs, to several very smart women in designer clothes. I felt very comfortable in my favourite old Monsoon silk dress whose packing-induced creases had responded neither to hanging unencumbered for a week nor to the application of Elizabeth's iron. It was a traditional communion service, with well-known, well-sung carols, and an apposite sermon given by Dr John Shepherd, Dean of Perth, drawing an analogy between the three wise men and scholarship, suffering, and prayer. The clergy shook hands with all as we left, and Ian and Elizabeth wished a Happy Christmas to many of their friends.

I had imagined that Christmas lunch might be eaten outside but when we got back to Palmyra I was thankful that we were to eat indoors with the air-conditioning. There was plenty to do but Elizabeth had everything under control. It wasn't easy for her, virtually running two homes and having to bring much of what was required from Coromandel.

It was quite a party with AnnaLou (Ian's first wife) and her sister Rosemary; Ian's farming son Michael, his wife Gabriel, and their four lovely children: Georgia 6, James 4, and

25 December 2000

After Morning Service - ST GEORGE'S CATHEDRAL

twins of nearly 2, India and Thomas; Ian's daughter Julia and her boyfriend Laurie; Elizabeth's mother Bernadine, and, of course, Elizabeth, Ian and me.

We had drinks and present-opening before the meal and once again I received far more than I gave. The meal started with a salmon mousse and cucumber salad, provided by AnnaLou. The assembled company then did more than justice to Elizabeth's turkey and trimmings with boiled potatoes garnished with cream and chives, and a salad from Julia. This was followed by AnnaLou's Christmas pudding, and then by strawberries and cream.

The children were delightful. Georgia and India danced till they dropped and were then content to sit and watch the TV. James seemed to be a quiet, thoughtful little boy, and his looks, especially his eyes, reminded me of my grandson Thomas, and I admit to just a moment's home-sickness, or should it be family-sickness .... This other, younger, Thomas enjoyed parental cuddles. It all went very well and I'm sure Elizabeth, for a number of reasons must have been very pleased and relieved.

In the early evening we drove to another part of the city, to a lovely house overlooking the River Cannon (I think), to have a drink with Laurie's parents. His jokey father and elegant mother Joyce were very welcoming, as were others - including Laurie's brother and his wife, and their young son and daughter who were riding new scooters.

Then it was home to Cleopatra Street again, where I tried to make a phone call on my mobile - which I'd transported, plus recharger, all the way from the UK after reassurance from BT that I would be able to use it to ring from Australia - with singular lack of success. I ended up using the house phone and spoke to Wendy just before she ate her Christmas dinner. I asked for a ring back with the cost of the call and was pleasantly surprised to find I'd had 4 minutes for only 2.8 Australian dollars. We indulged in lots of family talk and eventually turned in just before midnight.

Tuesday December 26th : Boxing Day

It was an 8 am start.

I packed, finding I had more than I came with, in spite of shedding the Christmas presents I'd brought. I was bound for Brisbane and the east coast today, and en route we visited the Bell Tower near St George's Cathedral, surrounded by the pleasant gardens. As I have mentioned earlier, it housed the old bells from St Martin in the Fields, London. When the St Martin's tower was showing signs of stress and it was realised that something less heavy would have to replace the bells, a certain Australian businessman called Laith Reynolds, who was in London at the time and who happened to be a campanologist, pulled financial and diplomatic strings to get the bells to Perth, in exchange for metal to be recast into lighter bells, more suitable for St Martin's.

The Bell Tower was a slim, elegant modern structure, six storeys high, and the bells could be viewed at the fourth floor level. The whole project had been completed and opened only very recently and entrance was free for a couple of months. We queued with predominantly Japanese tourists for just a short while. A maximum of a hundred

26 December 2000

BELL TOWER (housing bells from St Martin in the Fields)

visitors was allowed inside at any one time. The bells might be light in weight but they looked large and powerful, and the height provided panoramic views of the city all around.

At the airport we had a cup of tea, more chat and said our farewells. I felt quite emotional; it had been special to strengthen this neglected family link and they had made me so welcome. Once aboard, I settled into window seat 45A next to a young Australian who moved across the aisle and lay down on a row of empty seats: the plane was barely half full. I somehow became quite inept with my seatbelt and couldn't get it fastened. A steward came and helped me. Thereafter he was most attentive, possibly thinking that this elderly English lady was travelling by air for the first time.

An indifferent curry, with scanty salad, was followed by boring biscuits: my usual gin and ginger ale gave it all some life. We had been twenty minutes late setting off but had made up the time for the stop in Sydney. It seemed very late to me as I put forward my watch three hours to 6 pm to catch up with Sydney time. We waited longer than expected here because of a 'mechanical fault'. I had a wander round and bought a thin-strapped T-shirt. I crossed my fingers and presented my card, which was accepted without a murmur, so that was good news.

Once on board in the same seat on the same plane (so that I'd been able to leave my hand luggage) a happy-looking young girl came and sat next to me. She was a child carer at Sydney University so had five weeks' holiday over the summer vacation. She had lived in Kent until she was twelve but now regarded Australia as her country and would not want to go back. Her boyfriend was meeting her in Brisbane and she positively sparkled.

We landed around 8 pm (Brisbane is only two hours ahead of Perth) and my luggage came off the carousel very soon. I wasn't sure whether Wexas would have arranged for anyone to meet me from the Flag Airport International Hotel, so I walked round for a while but my name did not appear on any of the hand-held notices. I asked at the desk and was advised to get a cab - "about twelve dollars". I joined the Paddington-like taxi queue and got picked up by a ginger-headed, monosyllabic fellow who drove very fast but didn't seem sure of the hotel's exact location. The clock ticked up to '20 dollars 50' but I was relieved to arrive. In fact there was a little red bus, with trailer, delivering other passengers from the same flight but the driver had not been given my name. "We didn't know what time you were arriving," said the pert lady behind the desk.

The room was lovely but hot and humid and I couldn't work the air-conditioning. I went down for the night porter. If I'd put on my glasses I daresay I would have been able to suss it out. I thought that it was probably time to get varifocals and wear them all the time. The red bus would take me to the airport in the morning, leaving at 7 am ("be there at ten to", said the desk lady sharply), which seemed a bit excessive for an 8.50 am local flight. I requested a 6 am call: it was getting worse by the minute. I had a shower and washed my hair and helped myself to a rum and coke from the minibar.

I snuggled down into the very comfy bed at 10.30 pm - but what time was it 'really'?

Wednesday December 27th

I slept reasonably well, apart from an irritating selection of Mosquito bites acquired in Alphonse's garden on Christmas Eve. I checked out and waited outside for the (Australian) shuttle service. We went all round the houses picking up weary passengers. The suburbs were looking contrastingly cheerful with the Oleander, Hibiscus, Flame Trees and Wattle. There were lots of service stations scattered among the houses, and virtually indistinguishable from them except for their prominent signs for Dry-cleaning, Hairdressing, Sewing Machine Repairs, Masseur and so on.

At the Qantas Domestic Terminal I sat in an airy lounge to wait for flight 2372, and at 8.40 am boarded the little Twin Otter on which I had a single window seat 7A. The 'light refreshments' of biscuits, apple juice, and later, coffee, were very welcome as the first nutrition of the day. We stopped briefly at Maryborough for a lady of around my vintage to alight. We were about to take off when it was noticed that half her luggage had not got off with her and a casually-dressed airport employee came rushing to the plane to collect it.

Just another eight minutes and we were at Hervey Bay. A cheery chappy in brightly coloured shirt and shorts took us, and our luggage, to the harbour, where we had time to amble through the attractive little shopping precinct. I bought some 'shape of Australia' cards and then ordered fish soup and awaited its delivery in the outdoor cafe. It was more like a fish casserole with many different kinds of fish - tasty, filling, and very good value at nine Australian dollars. Colourful yachts graced the harbour with names like Achiever, Silhouette, Archimedes and Sunrise.

The green and white Kingfisher II Ferry arrived and within an hour we were being welcomed at the Kingfisher Bay Resort and Village on Fraser Island. My name was missing from the list of expected guests but all was well. I was in room 250 which was large and airy, and by now I was far enough up the learning curve to know that placing the room key tab into the little wall slot would bring on the air-conditioning.

I put on my bathing costume and trousers, went and booked several activities on offer, and then had a refreshing swim in the pool, which was being well used by lots of very active, very young. I had a coffee from the bar and lay back and revelled in the warmth. A cloudy sky was breaking me in gently. I went back to my room, washed some clothes and later shopped for fruit and ginger beer. I saw the Grey Shrike Thrush on the way back and heard its wonderful song. "It's called the Bush Canary," said another guest as we stopped to look and listen.

At 7 pm I went to hear Amelia, a lady Ranger, give an excellent lecture on the Dingos on the island and then joined her 'guided night walk'. We watched Micro Bats, Emerald-spotted Tree Frogs, a striped Rocket Frog, Wallen Rocket Frog, and Kallula Sedge Frog, most of which sat obligingly still in the light of Amelia's torch, while others, out of the limelight, croaked at various depths and pitches in the surrounding dark. The invasive Cane Toad got above average attention and the hazards of its introduction were much discussed. We were on the look out for snakes but saw only one thin red specimen and I've forgotten its probable name - Amelia said it was immature, so it was not possible to make a positive identification.

At 8.30 pm it was the excellent lady Ranger Amelia again, with a slideshow. She was doing this as a holiday job while completing her university degree course in 'Environmental Studies of Fraser Island'. It covered the geology, geography, Sharks on the east of the island, Turtles at the northern India Point, and plants such as the strange Banksia, the Dinosaur Plant - which seductively resembled the Pineapple, the Foxtail, and the Mistletoe, to mention but a few.

There were bird slides, including the weird Tawny Frogmouth, and covering the identification of Eagles from other birds in flight, the Eagles presenting a wide V-shape of the tail. We were also given a brief history of the logging trade on the island - which started in the second half of the nineteenth century using the Kauri Pines. But clashes with the Aboriginal people, and their clubbing to death of one of the logging fraternity, resulted in a halting of the business until the beginning of the twentieth century, when McKenzie Ltd were responsible for the only timber mill on the island, a jetty and a number of steam locomotives. Prior to this, the Pines had been punted and rafted by steam tug from the island to the Maryborough Mill. The McKenzie business became unviable and in 1925 they sold out. They had left quite a history and of course the splendid perched lake, Lake McKenzie, bears the name.

Finally, Amelia showed us a slide of the Maheno, a shipwreck lying off the east coast. Originally this had been guarded but the so-called caretakers gradually sold off anything of value. Amelia had visited an old man who had proudly shown off some of the spoils.

It had been a full day … ending with bed at 10.30 pm.

Thursday December 28th

I had a good night's sleep, with efficient air-conditioning. I rang the Ranger's office as instructed and confirmed that the Blue Dolphin Cruise was on. I walked to the Jetty Hut, located on the night walk, and went beyond in order to board the smart catamaran owned and worked by Peter alone, who was like a man called Arthur Lee back home in Devon. The vessel carried a maximum of twelve, I read on the side, but today we were only six. Two were young Americans: he was rather shy but she seemed more communicative and (here we go again) reminded me of Clarissa, our vicar's wife. A middle-aged Italian-Australian couple, who ran an Italian restaurant, were anything but shy and talked incessantly to each other in their own language, with occasional interjections in English to the rest of us. A lady on her own, and probably in her forties, made up the half dozen. She had come to see her daughter, who worked in the Ranger's Office and who was Peter's girlfriend.

The sky was grey and threatening. We had the usual preliminary life-saving talk and then set off towards Woody Island, looking round in all directions as we went, for Bottle-nosed Dolphins. The skies became more leaden and did what they had threatened to do in no small measure. The young Americans and I stuck it out for a while in the uncovered bow for it was very warm, but eventually the down-the-back-of-the-neck drips drove us inside, where the visibility was almost as good. This was the signal for the Italian lady to come over and talk to me. I had her family history and she asked about mine. She was proud of the family involvement in their business, but she herself was troubled with menopausal hot flushes: what did I think about HRT? She was unaware that I had anything to do with medicine in general, never mind Women's Health in particular, and I didn't let on. Finally she jumped up and down, taking a series of photos of her husband, asked me to take one of both of them, and then insisted that she take pictures of me, both with her camera and with mine. This helped to pass the time in the Dolphin-less grey water.

There were still no protruding fins at refreshment time, when we enjoyed a hot drink and a tempting selection of cakes. Then out of the blue (water) appeared fins - at the same time as the appearance of the only bird we saw: a Piebald Cormorant standing on a sandbank, its white front making its characteristic snaky neck even more conspicuous. It took off almost immediately and I missed it with the camera, but the unimpressive picture revealed later that I had caught the occasional Dolphin fin. It was hard to know where to look as their reappearances were so unpredictable, and this made it quite exciting and brought us all back to life. This was what we had come for.

"Now we can go home", said Peter with some relief. We had been out on the water for three hours before the Dolphins obliged, and it was almost another hour before we got back, later than scheduled. Peter had really put himself and his timetable out to get the happy result. Well, I suppose it was possibly because he had his future mother-in-law on board. It was still tipping down and I was soaked to the skin with warm rain just walking the short distance back to the Kingfisher Resort, but then I hadn't got much on. Peter was off on an Antarctic expedition in a sailing boat in the near future: we all wished him well.

My room was all beautifully tidied, with clean sheets on the bed. It was 1.45 pm and I was hungry so I put on dry clothes and went to the Maheno Restaurant, where I sat on the covered open deck and watched the swimmers in the pool as they got wet above and below the water. I had a bowl of curried tomato soup, followed by a generous helping of spaghetti bolognese, both garnished with large Basil leaves. I was surrounded by French and Italians, and Buff-banded Rails. Thus fortified I visited the shop and bought a poster, a calendar, and some cards, all depicting photographs by a local man, Peter Mayer. I had admired blown-up versions in the lounge at the Resort.

The rain continued and the night walk was very wet and very short. We saw only the Kulula Sedge Frog and just heard the rest. Poor Amelia had a bad back so one of the guests carried the heavy batteries for the powerful torch and the two walked in tandem. I was soaked again. I hadn't thought of bringing a mac.

I was in bed by 10.30 pm, anticipating a 5.30 am call for the morning early walk. I must have been mad. I hoped the rain would stop.

Friday December 29th

I was not called at 5.30 am although I thought I heard someone else's phone. It was still pouring down and I'd decided not to go anyway. I rolled over and went back to sleep. I heard later that the walk had been cancelled.

29 December 2000
Colourful Banksia

I had a continental breakfast with the company of the faithful Buff-coloured Rails and later, when the rain had stopped, I went and sat by an attractive window lake beyond the pool. I watched Magpie Larks, an Australian Spotted Crake and White-cheeked Honeyeaters.

I had booked a 4WD tour and joined the assembled takers behind the shop early in the afternoon. Bob, the driver, introduced himself and proved to be a well-informed enthusiast about Fraser Island. He gave us some history as we skidded along the sandy route. ("It's better than usual after the rain", he assured us). He talked of the dream of Michael Hackett to use Fraser Island in an eco-friendly way. This man gathered lots of supporters round him, all volunteers, and they were known as the Fraser Island Defenders' Organisation: FIDO, for short, with an appropriate Bulldog logo. In the seventies this group, with the single-minded support of people like John Sinclair and Ronda Cook, campaigned for the banning of sand-mining and logging. The battle was hard won eventually, with sand-mining ceasing in 1976 but logging not until 1991. The group really triumphed finally when Fraser Island was given World Heritage status. The narrator must have told this story to many tourists but it still came from the heart.

There had been considerable anti-propaganda at the time of Prince Charles' opening of Fraser Island as an eco-friendly holiday resort and fires had been lit by the protestors. And then the wind had changed direction and the protestors had to be rescued by people from the centre! Much research had been done comparatively recently and puzzling facts had come to light, such as that the sand, on analysis, was discovered to be identical to that found in the Antarctic.

Bob pointed out the Scribbly Gum Tree, a type of Eucalyptus (like so many of them) with the strange 'scribbled notes' on the trunk, giving fodder to all sorts of bizarre interpretations as to their origins: love letters, death threats, etc, when in fact they are made by hungry moth larvae who like only the Scribbly Gums. The attractive bright green Foxtail Fern had replaced the grasses in many instances and I think he said that this was also described as a sedge, the like of which was confined to Fraser Island and Cooloola - like the frog. It did look more like grass. Next he described the Grass Trees (not Eucalyptus). All this interesting commentary helped to take our minds off the very bumpy track. "The clutch is on the way out" said Bob, but whatever the state of the vehicle we were certainly king of the road. Oncoming cars were constantly having to back up on the narrow, slope-sided sections. I was relieved to get on terra firma. We took a walk along the side of a sandy-bottomed creek. The vegetation was thick and lush at all levels. The tall Eucalyptus Trees sported barks of yellow, orange, tan, black and all shades and states of semi-strippedness. The ground was a green carpet of Foxtails and other plants, and colourful fungi established on the rotting vegetation. Powerful climbers ran from under our feet high up into the trees above. Spectacular Stags Horn Ferns circled many of the trees, some at eye level, others high up in the canopy, all bursting with vulgar health. It was still very hot and humid in spite of the fact that the rain had stopped and the sky was overcast.

The vehicle had driven round to meet us and we were given very welcome cold drinks. Next we made for Lake McKenzie, a large perched lake in a lovely setting. Here some of us had a refreshing dip in the clear, clean, luke-warm water. I looked for the Turtles that lived in the lake but I didn't see any: too many human swimmers splashing about. A cup of tea and a slice of carrot cake and it was time for the jiggerty-jig home again. I was disappointed not to have had a closer view of a Dingo: there had been just one distant glimpse.

I called in at the seductive shop again on the way back and bought wildlife videos (which I would enjoy watching first), to take home for the family.

Late that evening I watched some TV: an Australian gardening programme, with their answer to Alan Titchmarsh - similar looks and accent - and then an old episode of The Vicar of Dibley.

Saturday December 30th

I woke up feeling tired, which seemed strange considering that I had had ten hours' sleep. Maybe the heat was catching up with me or maybe it was something to do with

30 December 2000

LADY ELLIOTT ISLAND

the air-conditioning, which is very drying. Anyway, tired or not, I'd got to get my act together and be packed by 8 am, when the luggage would be collected. I was glad I hadn't got to carry it the considerable distance from my upstairs room in the pleasant chalet block back to Reception. It was becoming steadily heavier with purchases towards Christmas.

I had my usual continental breakfast and settled my account. I'd paid everything via an in-house card, issued after my credit card had been scanned: all very efficient. I talked to Peter and Amelia and then walked to the jetty, hoping that my luggage would have found its way there, as promised. I wish I could feel more trusting when I haven't actually witnessed its transit. It was a warm, grey day and the boat trip across the Great Sandy Strait was refreshing. I sat next to a couple who worked boats along the coast of Hervey Bay where they lived. They had a dear little eleven-month-old daughter, Katie.

My luggage appeared reassuringly at Hervey Bay, the large bag in one container and 'hand' luggage in another. I waited until after 12 noon for the promised lift to the airport and used the time people-watching. A disgruntled family argued constantly while they waited for the next ferry: I marvelled at the patience of the mother. In contrast, a cheery family laughed and joked with each other: one of them, a young lad of about six, had an artificial leg.

A Kingfisher Resort driver arrived in a people-carrier: he looked half Japanese and had a smiley face: in no time I had his life history. He'd been born in Perth, brought up in Ireland, married an English girl in Southampton (where they were having snow at the present time, he told me), came with her to live in Australia and had worked in Sydney for nine years. Now he lived and worked in Hervey Bay, where he and his family were very happy. He admitted to having had a passive home-sickness for the UK but a trip 'back home' in November, when it was cold, and where heavy rain had caused flooding, "soon got rid of all that nonsense!"

We arrived at the homespun Sunstate airport at 12.30 pm but the office was not yet open. Eventually a young man opened the door, we paid our taxes and once again got temporary freedom from the luggage. The next phase of the holiday was beginning. The Twin Otter flight was uneventful, apart from the fact that the pilot was under instruction from a plump, older, jolly man, who every now and then said "No, no, no!" laughing reassuringly!

The sky was deep blue when we left Hervey Bay with just the occasional white fluffy cloud, but the clouds gradually became larger and greyer and ultimately confluent. The rain bucketed down as we landed on the earthen strip at Lady Elliott Island. We were surrounded by nesting Black (White-capped) Noddies, cackling away with their "Kir-kirring", and by other birds, yet to be identified. We had a warm welcome in the rain and followed the guide, who left each of us at our respective accommodation. I was in 'tented accommodation 9', which was spacious but the rain was already dripping through in a couple of places. Maybe I should have plumped for a cabin.,

I walked along the beach in minimal clothing. (No sense in getting everything wet.) Wonderful shells and pieces of coral lay along the tide line. I decided to go in for a snorkel. This proved to be easier said than done, for the rocks and the coral made walking into the water to a depth for swimming something of an assault course: flippers didn't help but the reward was great. There were many brightly-coloured small fish, the occasional large white one, and medium-sized Parrot Fish of different hues, plus several huge Sea Slugs: some of these were slinky smooth, others crenellated like a man's scrotum.

The birds along the beach were many and vociferous. Frigate Birds (of the Lesser variety, I think) surveyed the scene as they drifted about above the rest, Ruddy Turnstones nimbled purposefully at the water's edge, Bridled Terns hung about under the bushes at the top of the shoreline, and a great colony of Crested Terns, with eggs and youngsters of all ages, gave me an aggressive seeing-off, with messy souvenirs! It was magic and the rain had almost stopped.

I went back and dried, then showered in the washroom next door and changed for dinner. I went over to the restaurant, equipped myself with my favourite restorative and looked for somewhere to sit. I decided to make for a small table at the far end and sit on my own until I'd got the drop of the assembled company. As I did, a voice said, "Come and join us." It came from one of three people of forty-something, whom I'd seen on the plane. It was tempting. I said, "Are you sure?" and laughingly she said, "We'll give it a whirl". "And so will I then", I responded.

It transpired that they were British medics, although Peter and Lindsay - now consultant anaesthetists - had been working in Australia for nine years. Peter came from Birkenhead and had qualified at Liverpool the year before my veterinary son, Richard. The third was Cleo, over for a holiday, with whom Lindsay had qualified in London, where Cleo still worked - now as a consultant psychiatrist at the East London Hospital. A clever trio. They were utterly charming and proved to be excellent company and very tolerant of this Granny figure.

We were given a 'welcome' drink, a very sweet pink and orange fruit concoction, and then ate an appetising supper of ratatouille, young octopus with fresh salad, and followed by carrot cake and coffee. The younger medics bought and shared some very good Australian wine.

We went to the slide show and saw lots of pictures of life around the island, and in other places, with a preponderance of Whales. I turned in at 9.30 pm and was lulled to sleep by the Kirring Noddies.

Sunday December 31st

The last day of the year!

I felt great, having slept really well with the Noddies, and having been only vaguely aware of gale force winds. I had a light breakfast, accompanied by an alert little Silvereye who perched alternately on the table and on the back of the chair. It was very windy still but there were just a few white clouds and it wasn't raining. I booked for the glass-bottomed boat at 11 am and the island tour at 1 pm. It was high tide so I went for a snorkel: much easier to get in and out now. I had a good hour enjoying the fish, Pipe Fish, Demoiselles, Sergeant Majors and Groupers. It was so easy and productive that I was going off the idea of the scuba-dive, with all that gear and having to do the preliminary training session because I hadn't got my PADI certificate.

I got dried and went to the cafe for a cappuccino, where I joined Lindsay who was doing the same. She and Peter were keen divers, and when I told her of my thoughts on the diving, she said "Oh you can't come here and not dive on the reef. You must do it: it's not negotiable!" Powerful lady – and before I had time to change my mind again, I went over to the Dive Centre and booked an introductory course for 1.15 pm that afternoon. The island tour would have to wait. I was given a wet suit to put on before presenting myself. The glass-bottomed boat trip gave a good viewing of the coral but not much else, as the fish came and went across the small window almost before I had realised that they were there. I had an early, energy-giving, fish and chip lunch.

Just before 1 pm I put on my bathing costume and started to squeeze myself into the wet suit. It took me twenty minutes to get it as far as my hips. Thus half-clad I staggered to the Dive Centre where Justine, who was to be my instructor, decided it was far too small. (I'm sure it was only a size 8, or a size 10 at the very largest.) She produced something immediately more manageable and helped me on with the inflatable waistcoat, weights and cylinder etc. I walked to the pool with some difficulty and put on my flippers.

Justine went through all the mandatory points and I was pleased to discover that I could remember most of them. I must have had some benefit from the uncompleted PADI course at Barnstaple Leisure Centre, from which I'd opted out after three sessions because I just could not cope with the required waiting and walking round the pool with all that heavy gear. We did the airway, pressures, sharing air, changing air pressure at different depths etc, and the hand signals. Justine booked me in for the 'proper' dive from the boat at 2.45 pm.

Wet with sweat inside the non-breathing wetsuit, possibly with a little apprehension, I joined the large group of apparently experienced, blasé divers and a lovely young girl called Zoe, who had done her first dive on the previous day. Justine came over to talk to us both. The water was murky after the gales, it was low tide which meant we'd have to walk the length of the airfield over the Reef to get to the boat, and Justine didn't think it was the best day for a first (or second) dive. Would we mind leaving it until 9.30 am the following morning? I was mightily relieved and Zoe accepted the situation, so we disrobed and I walked back to my tent, feeling as light as air, and showered and washed my salt-sodden hair. I reminded myself that the experience was only postponed.

I took a long walk along the beach again and delighted in all the bird colonies. I came back and talked to Cleo by the pool. She was reviewing a book called 'Male Victims of Sexual Abuse'. Inevitably this led to a discussion on my one remaining professional commitment, Psychosexual Counselling (again). It was refreshing to talk to a consultant psychiatrist of the next generation, who was not only a respected professional but who also had an impressive breadth of knowledge of this neglected specialty.

I put on a dress for New Year's Eve and met Cleo in the bar. Lindsay and Peter joined us later. Peter had brought some rare sparkling red Australian wine from Sydney and it was really something. We each bought a bottle of sparkling something-or-other after dinner as the long night wore on. The music was excessively loud and as we were determined to talk we became quite hoarse. Every now and then one or two of us would join the movers and shakers and trip the light fantastic. It was a very friendly atmosphere, with many of the young staff looking lovely in their best bibs and tuckers.

I asked Cleo whether Lindsay and Peter were an item. She said she wished they could be and then told me that Lindsay had just got divorced from a "dreadful man", an obstetrician. Lindsay had not been able to get pregnant and had gone through no less than twelve unsuccessful IVFs. Cleo had come over to keep her company during this first Christmas and New Year on her own - a good friend.

I talked to Zoe, my diving buddy for the morrow. She was being slightly embarrassed by her very young-looking mother who was dancing the night away, but said with pride

"She used to be a vet, but now she's a sculptor." At midnight everyone shouted and cheered but it seemed strange without Big Ben or 'Auld Lang Syne'.

The three young medics were going down to the beach, but I opted for bed just before 1 am, thinking of the 9.30 am commitment the same day.

Monday January 1st 2001

The wind was blowing noisily when I woke up just after 8 am - with a slight head. A mesh-covered rectangle at each end of the tent served as windows through which the wind whistled: no need for air-conditioning or fans here. Did I really want to dive today? I got up and had a cup of tea, and then got halfway into the wet suit in the shower: easier if the torso is wet. At the Dive Centre Justine and Zoe assisted me to complete the dressing exercise, and then Zoe and I walked down to the side of the airstrip to the Coral Garden, where we hung about waiting for the others and the vehicle bringing all the gear. Once equipped, the short walk down the shore to the boat was crippling enough to make me glad I hadn't attempted the previous day's trek. On board we put on our flippers and went out some distance.

The boat stopped, put down the anchor, and it was getting off time. Being the new girl I was left till last. "Just step off, holding on to your mask," which I did. Oh! the bliss of the weightlessness of the tank, once in the water. Zoe and I travelled down the anchor rope as instructed. I had a couple of brief, painful bouts of ear pressure pain, but decreasing my depth for a matter of seconds and then going down more slowly must have equalised the pressure and I was able to enjoy the excitement comfortably.

There were shoals and shoals of little fluorescent fish, flashing like tiny electric light bulbs as they came darting from one direction to another, twisting and turning out of the coral: Parrot Fish, Triggerfish, Blennies, startling Yellowstripe Snappers and a large orange and black fish - some kind of Angelfish I think. There were too many to remember and I decided I must just enjoy them. Two very large pale fawn and black Batfish seemed to like our company and they stayed with us much of the way. We were down at a depth of 13 metres and had a good view of a Green Turtle just above us, and at one stage a large Manta Ray darkened the water overhead: it was like a plane flying over silently.

It was peaceful and quiet, yet teaming with fascinating life. I loved it. I was just beginning to feel a bit too cool for comfort when Justine indicated that it was time to go back up. We three had stayed near to each other and every now and then we had come across some of the other divers, in twos and threes. I wasn't sure how long we'd been down as I'd soon discovered that, without my glasses and even though the mask magnifies, I could not read the time, the depth, or the volume of air left in the tank. Mercifully I had Justine to keep an eye on things.

I was grateful for assistance up the little ladder, when everything again became unbearably heavy. Some of the others looked anxious when they saw me - I had blood round my mouth - but it was just that I'd managed to squash a small bit of my lip in with the mouthpiece.

1 January 2001

'Kirring Noddies' - LADY ELLIOTT ISLAND

Everyone had been told what time to return to the boat. I was surprised to find we'd been down for fifty minutes. We sat around on the little boat relating what we'd seen and waiting for one man who was missing. It was all very low key, but I could tell the staff divers were worried. One of them, who'd been in charge of the boat, put on full armour and went down: no sign. Then someone spotted what looked like a diver nearer the shore, and we went over and collected him. He was only mildly reprimanded for not staying with a buddy, and I thought the staff were very tolerant, especially when he started bragging that he'd been down longer than anyone else.

Then, it was back to the shore, where each of us filled in a form to say we were still alive and well, how long we'd been down and to what depth. I heard the arrogant chap say, "I was down an hour, you know." I walked back with Zoe. She'd been like a fish in the water, tall and slim, but her young body was obviously very strong, for she swung along with all the equipment. I wished I'd done this when I was younger.

I was hungry and surprised myself by having fish and chips again. I watched one of the staff trying to replace a Black Noddy chick in a nest where she said the adults had no young of their own. They were not too keen, although at one stage it looked quite hopeful, but when I went back later it was lying dead on the ground. I was tempted to say, "There's no shortage!" There must have been thousands of them on the island and most of them seemed to be thriving.

I located and photographed a rarer specimen, the Red-tailed Tropic Bird, its tail just one long, elegant, single feather. I went back to my bunk and crashed out for an hour. Later in the afternoon I took another walk by the water, revelling again in the turquoise sea, the white beach and, of course, all the birds. I had a cup of tea by the pool with Cleo, and then rang Wendy to wish everyone a Happy New Year. I think she said it was 6.30 am. This island is evidently ten hours ahead of the UK, not eight as I had thought.

We had a good beef dinner followed by individual Christmas puddings with cream. The staff held a quiz about Lady Elliot Island and we four came bottom - but at least I got the bird questions right. I must do that island tour and get better informed.

We went down to the beach and drank a bottle of wine, while we looked at the moon shining through the clouds on to the water. It was very peaceful and much less windy on this side of the island. We joined a couple of the staff who had lit a fire outside near their accommodation, and talked for an hour or so but went to bed before midnight.

I rang Charles but there was no-one at home. Richard and family were there so I guessed they'd gone out for a New Year's Day lunch together.

Tuesday January 2nd

I had a sociable breakfast with the three medics, and then a prolonged snorkel with the under-water camera. The water was less clear than yesterday but I saw nearly as many different kinds of fish as I had done when diving - but no Turtles or Manta Rays. I came back mid-morning for the mandatory cappuccino and to say farewell to the three, who were flying back to Sydney. I hoped I would see them again some day, somewhere.

I had a sandwich lunch and a half-hour snooze, and then joined the Discovery walk. I got acquainted with the Octopus Tree, which was bush-like and lined the top of the beach, providing a home for many of the Black Noddies. Casuarina (She-oak) had been planted to replace most of the hardwood, slower-growing Oaks - of which the island had been virtually denuded by logging. There were still a few of the old, indigenous Personea Trees around but these were very slow growing. The island had suffered another insult when the topsoil, and much of the fine sand, had been removed because of the rich fertilization value of the inseparable guano, provided by the heavy bird population. "Such things will never happen again", said our lady guide.

The water supply was all provided by desalination of the seawater, and all the rubbish, including food waste, was burnt on the far side of the island. Here the tour ended abruptly as someone came to give our guide instructions that she was to meet the new arrivals from the plane that was about to land. There was a hurried feeding of the fish, mostly Parrot Fish (a daily routine), in a lagoon close to the shore where they were waiting, and that was it! I continued along the beach and watched all the birds again: I could do this for weeks and not tire of it.

I rang Charles' number around Lady Elliott Island supper time, and it was good to speak to him and to hear in particular that he and Alison are expecting a third baby in July, which put me on a high for the evening. I also spoke to Richard, and they all seemed to have had a good Christmas, and New Year celebration.

I joined Ingrid (ex-vet, now sculptor) and her daughter Zoe (scuba-diving companion), and Jade for supper. They were more than interesting company. Ingrid was an impressive lady. She had done cartoons for a South African paper, generally depicting the slack and unpleasant way that many of the whites treat the blacks. As a result her house was trashed more than once and, fearing for the safety of her children, she left and came to Australia. They now lived in a converted Seventh Day Adventist Church in Sydney where she did her sculpting. She'd had a good year, with two special commissions, hence the holiday. I said I thought it sounded very exciting. "It's all right", said Zoe "and that's what my friends say, but there's clay everywhere!"

Before I went to bed, I rang Wendy (at a more civilised time), and Helen - from a phone box where only Australian phone cards can be used. I'd purchased a couple of 10 dollar cards at the island shop, the young assistant assuring me that I'd need more than one if I was going to ring England. I made 4 calls and still had 2 dollars left on the first card.

Wednesday January 3rd

I got up at 7 am for a snorkel before breakfast, found a peaceful lagoon and finished the under-water film. I came back for a shower and a hair-wash but had to wait for a while as the 'Cleaning in progress' notice was displayed outside the ladies' bathroom. That's what you get for getting up so early! All this activity had made me hungry and I ate a rare fried breakfast, sitting with Ingrid and co. Time here was running out. I packed and got generally organised. My tented accommodation had to be cleared by 10 am.

I did what I'd been intending to do ever since arrival. I went to the education centre and browsed through the history, getting a potted version, as below:

1816 Island named by a Captain Stewart who arrived on a ship, the 'Lady Elliott'
1843 Surveying voyage of HMS 'Fly'
1863 Guano mining, managed by Jack Askumas, with Asiatic labour
1866 First lighthouse built by Guano miner
1872 Lighthouse toppled by storm
1873 Present lighthouse built
1892 W Saville Kent's Naturalist Exhibition of the Island
1896 Phoebe Jane Phillips died on the Island
1907 Susannah McKee died on the Island
1930 Lighthouse keeper cottages built

1939 Weather station opened

1966 Lady Elliott Island under water for a whole tide

1969 Runway opened and last goats removed

1985 Resort opened

1988 Lighthouse became solar powered

1995 Lighthouse modernised

There were 127 known shipwrecks caused by the Reef and the weather around the Island. The last was the Apollo in 1980, during the Brisbane to Gladstone yacht race.

I would have been able to answer a few more of those quiz questions if I had come sooner.

I had a salad roll for lunch. It was a breezy day, which made my last beach walk very comfortable. I watched Shearwaters (I was not sure which kind), Roseate Terns and Brown Boobies. Some of the larger birds, including the Frigate birds, were riding high, gracefully, on the wind. I just lay down and followed their movements, which were beautiful.

I went and settled my bill. It was very reasonable. The dive was 121 dollars, about £48, which included my lesson in the pool, Justine's ministrations, insurance and the hire and use of all the complicated equipment. It was well worth it and I am so glad Lindsay ordered me on. The two New Year's eve bottles of Champagne which I'd gallantly said I would pay for, came to 46 dollars, £18, hardly over the top, for it had been really good.

I waited as instructed near the Dive Centre at the near end of the runway and Justine appeared, all in her gear, just back from a dive. I had been hoping to get a picture of her so this was good timing. She refused to be taken on her own, and I found someone else to take us both.

This was the beginning of the journey home. I found it hard to imagine snow in the UK. I heard someone report that it was minus 10 in the Cotswolds. Help! While I waited I talked to a couple of the young employees and commented that no-one was obviously in charge and yet everything ran so smoothly. One of them said, "He keeps behind the scenes: he's a really good guy that we've got here now."

There were two flights taking off before mine, one was returning from a day excursion to the Island with mostly Japanese, who had taken their snorkelling lesson so seriously, and the second was part of an 'Islands Tour'. At 4 pm the Twin Otter touched down and we flashed our vouchers and I got on board, having made sure my luggage had gone from the departure lounge. Ingrid, Zoe and Jade came to wave me off. I'd known them only a few days but they were somehow special and I felt quite sad. We exchanged addresses.

The short flight ended at Sunstate airport at Hervey Bay where there didn't seem to be anyone to meet me so I phoned the advertised taxi service, a bit anxious because my luggage had not appeared at the relaxed baggage collection point and the plane had made off into the blue horizon. It was only when the pleasant taxi-man arrived and said "These yours?" as he picked up my bags at a second collection point that I realised they'd been there all the time. He was "43-going-on-44" he told me, was never going to leave Australia to go to "your UK or anywhere else!" His ambition was to put by enough to travel the Bush for a few months when he retired. A very contented man.

He carried my bags into reception at The Sandy Straits Holiday Resort, where a smiling lady announced, "We've had to upgrade your room". This did not involve any added expense so I smiled as well. She took me, and the luggage, through a complicated system of passages and doors, using no less than three keys to gain access into Room 157. It was incredibly luxurious, especially in comparison with the tented accommodation on Lady Elliott Island, and housed a small, well-equipped kitchen, a large lounge with comfortable furniture, including wrought-iron chairs with inset glass medallions, a double bedroom, and a bathroom with a jaccuzi. The lounge looked out on to a small, colourful private garden. Unfortunately there was no food either in the kitchen or in the holiday complex, and the lady directed me to a fish restaurant over the road. I decided to go and hoped I'd be able to find my way back again.

I had the 'fish basket', which contained generous helpings of prawns, squid, crab and some white fish, plus more chips than I could eat, all for the equivalent of £5. I sat and ate outside overlooking the attractive harbour. Kingfisher I was waiting for the next day's trip to Fraser Island. I got back to 157 after a few wrong turns in the dark. I read all the literature there, advertising trips, eating places, cycle hire, tennis, fishing - lots of fishing – and then came across some anti-trawling propaganda. It maintained that, in trawling for prawns as they did, they took 20% of everything else in the process: even using the so-called 'quiet lanes' interfered with spawning fish, and so on. It was pretty convincing.

I watched the news on TV - nothing startling. I used the sophisticated bathroom and all it had to offer, but had difficulty with the sophisticated air-conditioning (what's new?) and the fan: eventually I got it sorted and sank into the very comfortable bed. I slept well until 3.30 am when I was rudely awakened by rousing pop music coming from the bedside clock/radio, possibly the previous occupant's early morning call. It took me some time to get rid of it and then I slept again till 7 am.

Perhaps there is something to be said for a tent!

Thursday January 4th

The taxi arrived promptly. The driver was an affable, middle-aged man who had "absolutely no English connections!" Sunstate was a friendly little airport. Two mums were making arrangements for their under-age daughters to travel alone. I handed in both lots of luggage and the man at the desk said "These will go straight through to Heathrow," so I apologised and quickly grabbed back the hand luggage which contained, as well as things I might need on and between flights, my warm skirt and jumper for the last lap. I bought my cappuccino but hardly had time to drink it before boarding. As the plane took off, and for a while afterwards, there were magnificent views of swirling sands, water and vegetation: I had no film left.

At Brisbane I waited with mostly Asian families for the bus tranferring us from the Domestic to the International Airport. Brisbane International has excellent shops and I tried on a T-shirt in a colour I'd always wanted, but although it read 'medium' it was (like that first wetsuit) far too clingy and it was the only size they had. "It's not really that small," said the miniscule Asian assistant unhelpfully. I bought two books, one 'A Return to Poetry 2000' containing the favourite ten poems of ten different Australians, and the other 'Hanna's Daughters' by Marianne Fredriksson, the story of three generations of a Scandinavian family told by the youngest: it looked promising. I also fell for three soft toys, one Kangaroo with baby (just its head, so I discovered later) and a small Koala Bear, with the birthdays of grandchildren Callum and Sarah-Jean in mind, and their imminent departure back to India.

There was a four-hour wait, but by the time I'd 'done' the shops, and sat outside and had, yes, a cappuccino, there wasn't much time to go. The flight was 3.30 pm and once on board I couldn't decide which seat was D and which was F in my appointed row. I chose the wrong one but an oncoming American family quickly put me right. We put back our watches another 2 hours: it was a long time and a long way to go.

I dipped into the poetry book. It was a very varied selection, something for every mood. I hadn't read any poetry since I'd been away and the rhythms set me to work on trying to write something about Philip as I had intended. We arrived at Singapore just after 11 pm, the early hours so far as my sleep rhythm was concerned, but we had only an hour to wait for the ongoing flight to Heathrow.

Everyone seemed very sleepy, and after reading a good section of my Scandinavian book, I slept on and off for a couple of hours. I woke to discover breakfast was already being served. I selected an omelette, which was bright yellow and leathery. The couple on my left had woken up and the man commiserated about the omelette, which he was also having. He and his wife had been visiting their son in Australia but had been away four months, making use of their time in the Southern Hemisphere to see other places as well.

We touched down exactly on time, 4.55 am, and I suddenly felt wide awake. My luggage came off the carousel early and I pushed it through 'nothing to declare'. There were numerous drivers awaiting incoming passengers, some displaying names in capital letters on large cards. I didn't see any of the Shuttle Service drivers I recognised so I put on my glasses and studied the names but 'Tyler' did not figure among them. Well, the plane had been dead on time and I hadn't had to wait for the luggage so I thought I should give them a bit of time.

I gave half an hour and then got anxious. The adrenaline surge was running down. I searched in my wallet and found the phone number, and gave the Ludgates of Brayford, the headquarters of the service, a call. I got the answerphone, which didn't provide immediate help. After rechecking all the held boards and enquiring at the information desk I was no further forward. Had I given them the wrong day? Or the wrong flight number? But no, I knew they checked everything meticulously.

I waited another long half hour and then rang again and got Lydia Ludgate, who had got my previous message and had been trying to contact her husband, who was supposed to be collecting me. But his phone was switched off! He was spending the night with their daughter in Ealing. She sounded very angry as she said, "I'll kill him!" I thought I might do that as well, if he ever turned up. As I came off the phone I recognised her husband, Bill, as he swung hurriedly through the doors. I reported her/our intentions. He was full of apologies - couldn't get the teletext, daughter had no alarm clock etc. I ventured to mention his switched-off phone, of which he'd apparently been unaware. Actually I was so pleased to see him, whatever the time was, that it no longer mattered. We got back to his car and the phone was ringing. It was Lydia and he didn't half get an earful. She hardly let him get a word in edgeways!

It was grey and damp and dreary, and in many areas there was still evidence of the serious flooding before, and again during, my time away. "You've missed the worst of the weather," said Bill. There'd been snow as well as rain. "It's much warmer now." It didn't feel particularly that way to me.

Bill and Lydia were keen, experienced scuba divers, as were all their family, and I told him of my comparatively lowly adventure - he was most impressed by the Manta Ray. It seemed no time before we were back at Heronslake, which also looked grey and wintry, but which gave me a warm glow nevertheless. I said farewell to Bill, who would be returning to Lydia …

I made myself a strong coffee - not cappuccino, that's just for holidays - unpacked, and began work on the enormous heap of Christmas and other mail, intending to complete the task before going for a sleep. However, I ran out of steam about 12 noon, when I was only about halfway through, and thought I would just have a couple of hours' rest. When I woke it was 10 pm! I had something to eat and finished the mail.

COROLLARY

It had been another good holiday experience, perhaps not as excitingly adventurous as some trips I've done, but I had really enjoyed it. I'd come back less exhausted than after other, more demanding, expeditions.

There are two main elements which make up any holiday so far as I am concerned. The most important is people, indeed Ian and Elizabeth were the whole reason for my visit, and the time spent with them had been wonderful. The welcome had made me feel a part of their extended family over Christmas. It had been therapeutic to talk about Philip, whom I'd never known that well. It had been our intention (John's and mine) to visit Philip in Australia before we were much older, but John started his year's final illness with an incurable cancer about three months before Philip died, quite suddenly, and we were not even able to go to Philip's funeral. Philip had a special love of Hadrian's Wall and its history and it was there that his ashes were eventually scattered. He and Elizabeth had got married from Heronslake and I'd taken to her from the moment we had met. Sadly, the marriage had not lasted and we'd lost touch with Elizabeth until she contacted us about Philip's funeral. Ever since there had been this kind of empty space, which none of us had felt able to enter comfortably. Now we'd talked about it, I'd seen the houses where she and Philip had lived, had visited his university department, and we'd called on the house to which he had retreated after the separation - a first time for Elizabeth, as well as for me. I now knew Philip better and had a new bond with Elizabeth, who felt she had lightened her sadness by sharing it.

There are people flashes which I shall always remember: Natasha the much-pierced hairdresser fellow passenger, the three medics and the Liverpool connection, Ingrid and family on Lady Elliott Island, and dear Justine, my diving instructor. She is the daughter of parents with a gypsy lifestyle and likes to 'move on' every couple of years. The world truly is her oyster.

As for places, the memories which are strongest include the beauty of Perth, especially that of St George's Cathedral, the walk through the tropical rainforest on Fraser Island, the beach at Lady Elliott Island, where all those glorious seabirds chuntered and busied themselves all through the day and night, the underwater scene with the Manta Ray, and the powerful effect of nothing but the vastness of space at the sheep farm - punctuated only by trailing Mallee Trees, the occasional Kangaroo, and thousands of majestic Merino Sheep.

All the shrubs delighted but many were also strange and 'foreign' but so colourful - and in December! The night sky was the wrong way up and I remember a moment of total bemusement when Bernadine (Elizabeth's mother) said how she had this lovely north-facing flat in Perth where she gets the sun all day … ?

I asked several times about the Aboriginals at what seemed like opportune moments and got some evasive responses. One Australian said, "Oh, most of them are unemployed, they drink all day and get more in unemployment benefit than anyone else." I'd read about the enforced exclusion of the Butchulla Aboriginals by the timber traders on Fraser Island and other accounts of ill-treatment. Elizabeth assured me that there were some good stories and showed me a book "Kings in Grass Castles" by Mary Durack, which gives an account of a family of early settlers who worked with, and were helped by, some Aboriginals. I've tried to order it but a 'reprint is under consideration.'

In the meantime, I've had all the photos processed and sent prints off to special people mentioned. And now, at 9.30 pm on Friday, February 2nd, I've finished writing up this diary, and I've still got a bit of a tan!

INDIA
and
SRI LANKA

with **WEXAS INTERNATIONAL**
- The Family -
and **THE TRAVEL COLLECTION**

INDIA and SRI LANKA
December 2001 - January 2002

Friday December 21st 2001

I'd just realised that this was the shortest day but I suspected that it might not seem that way. I was sitting at the Costa coffee bar in Terminal 4, Heathrow Airport. Lydia of the Shuttle Service had collected me and we had had a magically clear run of only three hours to the airport. I had been pleased to see that it was she, arriving spot on time at 4.20 am, and after a final visit to the bathroom (where I did a last-minute scoop up of the razor, remembering my seasonal unshaven armpits) I presented myself with completed luggage and locked up the house. We had enjoyed family and travel talk en route.

Arriving three hours before the scheduled departure time was uncommonly early for me and I was through the BA check-in desk No 19 in no time. Here a very helpful, probably African, girl reassured me about the weight of my luggage, which I had imagined might be over the prescribed 23kg limit. I'd always prided myself on travelling light and my uncharacteristically heavy load was accounted for by not only several kilograms of study material for Helen, but also by the Christmas presents to be delivered to the India-based family contingent from other members, of both sides of the family, in the UK. I'd never had such a weight and was thankful that I had at last invested in some lightweight, upright luggage on wheels.

In the wake of September 11th the security checks were understandably stringent. My Travelight handbag, with all its splendid zip-up compartments, was emptied completely by a plump lady attendant in white overall and black gloves. I had forgotten to put the nail scissors in my main luggage so she was obliged to confiscate these from my make-up bag. I offered her the tweezers as well but, after testing their sharpness on her hand, she replaced them. At least I'd popped the razor in the main luggage.

I was thirsty and tired. I'd slept fitfully until the prearranged BT call at 3.30 am. The large cardboard cup of coffee was good and was complemented by two crisp almond biscuits. The airport was buzzing with people, and with announcements from calls to missing persons due on flights to Amsterdam, and to New York, "departing in 2 minutes". I would nearly have died if my circumstances had resulted in such close timing. A delay of 40 minutes was announced on my flight to Mumbai (Bombay). Just before 10 am we were summoned to the waiting area of Gate 6, where I sat surrounded by Indians of all ages, many with mobile phones or laptops or both.

Boarding started on the hour and I was delighted to be offered aisle seat 48H, instead of 44E, which was in the middle of a row. Age has its compensations. I was on the starboard side at the end of a threesome. A voluminous Indian girl sat on my right, her left arm and shoulder spilling over on to mine but at least I could compensate and do the same over the aisle. Here I was, thankful to be on the plane even if, as yet, not airborne, for I had had a catalogue of domestic near disasters during the previous week. There'd been squirrels in the roof but I was reasonably confident that the local builder had wire-netted all their opportunist entrances over the gutters outside two of the bedrooms. I'd imagined them chewing their way through electrical wiring and all sorts.

The cover over a bathroom ceiling light had suddenly looked ominously singed and smelled of burning. Try as I would with levers, pennies and screwdrivers, I could not remove it so was obliged to call in the electrician and even he had difficulty in exposing and refixing the offending dangling light bulb, advising on new units in the new year. Then, only two days before departure, the central heating radiator in the living room had sprung a serious leak and by morning the cold water on the floor surprised my bare feet. The plumber, who had already installed a new hot water tank and a reconditioned pump for the water from the well this year, did come within 24 hours, by which time I had a heap of soaking towels. He put in some new piping, filled the system and tried out the heating. It wasn't working properly. He took up the floorboards and it was evident that the pump had had its day. He expressed surprise that it had been working at all, and I then remembered that on several occasions recently I'd checked to make sure I'd switched it on because the house had felt cold, so maybe ... A new pump was collected from the workshop and installed - so the two-hour quick fix became an all-day job, for which I was of course very grateful. During this coming and going I was busy trying to pack, move the sheep, process and freeze perishable food, check the e-mails, send Christmas cards and visit the neighbours, one of whom was going to keep an eye on the place. The small daughter of another neighbour, on being told, "Jean's going to India", announced knowingly "I was born there." I raised a questioning eyebrow to her mother, who shook her head, smiled and said, "She's always said that".

The final bit of trouble was to do with mice, who had been dismantling a small cloth frog in my bedroom for a whole week before I realised that this was the source of the stray red filler beans which had appeared, usually near skirting boards, in various parts of the house - where I then set traps. I was not very good at this, but after tempting goodness knows how many for several days, I eventually caught two, both dear little Woodmice, feeling sad about the first and sickened by the second, which was caught by just its jaw and still alive. I thought of releasing it some distance from the house but I could see it was probably too damaged to be able to eat, so steeled myself and knocked it on the head with the hammer. I felt sure there were more, so left several traps set in likely places.

I recorded all these events while the 747 was on 'hold'. It had been late in and so now we had to wait for a slot. We took off over an hour late at 11.30 am, being assured that much of the time would be made up as we had a tail wind. This was serious: we really were off! I had drunk plenty (no alcohol yet), taken my aspirin, and had a walk around: now that I'm approaching 70, I take the DVD thing to heart (not literally I hope). At 12.30 pm we were over Vienna at a height of 33,000 feet, travelling at 996 km an hour, with a tail wind of 70 km, and with another 3915 miles to our destination. I'm just amazed how the equipment can provide all this information but then it takes me all my time to do the basics on the computer.

A very beautiful air hostess in a sari brought a glass of good Bordeaux, and the lunch which followed was tasty and filling - although unless 'lamb' had been mentioned on the menu, I might have missed it. The generous scattering of red beans reminded me again of Kermit the frog and the mice. The excellent lime pickle was almost as good as that made by my Indiaphile sister.

The Indian lady got quite chatty. She was an insurance trainee and had been in London on a month's course at the firm's expense. When the young Indian on her right awoke for lunch, she understandably turned her attention to him. To my left was a charming French family, three boys ranging from around nine to thirteen, a mother who spoke English with a French accent, and a father who spoke perfect English and, so far as I could tell, perfect French to the boys. At one point the youngest boy got frustrated with the TV and radio buttons and said loudly "Merde", whereupon his mother saw my spontaneous smile and looked embarrassed. In front of me, a man of forty something, with long hair and a lived-in face – a bit like a Rolling Stone - cleaned out the plastic pudding dish with both forefingers and stuck his tongue into the red wine bottle!

At 4 pm it was 48°C outside and we were three and a half hours from our destination, somewhere between Kuwait and Abu Dhabi. I snoozed a little but it was impossible to sleep because of a very young Indian boy whose parents allowed him to roam the aisles, even when the seat belt sign was on. A Ghanaian-looking steward was very patient but firm and returned him to his parents more than once. It was this steward who kept coming round with the water supply and there seemed to be more awareness of the relationship between dehydration and DVT than I'd noticed on previous flights.

India was five and a half hours ahead of the UK so, somewhere around 10.30 pm their time, the noisy youngster fell asleep and so did I.

Saturday December 22nd

By the time I awoke, it was 1.00 am Indian time and I really did feel as if it was the early hours. Landing was imminent and we all obediently fastened ourselves in. The seat belt sign went off and there was an immediate chorus of clickings, first from the released belts and then from the opening of the overhead lockers as passengers reached for their hand luggage. We needn't have hurried for we stood around for ages before the doors opened to allow the five hundred of us to disembark.

The immigration and arrival desks were approached quite quickly via a tortuous arrangement of barriers. I think I got a learner who was being minutely supervised by an older, stern-faced man, as he processed every letter of my details on to his computer. I suddenly felt very hot and removed a sweater while I was waiting. Eventually I passed muster and waited again at the carousel for my luggage. I'd never before viewed this new luggage on its own as it were, and I wished I'd applied distinguishing tape or some such, as similar-looking bags made their appearance. I reminded myself that, as I remembered it, mine was black, had multiple side zips, a small padlock and a Wexas travel label. My vision of the luggage, never mind access, was hampered by a group of ebullient young men who had blocked the way with enough trolleys for a regiment. I was just beginning to despair, with memories of non-appearing luggage at Hyderabad all of twenty-seven years ago, when I spotted the appropriate label on a *navy blue piece*: it was mine.

Then it was through the Green Channel to the outside world, where I anxiously scanned the sea of waiting faces beyond the railings, but my searching gaze was only met by others demonstrating their own signs of recognition of friends and loved ones, to be followed by their joyful reunions. Towards the end of the line I was mightily relieved to sight (a slimmer) Mark. We met with luggage at the end of the barrier and walked the short distance to the white van in which we were to travel the four-hour drive to Pune. The arrangement for the vehicle had been made through one of Mark's students: his cousin was the driver, and another cousin and the student had come for the ride. These three sat in the front and Mark and I travelled comfortably in the back. We had no sooner got in and settled than the three Indians got out and abandoned us! After a few minutes Mark also left me and went to investigate, but they were just fulfilling some legal requirement.

An amazing new motorway was under construction but there was a singular lack of relevant directional signs in the environs of the airport. Taxi and rickshaw drivers helped us to find its beginning, where there was little traffic, and on completed stretches of open road and through well-constructed tunnels, the going was good. However, the intermittent half-finished sections, with bumpy diversions on to the 'wrong' side of the road, were treacherous, and the glaring, undipped lights of oncoming heavy goods vehicles temporarily blinded us to the presence of smaller vehicles, which had either dim lights or none at all. I was glad I wasn't driving but the excitement kept me awake.

We stopped for a very welcome small cup of sweet tea at a makeshift cafe, no doubt a precursor of motorway services to come. The student drove for a while, giving the cousin a break, but when it became evident that he was a learner and was having serious trouble with the gears on a particularly uneven section of road, Mark suggested that they might change back and leave the learning till the daylight. The road between the end of the constructed motorway and the Union Biblical Seminary (UBS) to the south of Pune was, without doubt, the very worst. By this time Mark and I were inclined to nod off every now and then but with the state of the road, the frequent veering to avoid enormous potholes, and the 'sleeping policemen' every few yards, it was impossible to grab more than five seconds' worth of sleep at a time.

Eventually, four hours from the airport as predicted, we arrived at the pleasant ground floor apartment in the seminary compound. Mark woke Helen gently: she looked well but much slimmer and it was great to have arrived and finally be there with them. I drank a very large mug of tea, unpacked essentials and went to bed. I felt it really was Saturday now. I couldn't sleep at first but eventually dropped off. I was vaguely aware of children's voices but I wasn't disturbed.

I felt really refreshed when I awoke around 11.30 am and got up and dressed. The warmth was lovely and made me smile as I put on my favourite ancient summer dress. Helen and Callum and Sarah returned from their walk, and I had a lovely greeting, being hailed "Granny Jean!", with arms in the air. We talked over a tasty, homemade quiche lunch, with cauliflower and roast potatoes.

Later I sat on the patio outside the house and wrote my diary to the sound of the Common Babblers, Small Green Bee-eaters, and the occasional noisy Parakeet: a

Common Pariah Kite swooped overhead making its eerie, shrill call. Helen had the sprinkler on the lawn which she was nurturing, having had sods of good turf laid. She had planted two Papyrus Trees, which looked very happy, as did a well-established Mango Tree, and a glorious flowering tree which I have yet to name.

We did a tour of the purpose-built campus and met some of the staff and students and their families, who were either permanent residents or had not taken the long journeys (like four days) home for Christmas. Flowering shrubs enhanced the well-kept grounds, and inside the railed area, outside the Principal's house, was a simple but impressive white centre piece representing Jesus washing Peter's feet.

We returned and had tea and, after story reading and an enthusiastic dancing session (to music of course), Callum and Sarah went to bed. I unloaded all the family Christmas presents and Bible study material, sent an e-mail to Wendy so that she and the others would know I had arrived in one piece, and thankfully retired to my comfortable bed at 10.45 pm.

Sunday December 23rd

I awoke at 2 am, my biological clock having not yet adjusted. I walked round (very quietly), read for a while, and then slept until 8.45 am. Mark was preaching at St Xavier's Roman Catholic Church, which was also used by the Naga Christian Fellowship Church, so he left early. We four followed on later, walking out of the compound and down the hill on which it is situated, into the outskirts of Pune, where we boarded a rickshaw at the head of the waiting queue of vehicles. The half-hour trip was full of interest, with buffalo, cows, dogs, goats, chickens, bikes, motor-bikes, rickshaws, taxis, not to mention pedestrians, all proceeding inexorably on their tortuous courses, rarely giving way but apparently never colliding!

The church was probably 100-150 years old, with handsome, sensitively-illustrated Stations of the Cross, with appropriate texts written underneath. Live music came from the gallery: the R C choir was rehearsing for Christmas and our service commenced when they finished with "Come, come, come to the Manger". So, in true Indian style the 11 am service started at 11.30 am, although it had to be admitted that we ourselves had not arrived until 11.10 am!

After a dramatic, recorded introduction, we all sang "O Come All Ye Faithful" and then a selection of choruses, easy to pick up even if unfamiliar, with their simple, oft-repeated melodies, and the words up on the screen, all accompanied on guitar. Mark used the Christmas story of Herod's unsuccessful searching for the newborn King to illustrate all-too-familiar present-day analogies of not finding what we are looking for, consciously or unconsciously, when it's right there under our noses and ready for the taking. It was a compelling address and one of the best I've heard for some time.

We emerged into the sunlight (oh how I loved this weather) for a refreshing drink and more introductions. I talked to the Pastor's wife (with young baby) and some of the students from Nagaland - those who had not braved, or could not afford, the four-day journey home, although the Pastor's father had made the marathon trip and had come for Christmas.

Helen went off without us in a rickshaw to do some shopping, while Mark, Callum, Sarah, John (from Ghana, who was one of the teachers at the college and an authority on Islam), his son Nathaniel, three other students and I all travelled in a people-carrier. We stopped en route at a pork butcher's, where many kilograms of meat were bought for the UBS, so it took some time. We admired the bizarre shop sign, which depicted pigs sitting round a table eating pork, served by pig waiters! The children were kept amused by loitering livestock - including a couple of pigs - and a very small, sleeping puppy lying underneath a cycle. I thought it was dead but it stretched itself, got up and walked away when someone collected the cycle.

By the time we got back, Helen was already home with a load of fruit, drinks and a duck for Christmas Eve, which I've just realised is tomorrow. After a late lunch, Callum sat quietly for his video time, Sarah had her afternoon nap and I made for the patio where the sprinkler sprinkled on optimistically over the sporadic grass, and Crows, Bee-eaters, Babblers, a lonely Hoopoe, and a variety of stunning butterflies visited or flew by.

We walked round other aspects of the campus later and met more family friends, adults and children. Well-harmonised carol singing emanated from the administrative block and gave me a feeling of Christmas in spite of the heat. We met the rest of John's family, including his wife Grace, who sported a wonderful hairstyle of tiny plaits, which revealed a draughtsboard-parting pattern beneath.

There was the usual story time after tea: those two had got some great books and I really enjoyed the exercise. Later, while Helen and Mark were busy, I watched a TV discussion about the Nobel Peace Prize. I thought one of the participants spoke very interestingly, with much basic common sense, laced with humour and optimism, which made for an engaging programme.

I had a chilly shower, probably because I did not wait long enough for the water to run hot. The plumbing took a bit of getting used to. We went to bed at 10.30 pm and I hummed quietly through some of Ruddigore and Carousel. (I knew I would be absent for several rehearsals, and I felt I needed some practice).

Monday December 24th - Christmas Eve

I slept until 8.45 am again.

This morning we were bound for the Snake Park. Mark had booked the van and he dropped us off after the fifteen-minute drive, while he went on to complete some secret Christmas shopping.

The park was impressive, with areas of well-established plants and shrubs, while other sections were still under construction. A central stretch of water provided a habitat for such birds as Cormorants, Pond Herons and Sandpipers. The bears were in hiding but we saw various Deer, Porcupines, Crocodiles, Tortoises (one very occupied in laying and covering its eggs - and ignoring the fresh fodder, and the fact that she was being walked over by her peers in their efforts to reach it), Turtles, and an endearing young Leopard. Birds included the White-throated Ground Thrush, a Great Pied Hornbill,

24 December 2001

HURRAH for CHRISTMAS! - CALLUM and SARAH

Pheasants, Peacocks, Vultures and Owls, all seemingly happily caged and in good condition. Women were doing all the watering in and around these enclosures. Today was the equivalent of a Bank Holiday, and the park was teeming with Indian families. Our uniqueness made us the subject of much interest so that we were photographed with an Indian family, and then while eating our picnic lunch, with six young handsome Indians. Sarah was not too keen on all this attention and managed to deter one or two other would-be camera flashers.

Helen and the children were frequent visitors to the park and Callum had a friend in one of the staff at the Snake pit, where he was allowed to hold a Trinket Snake. Sarah was discouraged as she was inclined to pinch and squeeze the reptile. Some of the other spectators drew back in horror at Callum's apparent courage. As we drove back to UBS in the death-defying rickshaw, I marvelled at the strength of some of the women labourers, carrying enormous loads of earth on either side of the main thoroughfare where the road was being widened.

Mark had just returned when we got back and had had time to hide the Christmas surprises. Ranjuna was there, Helen's Indian help. She wore a beautiful, shocking pink sari, which looked far too good to work in - but then even the lady labourers on the road had looked attractively saried. Ranjuna had bangles on her ankles, and rings on the toes of her enviably straight bare feet. I wasn't surprised to hear that she is a year younger than Helen: she has four daughters and one son. The eldest daughter of sixteen had just got married and the parents had provided the usual big wedding with all the attendant expense and, of course, the mandatory dowry. She (the bride) had gone to live with her husband's family. Mark and Helen had visited Runjuna's home, fifteen minutes away from the campus, where they all live in one room. "I wouldn't like their lifestyle", Helen admitted: who would?

We had a trip down to the swings before bedtime and a young student, who said he was from Mizoram, came and talked to me while I sat in a seat keeping an eye on the children on the swings. He wanted an English lesson but I found him very difficult to understand and handed him over to Mark. I hadn't heard of Mizoram before but studied Mark's map later to discover that it is up round the corner, to the right of the subcontinent as it were, not far from Burma.

It had been with some difficulty that Helen had got the frozen duck as a special treat for the Christmas Eve meal. It still had a head and sizeable webbed feet, which I supposed was reassuring as to its identity but, once thawed, it became evident that it was unhappily entire in every way, not even having been drawn. Helen coped well with its preparation and cooking, with her limited domestic equipment, while I was allotted the making of the stuffing. The bird had looked on the small side to begin with, but by the time all the inedible bits had been removed there wasn't a lot left. But the flavour was good and there were plenty of excellent vegetables, not to mention the stuffing, to go with it. The children had sausages, about which they were very enthusiastic.

Carol singers came to entertain us later. They sang with smiles and enthusiasm, accompanied by guitar and drums. I'd never sung "Hark the Herald" at such a rollicking pace. English words were on a carol sheet but, for a carol in their own language, a girl member shouted out each line lustily, ahead of the music. It transpired they were all from Mizoram, which was too far to go home, I guessed. They presented us with a Christmas Cake. Finally, there was a sorting of Christmas presents for Father Christmas, which was followed by a shower and bed at 11 pm.

Tuesday December 25th - Christmas Day

I got up at a time which was early for me - 7.45 am. There was great excitement at opening the presents: the children worked through stockings and smaller parcels until the last, the biggest: a sturdy three-wheeler bike for Sarah and an amazing remote-control car for Callum.

We rickshawed out to the other side of the city, a forty-minute drive, full of interest as usual, to the grounds of the Roman Catholic Papal Seminary, where we were to picnic with members of the Naga Christian Fellowship. Everyone was assembled under the trees where it was shaded and cool. Many were sitting in a large circle, playing a game in which the victim in the middle was gearing his answers to questions from the audience, acccording to a particular subject which he had been given: this differed in the extreme from the topic the onlookers had been dealt. This made for some hilarious possibilities. Other fun team games followed.

We had an excellent lunch of pork, chicken, beans, rice, and chutneys, cooked and eaten in the shade. Everyone was chirpy and obviously enjoying themselves, not least Callum and Sarah, who had an especially good deal from the Christmas sack as there were not as many children present as had been anticipated. I thought I'd take a little walk into the surrounding countryside to get a closer look at some of the birds and butterflies that I'd seen from a distance, but once beyond the shade of the trees it was unbelievably hot out there in the sun, and I was soon creeping back.

We had the maddest rickshaw driver back, weaving between all the usual hazards. There were lots of families out on motorbikes of all calibres, most of the ladies in gorgeous brightly-coloured saris. We passed slum areas where small children played in the dust at the side of the road: I wondered what the infant and toddler mortality might be. In spite of the erratic driving, and the bumps and potholes in the road, Callum and Sarah slept soundly all the way.

Later we walked to the Medical Mission Sisters' Seminary, situated high up on the hill above UBS, which was built on what was originally Medical Mission land. En route Helen spotted one of Runjana's daughters at a young people's day centre and stopped to speak to her. A photograph seemed a good idea but the girl said three other members of her family were there also and she would fetch them. By the time she came out into the road there must have been twenty to thirty smiling would-be subjects for a snapshot and, try as we would, it was impossible to get Runjana's family on their own, so I just took one or two random pictures. They all shouted "Happy Christmas!" and we shook hands with most of them.

Helen had been asked by a biochemist acquaintance to make enquiries about a lady doctor, a pathologist with whom he had worked on a project in India and whom he knew had been at the Medical Mission Sisters' Seminary but who had had a period of

25 December 2001

"TAKE MY PICTURE!"

ill health, with cancer. As luck would have it, two of the students followed us up the long drive and they confirmed that the lady, now seventy-three, was indeed there and still working. We were asked in, and met the lady doctor in question, who was charming and looked very well. The children were asked into the kitchen and given special star biscuits.

The light was fading as we walked back but we were able to have a view of the resident Spotted Owl in a high tree outside the main building. We'd seen a Plain Wren Warbler and a Black Drongo on the walk up. Even Callum had a go with the binoculars. The lights of Pune spread out below us and the pollution over the city softened the sunset sky into a mellow mulch of brown and orange: it was strangely beautiful.

As we neared the bottom of the hill two middle-aged Indian ladies caught us up, tapped me on the back and asked me some question. I summoned Helen, who had difficulty in understanding their Hindi-Marathi tongue but ultimately, with the help of a passing young man, discovered that they wanted to know how it was that Helen was so thin after having had two children, (I wondered that too.) They laughed and toddled off ahead of us, a couple of bats swooping in their wake. Back at the house, the lady upstairs (a headmistress) had brought down a plate of splendid Indian goodies, which were enjoyed by all, but especially by me.

25 December 2001
Grounds of the Roman Catholic Papal Seminary
MARK and SARAH, CALLUM and HELEN

Some time during the evening Mark did this clever thing of organising long-distance phone calls on the internet, and I was able to speak to the rest of the family around their lunchtime. It was exciting and I almost felt tongue-tied. Charles and family were enjoying Christmas at home, while Richard and family were at Wendy's for Christmas lunch. Helen joined in the exercise and she and Trevor had a pharmaceutical discussion. The world has become very small.

Wednesday December 26th - Boxing Day

I had a disturbed night with D and V and wondered whether it was over-indulgence in the Indian luxuries from upstairs, but decided, as Helen suggested, that it was more likely to be the 'traditional' Indian tummy. "You wonder when you'll get it, not whether you'll get it!" I felt distinctly limp and lifeless and decided it would be foolish to accompany the family on the planned temple and MacDonald's expedition.

I sat on the patio with my feet up and drank plenty of water. The temperature was comfortable and I half-heartedly studied any birds which flew into my field of vision: Jungle Babblers, Purple Sunbird, Jungle Crows, Pied Mynas, Rufus-tailed Finch-Lark, Roseringed Parakeet, Indian Myna, Indian Robin, and Common Pariah Kite all graced me with their presence. Ground Squirrels came and went and one chased a Babbler. (I do wonder why they are called 'Ground' Squirrels when they seem to spend much of their time leaping from tree to tree.) A Babbler that was trying to feed its demanding fledgling was hampered by equally demanding mating attentions from a male of the species. I heard the rising crescendo 'kuoo' call of the noisy Koel but didn't get sight of it.

A couple of Milkweed Butterflies** hovered around, and a large black and white Swallowtail flitted about in the shade of the Mango Tree, as did several speedy little yellow butterflies. A couple of children passed and called "Hello Aunty".

I skipped lunch, still didn't fancy food but definitely felt better. I slept for a couple of hours during the afternoon, being awoken every now and then by the silence of the fan when the electricity cut out intermittently.

Reunited later, we all went to Ghanaian John's for a cup of tea, where the TV showed wall-to-wall cartoons and the children drank coke. (John supported the Liverpool football team.) We left at 6.30 pm and it was dark and balmy. Then, more story reading and an early night..

*** On looking in a limited Indian butterfly book later, when I had returned home, I was not sure that these were Milkweeds: they could have been Danaid Eggfly females, mimicking the Plain Tiger variety of Milkweed.*

Thursday December 27th

After some discussion over the price of the hired vehicle, we left home at 10.30 am for a night away in the hills. I'd had a good night and felt sufficiently normal to eat some cornflakes. We drove out of Pune through the usual busy life of the city, past such memorable cameos as a Ladies' High Fashion shop, with pigs of all sizes foraging about outside, some children being stripped-washed with a bucket of water drawn from the road's standpipe, and a collection of very large Rubber Plants which were so thick with dust that they were barely recognizable. Mark sat in the front with the driver while Helen and I sat in the back with Sarah; Callum commuted acrobatically from one to the other.

As we drove away from the city there were areas of intense cultivation, sweetcorn and maize, and other crops I didn't know. The road was being widened in patches, and was single track for tree-felling along one stretch. We passed Bullocks and Buffaloes, a couple of Camels, multitudes of dogs - one strangely striped as if it had been crossed with Zebra - and a pile of broken glass, evidence that not all cavalier driving is accident free.

The journey to the Maidstone guesthouse in Panchkani (five hills) took less time than anticipated and we arrived just after mid-day, unloaded the car and were shown our accommodation by an Indian lady of mature years. The two rooms, one on the ground floor and the other up an outside staircase, each had three beds. It was suggested that I had the downstairs room and the family went upstairs but we decided to swap. We had a walk in the garden and ate a good lunch.

We visited the MAPRO jam factory and walked and watched from the visitors' gallery. Evidently this product was sold all over India ("bit sweet" according to Helen) and employed just twenty people to do the bottling, labelling and packing. The surrounding garden included a commercial nursery with hundreds of healthy-looking plants for sale, strawberries in profusion for the jam, and varieties of rose with outsize hips, destined for the company's Rosehip Syrup. A glassware outlet for a factory further north attracted our attention and Helen chose a couple of plain vases. We had a fruity strawberry ice cream. Once again the children, especially Sarah, attracted much unwanted attention from the indigenous population, some with cameras.

We were driven back to Panchkani and took a walk down the busy main street and then, a little way from the shops, went into the grounds of a Parsee Fire Temple but, not being of that persuasion, were allowed to walk only outside. It rained a little, which was refreshing. We stretched our legs again at a viewing point where a turbaned fortune-teller was busy with a couple of young clients.

We visited St Peter's Church and met its Pastor, Daniel, his wife Laura, and son Samuel, who were all very welcoming. They had accommodation on the premises and we sat comfortably on the veranda and drank coffee. Samuel demonstrated the wiles of his new remote-controlled car track to Callum and Sarah (Father Christmas had been very good all round) while the four parents discussed higher things. A Christian Missionary founded Panchkani and built the church one hundred and fifty years ago. The place was now very much alive with schools, thirty-two of them. I could see that it would be an attractive location for boarding schools.

The light was fading when we made for the Table Mountain with Daniel and Samuel. It gave wide views of the surrounding countryside and was something of a mini-theme park with pony rides, a big wheel, a train, a cave to explore (which served as a café during daylight), two men offering spectacular sightings through hired telescopes, undocked Sheep, a lady sitting cross-legged on the ground selling slices of her peeled cucumbers, and greedy, thieving Monkeys. There was a festive air about the place with lots of smartly-dressed families enjoying the facilities.

There were comments about it being "very chilly" because we were so "high up". I was comfortable in my short sleeves, while many of them wore their fleeces and Samuel wore a balaclava! The children enjoyed a ride on the train and explored the cave.

We dropped off Daniel and Samuel and got back in time to shower and change for supper at 8 pm. The children ate well as they had done all day and seemed remarkably untired. My guts felt rebellious again and I wasn't able to eat much of the meal, which was a pity because it was very good. I felt obliged to explain to the lady in charge, as she asked direct questions about left over food. The waiter was in a hurry to clear and Callum got the message early on, and clung on to his glass of water and his plate. The whole place had a faded Old Empire feel about it - gracious but neglected.

At 9 pm madam asked what time we were going to bed! Helen was still settling the children. Madam gave Mark instructions for locking up after I had left the dining room-lounge to go to bed. I mounted the dusky, moonlit staircase at 10 pm.

Friday December 28th

I had a dreadful night with an unpleasant taste in my mouth, stomach cramps, and long sessions on the loo every hour. I wondered how I'd get up in the morning. I stayed in bed till 8.30 am and then made an effort, and got packed and washed and dressed. Poor Mark and Helen had also had little sleep, with Sarah awake with a stomach-ache between 1 am and 5 am.

I opted to stay at Maidstone while they did their planned excursion. I couldn't face the insecurity of travelling in the van without a loo in sight. Helen made a diagnosis of Gardia, and produced eight tablets of Fasigyn 500 (Tindazole), four to be taken immediately and the other four to be taken in a fortnight's time. She also provided a couple of Loperamide because I'd left my Lomotil in Pune. Thank goodness for her pharmaceutical expertise and supplies.

I sat outside and watched the birds and admired the view. The ground ran away steeply from the back of the guesthouse to an expanse of water, beyond which one of the five hills marked the skyline like another Table Mountain. I felt weary and returned to bed where sleep was impossible because of a series of English lessons being given to young men on the balcony of the next room. The lady teacher had a very powerful accented (German, I think) voice. Under different circumstances it could have been quite entertaining. There was a series of phrases with like meanings such as "I am able to", "I am capable of", "I have the capacity to", and "I can". She got very cross with one student who had evidently not done his homework. "I do not want your money: I do not do this for the money ... you must do your study at home otherwise you will have to re-sit your exam. Learn all the irregular verbs by heart behind (at the back of?)

the yellow book." I did drift into sleep once but was rudely awakened by loud knocking on my locked bedroom door. I got up and admitted two gunta'd cleaning ladies, who swished about the floor with broomsticks and wet cloths.

I went outside again. I got a glimpse of the teacher as I left the room. She walked up and down as she taught, glasses perched on the end of her nose. Madam and her more charming husband came and asked me whether I wanted anything but I stuck to the bottled water. The teacher brought out her barking black and white dog (another disturbing factor during the night) on a lead and, after walking it round the garden, proceeded to let it empty its bowels within spitting distance of where I was sitting. She made conversation all the while, asking whether it was my first visit to India, why I was here etc. I was less than my usual communicative self and, after a silent pause, she concluded with "There are worse places to live: if you haven't got much money, it's very cheap here" and she was gone back upstairs. I wondered about her afterwards: how she came to be living here. Normally I'd have found out.

I sat with the binoculars and looked at Bee-eaters, Drongos, Sunbirds, Babblers and Mynas, nothing out of the Indian ordinary but I enjoyed them and was feeling better. Helen and family returned just after 2 pm and, after taking our leave, we re-visited the Table Mountain complex in the daylight. The Monkeys came very close and stole food from unsuspecting hands. An elderly lady in a yellow sari sliced the cucumber. I didn't see anyone taking advantage of her wares: how do these people survive? A man with a telescope made several unsuccessful approaches, mostly to men, until a very smartly dressed client accepted the challenge and in no time there was a queue waiting for the privilege.

The drive back to Pune was hairy and adventurous with at least three near misses - and there may well have been others for I was in dozing mode. We definitely hit a dog at one juncture. I hoped it was a fatal blow for I couldn't imagine anyone was going to take a stray animal to the vet.

A huge tree was felled as we approached and crashed right cross the road, but was moved very quickly. I commented on the dearth of crash helmets and Helen said a new law had been introduced on December 1st for all motorcycle drivers to wear such headgear, with on-the-spot fines for non-compliance. It had obviously not yet caught on.

The children ate a substantial tea and then it was story time again, which I really enjoyed. It was early bed for me as well. I washed my hair. I thought I really was better

Saturday December 29th

I felt almost well when I woke up, thank goodness. I had a quiet morning reading about Sri Lanka in anticipation of next week, and going through my music. Later the children joined me and we had a competitive session throwing half-inflated balloons into buckets. Helen made an appetising lasagne for lunch and I really enjoyed it: yes, my appetite had returned with a vengeance. Punchgani strawberries followed, topped with clotted cream removed from the top of the scalded Buffalo milk: delicious.

In the afternoon Helen, Callum, and I went to Jagtap plant nursery for me to buy Helen's Christmas present. The extensive nursery was packed with an incredible selection of plants suitable for the Indian climate. We bought a large (very large, by UK standards) Poinsettia, two hanging baskets of Petunias, two pots of Coleus, a Ficus Variegata - the most expensive of the lot at the equivalent of £10 - two Bougainvilleas, two Acalypha, an African Palm, and a Pharosuria. These were all to be delivered in the nursery van, and we'd imagined we might travel with them but there was just one seat and that was for the driver! The arrangement was that the van would follow our rickshaw. Not surprisingly, once we got into the heavy Pune traffic, where our rickshaw became one of so many, the van driver lost us when we turned left for the college. Our driver was all for following in hot pursuit, but Helen persuaded him otherwise and while she was making an opportune purchase of balloons at a nearby shop, he spotted the yellow van retracing its steps and rushed out into the road to redirect it. We'd chatted to the rickshaw driver in the interim: his English was limited but he did get across that he would never be rich and own his own rickshaw, as he had three daughters ... Mark admired the plants but thought the delivery charge of 269/- (£4) was exorbitant.

Helen joined Mark and Sarah at the opening of the Interserve conference being held here this weekend. We'd met several of the delegates on the campus as we'd started out on our afternoon expedition. Meanwhile Callum and I opened the new packet of Indian style balloons: varying shapes and sizes, multicoloured and with the odd hole! They were incredibly difficult to blow up and even more of a problem to tie with my stiff fingers and without any string. I finished up assisting the process with my teeth with some success, for which I received enthusiastic applause from Callum.

A lady called Denny (Denise) came and had a cup of coffee with us. She was a pharmacologist in Vellore, and she and her husband Jo, a biochemist, were organising the conference. I had this strange feeling that we'd met before, as did she, but after going through our life histories, it didn't seem possible.

Large blue bath time for the children was a noisy splashing affair but I did manage to get a few photographs. The ritual story time and bed followed.

I was left in charge while Mark and Helen went to an Interserve meeting. I joined them later for coffee and met a likeable couple from Canada who are doing a three-year stint as 'dorm parents' at Woodstock School in the north. Their three teenage children were with them.

I went to bed at 11 pm: nearly late, and was soothed to sleep by the fan and the comforting fluorescence of planets and stars on the ceiling of what was really Callum's room.

Postscript: I have discovered today that

(1) the Owl I thought I'd heard the other night was, in fact, the night watchman blowing some strange warning whistle,
    and
(2) the puzzling Guinea Fowl or Pheasant sound was the 'ribbet, ribbet' of the Frog bought from British Airways on the way over!

Sunday December 30th

Helen and I took the children to toddle around the campus and on the swings while Mark went to the conference. After a late coffee (the first session had overrun) I joined Helen at a seminar entitled 'Perseverance' given by a consultant paediatrician known as M C, who had known Anne and Murdoch (my sister and brother-in-law) in Madras, where he and his wife worked with handicapped children - he was inspirational.

I wished afterwards that I'd taken proper notes but this was the gist of it:

How should we persevere?

(1) be an incarnational presence with the people, rather than imposing our will upon them because of a better education, more privilege etc.

(2) seek for reconciliation, especially between Christian factions where differences and intolerances stifle the work

(3) await the resurrection - a long time in coming after endurance and hardship; compare a mother's delight at the successful birth of a baby after the discomfort and pain of pregnancy and labour.

(4) hold an eschatological vision: not to be occupied with the material world around us, to live in hope .

(5) help others, especially marginalised groups.

(6) self-giving: compare breast-feeding.

(7) maintain trust – compare children learning to walk: they falter and fall - into the arms of parents who keep an eye on them; they always get up and try again until they succeed. 2001 was a year of disasters, but don't give up trust and hope.

Why should we persevere?

Because we are concerned about the redemption of God's people.

(Could we do with an occasional sermon like this in Torrington? Yes!)

We had lunch in the hall at the conference and I enjoyed talking to the Canadian couple. The children ate well in spite of plenty of nibbles during the morning. Mark and Helen went to the Interserve AGM while I stayed with the children. That was no hardship. Callum watched his video, the delightful Dumbo, his Christmas present from Wendy and family, while Sarah had her afternoon nap.

Later we had a walk and a swing, and even Granny enjoyed some air-borne activity. The ubiquitous Abishake (that's how his name is pronounced, anyway), a young lad in his early teens who adored Sarah, joined us for a while. Sarah was busy drawing in the sand with a stick in her left hand. Callum was in one of his stroppy phases and I felt sorry for Helen, but he calmed down once we were back home. I watered the plants – there were more of them now!

Mark and Helen went to another meeting and once the children were settled, I had an in-depth look at Pune's Sunday Times. I was fascinated by the pages of 'matrimonials' where everyone was "fair" and/or "beautiful", had a string of professional qualifications, and came from "a good family." I found it sad that they all wanted to be "fair", their colouring was so lovely: was this all our fault from the days of Empire?

Sarah awoke and had a bit of a wobbly. She'd got a runny nose and couldn't breathe through her mouth and suck her dummy at the same time. The dummy was still a bedtime concession. She wanted to get out of the cot, so we sat on the bed in her room for a while. Needless to say she really wanted mummy and daddy but eventually she opted to return to the cot with clean nose, dummy and her water. Every now and then she would look up and give me a winning smile round the dummy: after a while her eyes closed and I was able to leave her.

Monday December 31st 2001 - New Year's Eve

My stomach felt slightly turbulent again this morning. I went to a conference session with Helen. It was a bit happy-clappy for my tastes but the address on some verses from Timothy emphasised looking for someone with whom to share one's work, someone who might eventually take over. (I thought about the Psychosexual Counselling slot which I had just relinquished and how I'd failed to persuade the authorities to train and put my successor in post.) The address was a bit long for a rumbling stomach on a Monday morning.

I joined Mark and the children in the pentagon where they played with, and talked to, others. We had a conference lunch and half a dozen of the conference people came back for coffee. I emigrated to the patio with Sarah, who was anxious to transfer water-filled balloons from one bucket to another. When we came back inside I talked to the young wife of the morning's preacher. They worked in South India, I think, although she was another migrant from Mizoram. They all appreciated one of Helen's good cakes, especially a Dutch lady who said the cinnamon made it taste "just like home."

I was a bit anxious about having to confirm my flight from Bombay to Colombo in three days' time, with Sri Lankan Airways. I hadn't got their phone number and the phone book referred only to Air Lanka. Dear Mark tracked it down and I was reassured when the pleasant girl said all was well and took my phone number in case there was any change in the flight time.

Helen and Callum and I happily picked up a rickshaw in the college grounds and set off into Pune on a shopping expedition. We called first at the security-guarded indoor cash-point where, after chatting to others waiting - two of them on a 'youth-with-a-mission' project - (only one punter was allowed in at a time), the machine had the audacity to refuse my card. Fortunately I'd brought some ancient travellers' cheques as well and we changed these at our next port of call - TATA FINANCE AMEX Ltd - and got 68.25 Indian rupees for £1 sterling. We walked through the busy street to Bombay Store, recommended by Helen, where I bought little presents for Callum and Sarah and other small items for gifts back home. Then I couldn't resist some Elephants on silk, suitable for framing, from another store nearby.

I'd expressed a wish for a Salwar Kameez, the combination of longish, gently-fitting top and matching loose trousers. Helen had purchased a lovely example of this traditional dress for Christmas from Westside, where I now had a look. I tried on a sage green example, the top with attractive embroidery, and a tuni (a sort of stole) thrown in. While I was in the dressing room Callum wriggled under the door to join me and said it was "All right". The trousers were far too voluminous for my taste and would have needed some radical surgery. At that time I wore a size 12/14 in the UK, yet this outfit was labelled XL, much to my chagrin! I decided to buy and parted with the equivalent of £16. We then went to investigate the advertised Grotto, but Father Christmas had sleighed back to Lapland, much to Callum's disappointment.

Finally we went to the Coffee House where Helen and I had fresh lime sodas, and Callum had an Apple Fanta and a dosa (a dinner-plate-sized sweet crêpe, covered in grated cheese). He consumed the lot, tearing off pieces in proper Indian style and dipping them into the chutney and the yoghurt. He, and the manager of this establishment, a dwarf (probably pituitary) called Niya, greeted each other like old friends, which they evidently were. As we left Niya commandeered a rickshaw for us and then bought two large heart-shaped balloons from one of the many nearby vendors on the pavement outside: "One for you and one for your sister Sarah."

It was 7 pm by the time we got back and Mark was a bit worried, having expected us earlier. The children were bathed and changed and dressed in their smart clothes for the New Year's Eve party in the conference dining room.

The hall had been decorated, the tables laid and adorned with lighted candles and flower heads, and it all looked very festive. Tonight we were served at table and relieved of the regular washing up of the individual stainless steel compartmentalised tray-like plate, sweet dish, and water mug. The food was as great as the company. The atmosphere was very relaxed and once the meal was all but over, a robust children's game of spontaneous football developed in the capacious building.

We returned to the house with two still very wide-awake children, but they soon settled down. Mark and Helen went off to the New Year's Eve Ceilidh, which was appropriately being oganised by Scots Mark, who did the same when I was at the Interserve conference with them in Hyderabad in 1998. They hadn't been gone long before the fans slowed to barely turning and the lights dimmed. The TV stumbled on for a while and at midnight I heard all the commentary on the launch of the Euro in nine different European countries. Sydney seemed to be having a very grand firework display in spite of the raging bush fires all around.

The TV went off, as did everything else except the two emergency lights, which came on exactly on cue. I heard a door open and an unhappy Callum appeared. I wasn't surprised. The fireworks and firecrackers had been making such a racket that the upstairs dog had barked incessantly, and of course the soothing noise of the fan, which comfortingly camouflages other more intrusive sounds, had stopped altogether.

We sat on the settee and talked. Callum was really waiting for his mum and dad to come back. I envied his apparent reserves of energy after all that had happened during the day. Mark and Helen returned. Sadly, because of the unfortunate timing of the electricity cut, it had not been possible to put on the Scottish dancing without the necessary music. We wished each other a Happy New Year 2002, the lights came on, and we all, including Callum, retired to bed where mercifully the noise of the fans drowned that of the continuing firecrackers.

Tuesday January 1st 2002

I had a really good night's sleep.

During the day Mark and Helen staggered their visits to the Interserve meetings and I stayed with the children. It was great to have the playground and swings within such easy reach and all so safe. We called to see Grace, who provided coke and orangeade. She was finding it difficult to discipline the children, now that John was in Australia. His conference was in Sydney - I thought about those fires again.

We lunched in the conference dining room, where I had a long chat with a very tall, very thin Swiss girl, who was doing six months' obstetrics in Utah Pradesh. Earlier I had talked to Maria, another young doctor, who was doing a similar stint in Vellore as an anaesthetist, before returning to New Zealand to marry a Chinese computer consultant who "is very interested in mission." Both these girls were working very hard and cramming in a lot of experience. I did my share of washing up and indulged in a good-humoured bit of banter with Jo, Dinny's husband, as we attempted to flush the grease away under the cold tap, into the lengthy sink.

After lunch I had another look at the badly-photocopied music which I was supposed to know by the time I got back to the UK, and then I hung out the washing. (No drying problem here.) It was the garden that could do with some rain: I did the watering. I did hope the tufts of grass would blossom into a lawn eventually: at present they could be aptly described as "poor little sods."

I bought some placemats, napkins and cards at the Oasis stall at the back of the church: so reasonably priced by our standards and good stand-by presents. I needed to watch it. My luggage would be getting as heavy as it was on the outward journey. I knew Helen had a few things for me to take back for the rest of the family.

Helen and Mark went to the last of the evening conference meetings and I stayed with the children - but neither of them woke at all.

Wednesday January 2nd

The final communion service of the conference in the church was well attended. 'Living Waters', a music group who had given their services throughout the conference, sang a truly lovely setting of the Gaelic Blessing, which I had not heard before. There were lots of farewells. Most people were leaving today, some going back to work but others, such as the Woodstock contingent, taking a break in Goa. Mark took back all the individual communion cups to wash at the house. (There was something to be said for having a communal one.)

We all took a break and visited the leafy suburb of Koregaon Park, the home of Osho Commune International, a 'spiritual health club' based on the teachings of Bhagwan Shree Rajneesh (1931-90), a controversial Indian 'export' guru who advocated, amongst other things, sex as a path to enlightenment. His 'mystic rose' technique embraced three days laughing and then three days crying, for weeks on end. However bizarre, there were hundreds of people willing to pay to experience the course at the centre and we saw many of them, mostly European-looking, walking in the vicinity of the ashram in their compulsory maroon tunics.

We took a walk round the beautiful gardens on the opposite side of the road. Well-established trees, an infinite variety of flowering shrubs and sheltered water features (great for Callum's stone-splashing exercise) made it pleasing and shaded, and an ideal venue for courting couples, of which there were several. I commented on the volume of water necessary for such an enterprise, and Helen said she had read somewhere of some nearby village being kept short in order to facilitate the project.

We also visited the Gandhi National Memorial over the Mula River at Yerwada, originally the Aga Khan's palace (built by Imamsultan Muhammad Sha Aga Khan III in 1892). It later became a school - lucky children - but in 1969 it was donated to India by the Aga Khan IV. After Mahatma Gandhi delivered his 'Quit India' resolution in Bombay in 1942, the British interned him and others there for nearly two years. Gandhi's wife and secretary both died during the period of imprisonment. We saw the samadhis (memorial tombs) where their ashes are kept. The building houses photographs of the highlights of Gandhi's life but it is the personal touches, like seeing his sandals and articles of his simple clothing, which I found very moving.

Coincidentally, it was announced only yesterday in the New Year Honours list that Ben Kingsley, who took the role of Gandhi so magnificently, had been knighted, and some of that film had been shot in and around this building.

It was dark by the time we stopped off at a little German bakery on the way home, where we relished the lemon cake, cheese croissants and cappuccino. Callum tucked into a large brown (heavy) sort of bap, made from buckwheat. All the world seemed to be in there including Osho devotees indulging in generous portions of calorie-laden foods, hippy-looking wrinklies, smart Indian businessmen, ageing European women with long, loose grey hair, and young Indian men who looked like students. There was a fair amount of embracing as some of the 'alternatives' came upon each other.

One of the students came over to speak to us and then I recognized him as one of the 'Living Waters' team, so I asked him about the setting of the Gaelic Blessing. It was original and had been composed by one of their members but he didn't think it was written down anywhere. Pity.

Helen shopped for vegetables and fruit from a roadside spread. Callum accompanied her and got rewarded with a carrot. Then it was the last story time, and packing for the next phase of my holiday, in Sri Lanka.

Gavin, who had a senior administrative role with Interserve, came in to use Mark's computer and update his e-mails, as he had done on previous evenings, and we all sat chatting afterwards. He wasn't going to bed as he had a night flight. My 'early night' was not as early as I had intended. Mark set the alarm to call me at 5.15 am.

Thursday January 3rd

I slept intermittently and awoke in anticipatory fashion at 5.14 am. The van arrived promptly at 5.55 am and I said goodbye to Mark and Helen. I was glad the children were still asleep, for taking leave of them could have been more difficult. I suddenly felt quite bereft, having imagined originally that Mark might be coming with me - but of course that was quite unnecessary and would only have prolonged the agony. It was the same vehicle as we had had for Punchgani and still housed most of the Christmas decorations, apart from the tinsel over one of the doors which had keep falling on my head, and some of the stars on the roof, one of which, a shiny green one, had gone into orbit via Callum. I had the company of two Nepalese students, a married couple who would finish their studies in three months' time. Mark was supervising their theses.

The cool dark gradually gave way to the warmer dawn as we emerged from Pune on to the comparatively quiet roads and the new expressway, where we overtook most of the traffic. In one stretch there was an attractive display of Bougainvilleas along the central reservation. About halfway, I guessed, we stopped for welcome chai and the driver produced chapattis from his squat tiffin carrier. There was also a loo: mine read "Latrienal's. Ladies".

The road became much busier as we approached the outskirts of Bombay. We passed crowded buses with nearly as many standing as sitting, and many huge, covered lorries loaded with goodness knows what.

We made the Airport Terminal 2 in four hours so that I would have another three hours to wait, I thought. I paid and said goodbye to the pleasant driver and the Nepalese couple who had not been home for two years, but were looking forward to making the trip after qualifying – a trip which would take a week by train. One of them got me a trolley, which I didn't really need with my luggage on wheels, and then a scruffy little chap commandeered it the very short distance to the entrance through which he was not allowed to pass, as he was not an 'official' porter - and then demanded 100/-... Oh well …

Once inside I discovered the flight had been delayed from 1 pm till 4 pm. No reason was given. I hoped that there had not been any shooting at Colombo airport and that the booked transport would still be there to meet me. Meanwhile I sat in the airport with a handful of others. Check-in was at 12.30 pm: it was now 10.30 am. I read another chapter of Rohinton Mistry's "A Fine Balance."

I got latched onto by a Muslim Indian, married to a Sri Lankan lady whom he described as "A wonderful business woman who gets visas for people. I help her". He spoke Tamil, Arabic, Sinhalese and English, the latter so strongly accented that I had to keep saying 'Pardon?' He returned the conversation constantly to visas and how he couldn't get one, (in spite of his wife) to go to England. "I'm a Muslim and I come from Sri Lanka and that seems to be a problem", he complained. "My wife goes to Israel often but I can't get a visa to go there either". After two hours I was getting a bit weary of this hard-to-understand one-subject conversation when it was announced that, because of the delay, lunch would be provided. So, after checking in and parting with the main luggage, going through customs and having hand luggage and handbag searched in detail, we enjoyed a very good self-service meal, although my Muslim companion still managed to talk constantly while eating. Thereafter I put myself on a very comfortable reclining seat outside the main lounge and read my book until 3 pm, when it was looking hopeful for the flight. I spotted just two other European-looking people.

I presented my boarding pass but was sent back to 'baggage' because I hadn't got the 'luggage identified' tag thereon: another security facet I had not experienced before. Handbag and hand luggage were again very thoroughly searched and the whole process added considerably to the waiting time. We boarded the plane at 4.30 pm for a 5 pm take-off. From my window seat I studied the extensive shanty town close to the airport. A few Christmas decorations sagged sadly between makeshift corrugated iron roofs. The usual collection of dogs searched piles of rubbish, grown men just sat about while some young lads played cricket on what looked like a mud pitch. I was seeing one of the sets of "A Fine Balance" for real. An Indian meal was served but I wasn't very hungry. I suddenly felt weary and catching sight of myself in the small screen on the back of the seat in front, wondered whether I should have a facelift! We landed at Colombo at 6.50 pm, having put on our watches half an hour.

I was highly delighted to get through immigration quickly, see my luggage arrive early on the carousel, find a choice of money exchange counters - I used the one which summoned me the loudest – and, best of all, catch sight of a young man in a yellow T-shirt holding up a matching card on which my name was boldly printed. He brought round a comfortable white car and we started our drive to the Pegasus Reef Hotel. He seemed anxious to make conversation and I thought he was asking whether I was hungry and I said I was not, explaining about the two meals. He looked puzzled and repeated the question, which I then understood to be "your country?" not "you hungry?". His mobile phone went several times and he said it was "the commander of the business". I asked him how long he had worked for the business and he replied "25 Kilometres", which I presumed was the distance to the hotel. I gave up.

The hotel was at the end of a long, bumpy, beach road. The receptionist and staff were pleasant and welcoming. The hallway was still decorated for Christmas, with an ornate Christmas scene: a bit incongruous for me, in this warm climate. My room was great and included a capacious bath. I'd missed my bath and had a luxurious lengthy soak, washed my hair, and then some clothes.

I then discovered one or two irritating factors in the room: the bedside light did not work, the fridge was locked, the bedside clock said 3.42 pm and try as I would I could not find a way to adjust it, so I studied my own watch to discover the proper time, only to find it had stopped. I made a rough estimate of what I thought the time should be, calculated the difference from that registered on the clock, and settled for doing a bit of mental arithmetic each time I needed to know. I could have called room service but it was late, I was really tired and couldn't be bothered. Just what was the exact time didn't seem to matter that much. No story time tonight, so I read to myself.

Postscript: There'd been some confusion about the cheap watch (£6) I'd bought not long before coming away, as to whether it was waterproof or merely water resistant: it was obviously only the latter.

Friday January 4th

I had a good night and worked out that it was about 8.30 am when I awoke. I washed and dressed and went in search of the Garden Restaurant where, for the first time for years, I had a full breakfast. I was just leaving for an exploratory walk when I stopped to talk to a couple of people, the man having asked me whether I had just arrived. He told me they came to the Pegasus every year for a month and were on intimate terms with the staff. He renovated and decorated for wealthy clients on his own, (he never employed anyone else) - in Finsbury, I think he said. He also 'did churches' in the area: "I hang on to the cross at the top of the roof" he said, which sounded particularly dangerous when he confessed to having "bad knees", which had not been much improved by arthroscopy. He asked where I lived and said he knew North Devon, where they sometimes visit. I suggested that they might call if they were anywhere near and if I was at home. I gave them my card and she said, "I don't believe this" - they were also called 'Tyler' - Robby and Raymond!

Over an hour later I took my walk and then went to ask at the desk about the expected time of arrival of my Travel Collection (Kuoni) group. Their flight was delayed and they were expected just before 2 pm. I went for a swim in the pool – lovely, and something else I'd missed. 'Flowers of the Temple' had fallen from the surrounding trees and floated on the water, adding a certain exotic something-or-other to the experience. One of the attendants came and chatted to me when I got out, and said how low his wages were. Robby and Raymond came for a swim. She aided and abetted his exercise programme, which he followed conscientiously three times a day.

A fresh lime and soda and a good buffet lunch were very welcome. The other Tylers insisted I sat with them, and he gave me his life history - with corrective interjections from his wife. He was a reformed alcoholic. He had had several unusual, but successful, businesses, including growing acres of flowers in Bogota, carnations, gladioli, roses etc, each flower being individually banded to prevent it opening too soon: the planting was timed according to need, for example: Mother's day, Christmas, Easter, and the majority had been sold to Covent Garden: three Jumbo Jets had been chartered to bring them over. Another of his enterprises comprised fishing for eels in Canada, destined for Billingsgate, where they were processed and sold as jellied eels - and so on. He'd made and lost several fortunes, had had at least two wives, with two sons by the first. He announced he was 54: I'd taken him for older. This dissertation was interrupted by Spencer, the Travel Collection representative, who told me that the group had arrived and that there would be a briefing at 6.30 pm. I spied two 'new' couples walking round the pool. They looked pretty staid and middle-aged: something like myself.

When I met the Kuoni bunch, I found that there were about seventeen of them, including me. The youngest couple came from London: she made clothes for the English National Opera and he was a civil engineer. There were two ladies travelling together and a handsome family of four who looked as if they could be Italian. Spencer gave us a good introduction to his country, which he obviously loved. The itinerary was to be in a different order from the original leaflet. He urged that we should "keep smiling like the Sri Lankans, whatever happens", "put up with little inconveniences" and not to expect everything to be perfect. I wondered just what he was knowingly preparing us for. "When you are miserable, you waste a moment's happiness!" ......

I had already eaten two good meals today so I settled for soup, salad and an unusual chocolate sweet. I asked for a gin - and a quadruple arrived, but it was local and said to be 'not as strong'. I prefer ginger beer to anything else with my gin, and the island's own was the best I'd ever tasted.

I made for bed at 9 pm as we were leaving at 7 am. I still had not got the clock sorted but there was a 6 am call anyway.

Saturday January 5th

I slept reasonably well although I woke several times and worked out the time. I had difficulty getting change of 1000/- for tips. I packed, and had fruit, a roll, and tea for breakfast. At 6.30 am it was still dark. We started off promptly at 7 am after a luggage check.

The coach was comfortable and Spencer embarked on a talk giving us local background information:

Rice:	was served in three forms - plain, string hoppers, and egg hoppers. It was grown in the mountains, two crops being planted with the two monsoons. It went into a nursery bed first, and was then transplanted when 8" high, and harvested at about four and a half months.
Breadfruit:	it had white pulp, was from a tropical tree, and was used as a vegetable.
Jakfruit:	it was very big, and could be used as both fruit and vegetable.
Other products:	these included cashew nuts, cane ware, and pottery.
Education:	there was a 90% literacy rate. School (free) was compulsory until the age of 14. Food, uniforms, books and medical treatment were also free.
Economy:	the major exports were tea, rubber, and coconut; the textile industry here worked for well-known brands abroad; one million people were working abroad and sending money back home.
Forest:	much had been lost because of the 'chop and burn' policy for ebony, etc but the remaining forest was protected.

The journey gave us, amongst other things, glimpses of fishermen in Colombo Harbour, views from the bridge over the Dutch Canal, heaps of pineapples on the pavement, and a close-up of a large majestic roadside Madonna. Betty, one of the two ladies travelling together, took advantage of a delay by a bus station and got her video camera into action to record lots of local cameo scenes.

Once on track again, Spencer started on the history of the country, and went through the arrival of the Portuguese in 1505, the Dutch in 1658, and the British in 1790 – who were there until 1948. They had captured Kandy in 1815 and had then built the road from there to Colombo.

I was happy to identify a Red-wattled Lapwing, a Purple Bee-eater and a Racket-tailed Drongo en route.

The lecture continued: it was a long journey!

The population was 19 million - and was mainly made up of 78% Sinhalese and 18% Tamils. The 7% who were Muslims - the 'Sri Lanka Moors' - went back to Portuguese times, being descendants of Arab and Muslim traders. There were also Burghers, who were the descendants of Portuguese and Dutch business people.

The majority of the population was Buddhist; of the Christians, most were Roman Catholics because of the Portuguese influence. 'Sri Lanka', which meant 'Splendid Isle', was its original name. At 25,000 square miles, it was 140 miles wide and 296 miles long. Green bunting along the roadside was a legacy of recent elections. Some white flags indicated the recent death of a popular government minister. "White flags for Buddhist deaths, black flags for Christian deaths", explained our guide. The election talk reminded me of the assassination of Bandaranaike back in the 1950s.

Money matters: there was a 5% tax on earnings over 140,000/- a year. Government pensions started between the ages of 55 and 60. Private pensions gave a lump sum at 55. He emphasised that it was the duty of the young to look after the old, non-pensioned relatives. Land costs were 3000/- to 5000/- per perch in country areas, as compared with 1,000,000/- in Colombo. (The perch was 25 yards by 25 yards.) Planning permission was only needed for 'permanent' buildings.

Spencer moved on to language and told us that there was no 'o' sound as in the word 'John'. The Sinhalese writing system came from the Brahmi script and had 56 letters, although that number was somewhat variable within the different regions.

We stopped at Kagalle and took photographs of Bible Rock and admired a statue of Captain Edward Dawson, a surveyor who did a lot for the town, we were told. Back on the road again, we passed a 'Fertility Care Medical Centre' with an impressive poster of the female reproductive system. What about the male?

We parked at the Peradeniya Botanical Gardens, where we had the Garden's own guide and took a pleasant walk. It covered 60 hectares and was almost encompassed by the Mahaweli Ganga River. As well as housing a giant collection of Orchids, and boasting a fine avenue of Royal Palms planted in 1905, it had a giant Javan Fig Tree, a huge Jakfruit Tree, and a Coco de Mer (with fruits almost divided into two by a deep cleavage and said to resemble a woman's buttocks). It also had a Knocknut Tree, a Butternut Tree, an Ironwood Tree of Ceylon - in which a Large Green (Brown-headed) Barbet perched obligingly, a Cook's Pine, China Grass, a variety of Bamboo which grows a foot a day (a painful property when attached firmly to victims as a method of torture), Indian Weeping Willows which do not weep, and a variety of trees planted by George VIth, Harold Macmillan, Yuri Gagarin, Princess Anne, and the Duke of Edinburgh, amongst others.

'Interesting plants' included the Sleeping Hibiscus, whose flowers never open fully, the Malagasy Periwinkle, looking like Busy Lizzie, and a shrub whose red berries were used as the measure for the original carat.

The attractive administrative buildings had been the residence of Lord Louis Mountbatten during the Second World War, and the place was used in the films 'Tarzan' and 'Bridge over the River Kwai'.

A great colony of noisy Fruit Bats flew about the tops of a collection of tall trees. Sadly we saw several of their corpses, in varying stages of decay, hanging from overhead wires. It was explained that they were large enough to contact two wires simultaneously and so electrocute themselves.

Back in the coach we couldn't help noticing, in Kandy, that there were streams of people of all ages walking in the same direction. Spencer explained that it was visiting day at the hospital and the Sri Lankans were inclined to make a big thing about seeing sick relatives, adding "even if they haven't seen much of them when they're well!" We were ready for the good lunch at a local restaurant, high up on a hill with good views over the city.

Close to Kandy's lake we visited the Temple of the Tooth, which, as its name implied, housed Sri Lanka's most important Buddhist relic, the sacred tooth of Buddha. It was reputed that the tooth was snatched from the Buddha's funeral pyre in 543 BC and afterwards was conveyed back and forth between India and Ceylon on the whim of invasions and political situations. Opinion stated that the 'tooth' was in a small golden casket inside a slightly larger golden casket, inside another golden casket, etc and might be a replica, but it had assumed enormous religious significance as evidenced by the many devout worshippers present: I felt uncomfortable and intrusive. Comparatively modern but clear illustrations of the life of Buddha reminded me again of the Stations of the Cross.

I indulged my habit of reading hoardings and advertisements as we journeyed on in the bus:

"Join the Team: Live the Dream" (advertisement for Players Cigarettes)

"Spoken English" which somehow implied the exclusion of written English

"Dangerous Seduction" (a film advertisement with a positively pornographic picture)

"Supported by Recket and Coleman" blazoned across a pharmacy window

"Daffodils" – the name of an Indian herbal massage parlour

"Contact lenses and hearing aid centre" seemed a sensible combination

There were lots of colleges of all kinds, and churches of every denomination. Our next port of call was a gem centre. I knew before we even got there that I'd succumb to making a purchase. Firstly, with the replica of a genuine mining situation in view, we were subjected to a detailed explanation of the laborious technique of mining the gemstones from seams of illama (a gravel-bearing stratum) in lowland areas along valley bottoms, riverbeds, and other very damp places. Someone had to go down to dig, another had to work the pump to keep the area relatively dry, another to wash the muddy gravel, and finally an expert to search through the pebbles for the stones which might make all their fortunes.

We were shown the fine handcutting and polishing techniques and then a collection of finished stones. There were the conundrums of pink (not red) rubies, and sapphires of orange and yellow as well as the better-known blue, the most valuable.

Chrysoberyl:	cat's eye with a ray which gives it its name, known as chatoyancy, in green and honey-brown
Alexandrite:	noted for its change of colour when moved from natural to artificial light
Beryl:	of a transparent green. Emerald is not found in Sri Lanka but the bluish-green Aquamarine is
Zircon:	in shades of orange, brown and green
Quartz:	in purple, brown and black, transparent to opaque
Feldspar:	is Sri Lanka's special Moonstone, grey, but the best have a suggestion of blue
Spinels:	are found in a variety of colours
Garnets:	of a deep red.

A great number of the stones can all be so many different, and the same, colours. How do they tell the difference?

After much thought and close study, I bought a pair of reputedly blue Topaz earrings with the Lakmini guarantee and receipt, believing that all the gems on display and for sale were local - only to discover later that Topaz was not found in Sri Lanka. But they are lovely, nonetheless. I was quite surprised to see how many of our party did buy jewellery, and we all sat about in the comfortable, air-conditioned showroom chatting and exhibiting our prize purchases. I talked to the family whom I'd considered might have had Italian connections only to discover that they were originally from Greek Cyprus, (wrong about the people, as well as the stones) but they didn't seem to mind. The father, Philip, was Professor of Business Studies at Kingston-upon-Thames University, having recently stood down as Dean. He was not buying his gorgeous fourteen-year-old daughter Irene anything, unless and until she passed her "A level" Greek later in the year! Son James was to be sixteen the following week. Mum Maria had a degree in Biochemistry and a teaching qualification, and ran educational courses at the family farm in Surrey. A charismatic bunch. We were all feeling culture saturated by this time, especially the rest of the group who had been plunged into the tour somewhat precipitantly, after overnight travel and a very short sleep: but the day was not over yet.

We journeyed on to the Spice Gardens and had a tour of the grounds, where we saw herbs growing, held plucked samples, and smelled such delights as Cinnamon; a Tree

Pepper from the Pepper Vine; Cardamom from a shaded perennial plant, the berries processed by drying in the sun; Nutmeg from a tree which could live up to a hundred years, the Nutmeg being the nut found inside the seed, and Mace the fleshy growth around the Nutmeg; Cloves, the nail-like flower buds of a tropical tree which starts flowering after seven years of growth; Ginger from smallish tubers of a perennial; Chilli (Capsicum) – curry: hot and kochichi; Tamarind pods from a huge tree; Vanilla beans/pods from a climber (Orchid family); Turmeric from a small plant with little yellow tubers (yams); Citronella from Lemon Grass; Curry Leaf from the appropriate bush, and so on… My mind and my senses were a bit overpowered after an hour of listening, tasting, and smelling.

The proprietor (I think) of this International Spice garden of Palapathwela then took us inside and gave us tastings of herbal tea and wine, and aromas of various medicinal herbal remedies. His students passed around the samples and then offered free massage. Takers were slow to respond so I thought I'd volunteer to have my arthritic hands and feet, and my face and shoulders done. A handsome young man with very powerful hands did the business over about half an hour using Sandalwood oil, and although the hands really hurt initially, they felt wonderfully free and flexible afterwards. Needless to say I bought some Sandalwood oil, a packet of the tea and a little booklet on the cultivation of the herbs themselves, as well as picking up free leaflets on the herbal medicines and the use of the herbs in cooking. One or two others eventually agreed to massage of one part or another and the coach had a very different atmosphere on the way to Habarana - as Spencer had predicted.

We arrived at Habarana Village at 8.30 pm, where I had a splendid room with an artistic pattern of fresh flowers arranged on the top of the bedcover, and was welcomed by a charming room boy called something like "Diarthe". I revelled in a long hot shower, enjoying again the Sandalwood aroma as it was washed away. A good supper, with background cabaret music, was followed by bed (I went to D4 instead of C4 at first and - surprise, surprise - the key reassuringly wouldn't fit!) and an excellent night's sleep.

Sunday January 6th

I woke at 7.45 am and, after breakfast, joined the optional trip (at extra cost) to the Cave Temple of Dambulla, which is situated high above the road in the southern part of the town. We walked up to it over a vast sloping rock face. Its history is thought to go back to the 1st Century BC when King Valagam Bahu, having been driven out of Anuradhapura, took refuge in these caves. When he regained his throne, he converted the caves into a magnificent Rock Temple.

The first cave housed a very long reclining Buddha and other seated Buddhas. The second cave seemed very spacious and contained two statues of kings, various Hindu deities and a large Buddha statue, with hand raised, under an ornamental arch. The walls and ceiling were covered with brightly-coloured frescoes, scenes of battles, good deeds, and the arrival of Buddhism in Sri Lanka, which was skilfully worked in to render seamless the irregularities of the surfaces: this latter, the Raja Maha Vihara, was undoubtedly the most spectacular. A small group of worshippers and two orange-draped monks were praying together in one of the smaller caves. Of the remaining two caves, the decoration in the most recently developed showed serious signs of

6 January 2002
DRAMBULLA - Hungry Monkey

deterioration. "They just don't know how to do the dyes these days," volunteered Spencer, who had given us a wealth of background information, "just think, those other frescoes have lasted in perfect condition for hundreds of years."

Swallows and monkeys added wildlife interest around the corridor of land outside. Only five of us had opted for this trip, Maureen and Peter, a well-rounded middle-aged couple from Cheltenham, Eileen, Betty and me.

I bought a few cards, photography being forbidden as evidenced by confiscated examples of negative strips displayed at the pay kiosk. This ban had been reinforced when some scantily-clad lady (?) tourist had been snapped sitting in the lap of one of the revered Buddhas: insensitive to say the least. I was also persuaded to buy some lumps of stone, pinkish and white Quartz, brown Chrysoberyl, and a greenish Spinel of some kind – I think! I bought a slim book at the entrance to the place, where a young girl was doing her literacy homework, while her mother worked in the shop with another beautiful young woman: a photogenic trio.

We got back about 12.30 pm. I had a walk round the lake behind the hotel and was rewarded with the sight of two Black-headed Orioles, and then had a refreshing swim in the rain before lunch.

The afternoon found us all bound for the Minneriya National Park in three open vehicles. We spotted two wild Elephants on the way and a couple of Spotted Deer near the entrance, which was just as well because we saw little else at the beginning of the afternoon. To be fair, a pair of Mongooses did come briefly into view later on, as did several Grey Langur Monkeys while we drove through the tropical rain forest. The Frangipani smelled wonderfully fragrant and Bee-eaters flitted about under the canopy. There was no sign of the Leopard or the Sloth Bear we'd been hoping to see.

The safari drive could sometimes go round the lake but the ground was so wet (one vehicle had got stuck, as it was) that today this was not possible so we stopped by the water and looked around. There were the usual Egrets and Cattle Egrets and the occasional Kestrel and Sea Eagle. I talked to one of the drivers who said the locals catch edible Eels and Perch in the lake.

Elephants were reported by bush telegraph in another area of the park and we took a speedy trip, the drivers taking short cuts in a competitive spirit. We were rewarded with some success: my camera battery gave up the ghost at the vital moment, but I reckon I got one shot: what timing.

During the drive back we got a puncture and the wheel was changed with all speed by the driver and his assistant, while we sat on a conveniently situated low wall and watched proceedings. The replacement tyre was almost threadbare! Shortly afterwards someone spotted "an interesting bird" by the side of the road. We reversed diagonally and dangerously to the spot. The bird had flown but only into the nearby forest where we were able to get a good view: it was a Crested Hawk Eagle.

We got back at 6.45 pm and, after a shower and change, I ventured to the shop in the grounds and bought a green cotton embroidered two-piece. Then, it was time for another good dinner - especially good were the vegetables, the fresh fruit (I'd had pineapple at every meal) and the imaginative sweets. Afterwards I sat with Philip and family and watched a magic show: all old tricks but I still didn't know how they were done.

I decided later, as I looked in the mirror while cleaning my teeth, that yesterday's face massage might have done some good - for a while anyway. I'd forget the plastic surgery for a day or two.

Monday January 7th

I was called by the room boy at 6.30 am. Today we were destined for an early excursion (before it got too hot) to the spectacular fortress of Sigiriya (Lion's Rock), built by Kasyapa when he feared revenge for walling in alive (!) his father, King Dhatusena of Anuradhapura in the 5th Century AD. When the expected invasion came, Kasyapa rode out at the head of the army on an Elephant but, in attempting to outflank the enemy (his brother) he took a wrong turn, became bogged down in a swamp, was deserted by his troops and took his own life. Sigiryra later became a monastic refuge, but eventually fell into disrepair - being rediscovered by archaeologists during the British period in the mid-nineteenth century.

Spencer's introductory talk as we drove along was quite compelling and held the mind but it didn't stop my eyes wandering: I had a good view of a Peacock and the endemic Jungle Fowl.

We approached the fortress through the elaborate gate and beautiful water gardens, and then from between the trees from which the rock rises, strangely sheer and unforgiving. A series of steps led on through the boulders at the foot and then ascended more steeply. About halfway up, a spiral staircase led up from the main route to a long, sheltered gallery in the sheer rock face whereon were painted a series of 5th Century (non-religious) beautiful women, the only such in Sri Lanka. In 1967 vandals reduced the number from 500 to the present 22 recognisable forms. Beyond the fresco gallery, the pathway clung to the steep rock and was protected on the outside by a 3-metre-high wall. This was coated with a mirror-smooth glaze, on which visitors between the 11th and 17th centuries had recorded their impressions in graffiti tradition. As well as provoking scholarly interest in the content - such as a male subscriber's guilt at viewing bare breasts and the consequent jealousy from his female counterpart - they charted the development of the Sinhalese language and script during that period.

The narrow pathway opened on to a large platform, and it was here, in 1898, that H C V P Bell, the British archaeologist, found the two enormous Lion paws while excavating: hence the name Lion Rock. Some of the sightseers stayed and viewed the rock and the surrounding countryside from here. Having got this far, I was determined to get to the top. A series of guides had been pressing their attentions and services upon us from the very beginning. I had refused their assistance repeatedly but as the climb became steeper and two of them latched on to me, one on each arm, it made the going so much easier that I succumbed. I had plenty of breath - it was just the knees .....

On the very top, there were numerous foundations - all that remained of the palace, which must have been quite magnificently situated, with views of all the surrounding jungle. Kasyapa knew what he was about! It was all very exhilarating to be on top of his world. On the way down we studied the Cobra Head rock, an overhang aptly named.

I bought the tourist booklet about the place and a few postcards with better illustrations than I could ever take, although of course I'd tried. I paid off the TWO guides over the odds, but I'm just no good at bartering and bargaining - and they had been very pleasant and helpful.

TEA LADIES

We were back in time for a swim before lunch. I surprised myself by competing with James, diving and seeing how far we could swim under water: I felt quite young for half an hour!

The afternoon offered another opportunity (optional): this time to visit the ancient capital city of Polonnaruwa, created by the South India Chola dynasty in the 10th Century AD. Its site was chosen because of its strategic position and the dearth of mosquitoes! The city was adopted by the Sinhalese King Vijayabahu I after he'd driven off the Cholas, and was then raised to greater glory by Parakramabahu I, who was responsible for the original 2400-hectare tank known as the Sea of Parakrama. I was up for it.

We visited the Royal Palace group of buildings and ruins. It was a dull day so the temperature was quite comfortable. The palace itself must have been enormous and was difficult to visualize in its complete three-dimensional form, with seven storeys and 50 rooms in the main hall alone. A thin little smooth-haired Terrier bitch was very relaxed and quite unafraid as she nursed her four plump, very young puppies by a wall in the shade of the ruins.

The Audience Hall had an impressive frieze of Elephants around its base, each in a different position and one with five legs. Stately Lions graced the top of the steps. The Prince's Bathing Pool still had one of its Crocodile mouth spouts.

In the nearby famous quadrangle we saw the Vatadage (circular relic house) and the Gal Pota, a colossal stone representation of an ola (palm leaf) book. Its stone inscription (the longest known) indicated that it was commissioned by King Nissanka Malla, that it extolled his many virtues and gave the weight of the slab as 25 tonnes:

96

it was dragged from Mihintale 100 kms away! Next, we saw the Tooth Relic Chamber (not sure whose), then the Latha Mandapaya - which consisted of a latticed stone fence round a small dagobah (Buddhist monument), surrounded by stone pillars shaped like Lotus stalks and topped with unopened Lotus buds. The king was said to have sat there to listen to chanted Buddhist texts. A curious, stepped pyramidal building was the Satmahal Prasada.

We walked a little way to see some extraordinary large Buddha images called Gal Vihara and forming part of King Parakramabahu's northern monastery. The reclining figure was the most fascinating, 14 metres long and worked in beautifully grained stone which somehow gave unusual expression to the face: the head rested gently on a compressed pillow. It was obvious that Spencer loved this place: he was a committed Buddhist and talked proudly of his son, who helped with the choir.

We took a walk near the end of the reservoir on our way back to the coach. I would have liked to have spent longer there for the birdwatching but we were behind time. As it was, I saw Grey Herons, Painted Storks with their bizarre pink splashes, Spottedbilled Pelicans, Large Cormorants, Pond Herons and, over on a small island, lots of soft brown Whistling Ducks.

Back in the coach, the Whistling Ducks obliged by doing a perfect fly-past in a series of necklaces above us. One of our group, who was uncannily like the original Victor Meldrew, said loudly "Jolly good formation, chaps!"

We arrived back at 6.45 pm in time for a shower and change before dinner. I was seated next to Victor Meldrew's (Mike's) little wife Patsy and she gave me her family's medical history. This included her recent knee replacement and that of her husband, his hypertension, and their anxiety about her infant granddaughter who had been diagnosed as having Turner's syndrome. I guess I was more aware than she of what this might entail and my heart went out to the family. I don't really mind being on the listening end on holiday - but who told her I was a doctor?

Tuesday January 8th

The 6.30 am call gave me time to have a short walk around the lake where Pond Herons and Painted Storks sat quietly on the water, and Ring Doves, a Redwattled Lapwing and a Brahminy Kite flew out of the mist.

I had my usual seat in the coach, about a third of the way down from the front on the starboard side. On previous holidays of this variety, I'd known passengers to take it in turns to sit at the front where the view was wider and not limited to one side of the road, but the larger Patsy (married to Chris) said she suffered from travel sickness and needed a front seat with her husband by her side. The other plum positions were taken permanently by the guide and the driver's helper.

Spencer asked whether we would like to call at "an ordinary family house" and this was what we did. The lady of the household obligingly demonstrated the preparation of chillies, rice and herbs in the dark interior of the house while we watched, admiring her skills and strength: she was fit! Her husband stood by smiling as he watched her

- and us - together with a clutch of family and friends. The children were charming, the women beautiful - a couple of them adorned with glorious gold earrings - but one young mum had scars from a serious burn on her neck and chest: "that's the danger with the kerosene", said Spencer, knowingly.

These people all looked well nourished, clean and properly clad. A small vegetable patch supplied many of their needs. The whole set-up had an air of content and normality about it. I wondered how many of us would be able to keep up our standards of hygiene and nutrition under the same conditions. This was discussed when we were back on the bus. Spencer emphasised their contentment and pointed out that they would probably find it as difficult to adapt to our way of living as we would to theirs. They had lined up smiling, and waved as we departed, unembarrassed by our tips, a small reward for the insight they had given us. Once my eyes had become accustomed to the dim light, I had spotted the children's school efforts at writing and drawing which adorned the walls. Would the compulsory education make for a discontentment with their lot when that generation became adult? I wondered.

A brief stop later on allowed a lady selling cashew nuts to board the bus with her wares. They were strung together in small packets of five. I really only wanted one but I had no change and surprise, surprise, neither did she, so I had the five but didn't regret it later: they were delicious. Heaps of Mangoes were piled by the side of the road but we didn't go for those.

There was some distance to cover now, so Spencer embarked on a dissertation on the domestic culture of Sri Lanka. He told us that when a child was born an astrologer was consulted and a horoscope prepared. Special significance was given to the addition of gold dust, which was added to the breast milk on one occasion. A baby's hair was left uncut until the child started talking: any earlier attention from the barber was said to lead to stammering. The horoscope's indications were strengthened by surrounding the baby with tools, books or whatever else might seem to reinforce the astrologer's predictions.

Once they started menstruating the girls were kept apart from the boys until an 'auspicious time', as suggested by the horoscope, when they were cleansed with herb washing under a Milk Tree, after which they saw their reflection as that of an adult woman. Later, usually in their twenties, advice was given about the kind of person they should marry, and the girl's father looked for a suitable partner, with a matching horoscope. Tokens were exchanged but the arrangement was in no way binding at that stage and should the couple find each other unacceptable, the tokens would be returned. (It all sounded very civilised.) A dowry system existed.

When the married couple went to live with the boy's parents, this was a 'diga' marriage: with the girl's parents, a 'binna' marriage. There was no living in sin and divorce was very rare. Parents had to be married for their children to be admitted to school.

By this time we had arrived at Kurunegala, at the cross roads between Colombo and Anuradhapura, Kandy and Puttalam. Large, rocky outcrops loomed over the low-rise buildings: these were named after the animals they were thought to resemble, such as Tortoise and Lion: they were said to have been created when animals which endangered the free water supply were turned to stone.

We stopped at the government-run Pinnawala Elephant orphanage near Kegalle, where we walked down the main street to see the Elephants - all rescued after having been abandoned or orphaned - being washed by the mahouts. We sat comfortably at the restaurant by the riverside and saw these healthy, contented-looking animals being swilled with buckets of water as they jostled for position. I sat next to Irene, and opposite Donald (the Les Dawson of the group), who now lived in Coventry but had a left-over Birmingham accent, and his wife Alice - whose accent reflected her Dutch heritage, as well as that of her French mother and having lived with Donald for 45 years.

One Elephant was shackled and kept apart from the rest and I imagined it might be a male, but we were told it was blind and so needed some extra care and control. Another had only three and a half legs, the missing section having been blown off during the Second World War. Some of us walked down to the river to get a closer look and take photographs. After lunch and this splendid viewing time, we walked to a covered area where three very young Elephants were fed milk from outsize bottles: one was quite stroppy with the keeper when he opted to feed one of the others first. It was very hot and, for the first time, I felt really uncomfortable.

Spencer, who was to finish his tour leader commitment with us at the end of the day, was anxious to complete his input for our Sri Lankan education and as we passed a small tea plantation he told us the history of its production.

Tea had replaced coffee as the main crop when a serious blight had destroyed the latter in the 19th Century; the plant required a warm climate, altitude and a sloping terrain, and was cultivated at three levels: the 'high level' tea (over 1200 metres) grew more slowly, but had the best flavour, the 'low level' tea (under 600 metres) grew more quickly and had more body, and the 'in-between' tea was a good compromise. I was surprised to learn that these bushes, which were pruned back to one metre every year, were members of the Camellia family. The buds and top leaves were plucked almost exclusively by women (who seemed to do most of the work here), were de-moisturised and crushed to start the fermenting process, and were then skilfully "fired" at the right moment to produce the final brown leaf, the varying quality being described by such names as 'flowery', 'pekoe' (eg Broken Orange Pekoe – BOP) and 'souchong'.

The relative merits of different kinds of tea drunk in the UK were discussed as we neared the end of our journey, and then completely out of the blue and appertaining to nothing in particular, Spencer said "Do you know that the most popular dish in England is 'Chicken Tikka'?" We arrived at the Swanee Hotel on the coast of Beruwela at 7 pm and said farewell to Spencer, who was bound for home in Colombo. He'd been an excellent leader, interesting, informative and helpful but never intrusive. He had accepted our tangible appreciation very graciously.

The heat was still oppressive as we waited for our room allocation and keys. My key plate said '33' on one side and '104' on the other: my room number was 104 and on the ground floor, its terrace being afforded privacy by a hedged corridor of green grass

8 January 2002
Pinnewala Elephant Orphanage

beyond. I was greeted by a welcoming arrangement of flowers on the bed and a small fledgling cowering and chirruping at the back of the dressing table! I lifted it gently and threw it to the sky and it took flight as far as the tall hedge, where it did a novice landing. One or two members of the party were disgruntled about their rooms because they couldn't see the sea or they didn't like the colour of the ceiling. My ceiling was blue and I was quite happy.

I partially unpacked and had the ritual shower and change. I enjoyed a drink, a (very small) gin with plenty of ginger beer, in the company of Don and Alice. Donald delivered an entertaining monologue on encounters with the locals in Sri Lanka to whom, it must be said, he was very generous. A nice man. Steve and Rita joined his audience.

The dinner was OK, but perhaps not quite up to the standard of cuisine to which we had become accustomed.

I went to bed about 11 pm I think: difficult to know exactly without a watch.

Wednesday January 9th

I got Alice, who had a room next door, to give me an 8 am call.

I had fruit, a croissant and some other fattening confectionary for breakfast. I then booked three beds near the perimeter of the hotel grounds and adjacent to the beach - like the Germans.

We met the local representative, Nigel, at 9.45 am and enjoyed a pineapple drink while we listened to his talk. He had a strange lilting to his strongly accented voice, which had a hypnotic effect, disturbed every now and then by a reverential staccato "Sir". Some of us booked for optional trips during the next (last) few days. Eileen and Betty and I then indulged in the luxury of using our reclining seats, where we sat and read. A White-bellied Drongo settled briefly in a nearby tree.

I went for a swim and then walked along the beach and swam out to the reef to inspect the underwater life, with the possibility of a scuba-dive in mind. The coral was all grey, colourless, and dead. I saw one pathetic little Parrot fish and some kind of eel and that was it: all very sad and disappointing. I couldn't help recalling the wonders of the Maldives and the Barrier Reef. I snorkelled for some time in the hope that I might find a healthy section, but without success. I returned to the hotel gardens and, together with Betty and Eileen, got seduced by three ladies selling lovely sarongs. We bought a collection between us.

Lunch was served round the pool after which we had a lazy afternoon, talking and reading until the sky clouded over and a storm seemed to be brewing. I went back to my room where the room boy had fixed the mosquito net and placed more welcoming flowers and a card. We three booked our seats for the advertised Culture Show by scattering our possessions about: Germanic tendency again.

The dinner was definitely better tonight and one of the staff kept asking whether we had any complaints: someone must have complained last night. The crab was excellent. The Culture Show, held outside, comprised dancing by beautiful girls in national costume, athletic male dancers, a dancer who looked like a Witch Doctor, a strangely padded masked man, and two drummers who provided the constant backing. I wished we had some sort of leaflet or spoken explanation of the story or history behind the acts. Donald was busy chatting up the Germans: a couple of them looked a bit puzzled.

The door on to the patio didn't seem to lock properly so I wedged it with a chair and decided to mention it in the morning.

Thursday January 10th

I arose at 7 am and left the key of the offending door at reception.

After breakfast those of us who had opted for the river trip left promptly in two People Carriers at 8.30 am. There was a roll call before we boarded and I was put in the front seat next to the driver, which made a nice change. It was a pleasant drive across the Bentota River, through Bentota and on to the Madu River, where we got into two boats.

We went through little tunnels of Mangrove Swamps and across stretches of open water studded with islands. Narrower passages were flanked by small prawn fisheries, where confident Cormorants stayed perched as we passed. A White-bellied Sea Eagle obliged by doing a perfect dive, came up with a fish rather too near our boat for its comfort, and flew off, leaving its prey in the water. Once we'd travelled some little distance, it returned and picked it up. We saw plenty of Pond Herons, a striking single Green Heron, a Little Tern and six different kinds of Kingfisher: White-breasted, Pied, Brown-headed, Storkbilled, White-collared and Small Blue. Impressive Monitor Lizards posed on the bank and swam gracefully through the water.

We went in to the Turtle Breeding (Rescue) Centre opened in 1978. Turtles come ashore to lay their eggs, around 120 at a time, and many are taken as a delicacy. Centre staff watch for the laying process, gather up the eggs of the different species - Green, Olive Ridley, Hawksbill and Loggerhead - and each clutch is identified, dated and labelled. We saw and handled these attractive likeable little creatures, at different stages of development in large tanks. One rescued albino Turtle had been kept at the centre permanently because it would have been so vulnerable if released: it lived until it was seven years old and was now preserved for posterity in a small tank by the door. Another albino was still quite small but would no doubt be kept at the centre and treated similarly in life and death. I did the tourist thing and had my photograph taken holding a large specimen: I was surprised at how heavy it was. The centre ran education courses in conservation, in the hope that the next generation (of humans) would, as the manager said, "behave in a more responsible way so that Sri Lanka will be proud of them". Inevitably we were taken to the on-site shop where I bought a Turtle wall hanging, which I intended to put under the glass on one of the dressing tables at home.

Next stop was Cinnamon Island. Here we saw the whole process of growing, harvesting the bark, making the sticks and putting them in the packet, which was sealed with a naked flame. I bought one of course. Some of us enjoyed a drink of milk from the freshly-cut coconut: 20/- and delicious. We saw the coconut fibre being teased out, dyed and ultimately made into stout mats, attractively coloured and representing Turtles and Elephants. I fell for one of these for a gift: each represented two long days of labour.

The next stop was at an island which housed a Buddhist Temple where five Buddhist Monks were permanently in residence. A large Boa Tree stood beside the impressive outdoor statue of Buddha. It was shown how its leaf forms the shape of a Buddhist Temple when folded over and held with the pointed end upright. The statue was flanked by the Sri Lankan flag with its orange stripe for the Tamils, the green for the Muslims and the big bold Lion for the Buddhists. The Buddhist flag has five colours - blue for the head, red for the blood, white for the tooth, orange for the skin, and yellow for I'm not quite sure what, but the combination is very easy on the eye. There was a wonderful fragrance of Balsa all around. The indoor premises were sparse with a very basic kitchen. I did notice a Girlie-type magazine on the small settee!

Then it was back to dry land and the People Carrier - still in the front seat, and why not. I noticed again all the hoardings advertising Vim, Sunlight Soap and Lifebuoy, products we seem to have grown out of. The school for the younger age group starts early and finishes at lunchtime so there were lots of youngsters heading for home as we drove through Bentota. Their blue skirts or shorts, and white shirts, were smart and clean, and one group of girls had bright red ribbons in their hair.

We arrived back at 1.45 pm. It was hard to believe it was only lunchtime: we'd done so much already. We sat round the pool and then sat in the garden in sight of the sea. A Jungle Crow dropped its calling card on my head. Ground Squirrels vied with Babblers with their noise and restlessness. Teatime offered the opportunity to indulge in banana fritters again around the pool: they were delicious and I had two. Well, this was a holiday. A very heavy grey sky made its afternoon visit again and I went back to my room. As I approached the patio entrance, I espied a Black-headed Oriole perched in the high hedge feeding a fledgling, which looked to me to be of the variety that had visited my room the night I arrived. The heavy sky shaded through soft grey folds to a stunning apricot on the horizon, as the sun set over the sea.

We were serenaded over supper by four young Sri Lankan men, the Raindrops, who told Eileen they sang in a local church: yes, I bought a tape. Later we repaired to Eileen and Betty's balcony and drank their gin with Steve and Rita. A landscape gardener, Cockney, from the adjacent room stopped to talk to us with his lady, on their way to bed. (They had a flight to the Maldives in the early hours: I remembered that scuba-diving again). He gave us his life history and talked very entertainingly, it must be said, until nearly 1 am, when his lady, who had left him alone some time earlier, summoned him to bed.

Friday January 11th

I got up early (7.30 am) and had a swim before breakfast. It was still quite fresh and I was alone in the pool. I felt hungry and indulged in several super croissants and then obeyed Nigel's summons to fill in the holiday assessment form for Travel Collection.

I walked along the beach to one of the small material and tailoring shops with Eileen and Betty, who had already been and got their eye in, as it were. There was an incredible selection of beautiful fabrics and after a long look I chose a navy silk and cotton material, with a pattern of outsize orchids in pale mauve and oyster, for a long skirt.

I came back and swam again, this time in the Indian Ocean. In anticipation of paying for the skirt, I changed some money at the desk.

After lunch we three took a tuck tuck (rickshaw) into Beruwela with Santha, the large taxi-man who hung about in and around the entrance to the hotel and against whom we had been warned by Nigel! Other guests' experiences seemed to have been favourable and we found him helpful and reasonable costwise: his size was the only daunting aspect. His vehicle was decorated with little skull and crossbone motifs, which might put some people off, I guess.

We asked to be taken to the harbour where many fishing boats made a busy and attractive scene. The crews all wanted their pictures taken. A large notice indicated that a 2000:200-2 marketing campaign was in force to improve the lot of the fishermen, the handling of the fish, and the trade in general: interestingly this was supported largely by Sweden. An amusing cartoon of four fish holding placards graced a wall near the entrance but the script was Sinhalese. We asked a group of men sitting opposite what it meant but their reply was "Take our photographs!"... so we obliged - snapping the cartoon.

We asked Santha to take us in the opposite direction and we saw impressive displays of fish of many kinds and sizes in the market in Aluthgama. They all looked so fresh and bright-eyed. Finally, we stopped at the Ceylon Tea House where I bought four little porcelain containers of different kinds of tea for presents, and Eileen and Betty fell for imaginative tea-strainers.

Tea was around the pool once more and I was at the banana fritters again. Afterwards, I was seduced into the pool for another swim. I felt that I could get used to this. After dinner we watched another magic show. The magician had amazing roaming eyes, more fascinating than his tricks - which followed the same routine as the previous magician: he had trained at the same school, perhaps. And so to bed, at 11.15 pm.

Saturday January 12th

I started the day with a swim, before croissants again, and then it was water aerobics, which seemed to be conducted for the most part from the side of the pool rather than in the water. I admired the smaller Patsy who struggled to follow the routine with her recent knee replacement. I left early to keep an appointment I'd made for a massage. The masseur seemed to be one of several young men who had premises in the hotel and who touted for business from the euphoric sun-worshippers scattered around the garden. I paid 500/- at reception and then 400/- to him personally. I wasn't sure about this 'business' arrangement but the energetic job he did on my arms, legs and back was well worth the money - the equivalent of £7 in English money.

I walked along the beach and took photographs and got back in time for a vegetarian lunch by the pool. The chef appeared with a cooked, beautifully presented, huge fish, for Donald who, with Alice, had been out very early in a local fishing boat and caught this "burra" (big one). We were all encouraged to have a taste and it was very good, soft and creamy. I swam in the afternoon and then picked up my skirt, with which I was well pleased. Steve and Rita invited Eileen, Betty and me to their balcony to share a very good bottle of Champagne before dinner: they'd also got the room boy to organise nibbles and set it all up.

I wore the new skirt at dinner and had to do a mannequin parade for our table. There was dancing after dinner and I really enjoyed myself with Chris and Steve. I thought of John and missed him. At midnight we celebrated James' 16th birthday and everyone sang 'Happy Birthday' - but no-one gave him the 'bumps'!

Sunday January 13th

It was an early start this morning for the last trip, due to begin at 8 am.

I think everyone had opted for this outing, so the coach was used and I was in my usual seat … We passed piles of yellow coconuts, avenues of green flags to remind voters of the Conservation Party in the recent general election, and De Silva's grave - which prompted cricket talk as Sri Lanka were playing Zimbabwe on home ground at that very moment. We stopped en route and looked at masks and striking batik work. I was fascinated by a huge golden spider, lingering in its web at the entrance. Some purchases were made, but not by me this time.

We continued on over a canal said to be 'spoiled by pollution' - what's new? Later we viewed the cinnamon processing (again) and heard about the production of kaolin (china clay) for pottery (and poultices), and then travelled on to a Moonstone factory where, yes, I did buy yet another pair of earrings, but with someone else in mind this time. A Giant Heron stood stock-still by a stretch of water outside, and a 'rescued', caged, pet Monkey provided entertainment.

We went through Kirinda, used as a land base by Arthur C Clarke's party in 1961 when diving for the Great Basses Reef shipwreck: there was a memorial to him. Hikkaduwa, with its long beach, was very popular with all kinds of tourists we were told. The scuba-diving was said to be good there but the drug culture had now taken hold. It was very hot and many of the locals were carrying umbrellas for their own personal shade. "We don't use sun-cream here: we use umbrellas!" We passed a well-kept Muslim cemetery and were reminded that Buddhists are, of course, cremated.

The port of Galle, 17Km from Hikkaduwa, is Sri Lanka's fourth largest town and said to be historically the most interesting. It was the major port before the construction of Colombo's harbour in the 19th century. It is even thought that Galle might be the Tarshish of Biblical times where King Solomon obtained gems, spices and Peacocks. The Portuguese came in the 16th century and the Dutch in the 17th century and it was they who built the 36-hectare fort which formed most of the older part of the town and which was now a World Heritage Site. It was peaceful and attractive, where Tamils lived quietly, and a variety of places of worship bore testimony to the religious tolerance for which the town was renowned. We took a very pleasant walk along the fort wall, where many relaxed Sunday locals were doing the same.

We viewed the cricket from a distance: it was evidently the tea interval or some such for a team of slim ladies in floaty dresses were formation dancing.

Other ladies were anxious to sell us articles with handmade lace inserts, and we stopped and watched some of them working the lace itself: I bought a short length which I felt sure would come in for trimming something at some time. We enjoyed a good curry and fruit lunch.

Driving back through the town, we saw more than one teaching hospital and numerous schools. The Hindi 'Cycle of Life' sign was much in evidence here: this is the one which resembles, or rather is resembled by, the swastika, and which Mark had explained to me when I'd registered some surprise at seeing it in India.

Stilt fishermen took our attention next. They each had a pole firmly embedded in the sea bottom, close to the shore, and when the sea and the fish were running right, they perched on their poles and cast their lines. This was a particularly interesting scene to watch and, needless to relate, cameras clicked and tips were thankfully received.

Then, it was back to the Turtle Rescue Centre, and those of us who had been before took a walk along the glorious picture-book beach. I have a very clear recollection of that scene.

Back at the ranch I had a shower and changed, and then joined Patsy and Chris with whom I had an interesting conversation, largely (and in retrospect inexplicably) about the Bench. A sitar group played and sang below the restaurant and I snapped Betty and Eileen taking part – well, holding an instrument anyway. I was then pushed into the limelight but no-one took my picture - thank goodness, I thought - but I received one through the post weeks later.

At dinner James was presented with a birthday cake and made a touching little speech. I thought his proud mum was going to cry. We all sang a rousing 'Happy Birthday'. Steve made a sort of speech and voted Donald the man of the moment and me the woman of the week. I was not sure why and felt a bit embarrassed, and uncharacteristically tongue-tied. This was the penultimate dinner and suddenly it all seemed to have gone far too quickly.

Monday January 14th

I have no diary notes at all for today or tomorrow, but I do remember the Monday as being a very relaxed day of swimming and chatting.

Mike and the smaller Patsy had rejoined us after a spell with their family, also holidaying elsewhere in Sri Lanka. Their son looked like his mum, and his wife was a beautiful

Sri Lankan lady whose parents were also in the party, together with the children, a handsome little boy with spectacles and a younger girl, who looked lovely but who was reputed to have Turner's syndrome which, as I've already mentioned, Granny had discussed with me. They all lived in London. When I first encountered Mike and Patsy, I thought Patsy must be deaf because Mike talked in such a fortissimo and exaggeratedly enunciated fashion, so I did the same - but I later realised that she could hear perfectly well. They would not be leaving with some of us tomorrow but had arranged to meet up once more with their family for a few days before they all returned together.

Chris and the other Patsy were to have another ten days here. They had an enviable lifestyle, having retired early, and were now living more than half the year in Spain, where they always 'ate out'. They let their Spanish residence during the holiday season and reckoned they made enough money to pay for their food the rest of the year. Patsy was very well endowed in the bosom department and sailed around gracefully in an impressive collection of kaftans. She had a powerful aura about her, and not just on account of her measurements - something recognized by Chris, who was pleasantly acquiescent, even to the point of obeying instructions to eat the rest of her dinner after he'd cleared his own plate, 'so as not to waste it', and to rushing down to the beach after dark when it was noticed he had purchased the wrong-sized shirt. They were entertaining company and talked of hard times when their three sons were young and Chris was still at university. Patsy has done years of work for an Oxfam shop, which she had 'totally reorganised and made it very profitable'. Chris nodded in agreement.

Pete and Maureen had also extended their holiday for a few days. They were exceptionally good at relaxing and were not infrequently to be seen apparently asleep on their sun-beds. Like most of us in this group, they had some good travellers' tales to tell. They also appreciated good food and demonstrated this very practically ... I talked to them at coffee time. Maureen wanted to slim but said she spent all her working days sitting in front of a computer and was 'too tired' to go swimming in the evening (as I had suggested). Oh, where had I heard this before? I did not dare to propose that she might eat less. They were not looking forward to going back to work, which they didn't seem to enjoy. I felt grateful for a mostly rewarding working life but, having done my last clinic just a fortnight before coming away, I suddenly felt very lighthearted and free … but then Pete and Maureen were probably only in their early fifties.

The surf looked good. Eileen and Betty had gone off down the beach to collect some made-to-measure garments, so I found a surfboard hire stand and got myself equipped. The surf was not as good as it looked when it came to hitching a ride, and I had less than a dozen really good trips right through the shallow water on to the sand: (I've had better at Northam Burrows at Westward Ho!). But it was so pleasant and warm, without the North Devon shivering, while scrambling back to mount another wave.

I got out the music for Ruddigore and Carousel which I'd promised myself I'd know by the time I got back, to compensate for missed rehearsals, and I spent over an hour going through it - silently, I thought. I became aware of the eyes of a large German gentleman upon me and realised that I was giving voice, smiled, and returned to the silent mode. I was quite looking forward to being at home again. By the time I got there I would have been away three and a half weeks, which was longer than I'd ever been away before.

So the day passed with lunch round the pool, fritters at teatime, and an excellent dinner. I would be going to miss the food, all so well-presented, the wide choice and especially the seductive sweets, including the bread pudding of all things, which was cut into light little blocks that just melted in the mouth so quickly that I would be bound to have a second.

I took a cursory glance at my luggage before I went to bed. The Christmas presents from Helen destined for the rest of the family, and purchases I had made in India, had remained at the bottom of my stand-up luggage on wheels, and I reckoned it wasn't going to take long to complete the packing exercise.

By this time tomorrow we would be in transit from Beruwela to the Colombo airport.

Tuesday January 15th

I swallowed the Swanee Hotel breakfast croissants for the last time.

There was much talk of packing among those of us who would be leaving tonight. Betty and Eileen were worried about getting all their goods into their cases. They had bought, amongst other things, a selection of the coconut mats whose shapes made them difficult to accommodate. They talked about the next meeting of their Stroke Club, which they ran in the Sunderland area. Eileen had taken mostly slides with this in mind, so that she could present an illustrated talk, and Betty had taken a video (for the first time). Eileen was a vicar's widow, her husband having died five years ago. When she found I was on my own it somehow gave us both permission to talk about our men's deaths: I could have cried when she said she'd been reading aloud St Paul's "nothing can separate us from the love of God" as he died, but somehow it was all very therapeutic. There are few occasions when I feel comfortable to talk about what was the biggest change in my life, and only those who have had the experience can really empathise.

Betty was widowed over twenty years ago and seemed a lady of integrity and good basic common sense, no frills, called a spade a spade in her homely Tyneside accent. When Eileen was relating some frustrating situation within the Anglican hierarchy, Betty said "Thank goodness I've always been a Methodist!" Like me, they both had supportive families.

Donald seemed very agitated and unable to sit down quietly. "He gets like this when he's excited", said Alice, as she tried to get on with her book in the garden. She had first left home in Holland at 19 when her parents split up, and had come to England as an au pair and had worked with a farming family near Crediton. During her time there, Donald was managing the construction of the extension to Torrington Milk factory and they met up. Small world ..... They had been married for 45 years. She now seemed the stabilising anchor for the hyperactive, restless Donald.

The day passed with more talking, swimming, eating and sunbathing. I changed large Sri Lankan rupee notes for moderate ones for tipping. The luggage was very tightly packed and I hoped no-one was going to open it. I gave a couple of my T-shirts to the room-boy for his wife, so that helped a little. We assembled at the entrance hall with luggage, said farewell to those who were staying on, and climbed into the coach for the drive to Colombo.

Donald and Steve had been celebrating the holiday somewhat indulgently, I suspected, and were full of silly smiles and bonhomie. Alice had wisely put herself in a single seat and so I was obliged to remove my hand luggage from the other half of my double seat when Donald appeared and said in slurred tones "D'you mind if I sit here, Jean?" After a while he studied me closely and then said "I think you're quite a nice person". I thanked him for the compliment. A pause, then "Have you ever been married?" Eileen and Betty turned round from their seat in front with looks of shock and sympathy, but I really didn't mind and found it all increasingly entertaining. "Yes", I replied. "Divorced?" he enquired. "No, he died ten years ago". Unabashed he continued, "Never thought of marrying again?" "Yes, but I haven't".

He settled down quietly for a while and then asked, "Do you mind if I hold your hand?" "No" I said: anything for peace and a quiet life. So that was what he did and then after a few minutes he turned to Alice, "Alice, I'm holding Jean's hand: you don't mind, do you?" Whereupon she looked at me, raised her eyes to heaven, and said, "Not if she doesn't!" Thereafter he went to sleep and, apart from being supported by Alice, on the other side of the gangway, to prevent him falling to the floor a couple of times, he was quietly away with the fairies.

We stopped at a very grand hotel and I'm not sure whether it was in Mt Lavinia or further on, in the outskirts of Colombo. The male staff wore turbans and white suits and it had a distinctly colonial air about it. This was the traditional comfort stop and several, including Donald who woke up with a start, took advantage. Boxes of Orchids, "one for each lady", were collected and distributed. They were very beautiful, one in particular in my collection with cream petals that looked like wax, and with vibrant crimson to purple centres. It was a great idea but they were eminently crushable and I hoped I'd manage to preserve them with all the other baggage, hand luggage, handbag etc. Donald stumbled back into the bus and opted for the empty two-seater behind me. "No offence Jean, but there's more room here". "Good idea," I replied, not without an element of relief. Alice smiled.

We arrived three hours before the scheduled time of take-off, as recommended, because of all the extra security since the bombing of Colombo airport and September 11th. My luggage was opened but not explored so thoroughly that it was difficult to repack. Hand luggage and handbag contents were examined in more detail. Security was indeed thorough. Betty and Eileen had strapped their coconut mats to the outside of their luggage and it was as if no-one could face disturbing all that: lessons for both sides! Donald and Alice had bought a lot of extra gear and another case to put it all in, so they got a lot of attention. I felt sorry for Alice: Donald was not in a state to be very helpful but she took it all in her stride. I guess she had seen it all before.

Wednesday January 16th

Wednesday dawned some time while we were waiting for the 2.30 am flight. I had a few Sri Lankan rupees so I thought I'd change them back into sterling, but the bank only dealt in dollars. I changed them anyway because the shops (after customs check) wouldn't take the rupees. I bought some chocolate and shared it around.

The boarding lounge was pretty full, very few Europeans apart from ourselves. Boarding was uncomplicated and, after a short trip in the airport bus, we settled down for the journey home. The meal was indifferent and I passed the time by dozing, reading the in-flight magazine, and going through that photocopied music again. Half the professor's family was sitting nearby so we had a few chats. They were unhappy to have been split up but the airline 'had not realised they were together' in spite of their unusual surname. Donald slept like a baby all the way back and I watched dear Alice as she folded the blanket and put it between his head and the window.

There were some very noisy customers sitting behind us, over-exuberant or drunk or both, and a family in front with two very young children, one or other of whom cried all the way back. I felt sorry for the mum.

The plane arrived more or less on time at 8.30 am and I felt quite emotional, as I always do, when it touched or rather, in this particular case, bumped down on to the tarmac. The carousel broke down so the luggage was some time in coming. I talked to Rita as we waited and then, when I spotted mine, she helped me lift it off on to the trolley. I walked towards the exit, saying goodbye to those still waiting and then I saw Donald being attended by Steve, standing in a pool of red liquid and thought for one moment that he'd had some terrible haemorrhage. Mercifully, no - he'd just managed to drop his plastic bag of Arrak (the local toddy which he'd purchased at the airport, a '3 for the price of 2' offer). I nodded sympathetically, and wheeled on through the Green Channel and out into the reception area, where I was pleased to see Bill of the Shuttle Service awaiting my arrival.

I was pleasantly surprised at the climate. The sky was blue, the temperature almost spring-like and I didn't feel at all cold, although I had taken the usual precaution of donning my faithful long warm skirt and jumper from my hand luggage just before arrival. Bill chatted amiably as we had a speedy journey back to Heronslake, arriving about 1 pm. He and Lydia were off scuba-diving with sharks, off Australia, in a few weeks' time.

I had a snack, rang my kind watchdog neighbour to report my return, and went through the enormous pile of mail, which included many of the Christmas cards, and that took most of the afternoon.

By 8 pm I was feeling the need of a good night's sleep, but I decided just to unpack the dirty washing, which I remembered was still on the top of the luggage, in spite of the airport's ministrations, and to put that in the machine before I went to bed. I was bewildered to find the key would not fit the little padlock and then when I read the label, in an alien hand, I realised why: it read "Wilson"! I just could not believe that I had brought home the wrong luggage. What was more humiliating, when I examined it more thoroughly, it didn't resemble my own that closely. For a start it didn't have wheels, and it was navy, not black, to mention just two differences. I came out in a cold sweat, collected myself together and rang Heathrow. It took some time to sort out the relevant number for the service I needed but after about twenty minutes, during which time the recorded message had assured me several times that they were sorry to keep me waiting, I got through to a very cheery Cockney fellow, to whom I pleaded crass senile stupidity but he just laughed and said, "Don't worry, someone does it every day!"

He took my name and flight number and the good news was that my luggage was still there. I'd already rung enquiries and got the telephone number for the name and address on the other luggage and I said I'd ring that person and apologize. He gently advised me against it, saying, "She's been on the phone all day!" I felt he was kindly protecting me from a very irate lady. In her place I knew I'd have been pretty worked up, too. "I'll ring her", he said. I remembered that Bill had said he was off to Heathrow again early in the morning – something like 5 am - and I said I'd try and make arrangements for a swap on the morrow. He said to be sure that whoever was collecting it had a letter of authorisation and some identity on him.

By this time it was 9.30 pm and the Shuttle Service answer-phone was on. I imagined that Bill was very sensibly preparing for his early start. I left a lengthy message, and the luggage in the porch, in case he was able to fetch it in the middle of my night. I quite expected the unpacking to be delayed for several days, but there were evidently two Heathrow trips scheduled for the Thursday, because the office rang me to make an alternative arrangement, through another driver. I was to take my luggage to the Little Chef on the link road, near the South Molton turn off, mid-morning and, if all went to plan, collect mine from the same driver at the BP garage, opposite Sainsbury's, at 7 pm. It did indeed all go to plan and I could have hugged the pleasant driver when he opened the boot. He had had quite a job in persuading them to part with the luggage, in spite of the letter and his identifying driving licence. The Shuttle Service were not asking for a charge for this special service but, from what I can remember, (for I didn't record anything at the time) I persuaded the driver to take £10: a bargain!

I went off to the 'Carousel' rehearsal in Barnstaple with the precious load in my boot and sang better than usual.

It had been my intention to write to the Wilson lady in Cheltenham to express my sincere remorse for putting her through such angst, and I had recorded her name and address on one of the many soon-to-be-discarded Christmas card envelopes lying on the table, but when I came to write the letter, a couple of days later, I genuinely could not find it. I still have guilt about that.

COROLLARY

This has been my tenth solo holiday since John died and many of the places I've visited are those we had planned to visit together. The first was Tanzania and Kilimanjaro, then the wonderful Galapagos Islands, Namibia and white-water rafting on the Kunene, a three-week excursion to the Philippines with its terraced rice fields and hyperactive Manila, Zimbabwe with memorable experiences on Lake Kariba, Ludhiana in India to see Mark and Helen just before Callum was born, then a trip which happily combined Botswana and the Okavango, and Namibia again, because I'd been so enchanted with

Etosha. Then, the foolishly short week in the Maldives where I'd scuba-dived for the first time, and finally, last year, in Australia, where the vivid memories are the Merino Sheep and more scuba-diving on the Barrier Reef.

Some have been pretty basic and physically demanding, particularly the Botswana experience where we erected our own overnight tents. I've joined some groups of people whom I've never met, for at least part of each holiday, and found them interesting - and a few of them scaringly like-minded! A new location and fresh people make for an exciting experience. I enjoy the opportunity to be relatively anonymous and share only parts of my life: for example, I rarely divulge that I am medically qualified until I am sure of the ground and the company.

The enjoyment starts for me as soon as I get on the plane for I am one of those strange beings who really like flying, but then my legs aren't very long. Not that I would want to be away all the time. My January break is my fix for the year. When I get back the snowdrops are out and it's not long to lambing. After two weeks away, I start to miss my home in Devon and all that goes with it, particularly my commitments to local community, the garden, music and drama. Mind you, now I'm back I'm missing Callum and Sarah - and their parents of course!

I've taken on board the idea of luggage on wheels, which I have always considered to be for the disabled old - but it was so much easier and, anyway, I am marginally disabled, and a bit old! And yes, I will have it swathed in large, colourful, identity tapes next time I go away. Something which I enjoyed for the first time was the massage, a therapy I've never considered before, but my hands in particular were so much better for several days. I could stretch at least an octave with my right hand, I think (there were no pianos around to try it). So maybe this is something else I'll consider now that I'm retired and have all this time on my hands?

It was a good trip and recent memories will be reinforced and perpetuated by the photographs. I would like to live long enough to do another ten adventures, but I'll do one a year, anyway, for as long as I am able. I still have a list of places to visit as long as my arm.

I think Madagascar might be next.

MADAGASCAR

with **WILDLIFE WORLDWIDE / TROPIC TOURS TRAVEL**

MADAGASCAR, MAGIC and MAYHEM
Prologue   Family Christmas
New Year   New Holiday

Although I had not had visitors for Christmas, the run up to the celebrations had seemed to be just as busy.

The two weekends previous had been spent, first, with Richard's family in the Cotswolds, where I'd heard Eleanor sing the first verse of "Once in Royal David's City" in the Church of St Matthew and St Mary in Cheltenham and shed the traditional Granny tears, and then studied Laura's splendid horse on a very cold Sunday morning. The following weekend at Charles' house, I'd revelled in Isabella's wickedness, Georgina's chat, Freddie's prowess on the clarinet, and Charles' cooking when he and Alison had entertained two colleagues to supper with their new baby. I arrived back home after less than 48 hours away to find the house had been burgled. At the time of writing this diary up, I have recently succumbed - under pressure from the insurance company (who admittedly paid up like lambs) - to the installation of something that I've always wanted not to have, a burglar alarm.

For Christmas, I drove to Wendy's in Wales where the views are wonderful, the space inside and out relaxing, and the Christmas excitement of Lily, Tommy and Genevieve engendered a certain nostalgia for when their mother and her siblings were children. Lily read the lesson from Isaiah in church on Christmas morning rather more effectively than some of the adult readers but there may be an element of prejudice here! There were convivial encounters with neighbours in nearby properties, and on Boxing Day about twenty of them, plus offspring, were entertained to lunch.

I drove home the following day to prepare for Charles and family and their friends, another family of five, who were scheduled to come and stay at Heronslake over New Year. I 'did' food and put up decorations to give the place a festive feel, but then it seemed unlikely that they'd be coming, as Charles' recurring back problem was in residence. I took down the hundreds of cards but left the bells and stars and holly wreaths. In the event, Charles stayed home and the family decided to come without him: I did not put the cards back. I rushed into town to do some last-minute shopping and got 3 points and a £60 fine for speeding near the police station!

The family of friends arrived early afternoon: it was probably three years since I'd seen them. The two girls were charming, helpful and chatty and their big brother had grown into a handsome lad. After the children had gone to bed, we sat up and talked late into the night - which was a mistake, for the girls were up by 6 am.

Sunday morning I kept strictly to the speed limit and realised how slowly one had to drive to be legal. I loved that morning's sung eucharist and gave all I had to the choir's "What is this fragrance?" - which should really be sung in French, I feel ..... Alison and co arrived in time for lunch. By this time half my mind was elsewhere, thinking about my luggage for the following day's departure to Madagascar, and the notes for care of the sheep, and the security and idiosyncrasies of the house while I was away, when my guests would be resident caretakers for part of the time.

Monday 30th December 2002

I changed into my favourite travel clothes - ancient Aztec skirt and vaguely matching top - and was on parade when Bill Ludgate of the Shuttle Service arrived, very promptly, at 2 pm, and I was waved off by the family farewell committee. It was a dreary grey day with bouts of heavy drizzle but a couple of brief, dazzling rainbows brightened up the afternoon. I was glad I wasn't driving and I anticipated warmer climes with relish.

We chatted constantly and covered subjects as varied as to whether we should play cricket in Zimbabwe in view of that country's potentially explosive political situation, the cynical idea that the AIDS virus could have been introduced purposely by some evil power, the ideal retiring age, the inevitable travellers' tales and, finally, the subject dearest to our hearts - our families in general and our grandchildren in particular.

We reached Terminal 4 at Heathrow exactly on schedule at 5 pm and I entered the reception area, making for gates 31-42. I had difficulty in finding my way into the maze of waiting passengers but, once installed in the queue, progress was surprisingly speedy. An Indian gentleman dealt with my ticket and I asked for my luggage to be checked all the way through to Antananarivo. He looked puzzled and asked "Where is that?" When told it was Madagascar he remarked, "I've never heard of it before."

I clutched my boarding pass and luggage receipt and went to find a decent seat in the departure lounge. Everyone looked as tired as I felt. As usual I wondered about the wisdom of this trip: did I really want to do all those internal flights in Madagascar? I have these eleventh hour doubts when I'm already committed and on my way. I reminded myself of sunshine and decided it would be fine.

The first leg of the flight was to Johannesburg and there were several South African accents around me. I regarded with incredulity the size of some passengers' so-called 'hand luggage', and its weight, as evidenced from the obvious effort made to heave it into an overhead locker. We were due to leave at 19.50 but it was obvious we were not going to take off on time. I started to have a niggling anxiety about catching my ongoing flight from Johannesburg to Antananarivo: there was only just over an hour's leeway and there are not many flights to Madagascar.

I had a pre-booked window seat, 44A, and settled myself in for the night. The screen flashed up information such as height of 33,000 feet and speed of 500 miles an hour, both of which I find it difficult to get my head round. (I understand 54 mph for which I incurred the speeding fine).

I put my watch on for the statutory 2 hours' difference in time and ate beef for dinner: overdone but tasty. I slept little and enjoyed the moonlight, and then the dawn, when it was announced that we were just over the equator, above Kisangani (Stanleyville), the Stanley Falls and the source of the Congo. It was the next day.

Tuesday 31st December 2002

I had a cheese omelette for breakfast. There was an empty seat next to me, which meant I could spread myself a little. The passenger on the far side of the empty seat seemed to have little English but had been kind enough to unscrew the top off my red wine over dinner.

We arrived in Johannesburg three quarters of an hour late but a personal message for 'passenger Tyler' was put over the Tannoy. I identified myself to the ground staff and was immediately whisked off in a people carrier to the Tana (Antananarivo) check-in: very good service by British Airways. Air Madagascar staff scanned my hand luggage and there, lurking in my make-up bag was a pair of nail scissors, which were immediately confiscated and added to those in an enormous waiting receptacle: what do they do with them all? I could have sworn I'd put the scissors in my wash-bag in my main luggage.

I talked to an Australian couple, Mike and Mary, who were to spend three weeks in Madagascar and then three weeks in Malaysia. He was a pony-tailed professor from the University of Adelaide, researching in evolutionary biology, special subject - insects. It was the Malagasy bees that were to be his particular interest, following up previous results from earlier forays. Mary was an attractive red-haired younger lady.

The bus from the terminal to the plane was very hot: I removed my support tights (whatever they say about DVDs) and my long underskirt at the earliest possible opportunity. Flight MD425 Madagascar took off on time and for a while I had a good view of the world below from 14F window seat and a row of empty seats behind me. I was beginning to think that not many people go to Madagascar: Tana unheard of by the Heathrow employee, and now a half-empty plane.

I couldn't face the lunchtime dry chicken, and just ate the salad and the sweet. We seemed to be over the sea for ages, and then above mountain ranges of clouds like Antarctic sculptures. We arrived after a flying time of just over three hours, having put on our watches another hour for the time difference between the island and the mainland. I was relieved to see my luggage with its newly-acquired bright green 'belt', purchased after last year's fiasco, when I'd brought home someone else's. The customs decided I should open it and I took out my key in readiness, but the padlock had done a disappearing trick. I explained this but they didn't seem to have much English. I tried it in French but just got a shrug of the shoulders. I did a thorough search myself but everything seemed to be in order. I decided that either the padlock had been ripped from the two zip-pulls by accident, or any intending thief had not had time either to complete the operation of theft or – even more alarming - the insertion of some illegal substance .....

Tropic Tours met me, brandishing a large placard saying "MRS TYLER". Jean-Jacques was the driver and the lady representative was Ooly. I had hoped to change some money but the airport bank was closed. No sooner were we out in the sunshine than a couple of touts were pressing me to exchange 8,000 Malagasy francs to the English £. Ooly said they would exchange money at the hotel so I decided to wait. She was very pleasant, spoke some English, and was anxious to tell me about her two boys,

Handy (3) and Racava (20 months): "Our names are Malagasy," she explained. We drove from the airport into Tana, which has a population of around 1,000,000, the total population of Madagascar being over 7,000,000.

I had first become aware of Madagascar at the London Missionary Society (LMS) conferences in Swanwick, Derbyshire, in 1948, 1949 and 1951 - what a long time ago. A certain Mr Burton, the Rev Leonard Hurst, and the Rev I T Hardyman told stories of the original missionaries, the Jones and Bevan families, who had all succumbed to fevers, apart from Mr Jones that is, who had gone on to found churches and create a Christian community. Four young Malagasy men were delegates with Mr Burton, two of them doctors, doing further training in the UK. I remember collecting 'ship half-pennies' for the maintenance of the missionary ship, the John Williams VI, which transported the missionaries to what seemed to me to be exotic and exciting places, but Madagascar had not been without its devastating periods of famine, persecution and rebellion. The brief references to the endemic birds, plants, and animals had fired my imagination. Ooly mentioned the LMS and the benefits it had brought but I could not get her to extend this conversation any further. She was very concerned about the time: we had been about a quarter of an hour late in landing because, according to the pilot, two private planes flying below the clouds had been allowed to precede us.

The nearer we got to the centre of the city, the thicker the pollution, much of it from the motor vehicles such as the many ancient and battered Renault 4s of every rainbow colour, and the equally eye-catching old Toyota pick-ups. There were people everywhere: cycling, walking, standing talking, running roadside stalls, or just sitting on the ground with a few wares to sell.

We arrived at the Tana Plaza, a rather more up-market hotel than I had expected, at the corner of a central square. The staff was very welcoming and I was able to change some money, getting the rather better rate of 10,000 Malagasy francs to the pound: I was glad I'd waited. I filled in the mandatory form and was shown to my room on the first floor, where I had the luxury of air-conditioning. I bathed and changed and then went for a walk round the square, looking for a valyha (a traditional musical instrument made from bamboo) for Wendy, who had become acquainted with such things when she had done a shore study on the island as a zoology student many years ago.

There were all sorts of crafts and seasonal goodies for sale but I didn't see what I was looking for; I took a couple of pictures. I was about to explore up round the other side of the hotel when the young man on the hotel desk evidently spotted me and came rushing out to warn me that I really should not walk about alone, especially when I was wearing jewellery (cheap silver earrings), so I did as I was advised and went in - and then had difficulty finding my room. I was informed that the next day's internal flight to Fort Dauphin had been changed from 11.55 am to 5.30 am - help! - and tonight was New Year's Eve. I lay on the bed and went to sleep and then had a job to rouse myself and go down and have a meal, which I felt I ought to do.

I had only paid for bed and breakfast at this hotel so I studied the currency: I had a collection of 25,000 Malagasy franc notes and, as the exchange rate was approximately 10,000 to the £, each of these lucrative-sounding pieces of paper was worth just £2.50! This was New Year's Eve and the dinner menu read as something very special. I had a gin and tonic and over-tipped the barman: his whoop of joy gave it all away. Oh well, it was New Year's Eve.

The dinner appeared to have nine courses. Did I really want this when I'd had hardly any sleep and needed to be up at 4 am?   But I had to give it a go. Everything was superbly presented, garnished imaginatively, and arranged artistically so that the salivary glands reacted to the sight as well as the smell. The meal was advertised as available from 7 pm but nobody seemed to be making for the dining room. No doubt they were all set for a long night and many were drinking at the bar. I bided my time until 7.30 pm and then strode bravely in as their first customer, to have the unrivalled attention of all the waiting staff, who watched my reaction to every mouthful.

I enjoyed the Kir Royal, the Gourmandise de la Saint Sylvestre, the Crayfish with Sesame seeds and a wondrous chutney of tomato and citrus fruits, and then a large portion of Daurade (Gilthead) fish, encased in ginger, lemon and fennel. I was struggling! And, after a refreshing sorbet au koombava, I opted out of the main course of Guinea Fowl (I have those at home) and finished off with the sweet terrine and the crêpe parcels. At the beginning of the meal we were entertained by three guitar-playing Malagasy musicians in striped George Melly suits: the rhythm was addictive and the melodies very sing-able. Later they were replaced by a duo of a man on a keyboard with a surprisingly good tone and another, very accomplished younger man, on a soprano saxophone: between them they created a comforting nostalgic mood with Evergreen Jazz.

I escaped to bed at 9.15 pm, prepared my luggage for the morrow and slept solidly in the neat, uninspiring little room until 3.30 am and then dozed until the wake-up call at 4 am.

The adventure had started
HAPPY NEW YEAR!

French for the day: reveiller - to wake up

MADAGASCAR
Internal flight from Antananarivo to Fort Dauphin
Journey to Berenty with Benoît

Wednesday 1st January 2003

I downed a minimum of the yoghurt, croissants and other pastries at this early breakfast and had a difficult conversation with the hovering waiter, in halting language. I was relieved to mount the minibus with John-Jaques for the trip to the airport. He came complete with large umbrella to protect me from the pouring rain. There was little traffic about at this time of day but plenty of people, some walking about as if they'd been up all night - maybe they had - New Year's Eve was only just over. Others were setting up their roadside stalls before 5 am.

John-Jaques insisted on waiting at the airport until I'd been checked in and we improved each other's language skills (I think). He had two girls of one and three years and spoke proudly about their early abilities. Most of the other passengers were with a group of French-speaking young people, and one older man who seemed to have little control over his frizzy-haired, handsome, hyperactive youngster called Sebastian, of about three years.

There was a dilatory air about the little airport, which was slowly populated by shuffling cleaners, two smartly-dressed ladies who took up positions at the check-in, and a man in a suit with a walkie-talkie. I thanked and bade farewell to John-Jaques, checked in and boarded the little plane shortly afterwards. It was less than half full and we could sit where we liked: I selected a window seat. Good coffee was served and a very hard crêpe. The flight took a couple of hours and somewhere in the middle I had a comfortable doze.

At Fort Dauphin I was met by Benoît, the guide, who spoke a little English, and the driver, Gaby, a man of few words in any language. Being the only passenger I sat in the front and had splendid views of the surrounding countryside. It was still raining but once we got to the other side of the mountains, Chaines Anosyenes, we were welcomed by a blue sky and I could feel the warmth of the sun. We stopped so that I could take a picture of the fan-shaped Ravinala (traveller's) Palm, which trees are said to align themselves on an east-west axis, but there appeared to be some defaulters. I saw my first Malagasy Baobabs on this stop: they looked like something from another planet. A clear little blue flower was called "Clitora", Benoît informed me, and to someone who is well acquainted with that area of female anatomy, it seemed very apt.

As we motored on we had sightings of Black Kite, a Yellow-billed Kite and what seemed to be apologies for Magpies in the form of Magpie Robin and Pied Crow. There were extensive plantations of Sisal, some of them replacing forest clearance (which was now monitored). These plantations bring some income to the island, where the crop is harvested twice a year for five years, the fibre being dried and exported for manufacture into twine, rope and fabrics.

Benoît was anxious to stop at a small roadside stall, where a group of adults and children watched over collections of little carvings and crude lumps of semi-precious stones. I was hardly ready for making purchases and, while I mused on the idea, knowing I had not got any small notes, we were entertained by the youngest child who was pressing her fingers on some de-winged cicadas which, not surprisingly, made shrill protest. Benoît explained that they were destined for the pot later. I bought two tiny carvings of Guinea Fowl and another of a chameleon and then, predictably, waited forever for the change as one of the middle-sized children went over the hills and far away to get it. We saw the real thing shortly afterwards in the forms of one small and one large Chameleon crossing the road in front of us. These sightings were closely followed by one of a thin grey snake, and all were given great attention by a carload of Japanese tourists ahead of us. Benoît explained that the Japanese government was involved in irrigation and conservation projects, which relationship seemed to attract quite a number of interested tourists from that country.

The final stages of the journey to Berenty took us along a wide, red earth track where we picked up a man called Sourloo whom Benoît described as 'the breakfast man', and which terrain flashbacked me to Western Australia. Berenty was a private reserve, situated on the banks of the Mandrare River and famous for its Lemur population. The Reserve was established in 1936, by a certain sisal planter, M Henri de Heaulme, who recognised that the 200 acres of Gallery (Tamarind) forest was worth preserving for its own sake. Thank you, M Heaulme.

I was escorted to Bungalow 9, which was near the breakfast place but a long trudge from the restaurant. The plan had been to visit the ethnographical museum of the Antandroy tribe but it was closed. I wasn't sorry, for although it was only 11.10 am, I felt like a kip. I organised my luggage, washed and changed, and dozed on the bed until 12 noon, when I went to the restaurant for some lunch. I had an enormous salad of fresh crisp vegetables, some of which I could not identify, a bottle of coke and a bottle of water, all for the equivalent of £3.50 - and that was expensive by Malagasy standards.

At 2.50 pm Benoît took me for a walk through the Gallery (Tamarind) forest. It got steadily cooler for which I was more than grateful, not yet being acclimatised to this change in temperature. Groups of svelte Ring-tailed Lemurs abounded everywhere: they walked elegantly without hurrying and were just so accessible and so addictive that I couldn't take my eyes off them. We saw them first. Then we saw the Red-fronted Lemurs (sub-species of the Brown Lemur) and finally, and most memorably, the Verreaux's Sifakas. Those handsome white creatures were so like humans as they danced about on their hind legs, that I found it difficult not to be anthropomorphic. They were incredibly agile and acrobatic, and hurled themselves across wide-open spaces from one Tamarind tree to another. All kinds of amazing vegetation grew around us and I just couldn't take it all in. A Sifaka ate enthusiastically from the centre of an insectivorous fungus. Benoît pointed out a smaller White-footed Sportive Lemur sitting above us in the fork of a tree: it was magic.

A beautifully-patterned snake slithered across our path. We had good views of a Madagascar Coucal, which reminded me of the Crow Pheasant I'd seen in Tanzania, a Madagascar Paradise Flycatcher, noisy Common Mynah Birds, Namaqua Doves, a couple of Hoopoes and a Long-billed Green Sunbird. After walking for about two hours, we had a brief sit down and Benoît talked about his family of three young children and his wife who helped at a nursery class at the school during term-time. Benoît was qualified as a teacher but had given up his poorly-paid school job to earn more money as a guide. He heard and spotted - and identified - everything. Then it was back to base. I'd been bitten in spite of the repellent. I would need to cover up for the night walk.

After a wash, and a change into cover-up gear, I sat by Reception for a while and took more pictures: one film gone already. Then I made my way to the bar and sat outside and drank my coke. Another pair of Hoopoes swooped in front of me and then a lonesome baby Long-tailed Lemur industriously applied its tongue to the licking of the wall opposite, for some mineral I presumed. Once it was dark, Benoît appeared and off we went with Gaby for a short drive to the Spiny Forest for the night walk. Benoît's torch lit the eyes of a Grey Mouse Lemur and followed its quick movements, so that we got a good view of this nocturnal aptly-named little creature. Shortly afterwards he picked out a White-footed Sportive Lemur and we watched that. I was wearing my head torch, which was excellent for looking up into trees, but I really needed to be looking where I was walking most of the time. The ground was uneven, unpredictable and crossed by sinewy roots from all angles. The head torch also interfered with positioning my camera correctly, so tomorrow I reckoned I would bring just the lesser variety (of torch), which would hang round my neck, and I would leave the higher illumination to Benoît.

We heard a Nightjar several times but didn't see one. Sleeping Chameleons were easy to spot, all pale and anaemic-looking against the dark forest, their special colour-change camouflage on hold for the night. Butterflies, similarly, slept motionless, blissfully unaware of our intrusive lights and comments. A nocturnal, very much awake, large blue-green Dragonfly flew back and forth through the beams of our lights. Other insects buzzed and flitted about, not all as innocent as they looked I discovered later, when I counted yet more itchy red bumps, especially round my ankles. We encountered the Japanese party, with another guide who could speak Japanese, Benoît confided. Two of the young men had bee-keeper-type nets over their heads and faces, which seemed to amuse Benoît, but as my bites began to take hold, as it were, I decided it was probably not such a daft idea.

We had wandered about for a couple of hours before Gaby drove us back to the campsite, where I went into the restaurant for dinner. The starter was a fruits-de-mer concoction, with paté, in an envelope of batter, something of a meal in itself. A generous portion of roast beef and boiled potatoes followed but I had to leave some of it: it was just too much. The fresh pineapple went down well: it was just … well … so fresh. It was very obviously the low season here. There was just one other lady eating and at that juncture I thought she was French: she didn't seem inclined to speak, which suited me well, as it was by now 9.30 pm and my brain felt it had closed its French language department for the day.

I was in bed by 10 pm, just before the lights went out.

Today's French word: la libellule - Dragonfly

Postscript

We had seen some Zebu during the drive from the airport to Berenty: they were like hump-backed oxen. My comment on their appearance prompted Benoît to tell me of their value. It was the ambition of every member of the rural communities to own Zebu. They provided good milk, good protein when slaughtered, could be sold when money was short or exchanged for other essential foods when the crops failed.

Wealthy men of one tribe would build themselves a large house, have up to fourteen wives, all dressed the same and whom they were obliged to 'satisfy' at the rate of one per night. Most importantly, a man would amass as many Zebu as possible for they were the true indicator of status and prosperity. When the man died, all his cattle would be slaughtered and given away - but not to his family - and the house would be burned down. He would be put in an ornate expensive tomb, considered to be more prestigious than the value of his house. It all sounded a dreadful waste. I wondered what happened to all those wives and their families.

In a second tribe, the Zebu was also of great importance, but the men were monogamous and when they died their animals were slaughtered and sacrificed and given to the family to eat. "They are more easily converted to Christianity", offered Benoît.

A couple of weeks after I'd returned to the UK and was writing up this holiday, I watched one of David Attenborough's "Life of Mammals" programmes on the TV Channel 4. It was the "Life in the Trees" episode and towards the end we had the "Lemurs of Madagascar", which made me smile all over again. There were some wonderful shots of several species, but it was those Sifakas (which he seemed to pronounce as "Shiffers") that took the biscuit, as they had done for me in real life.

Post-postscript

Over six years later - on the last day of April 2009 - when I was finally putting this material together for inclusion in my second travel book, I heard Libby Purvis interviewing Gerald Durrell's widow about his work in general and the Madagascar Lemurs in particular. They will haunt me for ever, in the nicest possible way. Gerald's writings gave the animals a personality and he has been criticised by some for being anthropomorphic, so why should I feel guilty at doing the same?

Lovely Lemurs (again), Antandroy Museum, Spiny Forest

Thursday 2nd January 2003

I slept well but 6.30 am seemed very early for the morning walk. It was pleasantly warm as Benoît and I started our trek in Berenty grounds. In no time we'd seen the rufous variety of the male Madagascar Paradise Flycatcher, the subtly-coloured greenish-blue Crested Coua hopping about in a tree above us, and the large Giant Coua with its startling blue elipse round the eye, feeding unhurriedly in a patch of sunlit ground.

Later, Benoît indicated a Madagascar Harrier Hawk at the very top of a tree: how does he spot them? I suppose for starters, he knows where to look. It looked something like a Kestrel to me until it took off with slow, sweeping wing-beats, when its long clean legs set it apart. We walked down to the side of the Mandrare River where a couple of Madagascar Bush Larks moved around on the dry ground near some Madagascar Green Pigeons. A colourful Broad-billed Roller seemed to observe us from a branch just above our heads. A collection of white Cattle Egrets was scattered along the far side of the river and ordinary-looking Plovers moved about on the near bank. I write "ordinary-looking" but studying Plover pictures later, I guess they could have been the similar Madagascar Plover but I never did ask Benoît. A male Knob-billed Duck sat on the water, looking for all the world as if it had some serious congenital abnormality.

On the return walk we saw groups of Lemurs, particularly the Ring-tailed variety, several carrying their young. One of the babies was tiny and carried in front of its mother: others were larger and had graduated to transport on their mothers' backs. They were all quite charming. One large Sifaka sat sunning itself in the middle of the track and another also sat in the sun, but at the top of a high tree where it fed its baby: a picture of absolute peace and contentment, which somehow reminded me of the Virgin Mary and made me want to cry - but I didn't: anthropomorphism or what. Hoopoes flitted prettily about, and Helmeted Guinea Fowl ran quickly for cover at our approach. A flamboyant Madagascar Red Fody caught the sun - and our attention - as it perched nearby.

We took a short excursion off the beaten track to see a colony of Madagascar Straw-coloured Fruit Bats, some hanging from, and some flying around, a stand of tall trees. Bats of all kinds seem to me to belong on another planet. We encountered some large spiders, one with a bright yellow back and another the weaver of the most beautiful silk web. A large-patterned gloriously blue butterfly settled long enough to be appreciated and then, finally, Benoît took me to a small enclosure in the reserve where are kept some Flat-tailed Tortoises (Kapidolo) and the Madagascar Radiated Tortoises, and a couple of Crocodiles.

We had walked for two and a half hours and suddenly it felt like breakfast time, or even lunch time. I sat quietly outside the breakfast bar with my coffee and rather dry bread and watched more Hoopoes and Lemurs in the area of long grass in front of me. The sun was well up but the temperature was still pleasant. This was better than I could ever have imagined.

At 10 am I met up with dear Benoît again, to visit the now open on-site museum dedicated to the local Antandroy - "those of the thorns" - tribe. It was really hot now and I was glad when the museum came into view at the end of a half-hour walk. The Antandroy are said to be one of the poorest tribal groups who live in the dry and desolate Spiny Forest, where water is very scarce. Hence they eat little rice but live on cassava and maize. They survive mainly by making and selling charcoal. Benoît said that many had left the land to find work and an easier lifestyle elsewhere.

The museum was set up in 1995 by an American lady called Fee (I'm not sure whether this is first name or surname), and a Frenchman who was married to an Antandroy lady. It was a long, hot walkabout round four large rooms downstairs and then an upstairs section as well. There were fans but the electricity was off in the morning so they were merely ornamental. Nevertheless it was an excellent hour and a half, which really put me in touch with where I was.

The large Voataro fruit was important for nutrition but also in the dried case form as Calabash for water carrying. There was a well-illustrated section about the Zebu cattle with predictable emphasis on their value. Each animal has a special cut in one ear for clan and in the other for lineage. Women were not allowed to milk the cows: they were considered to be too contaminated by menstruation and childbearing. After delivery they stayed indoors for three months with ashes on their faces. The placenta was buried in the garden and the site marked with a stick. The baby's fontanelle was rubbed with some special mixture to help it close. The Ombiasa, the medicine man, had his potions for treating the sick and there was considerable faith in charms (aolys) of various kinds.

A section was given over to the use of wood (now controlled) for planks for building and the charcoal business. A traditional farming tool, a fangale, was on display. The sisal planting was illustrated and the harvesting of the raw products explained, most of which goes elsewhere for cloth manufacture, but some drapes - for burial etc - are

SITTING SIFAKA

Oh you beautiful creature, protected and content
How you protect each other, on family closeness bent
So lithe and agile, leaping from ground to tamarind
Then climbing without effort to join some kith and kin
And sway on overhanging branch of some nearby tree
Thus mimicking a man on a high wire circus spree

You preceded man by many a million years
Your feet are like his hands but it's man who's in arrears
You've maintained your bonding throughout that space of time
And kept tribal commitment like creatures in their prime
Your beauty is a legend from wide-eyed gaze so sweet
To coat of grey white velvet and ballet on two feet
You seem to dance for joy, perhaps your just reward
For hanging on monogamous to your genetic cord

One very early morning just at the break of day
I spied a sitting Sifaka in the sun's first ray
She held and fed her youngster with human pose quite scary
So that my thoughts were turned to the nursing Virgin Mary
To be anthropomorphic may be considered foolish
A misconceived analogy, even a little ghoulish
But that's how I'll remember you in memory's sharp measure
Where you'll remain imprinted for ever and for ever

made on the island. This led on naturally to an account of the complicated funereal and burial preparations. There was an impressive skeleton of the relatively recently extinct Elephant Bird, so much bigger and more substantial-looking than the Ostrich, and photographs of a yellow-flowered plant called Aloha, from which paper is made.

Benoît stayed downstairs and talked to the museum caretaker and, judging from the laughter during their exchanges, they both enjoyed the company. When I was about halfway through my tour, some nuns in spotless white arrived, accompanied by a group of well-covered young adults and children. I suddenly felt uncomfortably conspicuous and wished I'd worn my long trousers instead of 'indecent' shorts. Most of the party studied me disapprovingly but one of the nuns did have the courtesy to say "Bonjour" and I responded accordingly, and gave her the best smile I could muster.

By now it was after 12 noon and definitely lunch-time. We walked back to the campsite where I ate a delicious tomato salad and a plate of fresh mango and then had an hour's essential kip. Then the tireless Benoît appeared again and it was time for another walk in the Spiny Forest. Gaby drove us the couple of miles to where two charming helpers were waiting to show us 'special things', as promised by Benoît. They located a sleeping Malagasy Eastern Scops Owl, which was sleeping as soundly during the day as the night-sleeping diurnal birds that I was to see later in the week. I was afraid I would waken it as I crept nearer with the camera, but Benoît assured me there was "pas problème" and sure enough the little creature sat motionless with its eyes screwed tightly shut.

Their next trick was to find the tree where the nocturnal Grey Mouse Lemurs spent their day. They were lodged motionless high up but a gentle shaking of one of the branches of the Euphorbia Oncoclada prompted some inquisitive head bobbing in and out of their hideyhole: I took a picture. A passing rufous flash belonged to a pair of Madagascar Paradise Flycatchers. Numerous lizards crossed our path but my attention was drawn constantly to the change of landscape provided by the wonderful views of the mountains in the distance. And so we walked for a couple of hours, the guides talking to Benoît, who did his best to relay to me their comments and observations on the terrain. I hadn't brought any money and felt sorry because these guys really deserved a tip. I said so to Benoît, who promised they'd get anything I gave to him after we'd got back.

I was very hot again and went under the shower before meeting up with Benoît outside the restaurant for a drink. The restaurant (with just one customer) was late opening and so we had time to talk politics, his and mine. He considers the new President to be good news and said everyone had high hopes for his term of office. "Better than the last one: he was too friendly with the French!" I couldn't understand why this was such a bad thing when after all Madagascar is a French territory. I mentioned that other French territory, Corsica, but he hadn't heard of it.

I didn't fancy a heavy meal, something to do with the heat I decided, and accepted the chef's suggestion of an Ostrich omelette. Also I felt under pressure not to be too long, knowing that Benoît would be waiting for the night walk. The omelette was light and frothy but the Ostrich was conspicuous by its absence. (It was only later that I realised that it would have been the egg from the bird which gave it its name.) I followed it up with a plate of fresh pineapple and then trailed back to my room for the torch and the big camera in which I had put the film most suitable for night shots (as advised by son Charles). Benoît was most anxious to show me the small Indian Civet which, although solitary and nocturnal, he said he was usually able to locate.

We saw a brown Big-headed Gecko rustling round in the undergrowth and a pale sleeping Chameleon with a helmet. The Fruit Bats were noisy but their sound was almost overwhelmed by another, like dogs calling and yelling. This, said Benoît, came from the White-browed Owls communicating across the forest. I got all excited when I spotted a small spiny creature scuttling along the side of the path. It was a very young Hedgehog Tenrec, which is supposed to sleep at night. As it was so young, Benoît was not certain whether it was the Greater or Lesser Hedgehog Tenrec. I took a picture.

Benoît shone his torch up among the trees constantly, and pairs of yellow, amber, orange, brown or reddish eyes were caught in its beam, some followed successfully to reveal the whole animal, usually a Lemur. One of the most amazing pairs of eyes belonged to a nocturnal Dragonfly. Benoît stopped suddenly and gave a grunt of satisfaction and I guessed he had found the Civet, but he shone his light on two Eastern Madagascar Scops Owls, high up in a tree ahead. I was delighted but for some reason the camera refused to bring them into focus. One flew away, and I despaired, but I thought I got a distant shot of the one remaining. I felt stupid that I'd had never learned how to override this camera when recalcitrant.

I had lost my bearings completely by now and was surprised but not too sorry when I realised we were nearly back at the campsite. We made a last little excursion into an area where Benoît had seen the Civet - but not tonight. It was nearly time for lights out so I got into bed and wrote up the diary by candlelight. I felt as if I'd been in Berenty for days, I'd seen so much. I slept soundly until the Ringtailed Lemurs did their early morning scramble up and down the roof.

Today's French word: la religieuse - nun (pretty obvious)

Le Dauphin Hotel: Antananarivo to Antsirabe with Edorique

Friday 3rd January 2003

I slept well until 7.15 am and then awoke feeling un peu malade d'estomac. I sat outside the breakfast area and toyed with the unspeakably dry bread but drank two cups of good coffee. It was so peaceful. Benoît joined me and I asked him if he would be kind enough to write down the Latin names of all the trees we had seen in the Spiny Forest and elsewhere. I passed him my notebook and he espied the family picture in the front. He studied it for a while and then said, "You all have the same faces." Well, I have the same trouble with the Malagasy … He wrote the neat botanical list without hesitation.

I went back to my room and packed my things together and then went and sat in the covered area near the Tortoises. It was very hot. I listened to Coucals and watched

Hoopoes, and wrote a poem about the Sifaka I'd seen feeding its baby at the top of the tree, before I'd forgotten how it had made me feel.

At lunchtime I had a drink with Benoît and then a light meal of cucumber salad and fresh pineapple: I think I could almost become a vegetarian if I lived here. Then it was into the Toyota pickup for the journey back to Fort Dauphin. After about half an hour we were stopped by the driver of a minibus coming from the opposite directon. Benoît was to return to Berenty in a following minibus, to act as guide to an English group. He was glad to earn some money but sad that he would not be going home to his wife and family near Fort Dauphin for the night. Until the previous year's political unrest and consequent dearth of tourists, he had had a regular wage of sorts, but now he was paid only when he was working.

I fished out his 'tip' and he seemed over the moon with the 15 dollars, which was only about £10. I counted myself exceptionally lucky to have had him as a guide, and as he got out to join those in the second vehicle, I told them how knowledgeable he was, that he spoke some English and had the enthusiasm of David Attenborough. They smiled and nodded. (Had I looked as tired and bored as they did, when I had arrived? I hoped not.)

Driver Gaby spoke no English so I tried to hold a conversation in French, starting with some remark about the potholes being "ralentisseurs naturelles" but it fell on stony ground, as it were. But we did manage short exchanges about the cattle on the road, the alarmingly dodgy bridges, and some very brightly dressed young girls who really took his eye and prompted a rare smile. There were groups of people all along the route going to and from village markets, carrying wood, charcoal, fresh fruit and vegetables, and other goods hidden in large plastic bags.

On the outskirts of Fort Dauphin, Gaby stopped near a school to deliver two sacks of charcoal and some correspondence we had picked up earlier at one of the villages. We stopped again to view some very large Pitcher plants, some of the flower traps heaving with doomed mosquitoes. " La meilleure place", I suggested. The unmade road took us along the beautiful coastline where inviting waves broke on to the white sand. I made the best of my view from above, aware that, sadly, there was not going to be time to explore or swim.

Gaby dropped me off at Le Dauphin Hotel and the sign of a leaping dolphin reminded me that dauphin means dolphin as well as heir to the French throne. Once again, the place was more up-market than I had expected and I was led along several short passages and mini-staircases, inside and out, to a room on the first floor - I think. It looked out on quiet gardens where, every now and then, heads and hands of gardeners would pop into view as they did the evening watering. Girls with brooms swept the tidy paths. I sat on a lounger and enjoyed the last half hour of sunshine.

There'd been no-one at Reception on arrival and I was anxious to know about the following morning's arrangements. An official-looking lady was sweeping by (not with a broom), brandishing a piece of paper in her hand, so I stopped her in her tracks to ask. The luggage would be collected at 6 am, breakfast would be at 6.30 am and I would be picked up at 7.30 am: the flight was not until 9.15 am.

I showered and changed and wended my way to the restaurant. My guts were still in a state of turmoil so I just picked a bit of fish and had an ice cream. The 'French' lady I'd seen at Berenty was the only other diner. She appeared to be trying all the courses but not eating much. She returned my smile but didn't speak.

I decided I'd better book a 5.30 am call and started the trail to reception but got lost. One of the waiters came to my rescue and escorted me there by yet another route, where a pleasant, elderly non-English-speaking man in a yellow shirt listened to my request and took for ever to write it down: I didn't feel confident that he had got or they would get the message! No-one here spoke any English and some of them didn't speak French either.

I found my way back to my pleasant room, drank plenty of water and, thinking about the early start, went to bed just after 10 pm.

Saturday 4th January 2003

I slept well and woke at 5.25 am in time for the early morning call. Sure enough, the luggage was collected at 6 am, and I presented myself for breakfast at 6.30 am but there was no-one around. A plump girl appeared behind the serving area at 6.50 am and then the silent, solo 'French' lady, who turned out to be Italian, and was really quite chatty in broken English. She taught in an Italian school in Addis Ababa and travelled twice a year. She had apparently done a pretty extensive tour of the island with a hired car and driver.

The breakfast crêpe was a long, sweet roll, which went down quite well with a tall glass of orange and a decent cup of tea. We then waited in the entrance until 7.45 am for the transport to the airport.

The small airport was very crowded with all sorts and conditions of men and women. There was a gathering of nuns who looked Japanese, one with a large tatty sunhat perched incongruously on top of her traditional headgear. A French Canadian family, or so it seemed from their speech, added interest to the waiting time. The three attractive young girls who had their hair in hundreds of tiny plaits, teased two younger boys whom I imagined to be their brothers from the family resemblance. As they talked to their parents they switched effortlessly from French to English and back again, as the mood took them. Oh, to be bilingual without even thinking.

When we boarded I made for a left window seat as advised by my Italian friend, and had wonderful views of the terrain below each time the white clouds cleared. One of the plaited girls said in English as we flew over a moderate mountain range, "Look, that's the ridge where we sat". I was a little envious for the second time. It all clouded over and I slept for half an hour. We were landing already: I was puzzled - this was too soon. But it was an interim stop at Toliary, over on the west coast and just above the Tropic of Capricorn I discovered, on consulting the map.

A few people got off and a handsome young dad and his little daughter took the seats next to me. She looked sad and weary and her hair was unbrushed. She obviously had a good relationship with her father and talked all the time. It seemed that her mother was ill and papa was taking her to other relatives to be looked after. After a drink and a trip to the loo, she settled down into a typical 3-4-year-old mode, clutching her doll with one hand and sucking the thumb on the other.

The next stop really was Antananarivo, where I was relieved and pleased to see a man with a "Mrs Tyler" placard - the Tropic Tours driver and guide with whom I was destined to spend quite a lot of time. This was Edorique, with a smatterng of English and an infectious smile. The bank at the airport was closed again (Saturday) but Edorique took me to the Tana Plaza, where I was treated like an old friend and had my financial batteries recharged at the very acceptable rate of 10,000 Malagasy francs to the £.

We then drove through the fascinating city, China town, and all, and picked up Esther, Edorique's wife, en route. I asked whether they had any children. "Pas depuis" responded Edorique, after some hesitation. Then he launched into a dissertation about children in Madagascar. "They make up 70% of the population and that's far too many". Education was not compulsory so many children remained illiterate. "People think the best thing you can do is to have seven sons and seven daughters: family planning is only just beginning here", added Edorique.

He then suggested that I should eat before starting the long drive to Antsirabe and at that very moment we came upon a discreet and, I suspected, expensive restaurant where he dropped me off. He escorted me in and the staff greeted me warmly. He said he'd return for me in about two hours. I protested. My stomach was anything but settled so that I didn't intend to eat very much, and in any case I'd no intention of being ensconced in this dim little hidey-hole for two hours. He said he'd settle for an hour and a half. I was directed to a table and sat where I could see the door - and Edorique when he returned. I also had a view of the swing door of the men's loo and its users zipping down and up as they went in and out: very French.

The drinks list came first. The gin was inordinately expensive so I had a Takila, which was dear enough at 16,000 Mlg fr (£1.60). The wine list came next: I opted for water. The menu was pages long and I went for the cheapest option, the menu of the day. The starter of Bouillon of Chicken with herbs was half an hour in coming so I began to wonder about the two-hour option. It was very good and a meal in itself with large pieces of chicken lining the base of the bowl - but I'd committed myself. I was surrounded by babbling French businessmen, and by two older women who were adoring and indulging a young child, in competitive fashion. The latter were evidently regulars, for Madame, in stunning black day dress and impressive earrings, kept checking that they were happy.

The second course, Porc Caramel with rice, was really very good and not too large which was a relief. I was mellowing, as was my stomach. The sweet was a delicious concoction of banana and lemon in out-of-this-world light pastry. I paid the equivalent of £9, including the tip, which of course was not dear at all.

I had finished just within the hour and a half when Edorique appeared: good timing. However, there was a problem: his people-carrier-type vehicle had broken down and would take an hour and a half to repair. (This was just one of the many unscheduled delays that I would experience during the rest of the stay). He commandeered one of the battered Renault 4 taxis and took me back to the Tana Plaza, where I sat in state in the reception lounge and read French fashion magazines and then had a go at understanding the Madagascar political scene. The new President seemed to be going down well, according to Edorique (as well as Benoît) who said "He is young, he is enthusiastic and was president of TEKO, a concern producing milk products " (touch of the Dairy Crest here, I thought) "so he should know about finance and business".

It poured with rain outside and a group of Japanese tourists stamped in and out, necessitating another wipe clean of the spotless floor by the conscientious young doorman. Edorique appeared on time again, and I was delighted to see him, albeit in a different, smaller Toyota. I checked my luggage was in the back. We left the smiling Esther on the steps of the Tana Plaza and I couldn't quite follow what Edorique said about arrangements for her.

Antananarivo was seething as usual and it took ages to crawl through, but I was happy enough to have time to look at all the shops and stalls in the narrow streets. The meat stalls were all open to the world - with its pollution, and visible swarms of flies peppering the poultry and sausages, and hanging over the pork, beef and zebu. On one counter I saw a heap of brains, now an unknown sight in butchers' shops in the UK.

As we left the city and drove out into the countryside, the rain came down even harder. This did not deter the roadside stallholders from offering their wares: small tables were covered in beautifully set out fruit such as apples, peaches and plums, in neat rows and clever patterns. Another displayed collections of bright orange mushrooms, which Edorique declared to be delicious. The mouth-watering smell of the freshly-cooked corn-on-the-cob emanated from the open fires burning at frequent intervals along the verge. A larger, more permanent-looking stall held stacks of flowering pot plants, some of them such as Fuchsia, miniature Roses and even Busy Lizzies readily recognisable, but others looking not quite like anything I'd seen before. On one stretch of road several men held out large bunches of beautiful Roses for sale.

The rain eased off and I enjoyed the glorious green of the vegetation on either side, most noticeably that of the rice paddies which swept along the bottoms of the valleys and up the terraced hillsides, studded occasionally with small groups of houses, all built from the warm red earth or of bricks made from the same. "La terre agitée." commented Edorique. Green daubed shutters hung in for windows.

People walked everywhere, mostly returning the 10-15 kms home after the Saturday markets, with parcels on their heads, babies on their backs - some of the women carried both - and many of the men and older children with huge bundles of wood on their shoulders and bags of charcoal on their backs. The legs of small children went like clockwork as they walked in single file between their parents. What stamina. I imagined them reaching their small, dark shacks soaking wet, and wondered how long it would take for them to dry out by the fire: they needed all that wood and charcoal.

The rain became very heavy again and some stretches of road were flooded, others had what I now realised were the mandatory Malagasy potholes, and some had both where the water made it difficult to spot the potholes. Driving was not easy and a couple of mad drivers made it worse. Edorique drove at speed but with reasonable care it seemed to me. The car did not have seatbelts.

On the outskirts of Antsirabe, in the dark, the unlit pousse-pousse (rickshaws) provided yet another hazard for the driver. We arrived at Arotel after 7 pm and I was shown to Room 107, pretty unprepossessing, but maybe it will look better in the daylight. I decided to have a light meal before anything else: otherwise I knew I'd go past it. I was the only taker in the restaurant and settled for a flaked fish dish, all impressively arranged in concentric circles, separated by others of carrot and sweet onion. The peach ice cream to follow was equally good, and was adorned with wafer meringues shaped like surfboards. I still could not face a 'proper' meal.

I had a bath and washed my hair and my friendly trouser suit. It had been a long but interesting day. I hadn't seen much in the bird department: Egrets, Pied Crows, Mynas, but then I hadn't really been looking. I'd been taking a more global view of the island - Richard and Charles won't be very impressed with that.

French word for today: les cerveaux - brains

Pousse pousse, Semi-precious stones, and learning about Edorique on the drive back to Antananarivo

Sunday 5th January 2003

I slept until 4.30 am, when the colonic turbulence returned and necessitated frequent trips to the loo. At 8 am I went to the breakfast end of the restaurant but it seemed to be closed. So I went and enquired at Reception and a lady came and opened the door. Two girls were sitting chattering behind the serving counter, possibly unaware that anyone was in residence in this out-of-season period. The cup of tea was welcome but although the bread and croissants looked excellent, I just could not face them. Eventually after a little silent French oral, I asked for a bag to put them in, explaining that I was "un peu malade d'estomac". (This was becoming one of my favourite phrases). I couldn't imagine I'd want a full meal today and thought that the delayed breakfast might just keep body and soul together. I knew I must eat something.

I went back to my room and searched for the Lomotil and couldn't believe I hadn't brought it. I thought I might start Metronidazole (which I had brought) tomorrow, if things were no better. The motions looked a bit gardia-ish … enough of that.

Edorique arrived promptly at 8.30 am and off we went. We took a pousse pousse each and went for a tour of the town. These rickshaw vehicles of transport were misleadingly named, I decided. The driver worked hard to pull them along, more tire tire (pull pull) than pousse pousse (push push). The temperature was pleasantly warm and the rain had stopped. The town was bustling with people, attending to their stalls but many walking about, some family groups in smart Sunday clothes moving to and from the

Catholic Church. We had several photo stops, one for an old colonial-type building overlooking Lake Ranomafana, another for the Roman Catholic Cathedral where I ventured inside and was quite moved by its beauty - lovely windows and drapes from the ceiling - but even more so by the backs of dark, worshipping heads of all ages, filling the place to capacity.

We pousse poussed on and I couldn't help noticing the names of some of the rickshaws such as Roses, Lily, Orchid, Texas, Diana, and an unimaginatively-labelled 'Titanic'. We went down a side street and Edorique knocked at the only painted, cared-for-looking building in sight. Eventually a bouncing, bald-headed enthusiastic little man welcomed us inside. Here there were many displays of semi-precious stones in their raw state, in small individual same-stone collections, in polished 'eggs' of different sizes, in ammonite forms and as single polished stones ready to be made up into jewellery. There was very little finished jewellery. The owner of the establishment presented me with a droplet opaque turquoise stone and then I was given the option to select small pieces of uncut raw stone, which took my fancy, from a huge pile in the yard. I fell for a citrine pendant and, as I'd brought little money with me, I decided to use my Visa card, which was promptly refused. Edorique came to the rescue and I did a brief borrow from him. After the complete city tour, we paid the fit pousse pousse men 25,000 MGF each for their two hours' labour, and then set off in the more traditional vehicle for Antananarivo.

The journey was through beautiful terrain as I'd discovered yesterday but today was bright and sunny, so even more enjoyable. The blue skies made the rice fields look even greener, if that were possible. I didn't have to concentrate on the driving and I allowed my mind to drift through flashbacks of Nepal's high views, India's small stall vendors and the rice fields of the Philippines, all evoked by my brief Madagascar experience. There were even more vegetable stalls today, tables of tomatoes and cucumbers, carrots and potatoes, and others I couldn't name, as well as the corn-on-the-cob collections and young boys with baskets of orange mushrooms.

Even on stretches of road which seemed to be miles from anywhere, there were people, some in family groups in Sunday clothes, perhaps walking back from church, or from visiting other family members, and mingling with men and women in working clothes, carrying produce and equipment, who had obviously not had the day off. The flood-waters had subsided and at least today the potholes were visible. A couple on a motor bike coming from the opposite direction with a child hanging out of the back, suddenly swerved to their left, right in front of us (we were, of course, driving on the right). Mercifully, Edorique had rapid response and good brakes but he did give them a mouthful of something-or-other as they passed.

The drive from Antsirabe to Antananarivo took about five hours, so as well as discussing the terrain, we talked about life in general. Predictably he said that should he and Esther have children, he wanted them to have a good education, but then went on to say he knew people qualified in medicine and law at Antananarivo who could not get relevant employment, and were working as policemen and tour guides. Edorique came from the very north of the island, Diego Suarez, home of the Antakarana tribe. The region was pretty inaccessible because of flooding on the badly-maintained roads for most of the year, so he seldom saw his family but was planning a trip with Esther in September. It

5th January 2003

ANTSIRABE - A full congregation in the Roman Catholic Cathedral

would take three days to drive there, even during the driest time of the year.

We got back to Antananarivo around 5 pm. I changed some more money at the Tana Plaza where I was to stay the night and then sorted my luggage, yet again, and packed away various small presents I'd bought for the grandchildren at roadside stalls of Edorique's choice, where he was always greeted like an old friend. These included two stylised birds (vaguely Cormorant-like) made from Zebu horn (for me), some little girlie, brightly-coloured sisal bags, a Ring-tailed Lemur made from raffia and an ammonite bought at the semi-precious stone centre.

I decided not to go down to dinner but to plod on with the bland left-over breakfast and drink plenty of water. I started the Metronidazole, hoping I'd feel better in the morning for the 4.30 am call.

French word for today: blé de mais au naturel - corn-on-the-cob

Airport delay … delay … delay …   Research camaraderie

Monday 6th January 2003

I had ten hours in bed, no less, apart from brief visits to the loo every couple of hours. I was already awake for the 4 am call but would have liked to have lingered. I'd asked for breakfast at 5.15 am, just coffee, but the dear waiter brought the full complement of bread, cake, croissants and fruit juice as well. When he removed all the solid stuff at my request I suspect it was contained in the personal plastic bag with which he drifted nonchalantly away: and why not? The fruit juice was a very thick combination of mango plus something else and it took much deep breathing and serious will power to keep down both it and the foul-tasting Metronidazole tablet. I'd barely recovered from this heady success when the porter reported that Edorique had arrived: he was early. In my anxiety not to keep him waiting I pressed the '0' button in the lift instead of '00', ended up on the wrong floor and then wondered why my key wouldn't open the wrong door.

The early morning drive to the airport was uncluttered. Nevertheless, I was amazed, as I always am on my rare excursions into the outside world at 5.30 am, to see just how many others had left their beds. Edorique seemed to have a runny nose and kept dispersing the snot with a series of rapid hand to nose to trouser movements. I was tempted to offer him a tissue but he unexpectedly pulled out a crisp white handkerchief from his pocket and did the job properly.

He accompanied me to the check-in and then I made my way to the departure lounge, where I was entirely alone for a while. I wondered whether I was in the right place, initially, because the flight was said to be bound for Antalaha, but I looked at the map and found it was north of Maroantsetra, which I therefore imagined would be our first stop. At 6.40 am a group of Malagasy joined me and we assembled for boarding. After twenty minutes, one of the group returned to sit down and I followed suit. She spoke to me and we had a good conversation in French and some English and she told me that she was with her family who lived in Antananarivo but they were going north to visit another branch of the family. They were all quite short in stature and their features reminded me of people I'd seen in Nepal.

An announcement was made which was unintelligible to me and everyone came away from the boarding gate. Presumably there was some delay: heigh-ho! The delay continued so I took advantage of the shop for coke (must keep drinking), some mints and of course the loo. Half an hour later came another announcement, which I understood to mean a further delay of three quarters of an hour. During this interval a smartly-dressed girl in red appeared and issued everyone with a ticket for a free 'petit déjeuner' at the airport restaurant, which she said was "en haut" and waved her hand vaguely towards the front of the building. I trailed off and got completely lost, and a young opportunist, seeing me wandering aimlessly and in possession of the conspicuous given ticket, offered to show me the way, for which I was grateful. He was very dissatisfied with his reward of 1,000 MGF, but I felt 25,000 (the only other note I had) was too much.

In the restaurant I positioned myself between a sour-looking French couple with their smiling toddler son, and a middle-aged Malagasy man with two youngsters, one of whom, a little girl, looked mortally ill. She was painfully thin and hollow-eyed and needed help up the staircase. She was wearing a witch's hat decorated with tinsel, which somehow added to the macabre appearance. I reckoned these people were all on my flight and would know the way back so I kept them in view.

I managed a small croissant and the coffee was good. The obliging waitress eventually found some hot milk, which aided the pill swallowing. An announcement, barely audible with the noise of international flights and associated passengers milling about (and which was, in any case, equally unintelligible to me in Malagasy, Malagasy French, or strangely accented English), prompted the French family to pack their things together, pushchair and all, and move. I did the same. I stopped to tip the milk-providing waitress and lost the trail-blazers, but never mind, there was the Malagasy trio, walking at the sick girl's slow pace. I followed them as the arrival of an international flight dictated we took completely different routes: I somehow found my way to the domestic flight area. The French family was there but they left quite soon on a different flight. I had hung around behind them at the boarding gate but then noticed that my boarding pass was a different colour. I was relieved to see the Malagasy family group and went and sat with them.

The piped music began to pall, especially "Where have all the flowers gone?", "I did it my way", and "Yesterday", which seemed to come round more often than other numbers I didn't recognize. I looked at my watch: it was 10.45 am and I'd been there since just before 6 am. It was all such a waste of time and was going to mess up the day's programme irrevocably … little did I know.

At 11 am, when I was in the loo again, I heard two American girls speaking glorious English. I hurried out to talk to them and had a pleasant conversation. They were not on my flight, which was definitely to their advantage as it turned out. I tried to be philosophical. Maybe it wasn't such a bad thing for me in my condition: resting, access to plenty of water, and the loo. I just hoped I'd reach the island of Nosy Mangabe at some time in the day.

And then, at 11.35 am, the flight was cancelled. I understood only too well the French "annuler". Help! What did I do now? I had spoken to a young man with the Malagasy family group who seemed to have more English than most, so I approached him to ask what happened next. We all queued at the counter to get our cancellation verified on the redundant ticket, and then I joined him with my luggage, and other members of this family, in a taxi (paid for by Air Madagascar), which took us back through the mid-day dusty heat of Antananarivo. I didn't understand where we were going and wished the airport had complied with my request to ring Tropic Tours from there.

However, when we arrived at the Air Madagascar office in the centre of the city (very near Tana Plaza, in fact) for a compensatory hotel booking and alternative flight, I accepted things were being done in proper order. My saviour then shepherded me to another office where non-nationals were dealt with, but at 12.45 pm the lady was just going to lunch: she'd be back at 2 pm. I sat on the cool steps rather than on the hot upholstered chairs, which kind people kept offering to this old lady. I had almost forgotten about my bowels which was just as well as there didn't seem to be a loo.

A young woman, a member of the family party, came and sat beside me. She was doing her PhD thesis on Gorillas. This revelation threw me for a while: had I missed something? Maybe it was Gorillas I should be looking for instead of the Aye Aye. But no, she worked in a zoo in Fort Dauphin. I told her about son Charles being engaged in research at Exeter University and she said she thought she'd heard the name and read some of his work. I guessed she was probably just being polite and friendly but then she said, "It was to do with fish and pollution". I was delighted to accept that she really did know of him. Small world. Her first name was Brigitte but the second name was so long, it didn't register.

At 2.30 pm the lady from the 'non-residentials' office returned from her lunch break and it looked as if there might be some hope on the horizon, but it was 3.30 pm before all the paper work was done. This was conducted in a singularly casual manner and at one juncture I rescued my redundant air ticket and recent attachments from the floor where they had floated, from their insecure position on top of the bevelled surface of the computer. It seemed to be the sorting out of a hotel which was taking the time. I suggested the Tana Plaza but it didn't find favour.

My helpful English-speaking academic stayed around until accommodation had been found. Brigitte told me that his name was Hada, and I asked her to write down her name and address for me. Her surname was Raharivololoma: small wonder I didn't get it first time round. And so I was now presented with my air ticket for the morrow, a pre-paid slip for dinner, bed and breakfast at the Karibotel Hotel, and a taxi to the hotel and to the airport in the morning. Needless to say a taxi-man was waiting. I bade au revoir to my Malagasy guardians, thanked them most sincerely and looked forward to seeing them for the flight the next day. The Karobotel was a few doors down the road from, and definitely down-market when compared with, the Tana Plaza, but the diminutive girl on reception was pleasant and spoke a little English. I had to fill in a lengthy document and leave my passport in their safe. A hesitant porter took me up to the third floor and then along dim passages to Room 35: no air-conditioning and an uninspiring view of room windows opposite. But I wasn't planning on being there long …

I did the necessary bit of unpacking and then went downstairs and asked to ring Tropic Tours. The girl looked blank as if she'd never heard of them. Fortunately I had the number and was relieved to find Ooly was in the office. I had imagined that the staff at the hotel in Maroantsetra might have phoned Tropic Tours to say that I hadn't arrived and, they would then have discovered that the flight had been cancelled, but this was Madagascar and if you will travel on your own in the off-season … Ooly was horrified to hear I'd waited 6 hours for a cancelled flight, asked if the hotel was OK, and said she and Edorique (VIP treatment) would collect me at 7 am – the last check-in time was 8.10 am for the 9 am flight: j'espère!

At 4 pm I wrote up the day's diary, so far. I'd already been up 12 hours but in spite of all the frustration, there were memorable things on the credit side, like meeting Brigitte and Hada, who had been my anchors, and just watching the go-slow worlds of the airport and the Air Madagascar office.

I washed and changed and went down to the restaurant, where I was so happy to see Mary and Michael Schwartz sitting at the only occupied table. It was therapeutic to give an account of my day in English and by now it all seemed quite hilarious. Three other members of their team joined them: John and Michael, PhD students, and a girlfriend. They were pleased with the bee population they'd managed to track down to date, some down a deep ravine. They were on a tight budget and were going out for "cheap Chinese" which they did, but not before we'd had a really enjoyable gossip.

I had a legume omelette and a mint ice-ceam and didn't have to make myself eat. I was in bed by 9 pm. Quel jour!

French word for today has got to be: annuler - to cancel

Maroantsetra   Rough night on Nosy Mangabe
More delay   Tamatave

Monday 7th January 2003

The wake-up call was at 6 am. I was almost getting used to these early mornings … but not really. I drank plenty of fruit juice and tea for breakfast, and Edorique and Ooly arrived promptly at 7 am. I think I could drive myself to the airport now. We dropped Ooly off at the Tropic Tours office. She must start her day very early for she takes her two young children to her mother's first.

Poor Edorique had evidently been instructed to wait with me until my flight took off but when Hada and co arrived, this hardly seemed necessary so he disappeared. Hada produced a book about birds, well illustrated, and in Malagasy from one end, and Japanese from the other, and written by himself. I asked him why he had not written it in French or English. "This book is for the Malagasy people and for the Japanese who are very supportive of Madagascar." I understood he spoke fluid Japanese and did his first degree in Japan. He went on to say how everyone wrote for the English and "they've got enough books." All the same I'd love to have an English translation of his book. We exchanged e-mail and other addresses.

We went through into the departure lounge, where 9 am came and went. I had a foreboding sense of déjà-vu. I understood Edorique to be on his way to Tamatave where he had a guiding commitment. At 10.00 am there was an announcement that there would be a delay: no reason, no time. I think it was at this moment that I thought I'd definitely join a group next year, although what difference that would make to recalcitrant internal flights I don't know - but at least there'd be someone else with whom to share the experience. A comfortable little cruise somewhere might be a safer bet.

Then suddenly, without warning, at 10.30 am, Boarding Gate 3 was opened and at least we were walking towards the plane. A familiar voice shouted "À demain!" and there was Edorique, leaning out of one of the windows waving me off. He'd taken no chances and I suddenly felt all reassured and quite tearful: get a grip. It was a small plane and I felt a sense of relief as we went along the runway but we were not through the wood yet. The plane stopped and a crew with a motor and a ladder came bustling out to do something to the right wing: ten minutes and we really were off and airborne. "Enfin" said a smiling Hada. The 1 hour 40 minute flight was pretty rocky but I slept a little. Papers and sweets were on offer.

At Maroansetra my Malagasy friends were greeted affectionately by a host of friends and relatives but there was no-one with a 'Tyler' board. I hung about for a while during which time I was approached by a touting driver in a white shirt. I said I needed to wait a while. I spotted a dynamic little fellow in a 'Tropic Tours" T-shirt and moved in his direction. He was meeting other TT clients (no doubt in a sensible group) and said I should take a taxi to the Relais de Masoala and it would be paid for. In the event, he arranged the transaction and I was ushered into the front seat of yet another battered white Renault 4, while two middle-aged Frenchmen were put into the back. I gathered from their conversation that they had not met before. We dropped them off, after a short ride, at the Hôtel du Centre, which looked like a not unattractive collection of basic bungalows. "Moins cher, pas pour le tourist," said the driver as we drove away. No, I bet they're not, I thought.

We stopped again in the primitive part of the town and picked up the driver's very lovely, well-rounded wife. I trotted out one of my favourite French phrases, asking them whether they had any children. (I really must stop doing this to every young couple.) "Pas depuis". He then asked me whether I was a clairvoyant! I must leave out the Family Planning bit. We arrived at Le Relais de Masaola, which was in a lovely situation up the estuary. It was very warm. I expressed my disappointment at missing out on Nosy Mangabe to the young lady at the desk who studied my voucher and showed me to Bungalow 9. It was spacious, had a fan that worked, and a wonderful view - a definite improvement on the Karibotel. I felt peckish and asked about coffee and croissants: no croissants so I just had a very large pot of coffee and piled in the dried milk and sugar.

I sat outside the dining room and a man appeared and introduced himself as Julian. He spoke a little English and said he was the guide for the hotel and promised to show me "Lemurs and Chameleons before dinner." The diminutive hotel lady, 'Clarissa' I learned later, took possession of my flight ticket to Tamatave for the following day in order to do the necessary confirmation, and very observantly noticed that it was dated for January 10th instead of the 8th - so I imagined the time might be wrong as well. I understood her to say that she would go to the airline office in the morning, but she had no English and I found her Malagasy French difficult to follow.

I retreated to the bungalow balcony, unpacked a little and then returned to sit outside the restaurant. I was enjoying the view, the peace, and feeling sleepy and detached, when along came Patrick, the Nosy Mangabe guide, who announced we were going to Nosy Mangabe for the night and to be "ready in a minute!" I said, "Give me ten". I collected my thoughts and packed the bare essentials I imagined I'd need into my small rucksack. We were to camp for the night and he asked me whether I'd brought a tent - and he wasn't joking. He thought he could borrow one for me. I was to ask the cook for whatever food I thought I'd need. I plumped for bread, bananas, pineapple, coffee, teabags, dried milk and sugar.

I was ready in ten minutes: he took half an hour. We walked about 100 metres to the water, accompanied by two of the staff carrying bed-roll, tent and food. I felt a bit colonial. We waited some time, (as one does in Madagascar) until a smart little motor-boat came zooming in. Patrick was not one to give assistance but neither am I one for asking and I put on my most agile front to climb inside. I was directed to the middle and then we all put on lifejackets.

The crossing to Nosy Mangabe took about 20 minutes and the last 10 minutes were very, very rough and reminded me that I had read somewhere that it could be dangerous at this time of year. We seemed to come out of the water completely as we rode each big wave. I loved it. This beat waiting about at airports. I was glad I was not prone to 'le mal de mer', but I did begin to think it might have been wiser to have left the big camera behind. On arrival at the steep shoreline there was no way I could climb over - or under - the high rail of the boat. Patrick noticed and fetched a stool, which he lodged insecurely on the coarse, shifting, orange sand, and I'd arrived. We were met by two (of the three) island staff and, once I'd signed the visitors' book, Patrick erected my splendid little tent on one of the several covered platforms, and I made up the bed.

It was about 3.30 pm by now and he suggested we go for a walk. It was extremely hot and humid and he asked whether I could "climb very high?". He wanted to take me to see some tombs and look for Lemurs on the way there and back. I said I'd give it a go and took my large bottle of water with me. We climbed steadily up twisting, muddy, slippery, root-strewn paths. The tropical vegetation was dense and wonderfully varied. I could put names to only a few. There were very tall buttress-rooted trees, Orchids, Pandanas and different kinds of Palms. Green-backed Mantella Frogs were easy to spot, although I think 'yellow-backed' would be more appropriate.

After over an hour, by which time I was as wet as if I'd been out in a tropical storm, we reached the collection of strange little stone tombs of an ancient Malagasy family, varying in size and balanced haphazardly it appeared, on and between huge rock boulders. There was a notice asking visitors not to touch the 'coffrets'. Inexplicably I suddenly had the urge to stroke the nearest but Patrick spotted my approaching hand and uttered a forceful "Non, non!" I withdrew with a shamefaced "Je suis desolée."

He suggested that we might climb higher but I knew my limitations, bearing in mind that the steep downward trek, although easier on the pulse rate, would be harder on the knees. This being the rainy season, the waterfalls were spectacular, but we paddled precariously over a wide expanse of water-covered rocks, which were evidently always wet and cool, whatever the weather: "les roches froides".

There were luring Lemur noises overhead and Patrick dived off into the hillside, obviously expecting me to follow - which I did with difficulty, after several temporary restraints by powerful creepers of one kind or another. We were rewarded (admittedly miles up a tree) with the sight of a family of Black and White Ruffed Lemurs. I attempted a shot of one of them, as its head became visible between two branches against a patch of sky when it gazed inquisitively down at us. I knew it was unlikely to be any good but somehow it didn't matter. I'd have that picture in my head for ever. It had been worth the scramble.

Later we had a less convincing view of a White-fronted Brown Lemur. It was by now dark in the forest anyway, the light fading fast from an overcast sky. We'd walked for four hours and I was ready to sit down for my light supper. We were to walk again later to look for the Rufous Mouse Lemur and THE Aye Aye. We'd finished eating when the rain started, absolutely pelting down. I'd never heard or seen such rain. It was impossible to see just a few yards in front. I returned to my tent with the torch. The rain continued all night long. Patrick said it would be a waste of time to go looking: nothing would be visible. In spite of my Aye Aye disappointment, I have to admit I did not fancy those muddy paths, probably young rivers by now, as well as a complete soaking of a different kind. I settled for an early night and lay down just as I was. I hadn't even brought the hairbrush.

Powerful flashes of lightning lit the tent into a sharp daylight every now and then, but there was no accompanying thunder. The rain did abate occasionally for a brief while, and then clouds of Fireflies, their fluorescence visible through the tent, did sparkling air dances all around. My bowels resumed their nocturnal turbulence. There was no way I could face a trip through the rain to the ghastly official loo some distance away across the mud, so I showed initiative and found a native way of dealing with the situation nearer home …

French word for today: les coffrets - the caskets

Wednesday 8th January 2003

It had been unclear as to what time the boat would collect me, because my air ticket to Tamatave had had to be checked and confirmed, and the chances were that the time would be different from the original ticket, which was dated incorrectly anyway. I had a niggling anxiety about this but as there was no phone or radio on Nosy Mangabe (the latter had gone to the mainland for repair) there was nothing I could do, and I tried to put it out of my mind.

We were to have had an early morning walk but – surprise, surprise - it rained heavily again. Patrick reckoned my flight would be either 10 am or 12 noon, and the pick-up boat would arrive at 8 am or 10 am accordingly. The rain stopped but we obviously could not go off hiking into the hinterland in case the boat arrived. I took a walk along the beach where I would be able to see and hear any advancing vessel. There were flowers, trees, sea-washed driftwood, and so many other things asking to be photographed and of course I obliged. The sun came out and enhanced the rare beauty of the scene.

A boat-less morning passed – and Patrick said, reassuringly, "Sometimes there's a flight at 3 pm." At 11.45 am there was the rumble of an engine. We gathered everything up and clambered aboard. The boatman said there would be a taxi waiting, which seemed pretty pointless, as we were never going to make a 12 noon flight. There was no lifejacket ceremony this time: no lifejackets, so far as I could see. This was a rough-looking workaday boat with a grumpy young man in charge. A violent argument ensued between him and Patrick about his being so late. Apparently no-one had told him and, in any case, it wasn't his job to pick up tourists etc. The other boat was evidently engaged elsewhere. He had DAAV splashed across his torn dirty T-shirt, and a tatty Yamaha flag rippled from the rail.

After an unceremonious landing, Patrick tore along the hot walk to the hotel and it took me all my energy to keep up with him. There followed another heated exchange in rapid Malagasy between Clarissa and Patrick, which wasn't very helpful to me, and I kept asking what was happening and what I was to do. Clarissa didn't exactly tell me to shut up but she did suggest in clipped tones that I went and had a shower and got changed. I knew I looked a sight.

I didn't dare strip off, take down my hair or get under the shower in case there was new information to change the plans. And there was. The plane had not yet come in, never mind gone out, so it was all stations go. I managed a wash, changed my clothes and sort of tidied my hair and off we went - this time in an orange Renault 4, in which the driver had to hold his door shut and drive single-handedly most of the time. Patrick and Clarissa sat in the back. We arrived at the strange little airport building with its food counter, open sides and big weighing machine. It was deserted and I suspected we were either too late or it was another 'annulé' and they'd all gone home. But all was well. The flight was now scheduled for 3 pm (clever old Patrick). Had it been on time, I'd have missed it. Patrick had another assignment and he had to leave, but not before I'd thanked him for the weird and wonderful 24 hours.

Clarissa insisted on staying with me until the plane took off and to be honest I was really quite relieved, for then if the plane did not come, I could go back with her to the Relais. We talked a bit. She looked so very young that I was surprised to learn she had an eight-year-old son. Her husband had died from cancer two years earlier, poor lady, and she and her son lived with her parents so that she could work and provide, while they collected him from school etc. She showed me a picture of her husband, a handsome Malay-looking man. She asked about me and listened intently as I did the French version of my family saga. She put an empathetic hand on my lap when I got to John's death.

We went over to the food counter, and the assistant rose up from her recumbent position across three chairs. I ate cake and bought some more water. Later we weighed ourselves on the luggage scales. She was about 8 stone I think: I still can't cope easily with kilograms. She said she was 5' 2" but she seemed smaller. I was more than a stone heavier but then I'm all of 5' 4"!

We snoozed a little and then at 2.30 pm things looked hopeful as passengers returned. At 3.15 pm a vehicle parked on the airport side of the building and out got an elderly white-haired man (not many people here have white hair) who shuffled arthritically into the office behind the scales. We were each given a warning notice stating that there were no loos on the plane: mercifully my bowels seemed to be in quiescent mode. This piece of paper doubled as a Boarding Pass. I gave Clarissa a hug and a tip, and thanked her for looking after me. I promised I'd send her a copy of the photo I'd taken of her at the airport.

We took off at 3.45 pm. I was hinged into an aisle seat next to a very large Italian man, who spilled over into my zone so that I had to hold in my left side every time a crew member wanted to pass. We'd been airborne only a short time when there seemed to be a problem. I had noticed areas of flooding when I'd craned my neck to see out of the window, and evidently the craft was unable to land at one of its destinations and I couldn't understand which. Some of the passengers seemed very upset. I tried to get some information from the Italian but he just looked at me blankly. The Captain passed so I managed to attract his attention and ask him "Tamatave?" "Pas problème" came the response. Thank goodness for that.

We landed sooner than I expected and, being near the exit, I was first off only to discover that this was Mananara North where most of the disappointed passengers were to stay the night, hoping to fly on the next day. I rejoined the few remaining passengers who were bound for Tamatave. We landed at 6.15 pm and for the second time, I was first off. I stood and scanned the waiting small crowd for Edorique in his donkey jacket, but without success. Had everything gone to the original schedule I should have arrived at Tamatave early afternoon to start the five-hour drive to Andasibe, so there was no accommodation booked here. I was just doing one of my silent French speech preparations to get myself out of this dilemma when I noticed, with much delight, a man in a white shirt waving vigorously from the balcony above. It was Edorique. I think he was as relieved as me, and we greeted each other with a hug. We collected my luggage and the drive started.

It was by now almost dark and it was certain I was going to see little of the anticipated impressive scenery as we made for Andasibe. The first stop was a garage where Edorique bought a lamp for one of the 'long' lights. The second was at a supermarket where I replenished my fluid supplies with two bottles of Coke and two bottles of water for less than a £. Then we moved on for some solid food in the form of 'sandwiches', which were in fact half-sized French loaves, deliciously fresh and prepared by a chatty man who was anxious to try out his English. He seemed to think England was synonymous with London so of course I tried to put him right. My outsize roll was filled with omelette, and Edorique's with toasted ham and cheese - a 'croque monsieur' - together costing under £2.

Once out of the town the road was comparatively quiet, apart from occasional collections of huge vehicles. Edorique explained that the railways, for the most part, had been allowed to fall into disrepair so that heavy goods went via the potholes. Inconspicuous children ambled along the unlit roadside in some of the villages. Long stretches were tortuous and very hilly and at one time it seemed we were going up to meet the newish moon. There was evidence of an accident and Edorique stopped to make sure no-one had been hurt, but it was just the vehicle which had been damaged and they were waiting for transport.

We were stopped for police checks no less than five times: all very civil but papers were scrutinised meticulously. Evidently there was a growing number of unlicensed drivers and vehicles. Some time during the late evening, Edorique asked whether I would like a rice dish. I declined but said he must stop and eat if he was hungry. We parked in a place called Ambinaninohy (I think), where I stayed in the vehicle and got the spicy aroma from the cafe as well as the flavour of the busy little place with its street stalls and walking vendors, including very young children selling bananas and other fruit. Some of them looked tired and weary. Edorique was back in no time at all and I suggested he must be a very quick eater. "Fast food!" he replied.

We arrived at Vakona Forest Lodge at Andasibe at 12.30 am. I was happy to hear Edorique promise me a 'free' morning. My bungalow was very pleasant and there was nicely-prepared food awaiting me. I put it in the fridge – yes, a fridge - this is really up-market. I cleaned myself thoroughly and did a bit of essential clothes washing, and collapsed on to the comfortable bed around 2 am where I don't think I moved until I awoke at 8.30 am.

French word for today: le gaspillage - waste (of time … today!)

Andasibe   Luxury of Vakona Forest Lodge
Exciting nocturnal wildlife   Perinet by night and day

Thursday 9th January 2003

I used the free morning to explore the lovely grounds and to write up my diary, which took ages, but I knew I'd forget what happened when and where if I didn't commit to paper. I ate the food which had been left in the room for my late arrival, for both breakfast and for lunch. The chicken was moist and tasty, and the black olive salad, with a superb indefinable dressing, was as good as I had ever had: my appetite had definitely returned.

I was on parade for Edorique at 2 pm and we set out to see the Lemurs at Perinet, the local private reserve. We were greeted by André, and some very tame, photogenic Black and White Ruffed Lemurs. These were then joined by Common Brown Lemurs and the good old Ring-tailed Lemurs. André took me round the waterways in a small boat from whence we saw Coquerel's Sifaka and the magnificent Diademed Sifaka. A strange-looking Lemur, with prominent white patches around its black eyes - which somehow reminded me of Mickey Mouse - was disappointingly called the Red-bellied Lemur.

André was a pleasant man. He had no English but he spoke French more slowly than some, said he'd worked there since he was "very young", and had five daughters (I didn't ask … honestly). He called out to a wooden house above the lake and his wife and three little girls waved to us. The other older two had walked to school just a kilometre away. They grew their own vegetables and rice. Not such a bad life I imagined. A minimum of cash no doubt but good fresh food, a nearby school, an element of security and a house in idyllic surroundings with the job. Magnificent Dragonflies swooped about among the rushes and plants in and around the water. Many of the flowers looked vaguely but not quite familiar. André described them all as "medicinal".

We left this section and moved on to another part of the reserve, where large clusters of shining Frogs' eggs hung from plants like globules of ice, and Crocodiles swam in the water and lazed on the bank. We saw Radiated Tortoises, Madagascar Tree Boa, and then, in a cage, there was an opportunity to study a Fosa pacing up and down (it seemed to me like a cross between a Fox and a member of the Cat family). We also saw White-faced and Knob-billed Ducks, Madagascar Kestrel, and the Greater Vasa Parrot. A Helmeted Guinea Fowl sat cockily (pardon the pun) on top of one of the cages, announcing its objection to the world in general. A Malagasy Kingfisher perched

9th January 2003
Uncommon Edorique with Common Brown Lemurs
PRIVATE RESERVE - ANDASIBE

conveniently on the bridge rail and a Cuckoo Roller also did a photo pose. With all the plants, Lemurs and other wildlife I hoped I'd caught on film, I'd suddenly used another two rolls. We bade André farewell after an excellent afternoon and returned to the hotel. Maurice was meeting us in Perinet for the night walk at 6.30 pm.

It was still light when we met up so we sat and talked in the car until it was dark. Maurice was very well acquainted with some of the internationally-renowned naturalists, including Nick Garbutt , the co-author of the excellent "Madagascar Wildlife" which is full of useful information and good photographs for the non-specialist visitor (like myself) but small enough to carry around in the daypack. Maurice then produced Nick Garbutt's classic authoritative "Mammals of Madagascar", on the flyleaf of which the author had expressed his thanks to Maurice for all his help in its compilation. (Edorique expressed a longing to own a copy.) Maurice had also met the late Gerald Durrell but didn't seem to know about David Attenborough. His English was the best I'd encountered yet.

The going was wet and slippery but not as difficult to negotiate as Nosy Mangabe. There were several Chameleons, conspicuous in their ghostly nocturnal bland colour. Sleeping Madagascar Blue Pigeon, Madagascar Paradise Flycatcher and three young Magpie Robins, huddled into an almost indefinable feathery blob, made easy still-life shots for the camera. We had a convincing view of a Rufous-tailed (Brown?) Mouse Lemur and a fleeting sight of a leaping Greater Dwarf Lemur - or so Maurice said. A Tree Boa slept disconcertingly on the ground at our feet. Malagasy Scops Owls called constantly to each other across the reserve, an eerie monotonous quavering sound. A bright moon shone through the trees and, as I looked up, I was temporarily confused by the 'upside down' star constellations. It started to drizzle but thoughtful Edorique had brought my mac out of the car. "Pour l'appareil", he volunteered.

It was after 9 pm by the time we got back. I took off my muddy shoes, put my muddy light trousers to soak and quickly changed for dinner. There were just five of us in the dining room: two young French guys who might have been an item, and two French girls who used the pool table noisily during and after the meal. I had selected the chicken after my good experience with the food in the room, but it was disappointingly dry and overdone. The two crêpes I had to follow melted in my mouth and went down well with a gin and tonic. The dining room was very grand, with a visible first floor and huge windows all round. The tables were all beautifully set and one of the waiters conscientiously turned all the wine glasses bottoms up while I was finishing my meal.

French word for today: l'appareil - camera

Reserve Peyrieras   Antananarivo

Friday 10th January 2003

I slept well, packed and had breakfast at 8.30 am, ready for the 9 am pick-up. Off we went, with Maurice again, to Perinet. It was a good day, pleasantly warm with blue skies. The loud call of the Indri (which carries for two to three kilometres) was heard almost as soon as we started walking, but we didn't see them for a while. Maurice pointed out, amongst others, a Parson's Chameleon and a Leaf-tailed Gecko, which I would never have spotted.

10th January 2003
Wonderful Western Grey Bamboo Lemurs
PEYRIERAS

The Indris were the main object of today's exercise and they were said to be amazing: I was not disappointed. They are very large Lemurs but their prominent ears made me think of Koala Bears. We spent ages just waiting and watching. They were mostly very high up in the tall trees. Their size did not limit their mobility or agility and they leapt from tree top to tree top, a couple of them carrying young. Sometimes they reciprocated and seemed to be watching us, which was good for a picture. I snapped away like a mad woman, knowing that the light was poor in the forest but using the recommended film and my 'big' camera, hoping that I'd get one or two recognisable shots.

We had rewarding views of the Malagasy Kingfisher, Cuckoo and Broad-billed Rollers and, as we stood on the bridge enjoying looking at the water, a Malagasy Moorhen put in an appearance with a host of chicks among the Water Lilies. It seemed a good place to take a picture of the two men. I had hinted that I might send Edorique "Mammals of Madagascar" which is unobtainable on the island and he opted to be holding Maurice's copy for the picture: a gentle reminder. Maurice knew of my Aye Aye disappointment and suddenly stopped to show me a hole in a tree made by the very same: this was the nearest I was going to get. He said there were very few of this elusive nocturnal creature in Perinet.

146

We had walked for three hours and once we came out from the forest, it was very warm. I bade goodbye to Maurice and tipped him: he gave me his address. I stopped at a café near the exit and drank a large coffee with evaporated milk and plenty of sugar, and replenished my water supply. I had not understood that we were to have lunch a short distance down the road, or otherwise I would have waited. It was a very pleasant lodge and we sat outside by the river to eat. Edorique agreed to join me and be my guest for the first time. He explained in his own way that guides and drivers are not supposed to fraternise with their clients. He had a zebu dish and I had a delicious sizeable 'Ocean Salade' of sweetcorn, rice, lots of prawns with chopped tomatoes, and slices of hard-boiled egg, all arranged on a rosette of lettuce leaves. The plate of honeydew melon, sweet red and yellow plums, and small mango was equally memorable.

A group of American researchers was seated at a large table further down the terrace. They were evidently staying at this place and, like us, had had a very good morning, looking at Indris, birds, reptiles and everything else. They'd collected samples of plants, fruits and seeds, which were contained in professional-looking packets. They were altogether very full of themselves and avowed they'd seen "everything" between them. They didn't speak any French but had an English-speaking guide whom I felt they were treating as an inferior. It made me feel uncomfortable and I had just a brief conversation with a large male of the party who had muddy trousers up to his knees, a serious limp which suggested he was ripe for a hip replacement and a huge file of papers. I asked whether he was writing a book but he said he "was just recording everything at present."

It was now time to start the drive back to Antananarivo, which looked about 100 miles on the map. It proved to be a winding uphill road with beautiful views, especially in the region of the Massif de l'Ankaratra on our left. After about an hour we stopped at the Reserve Peyrieras, near somewhere called Marozevo, which I cannot find on the map. This was Edorique's 'surprise'. A guide called Richard took me round to see a wonderful collection of housed Chameleons and Geckos, which of course I could not camera-resist. Richard was very keen to pose with a big smile and the creatures on his hand, one at a time. I would have preferred them on their bits of wood etc looking more natural but then they were being 'husbanded' anyway. We went on to see Crocodiles, Snakes, Toads, Frogs (including the spectacular Orange Frog), Stick Insects, Millipedes, Leaf-mimic Praying Mantis, Butterflies flying round freely, and the extraordinary large yellow Comet Moth, together with its caterpillars and chrysalises.

Finally there was an enclosure of charming Western Grey Bamboo Lemurs and Fruit Bats, and Knob-billed Ducks on the pond. It was all a bit concentrated but gave a chance to have good views of creatures I was unlikely to see elsewhere. I paid my 25,000 MGF for the privilege and the same to Richard, who had made strenuous efforts to show me everything, even if I'd had difficulty in understanding his English - as well as his French. Then it was Antananarivo, here we come. Edorique drove well, passing large polluting lorries as soon as it was safe, as we drove the tortuous high road. Near to Antananarivo they were busy in the rice fields, and the roadside corn-on-the-cob stalls were doing a good trade. Edorique bought some for Esther. Later we stopped to buy small bananas, which I'd said I liked. I remembered the sweet little numbers that used to come from the Canary Isles but I never see them in the UK these days. Edorique selected a great 'stick' of them which cost me all of 35p. They were perfect.

As we hit the city, the traffic was just incredible, with every kind of vehicle imaginable (but a preponderence of Renault 4s of course) being whistled on and off by numerous policemen attempting to keep some order and safe movement. I didn't mind the slow pace: I wasn't driving and it gave me the opportunity to look at all the tiny shops on either side. There seemed to be a disproportionate number of hairdressers operating from shabby, makeshift premises. So many people trying to scratch a living. An elderly couple sat hopefully on the pavement, with a small display of perfect tomatoes and little red onions. Nobody seemed to take any notice and I wondered how long they would have to wait for a sale.

Eventually we reached the Tana Plaza with which I had not been that enamoured originally but now the familiarity had changed it into an old friend. I gave Edorique most of the bananas, knowing that they would go bad in this climate before I could eat so many. I had to fill in all the hotel forms again. Edorique stood around and questioned the necessity when I'd already stayed there three times. But the young man on reception said that the police were "very strict at the moment". This was the last time I'd be staying at Tana so I collected my warm clothes to pack ready for the journey home in four days' time. Help! It was nearly over.

Edorique would collect me in the morning at the civilised time of 9 am for the flight to Morondava. I changed another £20, bathed, washed my hair, sorted my luggage, ate bananas and was in bed by 9.45 pm.

French word for today: fraterniser - to fraternise
                    (which Edorique said he must not do)

Valyhas   Flight to Morondava (late)

Saturday 11th January 2003

I got up at 10.30 am after a really good night's sleep and enjoyed a breakfast of fruit juice, fruit, croissant, biscuits and coffee. Edorique had arrived at 9 am, on time as usual, and we made for the artisan market. Antananarivo was not as busy as on a weekday. It seemed to be washday and there were clothes laid out to dry all along the river bank on the left, and people working in the rice fields on the right. When we reached the market, I marvelled at the covered stalls on either side of the unmade road. The main object of this visit was to buy one of Madagascar's strange musical instruments, a Valyha, which daughter Wendy had suggested I might bring back with me. (She had once possessed a small one, brought back from a student trip many years ago.)

We saw valyhas on the very first stall. The small ones looked a bit tatty and made a thin sound when the strings were plucked against the length of polished bamboo. We moved on to see carvings, semi-precious stones, pictures and then more valyhas. Some of these looked as if they were professional size and one in particular caught my eye with its rich colour and smooth surface. I picked it up and elicited a lovely rich tone as I 'fiddled' with the strings in amateur fashion, whereupon the stallholder came and handled it lovingly and played a charming melody, his fingers moving like lightning and plucking the strings with easy accuracy. It was very seductive. I had to have this one I decided and tentatively asked the price. It sounded expensive but when I did the conversion, together with an orange and shocking pink case, it was approximately £12.50. So of course I bought it and entrusted it to Edorique until I returned to Antananarivo for the very last time. I felt quite excited about the whole transaction. I went on to buy two packs of cards made from the plant Aloha, some embroidered with pictures of local scenes such as the rice fields, and others decorated with pressed flowers.

By now it was time to go to the airport. The traffic had increased considerably and it was a slow drive but we made it for 10.30 am, the flight being scheduled for 11.45 am. We sat outside until check-in time. Edorique seemed to know everyone who passed. The mechanics, easily recognizable in their blue boiler suits plus opened toolboxes, were lingering underneath and around 'our' plane. At 11.45 am our luggage had still not been loaded and that sense of déjà-vu parted bits of my brain. But suddenly all was pronounced well and just ten of us boarded the small plane. We started up the runway at 12 noon. This was the final leg of my tour, but no, we were not away yet. We were signalled to stop and a man with climbing apparatus was driven across the tarmac, and he and two ground staff spent several minutes doing something to the underside of the wing outside 'my' window: deep déjà-vu now. Passengers looked worried, but the 'Jim'll-fix-it' team did whatever was deemed necessary and eventually we were really on our way.

It was just a 50-minute flight to Morondava and we landed on time after some serious turbulence en route. I was more than pleased to see a tall thin man carrying a "Mrs Tyler" board. The luggage arrived and we drove to and through Morondava, avoiding the Malagasy potholes to the accompaniment of "shit" from the driver. He had a limited English vocabulary and "shit" was undoubtedly his favourite word and was used to describe the government, the Japanese, his ex-wife and life in general. I kept quiet. He explained that he would be driving me to Kirindy the following day and I was to be ready at 7 am. I indicated that the message was received and understood.

My room at the Baobab Hotel was Number 8, clean, basic and with a view of - oh yes - a swimming pool which I was soon enjoying. A Frenchman and his young daughter (I thought) were in the pool and another gent sat at a table in the adjacent restaurant. He was German but both seemed to be able to have a go in each other's languages. I had a luxury laze by the pool and ate little bananas. There was a gentle breeze but even so the mid-day sun was very warm. I pushed the lounger underneath a waving Palm. The German guy went in for a swim and came out in chatty mood: he told me he was 68 and married to a young Malagasy girl. The eight-year old 'French' girl was theirs. She spoke Malagasy, French, German and English he said proudly. She was very attractive and very articulate and spoke in one of her languages most of the time. His English was limited but I think he said he owned five houses for letting, just a few miles away.

He told me about a Scots lady called "Maggie" who had a small hotel a few yards down the road. John, the driver, had pointed out "chez-Maggie" just before we'd arrived at the hotel. I said I might go and see her (if only to have an English conversation, even if she did have a Scots accent). "She's quite old" he volunteered, "she's 60". I suggested this was quite young. "How old are you?" he enquired boldly. "Seventy". He looked (politely?) surprised and then said I needed six weeks in Madagascar. I wasn't sure whether this advice was related to my age. I had another swim, dozed a little and awoke to the sound of regular thudding. A young man was working very hard digging up a dead Palm tree by the pool bar. It wasn't that big but seemed to have disproportionately large roots. When he'd finished, he watered the living ones.

One side of the pool was separated from the road by a high fence, the other was adjacent to the open end of the restaurant, which looked over an inlet from the Mozambique Canal where two small smart cruisers, Baobab Fish I and II, were berthed. Further up the water young men fished from more primitive craft and Cattle Egrets flew up and down. This was a very welcome, pleasant, warm and restful bit of space after all the travelling about.

I started the evening meal with one of the generous tomato salads, exquisitively presented and dressed, and garnished with fimbriated green leaves, which I expected to taste like fennel, but it was more akin to mint. I'd anticipated crab for the main course but it wasn't available. Everything else was, explained the waiter. I didn't feel like pork, chicken, or zebu so I chose the fish dish, something called 'coca'. Half an hour later, an enormous portion of concentrically-arranged nuggets of fish, dowsed with an orange sauce and surrounded by chips was placed in front of me with a flourish. I did my best, the sauce was particularly good but there was no way I could clear the plate.

I was sitting on a small table next to the water and there was plenty of time between courses to get bitten to death in spite of my generous application of Autan repellent. I finished off with a chocolate mousse, which the French-Malagasy do so well, drank a bottle of tonic and a large coffee, and retired to bed at 9.30 pm. This early night was becoming a habit.

I mused how it was well-nigh impossible to get through a French meal in less than two hours when everything is so freshly and beautifully prepared.

French for today: caleçon de bain - bathing trunks
(from a notice at the swimming pool saying they were to be worn)

KIRINDY with driver John and guide Jean-Pierre
Indris   Baobabs   BBC Buddha

Sunday 12th January 2003

Last night was the hottest I've ever experienced. The air-conditioning was on what appeared to be the only programme, 'operation économique', which so far as I was concerned should have read 'operation inutile'. I had lit the anti-mosquito coil and in my semi-conscious state, imagined it to be giving out great heat. I lay naked and ultimately opened the window behind the bed: a few more mosquito bites wouldn't matter and I was taking my anti-malaria tablets. Later I opened the fridge door which I know was anything but 'operation économique' but it did give out a small draught of welcome cold air. I slept intermittently, getting up every couple of hours or so to refresh myself with water inside and out.

At 6.30 am I had a croissant and a very large coffee and, while I was waiting for John, I watched the water and spotted a smart Crab Plover turning over a couple of small crabs on the shore by Baobab Fish I. At 7.15 am John arrived and the breeze through the open windows of the Toyota was more than welcome as we sped off in the direction of Kirindy, driving through the unique and impressive avenue and valley of Baobabs en route. The whole area was studded with the strange outlines of these tall broad bare trunks, topped by unexpected spreading inflorescences of irregular branches. A Madagascar Jacana stepped gracefully across Lily leaves on a large pond, its clearly defined black, white and tan plumage looking as if it had been painted on. John said that particular pond was as big as it ever gets, after all the recent rain.

After a couple of hours' drive, we arrived at a clearing with covered platforms and some small wood dwellings. Insects of all sizes (and all bites, I suspected) were in noisy abundance and a pleasant local lady at this field station brought me out a voluminous wrap-around skirt to put over my shorts. I was introduced to a young man called Jean-Pierre who was to be my guide. He had a lovely smile but no English. We were to go looking for the 'white Lemurs' - I wasn't sure which. It was a very long hot walk and I drank lots of water as I stumbled along the woodland paths, gazing upwards most of the time. We saw Lizards, Snakes, outsize Millipedes, wonderful Butterflies, soft white eggs of uncertain origin, large empty shells which had belonged to Giant Landsnails and then a Madagascar Buzzard perched right above us. At one point Jean-Pierre stopped so suddenly directly in front of me that I nearly fell on to him. He pointed upwards and there was a Madagascar Harrier-hawk sitting even nearer the sky, with its wings spread like a skirt. We saw a pert little Sunbird-asity, the Long-billed Green Sunbird, Vasa Parrots, Kingfishers, the elegant Cresta Coua, and a Coquerel's Coua rushing off into the undergrowth along the forest floor. Shortly afterwards, obliging White-headed and Sickle-billed Vangas settled briefly nearby, their colouring almost identical but the sickle bill making for easy identification. This was definitely my best day for birds.

Millipedes rolled into impregnable balls, and a huge spider scrambled down a hole. Pink leaf bugs, appropriately named Phromnia Rosea, lined two sides of a twig, converting it into a convincing flower. It was impossible to catch the birds on film but I had a go at everything else. The flies, all apparently biting, were of every shape and size, from large black ones, which looked like a cross between a fly and an outsize beetle and really stung, through unimpressive grey-brown jobs with flaccid wings which also had a go, to tiny little fast-moving insects which inflicted pain out of all proportion to their size. Jean-Pierre led the way in his sensible (but thick) all-covering clothes, slapping his torso with a couple of branches.

He got really excited and said the 'white lemurs' were just ahead. In spite of my hot itchy body, his enthiusiasm was contagious and I got ready with the camera: and there they were. Four beautiful Verreaux's Sifakas up to their agile gambles high up in the trees. I found them irresistible and I was happy to stay and watch (and photograph) for ever. I even lay on my back for a while so that I could get a better view and also hold the camera more steadily. Eventually Jean-Pierre asked whether I would like to go and see the

12th January 2003

Baobab Avenue en route to KIRINDY

'brown lemurs'. I said yes, and drank another bottle of water. We walked until lunchtime and although we saw much of interest, those brown lemurs did not come our way. Jean-Pierre looked really disappointed and said they must have changed their eating place. I wasn't sorry to stop: we'd walked for over three hours and although my joints were amazingly obliging at this temperature, the rest of me was unhappily hot. We returned to the covered area and John produced a very good lunch of salad, bread, chicken, potatoes, jam, crêpes, and mango, and, somewhat to my surprise, I wolfed the lot.

I took my time in French-honoured fashion and got up several times to take pictures of groups of butterflies on the road below: yellow ones, brown ones, and a blue swallow-tailed collection hovering over and settling at the edges of large puddles left by the night's rain. John did his own thing at another table and played cards: looked like Patience. A group of six sat at another table with the lady who had loaned me the skirt. I wondered whether the two handsome young boys were her sons. A serious French-looking man had documents he was reading at the table and looked like a researcher, if you know what I mean, and every now and then he discussed things with a dark Malagasy, whom I imagined might be his assistant - all speculation. I couldn't help it.

Suddenly Jean-Pierre signalled me to come quickly for the brown lemurs, and of course I obeyed. They came steaming across the woods and then dropped down into the vegetation around the compound and just came so wonderfully, so photogenically close that I couldn't believe my luck. I had a slight panic when the film finished and I had to spend all of twenty seconds putting in another. These were, I discovered, handsome Red-fronted Brown Lemurs. Jean-Pierre had done a good job and I tipped him accordingly. He seemed as pleased as me, even before the tip.

It was time to leave Kirindy. I returned the lady's skirt, which must have saved me from a percentage of insect attacks. If ever I have the good fortune to come here again, I'll wear trousers. John drove at speed through huge puddles, round and sometimes over potholes and so we saw only such life as managed to scarper out of our path. Some Chameleons stayed put but I don't think we actually ran over any. Long-tailed Doves and Turtle Doves flew off in good time. We made a brief excursion off the main route to see a 'jumellage Baobab'. This took the form of two Baobabs entwined/entwinned from top to toe. They looked positively Siamese. John smoked and said he was not going to apologise because he was doing me a favour by keeping away the Mosquitoes.

There had been the suggestion in the original Wildlife Worldwide itinerary that we might be staying to see sunset in Baobab Valley, which I was sure could be spectacular. However, I must admit that I was not sorry when rainy season clouds spread across the sky, for not only was it pleasantly cooler, but sunset-watching would have been a pointless exercise. I was ready for 'home', a swim and a shower. We saw numerous Bullock and Zebu carts on the way back, some stacked with goods, wood, fruit and vegetables, and others with entire families. A couple appeared to carry both: a great method of transport. John played cassettes as we drove along and announced during one of them that he was the soloist. I suggested that he might have made a lot of money but he said, "Just a little". He went on to say that today was really his day off. His job on the Baobab Hotel's fishing boat as skipper, mechanic etc was finished for a few weeks - so he'd been informed by "boss", alias "Shit", and he intended to have a week doing nothing, after which he was planning on planting rice.

A hoarding, which informed of a cooperative between the Japanese and the Malagasy in relation to conservation, prompted John to reiterate his dislike of that nation. I ventured to say that another guide I had had (Benoît), who had seemed very well informed, considered the relationship to be beneficial to the island. John was not impressed. The Japanese were only in it for the money. The Chinese were all right, as were the Americans, "and the English are OK" he added, as a seeming afterthought, "but the Japanese … "

Back at the Baobab I did one of my packing exercises, showered and had a refreshing swim. I felt really hungry. I was making up for lost time, well, lost food anyway. The crab was on tonight. I asked the poor waiter what kind of crab it was. It was "rond" (round), "pas ovale". The round ones were the best he said. Whatever it was, it made a very special meal and I loved every mouthful. It looked like some kind of Spider Crab, served with fluffy rice and a sauce of tomato, melon and something else.

A large man on his own sallied into the restaurant and sat a couple of tables behind me. He spoke English with an accent I could not place when he talked to the waiter. I recognized him as the man I'd heard telling the porter somewhere in the upstairs corridor that the room was "All right but very expensive.", asking "What time does the restaurant open?" and saying that he worked for the BBC. This had aroused my curiosity. Would David Attenborough be coming next? He was now reading the wine list and asked for two bottles of rosé to be brought so that he could "study the labels". He didn't have any French and I wondered whether the waiter understood this instruction. I was tempted to interfere and tell him (quietly) not to open them yet, but I resisted. The waiter returned with both bottles opened, which evoked a throaty grunt of surprise. The man then requested a large jug of ice to go with them. This seemed to create a problem but eventually it arrived and he proceeded to pour off the water and add one bottle of rosé to the ice: he knew what he wanted.

When I'd finished my meal I walked over to him, intending to say how pleasant it was to hear spoken English. His appearance took me by surprise. I'd realised he was a man of substantial size from the profile I'd seen as he walked into the dim light of the dining room, but he looked even larger sitting down, with a distinctly Buddha posture. He could have been the Dalai Lama's younger brother. I said my piece and he was embarrassingly welcoming, rising up to his considerable height and fetching a wine glass from another table, insisting that I help him with his chilled rosé, which was very good. "Call me Chaw ", he said.

He liked to talk and without any prompting gave me his life history. He was descended from Moguls, which didn't surprise me, with family now based in Burma and the Yemen. He had been educated at King's College, London and he was so full of quotes from Shakespeare, Longfellow, Keats, Gerard Manley Hopkins, and others I wot not of, that I imagined literature to have been his subject, but in fact he had some sort of degree in War Studies. He was into Haiku in a big way and altogether I thoroughly enjoyed listening effortlessly to his erudite dissertation. He described himself as a freelance journalist and had recently done some work on Cheetah conservation in Namibia. He was now on a three-month mission to get what he described as "more background for work in Madagascar and parts of Africa", where he was certain that "changes are imminent". He returned to a monastery in the Yemen for a month every year to "collect my thoughts". Oh yes, I could visualise him in one of those orange drapes.

He was much better at talking than listening but was fascinating company. When he came to a temporary halt about himself, he asked, "Did you do a job or anything?" I confessed to being a retired doctor. "Oh well, that was a useful thing to do", and then he was on to his own next chapter. He was clutching a National Geographic magazine for one of the months in 1987, in which he shewed me an article about the Baobabs and the surrounding vegetation. He was planning a trip the following day and asked me to accompany him. I said I'd just been and he actually listened as I described the day's experience. I got the impression that he was not planning on going anywhere without plenty of personal care.

Around 9.30 pm I decided to make for bed and left him with a bucolic smile, the dregs of the rosé in one hand and a block of ice in the other.

I spread myself with Autan, lit the Mosquito coil, opened all the windows and the fridge door, covered my naked body with the sheet and slept well through the night. It's amazing how one can adapt.

French word for today: le papillon - butterfly

French and Scots resident encounters

Monday 13th January 2003

I woke with a niggling anxiety about the morrow's internal flight, which John had emphasised I must confirm. It was 7.30 am. I got up and was half dressed when there was a knock at the door. It was John asking for my air ticket. "I thought you were on holiday," I said. "My boss needs me to work for another two days". I wasn't sorry.

I was just finishing my breakfast when Chaw appeared in a bright yellow T-shirt with "9" on the back and "Ronaldo" on the front, with a pristine daypack and a smiling Malagasy aide. He and others were negotiating for a private plane from Tana (Antananarivo) to fly over the area for a couple of hours for photographs. The price was 500 dollars and Chaw said "Far too much!" We chatted while further bargaining continued. The aide was invited to sit with us but he pointed to his cigarette and sat some distance away. 400 dollars was agreed upon. "Today, now please," said Chaw, but he was told it was far too cloudy and they would try for early the following morning, depending on the weather conditions. "Come with me," he suggested and if I hadn't been commencing the homeward journey I'd have jumped at the opportunity. He was going to have to make do with pick-up transport in the Baobab Valley for today.

John appeared in the doorway. Tomorrow's flight was 7.45 am, an hour earlier than stated on the ticket, but at least it gave extra time for errors and delays. He would call me at 7 am. I could have hugged him but I didn't: I was glad I'd given him a decent tip, thinking at the time that it would be the last opportunity. Thus relieved and relaxed, I made for the pool, stopping to look at the boats and the activity on the water. I watched a Green-backed Heron, Sandpipers (I was not sure which kind) and a pair of Sand Plovers, and then had a swim. A French papa was reluctantly (or so it seemed to me) looking after his young son and daughter of about 4 and 7. He had great difficulty in extracting them from the water when it was time to go.

At lunch-time a young woman spoke to me in the restaurant in rapid French. Seeing my glazed expression, she tried English. She was Muriel from Nice, where she drove an airport bus. Travelling alone, she was staying in Morondava town for a week, had read that the Baobab was good for food but poor for service (!), and had stopped off for lunch. We sat together. She had already had a week in Tana and visited one of the reserves. She had this amazing French guide-book to the island, better than anything I had ever seen for anywhere in English.

We talked of France. She didn't think much of Torrington's twin town, Roscoff. She had worked at Heathrow and had a good command of English. She thought London had become "ridiculously expensive" and that once there was "more European cohesion" things would have to change. She was very critical of English cooking: I said little but did get on the defensive when she started on about the Health Service. She did consider the English to be "better at travelling", the French being too self-satisfied with their own country.

The service was slow but I enjoyed the omelette when it came. Muriel confessed to feeling unwell and left most of her coca fish. (I thought I knew how she felt.) She had a driver waiting and intended to spend the afternoon exploring the town and maybe book a couple of trips. I said I intended to visit "Chez-Maggie" and sure enough there it was in her wonder guide-book. The report was complimentary, said the accommodation was cheap, and that Maggie had lived in Madagascar for twenty years. So I wished Muriel "Bon Voyage", thanked her for her company and wandered down the road to Maggie's.

Anything less prepossessing from the road was difficult to imagine and the sign at the entrance to the small drive, flanked by small pots of rubbish and neglected grass was hardly inviting. I ventured down and there - lo and behold - was the most attractive lay-out of bungalows round a covered sitting area, well-kept gardens and a swimming pool. It was lovely. A Malagasy lady was watering the plants and I asked whether it was possible to talk to Maggie. She indicated the covered area further on and at that moment a tall, elegant, blond lady approached with a saucer of milk that, she explained, was for a very young kitten that she had been trying to tame since its mother had died.

When she had completed her RSPCA mission, she came and sat down with me. I admitted that it was curiosity, aided and abetted by the German gentleman's comments and the French guide-book, which had tempted me in. She had just the trace of a Scots accent and chatted aimiably. Her husband had been in the oil business and, after working in Europe had been moved to Tana where they had lived for eight years, during which time they had split up. His work had taken him back to Europe but she had grown to love Madagascar and decided to stay. She had bought land in Morondava and over the subsequent sixteen years had gradually built up her project, which had become a reasonable business: brave lady. Her French was good and she had European and Malagasy guests.

She had survived the serious flooding and cholera epidemic of two years earlier, when one of her daughters, who lived in Tana, had been staying there, with her three young children. Her other daughter, also a mother of three, who lived in London was, perhaps not surprisingly, nervous about visiting. Maggie had a house in Portugal to which in recent times she had managed to escape, two or three times a year. I was just thinking that if ever I came to this place again, here is where I would want to stay, when she announced that she intended to try and sell the business during the next couple of years.

She told a lovely story about her recently deceased dog's friendship with a couple of Brown Lemurs on the beach each evening. The day the dog died, they turned up at the compound as though looking for him. They now make daily visits. She was thoroughly charming and as I was leaving she called into one of her bungalows nearby to introduce me to Chris, a London eastender, and his very beautiful young bride of two weeks. They had been married in Morondava and had their reception at Maggie's. I was reassured to learn that they were booked on 'my' internal flight the next day, before flying to the UK via Paris. Madagascar Bulbuls conducted their own noisy conversation from the tops of the overhead trees.

I returned to the hotel to find Chaw was back and devouring an enormous lunch. He had been suitably impressed by the Baobabs, which he described, after a long pause, as "unique".

I donned the blue bathing costume and made for the pool. Early in the evening I packed as properly and completely as I could and wrote the luggage labels and had just settled down on the bed for half an hour when there was a knock at my door. The pleasant, plump room-girl came in with a pink toilet roll, which I didn't need. I wondered whether this was the hint for a tip. She had been very conscientious and I gave her two dollars, which may have been over-generous by local standards, for she got very excited and kissed me on three cheeks, if you see what I mean.

No sooner had she gone than there was another knock and there stood the slim, pretty non-English-speaking girl from the office. I presumed she had come for the voucher, which I had kept meaning to hand in, but although she took it, she indicated that I was needed downstairs. "You are a doctor?" she enquired haltingly. I nodded and hoped nobody had had a sudden collapse. I pulled on my trousers and accompanied her down to the entrance, where waited a deputation of formally-dressed, officially-labelled, middle-aged men. I was quite thankful when they shook their heads at the sight of me. I was the wrong doctor! The office girl was reprimanded by a pleasant young man, the manager I think. (The owner was an overweight man who dressed casually in long shorts and voluminous brightly-coloured, short-sleeved shirts: he smiled instead of speaking English.) The manager apologized and at that moment a young attractive Malagasy lady, with a file under her arm, emerged from the bar and was recognized and greeted enthusiastically: a much better bet in every way.

Buddha in the room next to mine was leaning out of his window, having a one-sided conversation with the swimming pool attendant. He said he was leaving for Tana the next day and going east.

The menu seemed to be the same every night. It was just that sometimes some things were not available. I selected Crevettes Provençal, served with rice and that splendid red sauce again. The dining room was empty, apart from one man on his own. Several locals at the bar gave the place a bit of life, while the gentle lap of the water, just below where I was sitting, gave an atmosphere of peace. Various craft passed along the water in the dark of 7.30 pm, small rowing boats, canoes, and sailing vessels of different sizes. The early evening sky had been full of sunset colours but was now overcast, apart from the upside down Great Bear. I was content in my solitary state and almost hoped Buddha had gone elsewhere for dinner.

I was nearly through my nougat ice cream when Buddha came and sat at the unset place opposite to me with a "Do you mind?" etc. He had had a good day with the Baobabs and had visited some of the nearby villages and taken lots of photos. We talked of AIDS, revolutions, poetry of course, and parental influence. He reckoned that 'Around the World in 1000 pictures', a book given to him by his father when he was a boy, had given him a thirst for travel. "I am so grateful for that", he said.

He was anxious that I should have a farewell drink with him but, thinking of that 6 am call, I declined. I felt a bit of a spoilsport, but after tonight (Monday) it was going to be Wednesday night before I had the luxury of another bed. He gave me his card, which read:

> BBC World Service
> U Kyaw Swa Thein
> Broadcaster
> Asia and Pacific Region

Quite impressive.

French words for today: coucher du soleil - sunset

Smallest plane yet - to Antananarivo   Valyho cassette   City tour Farewell to Edorique   Johannnesburg   Heathrow   Heronslake!

Tuesday 14th January 2003

Home James, I hope.

It was not as hot in the night but I think the Crevettes Provençale made my inside hot. I awoke at 5 am and heard Buddha gettting ready for his 6 am microlight flight: it would have been nice …

I was ready with my luggage at 7 am. John arrived at 7.15 am, said there was no hurry and to have a coffee, which I suspect he intended to do. The dear little girl behind the bar (6 am to 3 pm) obliged and, after some conversation, asked me to take her picture, which

I did. I wanted to finish the film so I went outside and took pictures of some of the boats on the water, and of two women in the water who were fishing with a sizeable net between them, placing the catch in the large baskets balanced on their heads. One of them was heavily pregnant. They seemed to be doing quite well and looked very happy.

Before we left at 7.45 am, John asked whether I had anything to pay and I was sure I had not. He went into the office to check and said I owed 22,000 Malagasy francs. I shook my head and then a little later realised it was probably for a Fanta and a bottle of water I'd had from my room fridge. I was going to say something to John but then remembered I had only 12,000 francs left anyway, so I quickly forgot again. (It is illegal to take any of the currency out of the country.)

The flight was scheduled, according to yesterday's confirmation, for 7.45 am (different again from the original 8.25 am). We arrived at 7.35 am to find an empty airport and the chalked up arrival time to read 8.25 am: I gave up. At 8 am I was joined by Chris and his wife Fara, who were obviously better informed. I had a pleasant chat with Chris who incidentally spoke no French. Fara had a minimum of English but it was obvious they adored each other. Chris worked for some 'Commodities Products' sugar company and spent a lot of time in South Africa, but had retained his Cockney accent, so I imagined that Fara would eventually speak his kind of English. Their idea was to return to Madagascar and set up some kind of business like "chez-Maggie". In the interim they would be living in a flat in Notting Hill. I asked about his family's acceptance of what he described as their whirlwind courtship and his marriage to Fara. He said he had no family, except for a couple of cousins with whom he had lost contact. Fara had lots of relations living in different parts of Madagascar, who had all come to the wedding and given them their blessing.

The flight actually took off at the re-scheduled time. We were the only passengers on the tiny plane. I wished them "Bonne chance" when we parted at Antananarivo. Their international flight to Paris was later than mine. In the meantime they were going to assemble their excess baggage, which held all their wedding presents, and have lunch with one of Fara's brothers in the city. I hoped things worked out for them.

Reliable Edorique was there at the ready and off we went on his promised city tour. First we went in search of a particular valyha cassette, for which I had given him the money but which he had been unable to find. The third place we visited in this quest was a neat little roadside stall, with cassettes and CDs stacked from earthen floor to canvas ceiling, and they produced what Edorique said I needed.

We took a great drive to the high part of the city, seeing the ruins of the recently burned Palais de la Reine, and a beautiful church being cleaned by a group of happily chatting men and women. Edorique said that the church had been started by British missionaries and I wondered whether they had come with the LMS (London Missionary Society.) As I have aleady mentioned, I recalled some of the LMS coming to talk about Madagascar when I was a youngster, in the Sunday School of Garston Congregational Church in Liverpool. Narrow cobbled streets took us past private schools, upmarket housing and foreign embassies. I photographed some of the wonderful panoramic views. We came back down to the noisy, vibrant, lower part of the city and had lunch at an airy spacious well-appointed eating place called the 'Big Bang', on the outskirts. I suddenly felt I hadn't eaten for weeks and devoured an enormous (half a loaf) camembert 'sandwich', washed down with coca cola, while Edorique got through a very large plate of chips and drank a glass of fresh pineapple juice, and then a glass of fresh mango juice: I wished I'd spotted those on the menu.

It was time to go to the airport now - 1.15 pm – with the flight scheduled for 3.25 pm. We called at Tropic Tours' office en route to say good-bye to Ooly, where I met the two male members of the staff for the first time. One was young and much bejewelled and the other elderly. A commemorative photo was taken.

Antananarivo airport was anything but deserted, with passengers already queuing at the desk. Edorique came with me as far as he was allowed, handed over the valyha (which almost made me feel and look like a local) and then we said goodbye - but he promised he would stay until the aircraft had taken off. He checked that I had not lost his address, that book in mind I guess. I almost shed a tear. One of the 'Hollywood'-shirted official porters, who are allowed to accompany passengers a little further, clung on to me like a leech and, once the luggage was loaded on to the scanner, I gave him my last dollar.

I wanted the luggage checked all the way through to Heathrow and kept a close eye on the man at the desk as he recorded this on the flight label, and then proceeded to attach it to the handle of someone else's luggage while he was trying to answer a query from another would-be passenger. I uttered a loud "No" before it disappeared from view, and he corrected his mistake, still talking, and without any change of facial expression. The embarkation form was so badly printed that I could hardly read it even with my glasses on. My hand luggage was opened and studied in detail, as was the valyha. My long warm skirt was shaken about and all the contents handled.

I settled comfortably into the departure lounge where all the fans were working. I repacked the disorganised hand luggage, had a wash and re-did my hair. In no time we were boarding, and my window seat 11D, booked by Sarah of Wildlife Worldwide, was near the emergency exit so that not only did I have a good view, but I also had room to stretch my legs - and nobody came to sit in E or F.

A group of white-clad Muslim gentlemen came and sat behind me and across the aisle. They fussed about with enomous bags of food and drink, some of which the stewardess confiscated and put in the overhead lockers just before take-off, doing the same with my small handbag. Two of these men were asked if they would mind moving so that two young children could sit with their mother, but they said they'd booked these seats 'specially' and had to stay together. Not very Christian I thought, but then they're not, are they! I offered my situation but the problem was solved further back.

The sky was blue and there was a wonderfully clear view of Madagascar as we left that special island. It was 3.30 pm and I felt a mixture of sadness that the adventure was in its final stages and a sense of relief that I'd actually got this far by today. I celebrated with the debs' drink of the 1950s, and had a gin and orange, there being no tonic or ginger beer.

It seemed no time before the evening meal was served. The overdone, sweet chicken was bonded to the aluminium foil but went down well nevertheless. A wicked white chocolate cream-layered bar and a good cup of tea finshed this repast and I suddenly felt very tired, but sleep did not oblige. The plane was nowhere near full, which I found surprising as this flight only operated every four days. It was just a two-and-a-half-hour flight and we landed on time at Johannesburg, where I was directed to a small Transit annexe. Here I joined the queue and a very helpful young man studied my passport etc, was reassuring about the luggage, which he said had the documentation to be checked through to Heathrow (and I knew the right ticket was attached to it), and told me to make for Gate 3.

Boarding was at 7.30 pm and, as it was already after 7 pm by my watch, it seemed I would not have long to wait. There were not many people about and I sat near Gate 3, next to a lovely little nurse from Namibia who lived near Windhoek - happy memories. She was visiting the UK for 2 weeks, staying with a friend in Bristol and going to see a teacher in Oxford who had been out to her village doing VSO and had become a great friend of the family. She intended to "do London": brave lady. She had a "little brother" working in Southport but didn't think she'd have time to see him. "A long time ago", she said proudly "my mother did a management course in Saffron Walden".

She said our flight was overbooked and unless you had a reserved numbered seat - she had just a ticket - there was no guarantee of a place. (Thank you, Sarah, for 49K.) There was to be another flight at 9 pm. 7.30 pm came and went and I asked a member of the airport staff what time we were likely to board. "Not yet" he said, looking at his watch; "it's only 6.45 pm". We'd forgotten about the hour's time difference. I put my watch back another hour, having already allowed for the two hours' difference during the flight from Antananarivo to Johannesburg. This was indeed going to be a long haul. I decided to go for a walkabout but the nurse stayed put, to be the first of those hoping to claim an unbooked seat.

I wandered around the airport shops and watched people buying great quantities of goods, from booze and jewellery to silk scarves, huge boxes of chocolates, cuddly toys and scented bunches of artificial flowers. By the time I returned to Gate 3, there was a queue of passengers having their hand luggage thoroughly searched, as was mine - again – including the valyha. We waited on the staircase leading down to the boarding corridor, while the old and infirm in wheelchairs, and mums with young babies, were escorted aboard. My nurse was still waiting.

Seat 49K was fine. The overhead locker was full so I put my hand luggage in 48K, placing the valyha at the very back where there didn't seem to be enough height for more luggage to be put on top of it. I'd just settled in nicely when one of the stewards came and asked if I'd mind moving so that a family could sit together. I was reluctant but imagining that there were children involved and remembering my harboured disapproval of the Muslim gentlemen who had refused to do this, I heaved a deep sigh and agreed. "It's another window seat" he said, and so it was but much further back on the opposite side of the plane, where the air-conditioning was not as efficient, and miles from my hand luggage. An elderly lady (whoops) was in the next seat to me and I started on a little grumble about the move. She looked at me blankly and I suddenly realised I'd spoken in French without even thinking. Success at last. I repeated it in English, which was a much better idea as she was from Buxton. Stella was nice company, had a daughter in Australia, another in South Africa, both of whom she'd been visiting, and was due back home on the very day her third daughter, who lived near her, expected her third baby. We dozed and talked.

I enjoyed the dinner of sweet and sour pork, bought duty-free gin and small toys, and decided to sleep - but my seat wouldn't recline and the one in front over-reclined, so that I was in a claustrophobic straitjacket and slept little. We neared Heathrow around 5 am, and I decided I must retrieve and don my warm clothes, so walked up to overhead locker 48K. I was very surprised to see that the family members who had 'needed to sit together' were all perfectly normal-looking adults. I took out my things, returned the luggage carefully (valyha seemed OK) and then couldn't resist an "Are you sitting comfortably?" - which was a bit unkind as it woke two of the men. They were lucky to be sleeping!

We landed on time but then there was some trouble with loading the carousel, which went round and round with three pieces of unclaimed luggage. I imagined them to be from a previous flight – which, I mused, was probably what mine had done this time last year. It seemed pointless standing there and I retreated with my hand luggage and joined a young woman sitting on the floor, backs against the wall, where we had a good view of the situation. She and her husband were leaving Zimbabwe for good. She had lived there all her life, as had her parents before her, but they just knew it would be foolish to stay. They could not sell their house but had been able to leave enough resources for their two sons to finish their higher education in South Africa. They were to have a holiday in France and then settle in London, where her husband had a job to go to. At the age of 43 she had enrolled as a mature student on a fine arts degree course. "So we're better off than many of our friends", she said, but the tears in her eyes showed her real sadness and disappointment. By the time we had exchanged our life stories, the luggage was coming.

I collected my emerald green banded pack on wheels, went through the 'nothing to declare' exit, and within seconds had spotted dear Lydia of the Shuttle Service. The rest was chat about our families and her business as we drove through a damp, grey-skied early morning, a stop for fuel and the loo, and then, within a few miles of home, a change of vehicle and driver as Lydia was driving back to London on another job. My new driver was very chatty, ex-RAF, personal friend of a couple of GPs I knew, and was keen to talk about his very successful triple bypass.

HOME

Wednesday 15th January 2003

By now it had been Wednesday for some hours of course, and it was mid-day when we drove into Heronslake. "What a lovely place." said the driver. "Yes, isn't it," I agreed

I'd had my annual 'fix', Madagascar had been extraordinary, one of the best, but this was where I belonged.

French word for today: rouspeter - to grumble (which I did on the plane - how pathetic.)

162

14th February 2003

Postscript

When I had announced to friends that I was bound for Madagascar, there were furrowed brows and geographical queries such as, "That's India, isn't it?", "South America?", "Africa?" - close!

Patient Sarah, of Wildlife Worldlife, had arranged my Malagasy trip in the rainy season and I wanted to do everything in two weeks. There was insufficient time and too much flooding to get to Diego Suarez in the very north, but I went just about everywhere else. The endemic flora and fauna (not to mention the guides) in the reserves in Berenty, Kirindy, Perinet and Nosy Mangabe were all exceptional, and I became addicted to Lemurs in general and Sifakas in particular. One of my most memorable moments was the sight of a Verreaux Sifaka nursing its young at the top of a Tamarind in the first light of a summer dawn: too far away for a decent photograph but it had left the most memorable image of them all.

Edorique was very special and was the constant I returned to after fraught excursions to other parts of the island.

Yes, I did send him THE book. It took an unconscionable time to reach Antananarivo, but eventually I received:

> "Grand-mère, bonjour!
>
> Je ne sais pas comment vous dire, je vous remercie mille fois plus bien reçu le livre "Les Mammifères de Madagascar", c'est vraiment du grand plaisir pour moi que Dieu vous benisse …
>
> Avec meilleurs souhaits pour vous et tout la famille,
> encore et encore et … merci!'

Edorique and Esther had a baby girl, Lairon Fenosoa Esdorinne, in May 2004 and I received a photo of this bonny little girl with the Christmas card in January 2005: no longer "pas depuis"!

27th May 2009

A PHOENIX   January 2004

VIETNAM

with **niece Ruth**
and
TENNYSON TRAVEL LTD

VIETNAM...?　WHY ARE YOU GOING THERE?

Wednesday 7th January 2004

That was just what I was wondering as I lay awake with indigestion because I'd taken my arthritis pills on an empty stomach, not having had time to get a proper meal. I would never have considered Vietnam as my January fix-for-the-year destination, had I not had a niece, Ruth, coming to the end of her two-year VSO stint in education: it had seemed sensible to take advantage of a personal family guide and she was keen for me to visit.

I had had a great time at Heronslake over Christmas and New Year, when eight of the grandchildren and their parents had come home, and I hadn't really given the holiday much thought until two or three days before departure. I checked the essentials like passport, tickets etc, but when I turned to the money, I discovered that I'd collected American dollar Travellers Cheques and not the dollars, as had been my intention following advice that the Cheques would be difficult to change in some parts of Vietnam. The local bank was very obliging and I had the dollars the day before I left. Then there was the Shuttle Service, which I'd booked earlier and, on checking the return date, I discovered that I'd given them the 22nd instead of the 21st, which would have been a long wait ... I'd totally forgotten about the nine hours' time difference so that, as our watches were to be put back, we'd be arriving the 'same day' as we'd left. Somewhat belatedly, like on January 5th, I spoke to the tolerant Lydia and she corrected the booking.

I started packing. I was going to travel light. I couldn't carry heavy stuff and it seemed I wouldn't need that much clothing in the warmer conditions. I tried on a couple of ancient sleeveless tops and didn't like the look of my white sagging biceps muscles. I'd have a sun bed at the local swimming pool I decided, something in which I had indulged before previous winter holidays in the sun. Brown wrinkles are best. I rang to make a time: they hadn't had a sunbed for over a year. It was suggested I went to a local hairdresser's and stood in the 'sun shower' for five minutes. I turned down that idea: half the enjoyment was lying down in the pleasant relaxing warmth.

I packed the hand luggage last: sponge bag, light change of clothes in case the main pack went astray and some small things which Ruth had specially requested. Then I went to bed at 7.30 pm, five to six hours earlier than usual, which no doubt contributed to my sleeplessness. I planned various projects I intended to do on my return. I felt I hadn't slept at all but I must have done for suddenly it was 1.30 am. The BT call rang faithfully at 3.30 am, when I got up and dressed, cancelled the answerphone service for a fortnight, ate a banana, and put some bacon of uncertain age on the bird table.

Thursday 8th January 2004

Bill Ludgate of the Shuttle Service arrived at 4.45 am. "Travelling light", he commented as he lifted the luggage. It bore my two startling green stripes for immediate unmistakable identification. The weather was atrocious: lashing rain, strong winds, spray from lorries that seemed like temporary mountain ranges, and a couple of fallen trees which made the journey positively hazardous. Bill talked cheerily and we covered the Bench (we've both been magistrates), the police and driving offences - penalty points in particular - grandchildren, the environment, etc. Bill drives 80,000 miles a year. And there was I, thinking how well I'd done doing 2,000 miles on a UK tour in the summer.

We stopped about 40 miles from the airport and, after mobile phone contact, I and my luggage were transferred to Lydia's vehicle while her passenger, whom she had just collected after a flight from Australia, and her luggage, were installed in Bill's vehicle ready for the drive back to Devon.

The rain continued - and more - and the traffic was very heavy. It was dark and dreary and I felt myself nodding off. As we neared the airport, Lydia chose to use the circuit for what will be the road to Terminal 5. We arrived at Terminal 3 before 9 am for the 11 am Singapore Airlines flight SQ 317 but I was somewhere near the back of the long, snaking queue in Zone E. It seemed the checking-in was behind schedule and the Raffles (1st class) desk had been brought into use for the economy class passengers. I was moved over, a sort of official queue-jumping. I smiled at the pleasant assistant and said how privileged I felt. "Don't get too excited", she said, "you haven't been upgraded". How right she was: 57F was a non-window, non-aisle seat near the back.

On my left there was a couple, probably in their late forties, who sounded like Australians and who were paying such constant tactile attention to each other that I imagined they might have only just got together. On my right was a young, dark man who had the biggest bottle of water I've ever seen and who spent most of the flight asleep underneath his blanket. We were all boarded by 11.10 am but didn't take off for another hour. The flight was 12 hours to Singapore, where the time was 8 hours ahead, so it would be 8 am Singapore time when we arrived there. It was dark by 3 pm.

It was a chicken lunch, preceded by a shrimp starter and followed by ice cream. I watched the flight screen and as usual marvelled at the information transmitted: position over Munich, Vienna, Budapest, etc., speed, height, outside temperature, tail winds, all reported. We've come a long way since Amy Johnson. The usual snacks, drinks, and papers were offered. I took the occasional walk, trying to time each one when neighbouring passengers were awake.

The stewardesses were all so beautiful, their lovely slim figures further enhanced by the neat patterned 'uniform'. One man walked up and down continually: he looked like John Alderton, the guy who died of cancer in the 'Calendar Girls'. The lights were turned off for a couple of hours and I think I dozed for a while. Breakfast was served at 4.30 am Singapore time.

It was of course now …

Friday 9th January

I'm not very good at being silent for long and felt I just had to ask the loving couple on my left if they were on their way home, as we downed the airline version of fruit and fibre. She was very chatty and a consultant in Obstetrics and Gynaecology in Perth, had qualified at University College, London, and had done her GP slot in Fleet. She'd met her mining engineer husband in New Zealand and they'd been to spend Christmas with his parents, who were now not well enough to make it to Australia. We talked shop: IVF, breech deliveries, elective Caesarians, water births etc.

We landed an hour late but as my onward flight to Han Oi was not until 10.35 am, I had time to shed some of my warm clothes, have a wash, do my hair and enjoy a cappuccino, (for which I reckoned, in retrospect, that I was overcharged). I walked to Gate 34, marvelling at the masses of orchids. I had a window seat this time, 51K, next to an overweight, coughing, German couple. I felt I needed waking up and ordered a gin fizz, and promptly fell asleep for an hour. Lunch came and went; I'd had so many sedentary snacks that I really wasn't hungry.

We landed on time but I waited an unconscionable time in the immigration queue. I suspected that the man at 'my' desk was a learner: he looked about sixteen and, even with directions from a supervisor, seemed to take for ever. Then my luggage was one of the very last to trundle through, so that by the time I got to the 'other side', four passengers were already assembled by a man with a Tennyson Travel notice bearing our names. I'd failed to spot any of the relevant luggage labels during the journey over and had wondered whether I was the only one in my 'group', as I had been in Madagascar last year, but here they were. The guide, Long, introduced David and Pam (lovely Welsh accents) from Bridgend, and Meg and her daughter Catherine from Gloucester: all seemed very pleasant and friendly.

It was about a 40-minute drive to Hanoi's Opera Hilton Hotel. The French influence on the architecture and the abundance of trees and lakes gave the city a romantic air. Some of the more modern, less attractive buildings, however, such as our hotel amongst others, and the tall office blocks, were hardly in keeping with the French legacy. Colourful flowering shrubs, and decorations and lights anticipating the New Year celebrations, provided a cheerful, welcoming ambience.

There were not many cars on the road, but there were hundreds of motor bikes and cycles, six to ten abreast on some of the wider stretches, travelling quite slowly and in an orderly manner. Our Hilton was amazing and after a protracted welcome with fruit juice, we were presented with our room keys: 607 for me with a large bath and a fresh rose. I threw myself carelessly on the bed and slept for two hours, after which I changed and went down to the bar and had a gin and tonic and nibbles for the equivalent of £1.40. I couldn't see the others but they eventually found me, having already located a bar on Floor 7 where a free drink was served!

I changed US$40 for Vietnamese money. 15,500 dong = US$1.

We went out to a nearby Vietnamese restaurant for supper. The food was delicious and I made an effort with the chopsticks. Sandra and Jonathon arrived from Laos and joined us halfway through the meal. Long seemed very disappointed that they were late: "Important for the whole group to have their first food together", he insisted. Well, they had done their best and had come straight from the airport in an effort to eat with us. After the meal, while we stood outside and waited for our transport, Long drew our attention to the Street Children's Centre opposite, run by a local charity and told us of its association with the 'Bookworm' next door, where the carers involve their charges in some basic education.

We had coffee and a congenial chat back at the hotel and I returned to the comfortable room and indulged in a long hot bath - and I did think about the street children. Then it was bed, at about 11.30 pm.

Saturday 10th January 2004

I woke occasionally in the early hours but slept pretty well. We met for breakfast at 9 am and then went to the Ho Chi Minh Mausoleum. The surrounding open space, Ba Dinh Square, was like an enormous parade ground and a small army of soldiers was going through a drill when we arrived. The uniforms looked to me like something from the Soviet Union.

Ho Chi Minh delivered Vietnam's Declaration of Independence here in 1945. We went into the Mausoleum and saw the embalmed corpse in a glass casket. He was dressed in uniform and guarded by four unblinking military men. Behind the Mausoleum was the basic Ho Chi Minh House, where he was reputed to have lived, in preference to the sumptuous Presidential Palace in the same grounds, during the war against the United States.

Next, we went to the Temple of Literature, built in the eleventh century and dedicated to Confucius. Above the main entrance gate an inscription requested dismounting from horses before entering. It was adjoined to the school of the elite of the nation, Vietnam's first university of the same period. Scholars aspiring to become senior mandarins studied for rigorous triennial examinations here, in Literature, Philosophy, ancient Chinese and Vietnamese history. In one of the courtyards the only 82 surviving stelae of the original 1000+, inscribed with the names, works and academic records of the scholars who succeeded in the examinations held between 1442 and 1779, rested on the backs of stone tortoises. The whole temple enclosure was divided into five walled courtyards and in one of these was a central pool, the Thiên Quang Tinh (the Well of Heavenly Clarity).

From the courtyard with the stelae, we crossed over to the House of Ceremonies, where sacrifices were offered in honour of Confucius, and where I was so busy looking upwards that I fell over the high plinth intended to keep out evil spirits. My camera crashed to the ground and the rewind mechanism went into action prematurely. (Later I discovered that the three-quarter-spent film had not rewound, but the panel registered 'E' for empty when I attempted to take another shot. I gave up and rewound it by hand in the dark, inflicted the machine with a sharp blow on the concrete floor and had no further trouble!)

We admired the extensive Hoan Kiem Lake and the Ngoc Son Pagoda.

We visited the One Pillar Pagoda (Chua Mot Cot) sitting in a lotus pool, having been reconstructed after departing French soldiers blew up the original in 1954. In the Kim

Lien Pagoda we enjoyed an excellent lunch in which vegetarian ensembles had been imaginatively prepared to resemble meat and fish dishes. A corn concoction with lotus seeds somehow seemed like fish, and cauliflower was cut in a way to make one think of squid. The spring rolls were minute, delicate and delicious, and the whole meal was garnished with coriander, which I love. Energy thus restored, we made for the Museum of Ethnology where full-scale models, crafts, musical instruments, housing and clothing representing 54 ethnic groups, were on view. It was funded by the French.

An hour's cycle round the old city gave one the feeling (fear?) of what it was like to be really close to the organised chaos of the traffic, mostly motorbikes, which drove at a moderate speed. There was an abundance of zebra crossings, which were completely ignored, and the advice from Long was to "cross the road slowly, never run, never stop, never turn back and you'll be fine!" If any pedestrian was hit, the vehicle driver was always to blame. We were riding single file so the seven of us made quite a crocodile. We went through a whole street of small welding businesses, with work being done outside the premises, sparks flying everywhere. Another street had nothing but bag shops, another with gift shops, and the next had people cooking all along the pavement, and so on.

At 5 pm we arrived at the Thang Long Water Puppet Theatre to watch an incredible performance, which ran through no less than 17 different scenes as itemised in the programme. The puppeteers were more or less concealed behind a screen beyond the lake, the control seeming rather remote, and yet at times there must have been up to 20 puppets in action. A group of musicians played a musical prelude and then appropriate accompaniment throughout, with several vocal solos.

Back at the Hilton there was a message for me. Ruth had rung. She'd had some trouble finding me as somehow I'd managed to give her the name of the hotel where we were to be staying two days hence. So, I telephoned her, apologised for making a muddle, and she welcomed me to Vietnam. I looked forward to seeing her later in the week. We had not met since my mother's funeral in 1994.

The group all had a drink in the bar (no free ones tonight) and then we made for the Nuam Douange restaurant, recommended by Long: "turn right out of the hotel, then left, then 2nd left, etc …". We made a couple of false starts but once there, we enjoyed an excellent meal at around £4 per head, during which my chopstick dexterity definitely improved. It was a chance for a chat and suddenly I felt we were all happy to get to know each other: that is, apart from Sandra and Jonathon who did not show up. We finished off with coffee at the Cafe de ling, among lots of noisy locals.

It had been a full and fascinating day, a steep learning curve - for me anyway - in Vietnamese history and culture and I was thankful to collapse on my great bed at midnight.

Postscript:

Long was to be our guide for the northerly parts of the tour and was fiercely loyal to this, his area of the country. His father had been a colonel in Ho Chi Minh's army, which meant that Long himself was exempt from national service: interesting logic. He was 32, had a university degree and was busy doing further study, for which he attended evening sessions. He talked of the low salaries in Vietnam and how no-one could afford to buy property unless they made money in some sort of black marketing, which he said most people did. His father had helped his siblings to buy houses but he, Long, intended to stay in his parents' home, and when he married his girlfriend – a very attractive photo was displayed – they would both move in with them, he said - but he was "not ready yet!"

Sunday 11th January 2004

Fortunately I had more or less arranged my packing and possessions the night before, for I overslept until 8.29 am - I couldn't believe it. After a breakfastless almighty scrum I somehow managed to be down in the hotel lobby by 9.20 am, where I paid the US$1.25 for my phone call, and collected a receipt for my luggage which was to remain there during our sojourn in Halong Bay until we returned the following evening. I hoped I hadn't left anything. My overnight luggage seemed very small.

The roads were crowded with weekend traffic: "Everyone, except the young people, going home to the country for the weekend," explained Long. There were no cars, just cycles and motorbikes. No heavy traffic was allowed on the roads between 7 am and 9.30 am. We saw police trying to arrest someone but they seemed to be losing ground as he fled away at incredible speed.

Long talked as we drove. We were not that far from the Chinese border. "We export everything to them," he claimed proudly: "rice, chillies and all agricultural produce. They come here as tourists, mostly on the cheaper trips." We travelled along Highway 5 and as we turned left for Hai Phong, I noticed an impressively elaborate graveyard on the right. I wished we could have stopped.

"There's no unemployment here", continued Long, (there's no unemployment benefit either), "families all help each other. Every child goes to a village school between the ages of six and twelve years". We passed several graves scattered across agricultural land, and then some open cast mines. These last interested David, who had been a miner for many years, until the mine in his valley closed. He struck me as a man of substance, and it was evident from a few casual, unboasting remarks that he had encouraged his peers to join him and strike when the conditions had become intolerable. He now worked as a maintenance electrician at an RAF station but still talked nostalgically of his earlier career, in spite of all the problems. Long explained that the dust and mud from the excavations here were used for cooking.

We passed acres of rice fields at various stages of cultivation. Those packed with plants ready for transplanting were like the greenest of green lawns before its first damp cut in the spring. Hard-working (mostly) women, in their pointed straw hats, planted the little green sprays into adjacent flooded fields at amazing speed. Mercifully no machine has yet been devised to do the job as efficiently. "The land was given to the People in 1994", explained Long, "and they work very much harder now than they did when they formed part of a farmers' co-operative. By 1998 the production of rice had increased so successfully that we are now the second biggest exporters of rice in the whole world." He raised his arm demonstratively and gave a big grin.

11 January 2004
JUMA IN HALONG (Ha Long) BAY

His commentary was brought to a close as we arrived at the Humanity Centre, where shelter and employment was provided for disabled, mostly young, people. They were a cheerful bunch working diligently at sewing, embroidery, painting etc. Some of them were minus limbs and I imagined this could be the result of exploded mines, the aftermath of the Americans' ' interference'. Others had obvious congenital deformities and I wondered how many of these were the consequence of the Americans' use of chemical defolients such as Agent Orange, used in an attempt to deprive the Viet Cong of ground protection and cover. There were some magnificent huge embroidered pictures, which looked for all the world like sensitive paintings. The effects of light on the water around fishing boats and on the rice plantations were particularly convincing, and I couldn't resist buying two small examples of such.

Then it was back in the bus (a 26-seater, incidentally, for the seven of us, plus Long, and plus, of course, the driver) and on to Halong Bay, the main objective of the day. It was very cool and UK-ish, misty and damp. There were many boats waiting to be hired but Long obviously knew which one to engage: maybe it was pre-arranged. Anyway we were the only party on board as we chugged out to become part of a breathtakingly beautiful landscape. I was surprised to read that the bay encompassed 1500 square miles. Ha Long means 'dragon descending', from a local legend which tells of a celestial dragon and her offspring being ordered by the Jade Emperor to halt an invasion from the sea. The clever dragons spewed out lumps of jade which turned into wondrous islands and karst formations - (limestone regions with underground streams and caves) - thus scuppering the enemy ships. The dragon was said to be so happy with their work that she settled there for good and still lives under the bay.

The limestone islands (of which there were over 1600), with their bizarre sculptures, made a magically mysterious backdrop for the sails of the junks and sampans gliding among them, all made more unreal by the shifting mists. We visited one of the many caves and grottos. I think it was Hang Dau Go. Stalactites and stalagmites could be construed to resemble birds, beasts and humans, and all was sensitively footpathed and cleverly lit so as to enhance, rather than detract from, the natural miracle. The ceiling of the cave was like the surface of a moderately choppy sea, as if somehow we were on the underside of the waves. No wonder the whole area had been included in the UNESCO World Heritage Sites. I loved it.

There were two disappointments: one was that the weather was so chilly I was not enticed into the water for a swim, although I'd remembered to put on my bathing costume in the morning (in spite of the rush). Ruth's husband, Chris, who had visited Vietnam more than once, had lent me a splendid map of the area which he had annotated, and the 'we swam here' had made me optimistic. The other disappointment was the dearth of birds. It wasn't surprising that Long knew nothing of them: there weren't any. I did spot two large birds in the distance which Long said were "Sea Hawks" and an even larger, darker specimen which Long said he couldn't see. We had an excellent lunch on board, including delicious fresh crab and king prawns. Meg and I shared a good bottle of French wine: the others were all into the local beer.

It was virtually dark by the time we arrived at Saigon Halong Hotel. I bathed and changed in Room 1104, and then got into the staff lift by mistake as I attempted to join the others for a free drink. We walked out to a local restaurant recommended by Long, turning left and passing through the very overt red/pink light district, and had a good meal of lots of local dishes, pleasant red wine of unknown ethnicity, and convivial company. Sandra ate little, explaining that she ate just one meal a day: so do I really! Catherine propelled a glass of red wine over her mother, who was remarkably unphased. We were all better at the chopsticks manoeuvres, but with David still the best.

A very large healthy-looking rat was spotted scuttling across the restaurant floor as we left. Too late to be squeamish: we'd eaten!

I walked back to the hotel with David's wife, Pam. She talked about her father of 81, who lived in nearby sheltered housing and whom she visited every day after work: lucky man. We then had a discussion about HRT and how long one should stay on it: I'm never allowed to forget my 'life's work' wherever I am.

Bed was at 10.40 pm, in preparation for an early morning. I was determined not to oversleep again. It said 3 am on the lobby's 'London' clock.

Monday 12th January 2004

My sleep was disturbed by the room's heat, in spite of having the air-conditioning full on. I breakfasted with Catherine and Meg and then returned to my room, haltingly, in a lift which must have been having repeated conflicting signals from inside and out. I made it to Reception with my hand luggage by 8.25 am, five minutes before the appointed time, but I was still the last.

We were hardly into the day's drive when Long indicated that we were passing an army training centre. The compulsory national service (for those not blessed with a Colonel for a father) was two and a half years. I got the feeling that Long did not get along all that well with his father, as he muttered, disapprovingly, "He still behaves like a Colonel." We passed more graves, more rice fields studded with the bobbing conical hats of the workers and then three women, in the same headgear, balancing heavy loads over their shoulders on each end of a bamboo pole, in baskets shaped like inverted conical hats. I found myself dozing a little, which made me feel guilty. I awoke as two noisy, substantial, Hyundai vehicles sped by and I wondered what I had missed.

We stopped at a village in the Bac Ninh province and were driven in a pony and trap through the narrow approach to a delightful open air theatre (pagoda) where four lovely young women, and a handsome man, performed what I imagined was the local folk music (Quan Ho) - songs of love and place, accompanied by two musicians and preceded by a translation from Long. It was quite compelling on the ear and the eye, and their obvious enjoyment and enthusiasm transmitted directly to the audience.

This was followed by a visit to a nearby temple of the Ly dynasty, where their enormous portraits all looked remarkably similar, except that the first Ly (of the 11th century) was in red while the other seven (covering 11th to 13th centuries) were all in yellow. We lingered for a while and were allowed to take pictures: I rather liked the Ly dynasty portraits and bought a pull-out series of the eight kings. I could see Sandra frowning

12 January 2004

YOUNG DANCING STUDENTS

and suspected that she disapproved of such extravagance but I think I'd have regretted it later if I'd resisted.

We then had another short trip in the pony and trap to a nearby restaurant for a very good lunch, preceded by a slurp of powerful rice wine, which was a shock to the taste buds on first encounter. The meal included the usual tasty soup with noodles, some unusual vegetarian sausages, a superb cabbage dish with olives, salt and tomato juice, a slab of a white'ish sweet that combined a fudge-like appearance with a pull-out tenacity far beyond any known chewing gum, and juicy kumquats. I knew I was going to miss this adventurous food with its presentation, flavours and imaginative combinations.

We walked through the village streets back to the bus. Little piles of bricks were lodged against the back walls of the houses: "ready for when they want to build on", offered Long. On arrival at the Hilton Opera Hotel I could not for the life of me find my luggage receipt. Long came to my rescue, murmuring that this was why he liked everyone to give themselves plenty of time and be ready early. Needless to say, once I got up to room 116 on the first floor, I discovered the little white slip in with the change

12 January 2004

PROUD AUNTY - HILTON OPERA HOTEL

I'd received when I'd made the phone call. The room was basic, not as luxurious as before - when it was disclosed that we had had the executive suite by default! After a quick luggage sort-out we had a walk round the Lake of the Restored Sword, Ho Hoan Kiem: another lasting legend behind the name. King Le Thai To used a magic sword to liberate his country from the Chinese Ming in the early 1500s. He returned it to the Divine Tortoise in the lake from whence it had come: the animal was said to have snatched it back gratefully.

We ambled along the streets, browsing in and out of shops. I bought a couple of little wooden dolls and a set of lacquered bamboo trays. The atmosphere was pleasant. Old houses were jumbled between new developments, some of the latter very tall and slender and brightly painted. Groups of school children waved and shouted "Hello!" and we all got braver at crossing the roads. Back at the hotel I bathed and washed my hair ready to meet Ruth, whom I had not seen for so long: first impressions are everything. She arrived promptly at 6.30 pm, looking great in a red jacket, crash helmet in hand: she'd come by scooter-taxi: all VSO workers are required to wear crash helmets - not many others do. She looked lovely, slimmer than I remembered, well and attractive. I felt quite emotional. We went up to my room, where she left her crash helmet and set the camera for an arrival photograph of us both sitting on the bed. The last picture I have of the two of us was taken on the lake in Kodai, India, 26 years ago.

We joined the others in the Sports Bar where we all had our '50% off' drink of the evening: a gin and tonic each for Ruth and me. The group chatted and asked Ruth about her work and then went off to the Nuam Douange restaurant of two nights ago, while Ruth took me by taxi to a VSO associated restaurant. I started with a seafood soup, which put me in mind of bouillabaisse, and followed it with a tasty flat fish in a delicious lemon sauce, with rice. We talked incessantly while we ate and then walked back through the still bustling, but now quieter, streets. It was good to catch sight of St Joseph's Cathedral, which looked truly beautiful in the floodlighting, as did the lake. Back at the hotel I off-loaded the modest bits and pieces I'd brought for Ruth before she went off on another scooter-taxi. It had been such a memorable evening with Ruth and I felt proud to be her aunty.

I did the luggage 'thing', including the labels for the morning flight to Danang, and climbed into bed at 11.30 pm. I attempted to book an early morning call through Reception but there was no response, a bit late I suppose - which was what was worrying me. I'd have to trust to luck. I'd mislaid my nail-scissors and just hoped they weren't lurking somewhere in my hand luggage, to be picked up by the all-seeing scanner.

Tuesday 13th January 2004

I awoke at 7 am after a reasonable night's sleep: I didn't usually wake spontaneously at that hour: was this what they called 'jet lag?' I'd never had it before. I breakfasted alone in the restaurant. Some of the other guests were obviously business people, in earnest discussion as they ate. I met up with the rest of the group, with luggage, at 8.50 am, ready for the transfer to the airport for the flight from Han Oi to Da Nang. I was thankful that our internal flight had been changed from 5.30 am to something more civilised.

As we drove along we saw great spreads of fruiting kumquat trees and flowering 'peach' trees which bore no resemblance to those others of the same name, but which had pretty pink flowers. Both the kumquat and peach trees were pruned and trained with wire into the shape of Christmas trees. Many were in pots for sale by the roadside for the celebration of the rapidly approaching Tet, the lunar new year, and we saw many of these sizeable purchases being transported by the buyers, balanced precariously on the backs of motor bikes, sometimes two to a vehicle. It was mind-boggling to view some of the luggage carried thus - computers, mattresses, large glass doors, to mention but a few.

Long organised all the luggage at the check-in, so that the total weight of the group's luggage was not overweight, as was some of the individuals' luggage. The latter benefited from the likes of me, with my underweight contribution. We said our good-byes to dear, helpful Long, our guide for the north. We had all benefited from his impressive command of English through which his pride in the homeland, as well as his considerable knowledge, had been easily understood. I chatted happily with Catherine on the plane. On landing we were whisked off immediately towards Hoi An, having lunch en route, sitting in Mackintosh-style chairs and devouring, among other things, yet another variety of spring rolls, with duck and a spicy red pepper sauce.

We had a walk round Hoi An market, where the amazing diversity of vegetables and fruit, known and unknown, was fascinating. I loved the dragon apples' shading from green to a fiery pink and punctuated with strange little protruberances. They had small dark seeds scattered about in their white flesh inside and were sort of melon-refreshing to eat. I suddenly realised how pain-free were my normally aching joints.

Next we visited a Cantonese Community House. I should have mentioned that we now had our new guide, for the south, Le, with a brilliant smile and a differently-accented English - not surprising I suppose, but it was not as easy to understand initially as had been Long's.

The House (temple) was in honour of a good mandarin, who had supported the emperor and become a god. There was a wonderful dragon, and a sea goddess who could see and hear for a 1,000 miles. An ancient Chinese house had our attention next, which embraced a curious collection of different architectural styles. We had a welcome cup of green tea in the homely middle section. The back of the house opened on to the river.

We walked across a bridge, which displayed Japanese monkeys at one end and shrimps and dogs at the other (Chinese) end. We strolled by the river, now silting up and flowing on a different course from the original. This one-time port was no longer able to accommodate large craft. There were stalls along the roadside and I bought a sweet little blue and white doll's teaset.

Finally, we went silk shopping. I had a plan in mind to buy, or have made, cream silk trousers to be worn under a navy silk mandarin-collared dress, long-sleeved, with the skirt slit from the waist on each side. The girl drew the outfit, I selected the fabrics and she then measured me in some detail in full view of the group. This included the distance between the nipples, which seemed to amuse one of the male members of the party. She said it would all be delivered to the Furama Beach Hotel the following day. This sounded incredible: apart from staying up half the night to do the sewing, it was quite a trip to the hotel, as we were to discover. This was too good a chance to miss.

I think most of us had a sleep in the bus and it was dark by the time we reached the hotel, which was lovely and open, with the sound of the sea on the nearby beach. It was time to eat, so no time for a bath: just a quick change of clothes, food, and then bed. It had been a day crowded with memorable sights, sites, and sounds.

Wednesday 14th January 2004

We had an early start and, as neither I nor anyone else had that much confidence in my ability to wake on time, David had promised to knock on my door at 6 am (the middle of the night to me): they had the room next door. I surprised myself by waking before the summons. I had fruit and croissant for breakfast and then Le came and told me he had confirmed my flight for the morrow, when I would be leaving the group for Saigon. And he had also confirmed my home-going flights for the following week, good man! It was a grey, drizzly morning but the pool and the sea looked wonderful.

I felt quite weary as we climbed into the bus. We visited a huge sculpture emporium, where detailed and intricately designed lions and dragons sat next to simpler, smooth representations of other iconic figures such as the Virgin Mary and the Christchild. They are evidently known for their CHAN reproductions. We spent some time browsing round, while Sandra and Jonathon went to the office to discuss the possibilities of purchase and delivery of one of the exhibits. They said it would look good in the middle of their front lawn. The whole exercise of getting it from the yard to their actual home would cost something in the region of £1,200, which seemed more than reasonable to me, but they didn't make any definite arrangement.

We started up the Hai Van pass on our way to Hue. We stopped on the top with wonderful panoramic views, and I bought a bracelet from a young girl who spoke

14 January 2004
PREPARING THE RICE FIELDS

excellent English and said she hoped to be a teacher: her peers stood around, in admiration I think. There were bottles of snake wine with the curled forms of that animal very much in evidence in the pale yellow liquid. "That's like viagra", volunteered Le.

Back in the bus, Le gave us some background. His family, whose sympathies were with the south of the country, lived on the border between the north and south, which made life very difficult for his parents when the family (eight of them) were all young. His father faked a loyalty to the north occasionally, when it seemed he might suffer (like being shot) if he admitted his southern affiliation. On one occasion, aware of imminent trouble, he ran away, and Le told how many of the men of their village were killed that night. His mother prayed, and then went and turned over the corpses lying around. Her husband was not among them: he re-appeared two weeks later. The family were committed Roman Catholics and his father felt that the most important thing was to protect his wife and children. Schools closed and, as he was a teacher, he had to find something else to do. He learned to plant rice, as did the young Le, to feed the family and earn some money. His father's brother-in-law had been a Captain in one of the armies and once the war was over, he was sent to an 'education camp', ostensibly for two weeks: he was not seen again for five years until he knocked on the door of Le's parents' house. These were revealing, if disturbing, little windows on the lives of the ordinary Vietnamese people. Le smiled at the happy conclusions to this family saga.

Once at Hue, we visited Dai Noi, the Imperial City, some parts of which amazingly survived the destructive offensive of the Viet Cong and the Americans. We saw what remained in the Yellow Enclosure, the Hoang Thanh - there being little left in the other two walled areas. There were temples, palaces, flower gardens, decorated gates, green and yellow tiles, and, in the first enclosure, the nine deities' cannons - five on one side representing the primary elements, metal, water, wood, fire and earth, and the four opposite depicting the four seasons. There was an electric blue in some of the paintings by one of the gates – so, busy camera. We were more than ready for lunch by now and were not disappointed by the tasty soup, ubiquitous spring rolls, chicken, rice chips, fish, fruit, and green tea.

A trip on the Perfume River gave a chance to see all the permanent boat people delivering, collecting, selling, taxi-ing, fishing and just living. One of the most memorable cameos for me was the sight of two small children leaning over the side of their boat, cleaning their teeth under a line of white washing, as sparkling as seen in any detergent advertisement. We stopped and went ashore to see the Thien Mu Pagoda. The octagonal tower had seven tiers, each representing a reincarnation of Buddha. There were guarding statues of deities, a laughing gilt Buddha, three glass-enclosed statues of Buddha (not laughing), and a fine bell whose toll is said to be heard ten miles away. The sad thing is I cannot remember hearing it. The garden's collection of ornamental shrubs and trees, including bonsais set out in pairs, had attracted some Milkwood butterflies.

It was a long drive back to the Furama Beach resort. People were still busy in the rice fields and we saw one field being prepared with a pair of buffaloes. A few Cattle Egrets poked about. Le talked about religion. His uncle and a brother were Roman Catholic priests and he had an aunt who was a nun. "But we are very respectful of other religions", he assured us: "Buddhism, Confucianism, Daoism, Islam. People here are either very rich since the tourism, or still very poor, but the poor are not resentful. The underlying culture is Buddhism, which is very calming".

He talked of his two young sons, who were allowed to ring him on his mobile at any time, to make up for the fact that some nights he had to stay away. As we talked, darkness descended and our driver showed incredible skill as he coped with being overtaken by empty buses driving south to Saigon, having deposited their going-home-to-the-country-for-Tet passengers further north. This they did on hairpin bends with positively (or negatively) absolutely no visibility, and heart-stopping drops on either side. Le asked me what I meant by a 'hairpin bend': I removed one of my hairpins from my bun in explanation.

We arrived back at 6.30 pm and I was tantalised by the seductive noise of the ocean, which it was becoming increasingly obvious I wasn't even going to have time to walk by, never mind swim in. The silk goods ordered by Meg and me had not arrived. I had a quick wash, changed, and wrote a bit of farewell doggerel, as is my wont, as I will be leaving the group early in the morning. I joined them in the bar and, after the first mouthful, Le appeared to say the dressmaking had arrived. There then followed a mandatory trying on and mannequin parade. We were both delighted, and stayed thus clad for dinner, which we ate in the beach bar where the warm air blew in kindly and made me wish I was staying there another day. I enjoyed mussels and then a duck salad. I felt really sad to be saying goodbye to my travel companions (easier in verse) and, when Catherine gave me a hug, I nearly cried.

I paid up, arranged for an early morning call at 5.45 am - help! - packed, bathed and tumbled into bed.

Thursday 15th January 2004

I obeyed the early call, listened to the sea for the last time, and had a light breakfast of coffee and fruit. When I got to the entrance, Le was there. I hadn't expected to see him, as this was his day off. I appreciated his accompanying me to the airport. To my shame, I found I still had the room 'key' (piece of card) in my pocket, so he was able to take it from me. I thanked him and he seemed to appreciate the recommended tip.

We took off promptly for Saigon and, being on my own, I sat thinking about the country and its people. They were naturally charming, beautiful, slim, unsophisticated, uncomplicated - almost childlike and naive - industrious, cheerful and helpful but not intrusive.

I was met at the airport by guide number three, Thanh - with his 'Videtour' placard and my name spelt correctly. I had imagined I'd be joining another group but it seemed I was 'the group'. The driver was Duc and we set off, not to the city, but to Cy Chi to see the labyrinth of tunnels used by the guerillas during the war. We passed a great pile of sea-shells by the roadside. These would be powdered and used to make paint, explained Thanh. (One of my granddaughters, who collects shells, would have considered that a dreadful waste.) There was a fair bit of road-widening going on, and some of the houses had had to sacrifice their front rooms, which were being demolished. "The compensation is costing more than the work on the road", said Thanh wryly. He spoke good English, with an accent different again, but was easy to understand.

We stopped at a rubber plantation and I took a couple of pictures. The trees were tall and the avenues long, somehow presenting a graceful scene.

At the tunnel complex I joined others to see a film giving the background information. The idea of survival, plus carrying on with the ordinary essentials of everyday life was well illustrated by the phrase "a rifle in one hand and a plough in the other", and by pictures of a man planting rice with a gun on his back. The tunnels themselves were small and narrow and went on for miles. There were disguised vents every so often. I wriggled down into one tunnel as tourists can do. It was only just wide enough for me to move along in a half-crouched position and I'm not that big, but then the Vietnamese are so small and neat and these were their passages. There were horrific man traps with spikes to hold and perforate until the intruder was found and finished off, underground meeting rooms, and primitive provision for a whole life on this lower plain. We had a break and a cup of green tea. A group of noisy Americans were competing against each other at a tourist firing range .....

From here we went to the War Remnants Museum, where the mostly black-and-white photographs of the devastation and personal tragedies of the war moved me to tears. (Oh, why did we go into Iraq?) The picture that made me cry, as I am sure it has done to many - and partly, I guess, because of its awful familiarity - was that of the young girl fleeing for her life from the effects of the napalm bomb. After four rooms of illustrated reminders, including limbs amputated by exploding mines and the delayed legacy of congenital deformities caused by noxious chemicals, I had had enough and returned to the waiting Thanh and Dud. For a split second I did not recognize them as they sat among other Vietnamese, but then Thanh spoke and suggested I go on to Rooms 5 and 6. (They'd obviously been keeping an eye on me). I said I'd got the upsetting message and he nodded understandingly. Back in the vehicle, my mind dwelt on Vietnam's suffering from wars, the French, the Americans, north against south and marvelled at how they'd apparently risen like a phoenix from the piles of ashes.

We drove to Saigon city and stopped to look at Notre Dame Cathedral, a beautiful brick building completed by the French in 1883. I took pictures of some of the lovely stained glass and of a statue of St Anthony. There were hundreds of small memorial plaques applied to the stonework of the recesses round some of the windows, commemorating those who died in the war. Thunh, a Roman Catholic, crossed himself as he said how he loved his cathedral.

I bought one of the conical hats at a street store for the equivalent of 40p. I'd fancied one of these ever since my arrival. I suspected it might be regarded as comical rather than conical back in the UK but I'd wear it here, anyway. We went into the impressive, high-ceilinged post office, which was more like a large railway station, where I bought some cards. Then it was back to the car. This city did feel French with its colonial architecture and wide tree-lined avenues. The New World Hotel was opposite a great flower market where the potted peach trees, lemon trees, yellow, orange and red chrysanthemums, and yellow, red and orange salvias, to mention but a few, were spread out for sale by numerous stall holders. Tet was going to be very colourful.

Room 710 was equipped with noisy and, I think, efficient air-conditioning but I did long to open a window. I read the hotel blurb and discovered that there was a swimming pool on another floor. Just what I needed: it was 4 pm. I was in there by 4.10 pm, enjoyed twenty minutes' exercise and then lay on a recliner in the evening sunshine. At least I'd had my swim, even if it hadn't been from the beach by the Furama Beach Hotel.

I returned to my room to find a message from Ruth, who would be calling in after 9 pm. I had a bath, sorted my luggage and put all the bits of paper, cards and other memorabilia in some sort of order. I used the hotel safe for the first time, using my home burglar alarm number, which I reckoned I was unlikely to forget. I watched the news and found that Dr Shipman had committed suicide. He had more than tarnished the "Trust me, I'm a doctor" idiom. Bush had announced that the USA Mars probe was successful. I felt sorry for the Brits team and their failed space project. Once again I was relishing the painlessness of my joints in spite of early rising and all that walking around.

There was a knock on the door and I was handed a small package: it was a 'welcome to Vietnam' present from dear Ruth - an attractive desk calendar with views of Vietnam and a lovely silk card to go with it. I rang her from downstairs but could hardly hear her because of guests at a noisy wedding reception, who were having their pictures taken on the stairs. The bride was in a white wedding dress but I was told that there had been an earlier ceremony in traditional Vietnamese costume.

I sat downstairs in the huge entrance and watched the world go by while I waited for Ruth. There were big Germans, suited businessmen, superbly costumed girls on the large doors, and a few sloppily-dressed Brits. Ruth arrived about 9.30 pm and we had a drink and lots of chat. We had plenty to say to each other.

I thought she was finding it hard to say goodbye to people with whom she had worked, and some of whom she would be seeing for the last time, as each day passed, from now on until she would be leaving on March 11th.

Friday 16th January 2004

I got up at 7 am, had croissants for breakfast, and observed the inexpressive, unflinching faces as I came down from the seventh floor. Thanh was on parade promptly at 8 am. I gave in my (proper) key at the desk. We got into the car - with seat belts - and Duc, the driver, gave us a big 'Good Morning' smile. We drove through Chinatown, where lived 700,000 Chinese people. There were colourful Tet decorations everywhere. Out in the country there were fires of rice straw, which would yield fertilizer, and a few birds sitting in trees and on the overhead wires. Thanh couldn't identify the moderately-sized black one with a white chest, nor the bronze-headed yellowish bird.

There were more crash helmets about today, although generally the motorcycling population seemed to be primarily concerned about the pollution and many wore scarves around, and hiding, most of their faces. Then again it was suggested that this was more to do with protecting their skin from ultraviolet light, as beauty is associated with a pale complexion - and there was me, hoping to go home with a bit of a tan.

We passed a flamboyant Cao Dai temple, this religion being an amalgamation of Buddhism, Confucianism and Christianity, with a touch of Islam, animism and ancestral worship thrown in. Adherents believe in one ultimate deity and practice meditation and vegetarianism. It doesn't sound such a bad idea, except for the vegetarianism!

We passed a Madonna decorated for the New Year, great heaps of water melons being sold at the roadside, a Viet Cong cemetery, a large bird-frightening effigy in a field of newly-planted rice (there must be a few birds, then .....) which looked more like a scare Buddha than a scarecrow, elaborate funeral vehicles, one driven, one pushed, and a huge tree balanced on a bicycle and being pushed by a small man in a nearly horizontal position – and Pedigree Chum and Omo advertisements in abundance.

We had a brief loo stop at the 'Happy House', where two healthy-looking black-and-white monkeys swung about with enviable agility in a roomy cage at the entrance. I wondered whether they were always there or just in celebration of the Chinese New Year of the Monkey. Nearby was a charming pink flower with thick succulent petals, quite different from anything I'd seen before. Thanh said it was the 'Fairy Flower'.

Back on the road again we passed an abandoned Big Wheel, which seemed so incongruous towering above the surrounding countryside: evidently the legacy of some bankrupt enterprise. Nearby was a colourful expanse of glorious Lotus flowers, the seeds and roots of which provided food. Thanh was anxious to inform about everything in view, including a plant that was used for 'incest' - although I'm sure he meant 'incense' - and another from which came kapok filling. The main object of today's trip was to spend some time in the Mekong Delta, and in the late morning we arrived at Vinh Long where we boarded a little boat and met Miss Dam who was to be my guide on the river. She was a tiny, beautiful, young lady who looked about sixteen, with an excellent command of English. We went ashore on a small island to visit a rice factory. We watched the making of 'poprice' (cf popcorn). Hot sand was used in this process and the sand was heated by the stones of a local fruit. The poprice could be mixed with a caramel which included coconut milk, pressed, rolled out quickly, cut, and packeted. We saw a similar process with maize, to which nuts were added to make a delicious toffee. Perhaps the most vivid memory would be the sight of the lady (she was 44 she told me, having first asked me my age) who gently threw ladles of rice milk on to a piece of stretched silk over a heated pot, allowed it to linger for a matter of seconds and then peeled off the dinner-plate-sized circle of rice paper, and added it to the tall pile beside her. She produced 800 sheets a day but had time off between rice crops.

We drifted on in the little boat through narrow canals with named dwellings on either side, protected by planted Mangroves at the water's edge, which reminded me fleetingly of the Philippines. The vegetation was lush, exotic and various. There were trees hung with clusters of vibrant pink Rose Apples - which I felt should be called 'strawberry apples' on account of their shape as well as their colour - Langon Trees, Capon Shrubs, and so many others that neither I nor Thanh could name.

We stopped at the Landlord's House, a 1920's building with Victorian, French and Chinese architectural influences, so I was informed. Two ladies sang sweetly to us of the relationship between mother and daughter, Miss Dam giving us the translation. The ladies were accompanied by two smiling men on (sort of) guitars. It was all very

16 January 2004

MAKING THE RICE PAPER

pleasing and relaxing as we drank tea and ate prickly-skinned, big-stoned ramputants, and water apples that looked like white pears, while we listened. At the end of the recital, the guitarists struck up with a strange version of Auld Lang Syne and I couldn't resist providing the voice. They seemed delighted and wanted a repeat but Thanh said it was time to go!

Back on the river, Dam told me she was 26 and she enjoyed her job because it gave her financial independence, but she was tired of everyone, particularly her mother, telling her to find a good man and get married, saying, "If you have no children, you'll have no-one to care for you in your old age, and you'll wander about on your own in the next world ...... "

We had a break for lunch on another island at a restaurant with a well-established bonsai garden. I was ready to sit and eat in spite of the heat and did justice to the tiny spring rolls, two huge prawns, a whole carp-like fish served upright in swimming position, as it were, vegetable soup, an abundance of rice, various fruits and a drink of hot fresh lemon juice. I walked round the garden while Thanh and Dam talked to other guides. I'm not really that taken by bonsai trees but they did seem to be attracting a wealth of butterflies, which I did enjoy.

A relaxing one–and-a-half-hour trip took us back to the road and we started the long drive back to Saigon. The roads were even busier, crowded with pre-Tet traffic. I sat, seat-belted, and observed some amazing driving skills and lack of skills, but the only possible evidence of an accident was a lonely rider-less bike in the middle of the highway, surrounded by police.

We got back just after 6 pm. I said farewell to the pleasant driver Duc, and to Thanh, who had been a helpful and conscientious guide, then collected my key, bathed, and changed in time for Ruth's arrival at 7 pm. We then walked to an atmospheric vegetarian restaurant, where we were joined by Bich, Ruth's previous translator, a lively lady who supported and helped many of her family on her income. The meal was very good. It had been an education here to discover just how appetizing, and imaginative, vegetarian food can be. (Maybe I could be an adherent of the Cao Dai temple philosophy after all). I magnanimously insisted on paying the bill, which came to under £3 for all three of us!

We had a chat with the lady owner of the establishment, who regularly got up at 4 am to buy the vegetables, as well as supervising the running of the business all the other hours of the day, and had a brief encounter wih a deep-voiced, brightly-clad lady who did massage.

Ruth and I walked back to the hotel via the flower market and, as well as admiring the potted plants and trees, we had a closer look at the ingeniously sculptured trees in the shapes of dragons and reindeer and the like, and took pictures.

I bade a temporary goodbye to Ruth, paid my bill, asked for a 7.30 am call and was in bed by 10.30 am. Quite a day.

Saturday – already! – 17th January 2004

I was packed and ready for collection by 8.30 am. I stood outside with luggage in the morning sunshine until Ruth arrived. The car was very comfortable and I climbed in to sit on the beaded seat cover. The chauffeur was Bich's brother-in-law, married to her younger sister. We drove some of the same route as yesterday, and stopped off at lunchtime at a roadside cafe for generous helpings of pork and noodle soup, and a drink: less than £3 for the three of us.

As we drove on, Ruth and I chatted about the family, Ruth's work in Vietnam and the resilience and survival of the Vietnamese through all kinds of change. The countryside got greener with fewer houses but there were often stalls by the roadside. Every now and then we would pass a new, large, showy house, often built backing on to older small properties, with some kind of business being conducted from the front.

The skies were blue and clear as far as the eye could see, and there was a pleasant light wind as we arrived at Ruth's little blue house in Duyen Hai. It was cosy and compact and welcoming, with familiar family photographs and local memorabilia on display. I sat outside at the back having two cups of (UK) tea and a piece of shortbread I'd brought with me on behalf of Ruth's Oban friend, Libby. A few hybrid ducks ran about. They had little life left, Ruth explained, as they were being fattened for Tet. A neighbour, who was washing dishes outside, near the water pump, came over and talked to us – well, she talked to Ruth, anyway, in Vietnamese. She was Tuyen, seemed a lovely lady, unmarried and a teacher. She lived next door with her brother, Mr Danh, a senior teacher and also unmarried, and with their eleven-year-old nephew, An, who lodged with them during term time so that he could go to the nearby secondary school.

We were invited to their house for supper, so I roused myself and had a cold shower and a change of clothes. They put on an amazing spread and we all (including other members of the family and Phuoc, the driver) sat round the table, filling the little room, while Mr Danh periodically made visits to the adjacent kitchen where he crouched on the floor to collect fresh supplies. (The whole race seemed to spend much of its time in the crouching position for long periods, as the people worked or did routine chores. They were all so fit.) They ate and talked and every now and then Ruth translated to keep me in the picture. She was giving extra English lessons to An and suggested that I asked him a few simple questions in English, such as "What's your name?   How old are you?   Are you happy?" He answered well, and then I asked him whether he knew what his T-shirt said. He shook his head: it read 'Travel Round the World '.

I copied the others, laying some of the tasty titbits on rice paper or large leaves and then rolling them into something which could be managed by hand: it was easier than chopsticks. Even so, I was a bit slower than the rest and every now and then someone else did one for me. There was a great sense of hospitality and in spite of not speaking the language, I felt a real part of the company and remember it as if the entire conversation had been conducted in English. I was thirstier than I had realised and I drank the orange provided very quickly. Before I could blink, it was quietly filled again and then I remembered that it was good manners to leave a little of food or drink unless you were desperate for more immediately.

It was an early evening meal so that afterwards there was time to go and visit Phong and Nhung, married teachers who lived a short walk away. They were out but a 15-year-old brother (another term-time lodger for educational reasons) asked us in, made us tea and uncovered a box of Tet coconut tasties called 'mut' I think, but pronounced 'muck', which they most certainly were not. The whirr of a motorcycle engine heralded the arrival of Phong and Nhung who came in, with their dear little baby girl. They were so pleased to see Ruth and wanted us to stay for a meal. Ruth explained that we had eaten. They suggested the following day but Ruth had plans and there was no time. Ruth produced the Tet presents for the family, with which they were delighted, especially with a Scottish flag depicting a dragon.

We walked back in the pleasant warm evening air, had a coffee and another chat and a knobbly custard apple. I was in my comfortable, mosquito-netted bamboo mat bed (dear Ruth's really) by 9.30 pm.

Sunday 18th January 2004

I slept really well apart from loo trips – well, I did drink all that orange and a cup of coffee last thing. I'd been vaguely aware of quacking ducks early in the morning and Ruth informed me that those I'd seen running round behind the houses had been captured and stitched into individual bags (with their heads free) and taken off on the neighbours' motorbikes to the family Tet celebrations some distance away. At least it sounded to be a more humane method of transport than for some I'd seen, which were hanging live upside down with their feet tied together on the backs of bikes. Another distant intrusion, which had pounded away on the perimeters of sleep, had been an unforgiving news broadcast (I learned later), interspersed with blasts of popular music and delivered over a Tannoy, voluble and impossible to ignore. This commenced every morning at 5 am, Ruth told me, and continued for an hour or so. It smacked seriously of the underlying Communism which, for me, had been comparatively low key up to the present.

Ruth had been out early and got some lovely fresh bread, which we ate with fruit for breakfast. I sat reading in the front room by the open window while Ruth did her washing and then we called at the OXFAM building, where she had her own space and desk: hers looked tidier than the rest. This visit was followed by a walk to the local market where, once again, I was mesmerised by the variety of superb fruit and vegetables: I still can't name them all. There were great flashes of colour from the flowers and, further on, compelling displays of more subtly-coloured fish. All was supervised calmly and quietly, mostly by women, of all ages. They knew how to produce beef and pork here. Not only did they use every part of their animals including the offal, intestines, pigs' ears and heads, (I was reminded of that wonderful brawn my mother-in-law used to make) but all the meat was enhanced by a decent layer of fat. Ruth was busy distributing small Tet presents to her favourite stall-holders, with whom it was evident she had a great rapport. As I drifted along behind her, I was very much aware of being the focus of attention - there were not many Europeans about - but it was a kindly curiosity and not in any way intrusive.

We walked back to the house and then went to a nearby restaurant, me on the back of Phong's motorbike – it took me back 50 years to John's BSA bantam days - for lunch being provided by Ruth for a collection of grades 1 - 4 teachers. They were a happy bunch, just three of them men, who had some English, which I have to admit I sometimes found as difficult to understand as the Vietnamese. There were three children in the party, a girl of eleven and two younger ones of possibly four and three, depending on how the age was calculated. You could be one already should you be born just before the lunar New Year, when you would become two - or even three, because you'd been 'alive' for nearly a year before you were born, anyway! Whatever their recognized age, they were remarkably well-behaved. Once again I was required to ask simple questions, this time of Bi, the eleven year old, who also had extra English lessons with Ruth.

The meal commenced with wrapping rice paper parcels of mountains of fresh shrimps, noodles, herbs, pork etc, many of which were embarrassingly done for me so that I was reminded, once again, to eat more slowly and pre-empt mandatory refilling when my plate became empty. A hot dish of fish balls was served from the centre of the table - this reminded me of the expensive crab balls I made years ago - with options of various sauces, mostly pinkish and some with chilli influence. I was glad of the balancing effect of the chunks of huge juicy grapefruits to finish off the meal.

It was obvious they all enjoyed themselves and indulged in lots of in-jokes, of which I felt I sometimes got the gist in spite of the language barrier. As they departed, mostly on motorbikes, one of the lady teachers not only donned a face-covering scarf but also a pair of elbow-length gloves. After lunch I sat in my favourite spot, outside at the back of the house, wrote this diary, missed the ducks, and saw a little Flycatcher. Then it was off in the car driven by Phuoc and accompanied by Bi, Hoang - a neighbour's young boy whom we had seen being scrubbed for the outing by his mum behind their house - and Cam Tien, whose mother was a teacher and who was a niece of Mr Danh's, I think.

We were en route for the beach but stopped first at Long Khanh, where we took a short walk to the Roman Catholic Church, which sported an impressive fish symbol on its tower, the motif used by so many of the more relaxed Christians in the UK. There were people gathering inside and out, all in their Sunday best and we left as a service was about to begin. I had almost forgotten it was the Sabbath and wondered whether they'd had a decent choir for the Sung Eucharist at St Michael's at home in Torrington: then I realised that it was still only 6 am in the UK.

We motored on to Long Vinh School where another group of teachers had collected to see Ruth and her aunt. The school holidays had started so there were no children to see. Some of the staff had stayed behind for an extra day before going home for Tet. One lady teacher was about to get married to a deputy head somewhere else in the province and she put up with a fair bit of teasing. Another very lively lady teacher said how young and happy and beautiful I looked - I love this place! A male teacher was dark and, to my way of thinking, very handsome, but evidently his colleagues ribbed him about his looks. He probably had Kmer blood in him it was explained and he was regarded (not unkindly) in the same way as ethnic minorities are in any other country. They did admire and envy a pale skin here. It was obvious that a chunky member of the group was a bit of a lad and, as he lit his cigarette, he made remarks and jokes which of course I did not understand but which brought reactions of shocked amusement from his colleagues. Tellingly, no-one offered to translate.

The head teacher was a quiet man who sat authoritatively at the head of the table as yet another roll-your-own rice paper meal with my favourite shrimps was unexpectedly served up. He had survived the recent death of his young wife with an ectopic pregnancy and his other children were still very young: he looked sad. 'Our' three children behaved impeccably as they tucked into the food and I envied their skills of such rapid deheading of the prawns, and the neat rolling of the filled rice paper and leaves. I suspected we had lingered longer than Ruth had anticipated and I wondered whether we would ever get to the beach, which I was anxious to see, not yet having walked along a sandy shoreline. We had commemorative photos taken and were then allowed to depart.

The beach stretched as far as the eye could see and the sand was generously scattered with long thin shells of the Turritella variety, and there were the tell-tale sandy tracks of the secretive shore crabs. We paddled and the children jumped about in the in-coming tide, Hoang getting his trousers really wet. I asked Ruth about swimming. It seemed that bathing costumes were a rare sight. On the only two occasions when she'd been swimming in the sea, she went in fully clothed, as did her associates.

It was time to go but the children pleaded for another five minutes, which they were granted. For one of them this was the seventh visit to the coast, for another the second and for the third I think it was the first time. It was certainly the first time that one of them had ever travelled in a car. Phuoc had waited by the car and being acquainted with sand, he had spread papers on the floor of the vehicle. We dropped Bi at her father's (Son's) new house, where we were met with buckets of water to clean our feet once we'd removed our shoes, and then Son and his wife welcomed us, carrying their new baby son of whom they were very proud. Cam Tien was also left here for collection by her mum. More food appeared - help - but fortunately not too much.

Once home, we had a quick shower and change and took the short walk along the main road, and then along a sandy track (my joints were still good!) to Chi (Tu Be's), a sandy pleasant cafe where Ruth had her evening meal fairly regularly. We sat at a table separate from an extended family and a dear little boy came and studied us. The food looked good but I could eat little after the day's hospitality. There were three birds in large cages but two were covered for the night. The third was large, black and white and responded in mimicking fashion to my whistling advances. As we left, the little boy, now very smartly dressed, was being lifted on to his parents' motorbike and the three of them took off into the dark. "They hardly ever go out at night", Ruth volunteered: "it's Tet".

We walked back. I was glad Ruth had a torch. I sat and drank a glass of Da Lat wine and considered what a lot, thanks to Ruth's wonderful planning, had been packed into the day. I realised that this was the last time Ruth would be with these people at this time of year and, in fact, the last time she'd be seeing some of them at all. She did the ironing while I mused.

Monday 19th January 2004

I slept really well again. The bamboo mat-mattress cover was made up of tiny bamboo smooth squares, which slotted into a flexible framework. After a breakfast of fruit and good coffee, we prepared for the day's journey south. Phong came to say goodbye and brought Dung, a friend of his and Dung's son who were to travel with us in the car driven by the faithful Phuoc. The young boy was a handsome clone of his father but soon looked much paler as we started on the road to Saigon. He was very travel sick, poor lad, on this his first trip in a car.

We went through Vinh Long, then on to My Thuan and across a magnificent bridge over the River Tien, to which hundreds of Vietnamese had flocked to witness its recent opening. It was a joint project with the Australians. We revisited the roadside cafe at Vinh Long and I found I was salivating at the now familiar cooking smells as we entered. The noodle and beef soup was tasty and satisfying and I washed it all down with plenty of iced green tea.

We drove on through increasingly heavy traffic, with a visible build up of Tet preparations all the way. We arrived in Saigon just after 3 pm and booked in at the Southern Hotel where we had Room 702, which was reassuringly near the fire escape. This consisted of a ladder fixed to the outside wall of the hotel, and which was enclosed by rings of metal to confine the escapee to the tube. It was to be entered on this, the seventh floor, through an open window.

We showered and changed and visited the Bodhi Tree, where we had eaten with Bich. I had an avocado shake, which was another new but delicious experience. Then we went to an Internet cafe where Ruth caught up with her e-mails. We walked round the town and the flower market: there were more flowers than ever. The hundreds of motorcycles revved their way through the busy streets, many just incredibly heavily laden with people and goods. By 4 pm the street market had been set up with elaborate awning structures, shelves, racks and piles of goods all along the side of the busy road. Ruth said that by morning you'd never know they'd been there. We also browsed round the permanent day market, where the bewildering range of perishable and other goods was interspersed with various instant personal services such as manicure of hands and feet, and removal of facial hair with razor.

We went into the embroidered picture shops where huge works were displayed, many of flowers and scenes of Vietnam. There was one I particularly liked, of a woman in Vietnamese dress walking into the distance down an avenue of trees swaying a little in the breeze, as was her skirt. It was just so beautiful, emanating an atmosphere of gentle calm. Another large embroidered water scene was similar to the small one I'd bought at the Humanity Centre. Two young women stitched away speedily, at a table near one of the entrances, with the finest of silks in what seemed a poor light: they did not wear spectacles - yet. The jewellery shops were equally enticing. Ruth was thinking in terms of a traditional gold bracelet. Some of them were in sets of seven, called 'semaine', maybe a legacy from the days of the French.

Ruth had arranged that we should meet Phuoc and his wife Tu, Bich's younger sister, at the Quan An Ngon restaurant for supper and when we arrived they were standing outside looking in the opposite direction. It transpired that Bich had told Tu that I was 71, and she insisted on taking my arm and almost carrying me up the stairs as we were directed to the upper floor of the restaurant. They were a lovely couple. He had distinctly different features from other Vietnamese I had met: a longer face, which somehow reminded me of Thailand. They had one son, little money (the owner of the car hire business gets most of Phuoc's takings) and Bich had advised them not to have any more children, which neither they nor she could afford.

The place was buzzing with families having celebratory meals: a happy festive atmosphere. It was back to the chopsticks tonight for rice, with vegetables, noodle dishes, and dainty spring rolls. I loved the refreshing lime drink they recommended and also the sweet of chocolate brown rice covered with an even sweeter white sauce: it possibly sounds boring now, as I write this, but it was delicious - the sort of thing I could try at home I thought, except that I had not identified the added flavours which were probably the making of it.

We bade farewell to Phuoc and Tu, who gave me a memorable hug, and then took a taxi back to the environs of the hotel, where Ruth visited the photographer's with some films. The lady also 'did' beaded bags, which adorned the showcases. Several people hailed Ruth on the streets, including her favourite scooter taxi-driver and she stopped to chat more than once. It was obvious that they all loved her. The fact that she had made such efforts to speak the language was, I am sure, just one of several things which had endeared her to the locals.

We'd had a great day again. Tomorrow would see the start of my journey home.

Tuesday 20th January 2004

I had a good night's sleep, got up 7.30 am and walked up a couple of floors for breakfast. The Southern Hotel was one of those typically tall, thin buildings where the accommodation didn't start until the first or second floor, with chiropody and massage and other services being housed lower down. Ruth used to stay elsewhere but that particular hotel, like several other similar buildings in the city, had been forced to demolish some of its top floors to bring its premises into line with new safety regulations: it had now reopened but Ruth had stayed with the Southern. Being Ruth, she had confessed to feeling quite guilty when she had met and talked to the former hotelier in the street yesterday. We enjoyed French toast and coffee with milk. I also had fresh lemon juice: the girl apologized for running out of sugar, which is generally offered with the juice. I was more than happy, but the drink was not charged for!

We walked round the market. I didn't think I'd ever get bored; it was so huge and there was always something fresh to see. I bought a few fancy Tet envelopes at the entrance. There was less poultry but more hearts, livers and kidneys than I'd seen before - but no sign of any lamb, just a few joints of goat for sale. Incredibly, there were no flies to be seen on any of the meat slabs. I remembered India and how sometimes one almost had to wipe the flies away to identify the meat underneath. It seemed all the more extraordinary because there were so few birds about to eat the insects - but maybe that was why the birds weren't there: there weren't enough insects? The fish were all fresh and bright-eyed, some very much so as they swam their last moments in bowls of water. A cluster of what I can only describe as tortoiseshell-carapaced lobsters was evidently a pretty rare luxury and was exhorbitantly priced, by Vietnamese standards, at the equivalent of £10. (Charles, with his expert knowledge, later identified these from photographs as crawfish.)

I bought a large chunk of fresh ginger root, which was very cheap, and some Vietnamese coffee beans, which were expensive, relatively speaking. I was so busy taking pictures that I almost got mown down by a damp man carrying an enormous block of ice across his uncovered shoulders.

A last amble through the town reinforced what I was sure would be indelible memories of the flowers, the traffic, and the disabled: struggling with absent or damaged limbs – and often with both. We had a thorough look round the jewellers which sold the gold bracelets and Ruth was at last persuaded to have one of a semaine collection: they were on the small side, obviously geared to the local populace, but Ruth was determined to have the authentic design, which does not fasten. The sales lady was charming and patient and selected one to fit. We were both pleased.

Our intended restaurant venue had closed early for Tet so we returned to the now familiar Bodhi Tree, where I had a vegetarian (?) Shepherd's Pie and a fresh lemon and lime drink. Then it was back to the hotel to collect the luggage, pay the US$20 for the two of us for bed and breakfast, and the US$5 for the taxi they had kindly arranged to take me to the airport. It was 2 pm and I felt quite tearful as I said goodbye to Ruth: I was glad she wasn't coming to the airport. She was taking the scooter taxi, with her favourite taxi-man, to the bus station in order to get the bus to Phong's parents' house in the Vinh Long for the Tet New Year. She had tried to identify the turn-off to the house

20 January 2004
HO CHI MINH CITY MARKET

20 January 2004

TET FLOWERS Favourite colour - Yellow

during our long drive from Duyen Hai, so that she would be able to stop the bus at the right place: brave lady.

It was just twenty minutes to the airport and I was in plenty of time for the Singapore Airlines SQ173 flight. Once cleared through check-in, and scanned with my ding dong hip, I had a cappuccino coffee, browsed round the airport shops, and watched a convincing Vietnamese film - about a very sick street child who was found in a rubbish trolley by two refuse-collecting women. The street scenes of the stalls and the traffic, and then the refuse lady staggering up several flights of stairs with her bicycle to her small appartment, were very convincing.

Time was going on but there was still no indication that boarding had commenced at the named Gate 6. I took a walk only to find that there was a substantial boarding queue for my flight at Gate 4. Shoes were to be shed. Such moments as this make me feel geriatric, having lace-up shoes because of my arthritic feet, which are slow both to undo and to do up again on account of my arthritic hands. A pleasant young German lady made sure I didn't lose my place in the queue. We were just twenty minutes late taking off and I put my watch on an hour for the time difference. A helpful man next to me brought down my hand luggage: there are some advantages to being old and alone. There had been an empty seat between us.

I was near the front of the immigration queue but hadn't filled in the relevant document, which was mandatory even for the one-night stay, so I finished up at the back of the queue again. My luggage came through really quickly and I was soon on the other side and waiting in another well-organised queue for the taxi. I was directed to Bay 7 where a pleasant lady taxi driver took my luggage and settled me into her comfortable vehicle. She was Jackie Loh, 51, she told me, very chatty, with good English, and anxious to promote Singapore, pointing out the floodlit St Andrew's Church (having first established that I was a Christian), the tallest 72-floor building in the city, and then the colourful and imaginative decorations for the Chinese New Year of the monkey, as we drove through the city's Chinatown. From Tet to this!

She asked for 15 Singapore dollars. I had only American dollars, which I handed over happily: it was quite a distance and I had felt very comfortable with her. She said it was too much but I wished her a Happy New Year, whereupon she suggested that I might book her for the taxi the following morning: she said it was "very busy' and everyone was "on holiday - except me", she laughed. She said she could come early and give me a tour of the city, which didn't seem such a bad idea. I promised to ring the number on her business card to confirm the booking and give her my room number.

The reception at the Peninsular Excelsior Hotel was in the lobby on the first floor. The girls were a bit offhand and seemed distracted by a private row. I had Room 1333 in the Excelsior Tower. I opened the door with my card key (I was getting better at this) and after waiting what seemed like ages for my luggage, I rang down, quoted the very long number on my luggage receipt, which I had difficulty in finding, and the wheely luggage arrived immediately. I sorted it, had a rum and coke from the minibar and a bap I'd secreted away on the plane. I rang Jackie and climbed thankfully into bed.

Wednesday 21st January 2004

I had ordered a breakfast of fresh pineapple and croissants in my room, obeying the instruction on the menu card to hang the order on the outside of the door before 3 am. I hadn't located the restaurant in this vast emporium and I was worried about the time it might take to find it and then be served. I paid the bill, forgetting about the cashew nuts I'd consumed - but they hadn't! I noticed an entrance to the swimming pool on the lobby floor and went to investigate. I sat there for about twenty minutes, taking in the amazing view of the city, including the 72-storey building, and wishing that I'd had the time to use the nice little pool.

I rang down for the luggage to be collected. They're always surprised that I have just the one bag. Jackie Loh was waiting. She told me she was Chinese, a Buddhist and went home to China occasionally to worship her ancestors, her parents in particular. She lived in a 17th floor apartment near the airport. She had two sons, one in the navy and one about to get married, which seemed to please her. There was no mention of a husband so I didn't ask.

She gave me a good tour: the wide roads were very clean - some flanked by avenues of trees but with fewer flowers than in Vietnam - and with fewer motorbikes. Some of the high buildings had spectacular fronts of coloured glass, and roof gardens and verandas somewhere near the sky. We drove up a hill to view the nearby island, and the cable cars travelling in between. I seemed to remember that some members of the Tennyson Travel group were scheduled to take the cable-car trip. Jackie dove me round for three quarters of an hour, being allowed freely past a couple of toll booths, explaining that she was just taking me for a look. Then it was to the airport, all for 20$US. My picture of her in the driving seat was one of the best my recalcitrant camera took and I planned to send her a copy.

I went through the usual rigmarole at the airport, amongst a goodly number of UK backpackers, some with showy tattoos and dreadlocks. Singapore airport must have the biggest collection of orchids of any airport in the world, so many in fact that the first time I saw them, when I was on my way to Australia, I thought they must be artificial. They are vulgarly magnificent.

I sat and read but was distracted by the penetrating chatter of a flamboyant blond/grey-haired Brit, probably in his late fifties, who was accompanied by a very young, very attractive Malay girl who was worried about her anticipated stay in England. He kept telling her not to fuss, saying over and over, "Oh you'll be OK". I wondered.

The flight was late taking off because someone had announced as they boarded the plane that not only were they seriously allergic to peanuts but neither could they travel with anyone else who was eating peanuts. This extraordinary state of affairs meant that the caterers had to come on board and replace the whole flight menu. An agitated Malay lady was constantly disturbing the stewards about something and a younger woman demanded a change of seat because she said her video was not working. A patient stewardess found nothing amiss with it. I felt sorry for the staff.

I was seated on the aisle, to the left of the centre four seats, with an empty seat on my right and a pleasant couple beyond. Newspapers were offered and I selected a copy of the Asian Wall Street Journal. I was horrified to find a sizeable front page cover dedicated to what I thought at first was "Asian Flu" but on closer inspection found it to read "Avian Flu Epidemic - in Vietnam", with an account of thousands of poultry being slaughtered - and of thousands more which should have been slaughtered but which had mysteriously disappeared. I thought of all the poultry I'd seen for sale in the markets, not to mention hundreds more being taken up river in small boats. Did they know about it, I wondered, and was that why they were whipping them off somewhere out of sight?   I was just attempting to follow the article on the next page when I knocked or rather propelled the orange juice off my table and all over the lady two seats away. I felt dreadful and called for the stewardess, who arrived with lots of hardly-absorbent paper towels and between us we mopped her up. (Something to be said for the more easily manageable tabloids, I thought.) The 'recipient' was a very pleasant lady with a Halifax accent, who was remarkably tolerant and unphased by the whole episode. We started talking: she and her husband had just visited Australia to see his elderly mother.

I think I dozed occasionally. I studied the flight screen and, when over Bengal, I fantasised that I might drop down and see Helen. We were travelling at 887 km per hour, the outside temperature was -39'C, and our expected time of arrival was 6.37 pm. There were another ten hours to go, which meant that it was still only just after 8 am in the UK but was 4.10 pm here in seat D61. About an hour before landing I repaired to the loo and put on my traditional warm travel skirt and sweater.

We landed promptly, having made up the 'peanut' time with a tail wind. I was more than delighted to see Lydia of the Shuttle Service waiting at the barrier. I don't know how she and her husband cope with this business, up all hours of the day and night: she'd done the Heathrow pick-up four times this week. She said she and Bill had tossed for who should collect me, in view of the much-reported Avian Flu! The drive home was uneventful and, as usual, we talked as we went.

Back at Heronslake some time before midnight, I switched off the burglar alarm which Rachel, my voluntary house-minder, had left on having gone back to her own bed tonight, thawed out some milk and had a drink, watered some sad house plants and welcomed the feel of my own bed.

The next day I felt the need for a rice pudding, which I had not made for years, then made a lemon and lime drink, and vowed to use more fresh coriander. I had really enjoyed the food but doubted I would ever get into the way of serving the fish and meat together: that belonged to Vietnam.

A walk around found the sheep and the guinea fowl well, snowdrops out and some early black-faced lambs in a neighbour's field. Not a bad time to come back when everything is beginning again.

A PHOENIX

So you're going to Viet Nam this year
Well whatever for?
They you should pay to go that way
It's war-stricken and poor

True, I knew so little
Of this coastal strip of earth
Winding by Cambodia, Laos
To northern wider berth

But the scenery is spectacular
From mysterious Ha Long Bay
Through Hue, Perfume River
To the Me Kong Delta day

The Pagodas are enchanting
With much of red and gold
The museums thought provoking
War Remnants took a hold

On the imagination
Disturbingly well told
In pictures, stories, weapons –
So many won't grow old …

Others who've survived
Are minus limbs from mines
Or live with life deformities
From Agent Orange times

And yet this race has risen
Like a Phoenix from the ashes
Optimistic, visionary
With inspirational flashes

They know well how to work
Apparently a pleasure
It merges with quiet subtlety
Into a gentle leisure

They're such a handsome race
The women truly beautiful
As parents, so attentive
Loving, tactile, dutiful

They have a naïve charm
They help but don't intrude
They smile and ask how old you are
From them it isn't rude!

Ho Chi Minh, their hero
He's sculptured oft this man
Usually with children
(He was married to Viet Nam)

His philosophy was humane
Somewhat a Gandhi figure
Let's hope it will remain
Snuff out a current trigger

Which smacks of some corruption
With high places connection
A tempting to reform
Kowtow without objection

Change the things which need attention
The poverty, pollution
But let the people stay the same
Within the constitution

You lovely laughing people
Treasure what you've got
Don't let it be tourists like me
Can start commercial rot

January 2004   VJT

ANTARCTICA

with **NOBLE CALEDONIA**

PROLOGUE

I had made this radical decision, nearly a year ago, to spend Christmas and New Year in Antarctica and confirmed the same by paying a deposit for a holiday with `Noble Caledonia' leaving the UK on December 18th. My younger son, the only member of the family to have visited that part of the world, to give lectures on a ship as it cruised near the South Pole, had inspired my interest with his pictures and travel talk. Nevertheless, he questioned the wisdom of such a trip for his (elderly!) mother who was known to fall about for a pastime, and reminded me that it would be "slippery" and "very cold" for my arthritis.

By sheer good fortune I met a man in South Molton Parish church while attending a 'Tsunami' concert given by the Winkleigh Singers, whom I much admire. He was with a long-time lady friend of mine who introduced me as "someone who has travelled the world" - flattering but hardly true - and his immediate response was "I've just been to the Antarctic." Not only had he been there but he had taken virtually the identical trip with the same travel company! I fired him with questions and the one-to-one monopoly would have spilled into the second half of the concert, had the director not been properly disciplined over the length of the interval. My new acquaintance, Chris, was not that much younger than me I reckoned, and had a slightly halting gait, so I asked him about his joints and the low temperatures. He said he'd been as good as he ever was: it was a dry cold.

The greater part of this holiday was a cruise with excursions in zodiac craft and optional walks from the landing sites on the majority of days. I wondered about the walking and my mind went back to my last so-called 'adventure holiday' when I knew for a fact that I'd held up the rest of the (younger) party on one particular day: they'd been pleasant and forgiving but I had vowed never to do that again. Adventure holidays are comparatively cheap, travelling in small groups, cooking your own food, putting up tents etc, and this Antarctic job was costing me more than I'd ever paid for a holiday in my life, even though I was having a basic inside cabin - but the 'single' aspect always sends up the price.

Still having some qualms about the adventure, I rang the company before committing myself for the full cost. I got a "Sharon speaking, can I help you?" lady and I asked her the average age of those two hundred or so passengers travelling on 'my' trip. She was gone for ages but eventually came back apologetically with "I'm afraid they're quite senior". "Oh dear," I said wickedly, in as young a voice as I could muster, "Sixty-five to seventy!" "Thank you". At seventy-three I felt I wouldn't be that geriatric in comparison so, feeling reassured, I paid up.

Nearer the time, a suggested kit list arrived and I purchased a new pair of waterproof trousers (sufficiently large to go over thermals, silk socks, long wool socks and woollen trousers) and a couple of fleeces on special offer, bright, light, warm and easily dried. I devoured various wildlife books and guides, read a sensitive book by Jenny Dinski who was getting her own mind and life in order as she penetrated further south in the white landscape, and felt something of a wimp as I read the story of Shackleton's incredible journey over frozen wastes of land and water.

A few weeks before departure, the lady who had introduced Chris in South Molton, rang to say that, incredibly, her sister and husband, Jill and Richard, were going on the identical cruise and that we should all meet up for lunch. Then I read that a Pam Kemp was giving a morning lecture on the 'Antarctic Experience' at Rosemoor on November 1st. It seemed somewhat unusual I thought: there couldn't be many plants there, the usual subject for RHS lectures. We all attended. The lady had been to the Antarctic several times as a guide and courier and had taken some good pictures, which we enjoyed. She was also helpful about practical aspects of such an expedition. We stayed at Rosemoor for lunch and savoured the Antarctic anticipation, with helpful input from the experienced Chris: all very convivial.

The build-up to Christmas is always crowded with functions and preparations whether one is at home or away. The Barnstaple and North Devon Arts Festival took up some of my time in November. The standard of the younger competitors seemed to be getting more and more professional, as evidenced by the final cupwinners' concert at the end. I landed the cup for original poetry, again: no competition, so hardly an accolade - and then paid £10 for the engraving and £5 for a repair! I'd been involved with the Hospice since the poetry book and I went to their 'Rossetti Requiem' at the Plough in Torrington, where I was moved and enchanted, in particular by a lady who'd come straight from her chemotherapy to sing her own song, and a sculptor who'd traced in three dimensions his emotions from diagnosis of a life-threatening cancer, through treatment, to recovery. The whole experience came over as a celebration of life. This was followed later by a memorable 'Light up a Life' Christmas service in the Pannier Market. The church choir sang at the Torrington Cemetery Chapel, at the funeral of the husband of one of its members. She was a Ukrainian lady, who sang and had a store of delightful Russian folksongs, and her husband had been her UK anchor. Two elderly ladies, living in St Giles, died just before I went away: neither had been having much quality of life but a Christmas leaving always seems sadder.

I got on with the cards and presents early, noticing as I do these days that an increasing number of friends and acquaintances have left the list: all the more reason to make the best of the time that's left. There was cheerful drama from the Torrington Players with their splendid production of "The Happiest Time of Your life"; The North Devon College drama students staged an impressive "The Lion, the Witch and the Wardrobe"; the infant school gave a charming Nativity play, with a preponderance of sheep; the Barnstaple Amateur Operatic Society fulfilled their annual commitment at Meddard House, where we loved some of the audience entertainment, rehearsed and unintentional; I enjoyed an excellent lunch with the Community Development Trust at the Black Horse; and 'Torrington Together' happily inspired representatives of more than thirty different local organisations to attend their inaugural meeting.

The tenth annual 'Big Sing' with local band, choirs, clergy, mayor and speakers was held in the Pannier Market, with a good congregation and enthusiastic participation by some of the younger members. I managed to fall up the platform and rupture some superficial blood vessel on the front of my left leg. I could feel it swelling to alarming proportions as I stood there listening and singing and doing the poem: I did not go to the pub afterwards but hurried home and renewed ice packs through the night. This treatment and a crepe stocking reduced the swelling considerably, which was just as well, for this was three days before take-off. The same leg had only just healed from a lower shin injury when I carelessly fell up the steep steps at the Minack Theatre seven weeks earlier: old women's legs take for ever to heal and it was fortunate that this time there was no open wound.

When the weather had been really cold about ten days ago, I'd thought, "Do I really want to go to the Antarctic?" but mid-week it warmed up and I decided to give the grass the last cut of the year. It was quite muddy and when the machine slipped onto the rosebed, I had to drive the car across the front lawn to tow it out. As I removed my Wellingtons after this exercise, one of them split down the front. Boots are a vital part of the Antarctic kit, especially for the wet landings, and I was relieved to discover that a local tradesman now stocked this countryside footwear.

17th December 2005

I always dread the day before departure in case I think of something I must do for which there isn't time. I took my Black Labrador, Chester, and all his paraphernalia to his holiday home where he was warmly received. I had intended putting him in kennels but some friends in Beaford had persuaded me to let him stay with them, although I did wonder about the wisdom of this decision: they have a charming but distinctly neurotic spaniel, undergoing professional obedience training. Chester had sensed something was up when I gave him a good brushing and washed his bed, and had followed me round all morning, but he was happy to be left. There he would have the run of the house with a beanbag in every room: I hoped he would adapt to the Heronslake more severe routine after such indulgence.

A farmer friend (my 'agricultural advisor') would keep an eye on the sheep and a neighbour would feed the guinea fowl. I was cleaning out the fridge when my retired bread roundsman (and unpaid social worker) paid a social call. We had coffee and sat and talked for an hour.

I cleaned the floors, watered the plants and had a light meal. I then retired early to bed with the radio, only to be disturbed (although I wasn't asleep) by a thoughtful farmer's Mum to explain the movement of sheep, with lots of lights, along Stevenstone drive at the front of the house, "in case you thought anyone was stealing them." I hadn't noticed but I might have done. I thanked her.

At midnight I had a bath, changed into my travel clothes, packed the last-minute bits and pieces and forced down some toast, which I was eating when the alarm call went off. This was it! The hour had come …

ANTARCTICA
White Escape

Sunday 18th December 2005

The Shuttle Service arrived promptly at 1.50 am, driven by Clive, a pleasant chap, and we chatted freely as he drove along the empty roads, which became a bit busier as we neared Heathrow. I admired the way he coped with the new glaring lights on the approaches and knew when to ignore 'No Road' signs. Just a three-hour trip; good going.

At Terminal 2, I was allocated to a 'group' queue at Desk 49 by the Noble Caledonia representative, Angela, who was to travel with us: re-assuring. Fellow passengers looked pretty ancient (like me) and there was a preponderance of females. The coffee bar was not open so I drank my Sparkling Appletizer, which I had uncharacteristically thought to bring.

During the hour's wait for the flight to Madrid, I became acquainted with some of the passengers: Dilys, a Welsh lady with long 'blonde' hair which she got away with, in spite of being my age, and who had just done her 130th skydive; and Betsy, a gaunt and keen retired pharmacist, who insisted I put my luggage on her trolley with which, between us, we managed to bombard waiting passengers at the crowded airport. I eventually rescued my more manoeuvrable wheely version and did my own thing. We had similar tastes in music, and enjoyed choral works in particular: we each did a bit of professional name-dropping. She had upgraded for the flight so was called early to board. And a pair of retired medics – Ann, a surgeon on casualty and orthopaedics, and Bryn, a GP (retired at 55), were fun to be with. Needless to relate, we discussed the deterioration of the health service in general and of the GP in particular.

I sat next to a pleasant plump lady on the plane: she and her husband and their daughter were on their way to spend Christmas in Mexico, in the daughter's house with her own teenage family. She (the daughter) looked like a teenager herself. It was a shortish flight, made confusing by constant changing of the clocks: I can never get to grips with 'summertime' - and did I really leave Heronslake earlier today?

Madrid airport seemed pretty chaotic. I had several euros' worth of coffee and applecake with Dilys, and a Polish 'Legal Counsel/Advocate' came and joined us on the only seat available and gave us her business card. I had been allocated seat 41B on the Buenos Aires flight but a Japanese gentleman was already installed and seatbelted: 41C, the aisle seat was vacant and he seemed pleased that I agreed (and preferred) to sit there. He and his lady had little English and seemed very tired - so was I. The earlier flight had been with Iberian Airways but we were now travelling Argentinian Airlines: the stewardesses were not as smartly dressed or, more important, not very helpful, and the food uninteresting and dry: but this was a long flight so we had to make the best of it. Some time in mid-flight, a young American sitting across the aisle got up and I alerted him to the fact that dollars were literally spilling out of his back pocket. He went a bit over the top with gratitude! I dozed, took the obligatory walkabouts and we arrived late at 12.15 am.

Antarctic Escape Day (2)

Monday 19th December 2005

We waited in the bus for people and luggage to arrive: there seemed to be an awful lot of us. We were all identified and ticked off: someone was thought to be missing but they were in the second bus. A local courier with a good command of English, made all the better with her charming accent, gave us some advice about visiting Buenos Aires the next day – or, rather, later the same day. During the 45-minute trip, she identified points of interest in the city, but it was dark and my brain was not very receptive.

The Melia Hotel was spacious, warm and welcoming and I was given the (key) ticket for Room 814. It took me a little while to discover that the same bit of plastic had to be slotted in for the lights. I did a minimal tidy of the luggage, removed multiple cushions, and rolled into the kingsize bed at 3.10 am 'their' time, I think, and died till 8 am.

At 9.30 am I had a light breakfast with Dilys and then we found our way across seven-lane roads and roundabouts, and the docks, to the eco-reserve, only to discover that it was closed on a Monday. But we had a good walk and then opted for lunch in the sunshine at a restaurant which backed on to the docks. We took the opportunity to exchange life histories. Dilys had worked in education all her life, teaching movement and dancing. Since her 'retirement' she had established a school for the disabled, where her long-time skills had helped them to move more evenly and confidently and the classes had provided some sort of social life. She was a fascinating lady of energy and commitment. We ate a Mozzarella Pizza of a kind that I'd never had before - three slices each. Everyone at the restaurant, staff and clients, seemed very relaxed, as they did also in the streets as we walked back to the hotel, where we sat at the bar and had a drink.

Betsy appeared: she'd been studying the shopping options and intended to buy a leather jacket. Jean and Avis, retired headmistresses, came and chatted and then we all decided we needed a kip before going to see the Tango dancing in the evening. I enjoyed a long luxurious bath first.

The Tango dancing at a local downstairs venue was something else. Four couples made up the performance, sometimes dancing together, sometimes just a single couple. Their movements were wonderfully sharp and exact, giving the occasional impression of being double-jointed at the hips. Their performances were interspersed with songs by two excellent vocalists, a glamorous lady and a handsome man. Music was provided by an amazing group: two violins, one viola, one cello and four accordions. The leader (one of the accordion players) didn't use a note of music, wore a sparkling white jacket and had a wonderful smile like George Melly.

An enjoyable meal with wine was provided during the entertainment. I was seated opposite a man called Henry who seemed sad, dealt in agricultural machinery but was not as talkative as the Grundy's. Next to me was Tom, ex-forces, then police, and now in 'crisis management'. An interesting guy.

I was more than ready for bed at 12.45 am.

Antarctic Escape Day (3)

Tuesday 20th December 2005

I had a light breakfast – and afterwards met up with Richard and Jill who had come on a different flight, after spending the night in Madrid. I talked to Avis and Jean, and a young couple, Lyn and Andy.

There was a lot to see in the city but progress was slow on the organised coach trip and stops carefully planned, because this was a special pre-Christmas shopping day, when traffic had free parking anywhere. We saw the smart Pacifico shopping centre – we were told that this had made imaginative use of an old railway station; we drove along the prize avenue which the guide said was longer and wider than the Champs Élysée; we passed by the Opera House which seated 3000, had wonderful acoustics and its own theatre 'factory', making all the costumes and wigs; and we admired the impressive Obelisk, May Square, the blue pinnacled Russian Orthodox Church, and many magnificent statues including a comparatively modern one of many men pulling a huge boulder - said to represent success when everyone worked together. In fact, we did stop at the Cathedral, where we had a few minutes inside. There was a reverent but not austere atmosphere, lovely statues, and local worshippers praying amongst interested but respectful tourists.

As we drove round, our guide filled us in with historical facts. Buenos Aires was founded in 1526 but did not gain independence from Spain until 1816. In 1871 the population was decimated by both a serious Yellow Fever epidemic and a massacre of the Indian population, and subsequently Spanish and Italian communities were encouraged to come from Europe and regenerate the city.

We went to the Italian quarter, La Boca, north of the river and famous for its junior football team which had just had a great victory, as evidenced by all the yellow and blue flags on display. There were interesting shops and stalls selling paintings and photos. I fell for two black and white prints of a couple of street Tango dancers, and then watched it live in a square nearby. The buildings were brightly painted, many with a corrugated roof. The La Boca River flows into the Parana Delta where, with other rivers, it forms the Rio de la Plata and separates Uruguay from Argentina: 160 miles across in its widest part.

Argentina was thus named because it was originally thought to be a source of silver in the area but, in fact, it was the precious metals which came from Uruguay that were processed in Argentina. Gambling was forbidden in Argentina but was permitted on a floating casino on the river. Buenos Aires meant literally 'good air', translated as 'fair winds'. We passed an 'expensive property area' of converted warehouses, which put me in mind of Liverpool's refurbished Albert Docks. Some of the skyscrapers were of extraordinary heights and shapes. A very tall blue building was owned by a lady entrepreneur, who dealt in concrete; a strange round skyscraper was known as 'the cigarette' or the 'curler'. A shallow parabola of a building, with a flat back, looked for all the world as if a breath of wind would have blown it down. I wondered whether they ever had earthquakes here. The British Tower was pointed out to us: it was said to have bells like Big Ben but we didn't hear them.

We saw a huge flower memorial which was lit up at night, a huge fig tree, a Rose Garden viewed from the coach (cf Rosemoor), "Little Palermo", crossed wide one-way streets with several lanes, some of which changed direction at business times, and were intrigued by the dog-walking culture. Many business people lived in city flats but seemed to have such a great love of dogs that they were prepared to pay handsomely for dog-walkers to exercise and look after them during the day. Some of the minders had nine or ten dogs on leads in the park areas. There was evidently a great camaraderie between these people (some of whom earned more than teachers we were told) and they were like mothers with their babies, comparing notes. There was no doggy bag rule!

We visited the La Recoleta Cemetery, which housed 6000 mausolea, including that of Evita who died of cancer in 1952, aged 33. She had originally been secretly buried in Milan, but was then brought back to Argentina in 1974. Her mausoleum was decorated with dead 'fresh' flowers.

We were dropped back after this four-hour, fact-filled tour at 1 pm. This gave us just an hour for lunch so we made for the coffee bar upstairs where service was said to be quicker than in the restaurant. I delighted in a plate of smoked salmon topped with mushrooms and a poached egg: $a20 in local money (pesos) = $7 American: excellent value.

Erica was our guide for the afternoon tour, which started promptly at 2 pm. She talked of the Buenos Aires Province, its Delta's 21,000 sq km: the green area between the rivers was Mesopotamia (different from the similarly named in the Middle East). Many islands had been formed by the silt from the Parana River. Erica talked about local customs such as drinking 'shirtimatti' (?) which is 'better than tea'. A local girl was arrested at customs for carrying this herb, which was thought to be cannabis, but released after her flight had departed. Someone commented on the abundance of hydrangeas in flower: "If you always have them flowering in your garden, your daughter will not get married", Erica informed us. There was some suggestion that they were quickly cut back when the right man came along!

I sat by Dilys and, when Erica was not talking to us, we talked to each other. Dilys told me of the Green Tortoise bus tour she had once done across America.

We reached the landing stage from whence we were to embark on a trip up the Parana Delta. The photographer was waiting. Background information: the Delta starts to form near the city of Diamante in the province of Entre Rios and finishes in the Rio de la Plata. It is made up of over 5000 waterways and its islands are inhabited by 3000 people, working mainly to supply the pulp and paper and plywood industries. Wicker plantations supply most of the country's produce for its arts and crafts.

This was a lovely trip in pleasantly warm sunshine, on calm waters through banks of green vegetation with trees beyond, passing interesting dwellings which ranged from basic structures to really beautiful houses, many of which were second homes for wealthy business people. They were comparatively cheap to buy but costs were incurred for transport for supplies and material for barriers to be put in place, to keep surrounding territory from being washed away.

20 December 2005
LA BALA Italian Quarter, Buenos Aires

There were flamboyant butterflies, Cormorants, Shags, Egrets, and an unidentified apricot-brown thrush-sized bird. A welcome cup of tea and a crumbly snack were served on board.

The photographer had his prints at the ready. I bought one of Dilys and myself coming down the steps. One female member of our party was extremely rude to the photographer, who was not particularly pushy: all she needed to have said was that she didn't want her picture, but she went on and on in a loud harsh voice about him 'taking advantage'. Just occasionally I pretend I'm not British.

Back in the coach we were driven to a vantage point to see Buenos Aires at a distance, and Uruguay at an even greater distance on the other side of the water, but the latter was too far away to be convincing. I picked a pink bottle-brush type blossom and was informed that it was from an 'Acacia Constantinople tree'.

We returned to the hotel through heavy traffic. I settled my account, had a bath and washed my hair and packed ready for an early start in the morning.

Finally, I wrote up the diary. It had been quite a long day.

Antarctic Escape Day (4)

Wednesday 21st December 2005

I thought I'd booked an alarm call with the switchboard but nothing happened: fortunately I awoke spontaneously at 4.30 am and had my luggage all sorted with a couple of extra labels in time for the collection from outside the bedroom door at 5.30 am. I had mouth-watering croissants for breakfast with Melanie, who was in her forties I imagined. She'd been a travel guide but was now doing freelance artwork.

Angela was acting check-in and I collected my boarding pass from her - seat 19D. It was a pleasant drive to the airport, where we identified our luggage and then stood around for ages. I talked to Jean and Avis and predictably we homed in on education: they discussed the paperwork overloading and how their roles had changed during their working lives. Avis thought I was very brave to be a school governor, which immediately made me feel that maybe I wasn't as aware as I should be.

Jean had the seat number next to mine. The crowded airport bus picked us up and as we made our way slowly up the steps of the plane, a tall slim lady asked Jean and me whether we would swap seats with her and her husband. They had "been together for 51 years" and didn't like being separated at meal times. I suspect we exhibited an element of reluctance in our response …

I finished up with a window seat next to Cynthia and Chris. He had been with the Africa Rifles, I think, in his youth and then, I believe, had become a school teacher. He was a charming man and still had a military air about him. He and his Cynthia spent the summer in a campervan in Europe, and took two holidays further afield in the winter. I admitted to a touch of envy, not so much about the holidays but of their companionship. We talked of the NHS (can't escape) and private medicine. He was awaiting knee surgery and cataract removal. Yes, we're mostly pretty senior!

I couldn't make out why Richard was walking up and down in an agitated fashion before we actually took off: it transpired that he and Jill had been allocated non-existent seats, but it was eventually sorted out through Angela's intervention. We had an enjoyable late breakfast-brunch during the flight. By mid-day the terrain had become very bare and cold-looking as we came down to a barren-seeming little airport, somewhere in Patagonia, to let off a few passengers and pick up replacements. I took a couple of pictures before we landed.

There was a fair bit of bird talk (feathered variety) in front of me. One man (whom I think I identified later as Martin) appeared to be giving a tutorial to Tom, standing in the aisle, and then a sizeable man called Ted, with an impressive crop of white hair, came and joined the bird name-dropping discussion.

I think it was about now that Angela informed us that the cruise itinerary had been changed and we were going 'the other way round', so that we would visit the Falklands first, and then South Georgia, before going south to Antarctica: it was all to do with re-fuelling. I didn't know enough to judge whether this was good or bad news but some of the others got very worked up about it, deducing that less time would be spent further south. Time will tell.

In Ushuaia, the southernmost city of the world, at the extreme tip of South America (El Fin del Mundo) we were taken on a tour, aware of the spectacular backdrop of the mountains and the Beagle Channel running in front of us to the south. We drove up a winding road through forests of Nothofagus Trees, which looked more like beeches than the oaks to which they were related. We took photos from a high vantage point and admired the brightly painted houses and the ubiquitous lupins. We visited a splendid tourist souvenir shop but I didn't add anything to my luggage. I was tempted at the sight of a carved photoframe with 'holes' for eleven grandchildren, but it was large and fragile.

British Christian missionaries had come to convert the Indians in the 1800s and some of their descendants were still here, having been given land outside the town and known as 'little England'. Our guide said they were not really integrated and were connected with the tourist business.

We were taken to Explorer II, where our luggage awaited us. I'd been 'upgraded' from B7 to A7 and I imagined I might have a porthole. (I'd been too mean to pay the considerable extra.) But no, it was just one deck higher – nonetheless, very comfortable, and would have taken two persons so I had plenty of room.

A few of us sat and had tea together and had a brief introduction, followed by an emergency drill with lifejackets, having managed to find our way to the lounge. I unpacked, changed, and we all reassembled for an introduction to the Expedition staff by Cruise Director, Jannie Cloete, a charismatic man with an alluring South African accent. Suzana Machado D'Oliveira, an attractive blond Brazilian lady, our Expedition Leader, spoke next. She was equally compelling, and the passion, enthusiasm and experience of the entire Expedition team was impressive and exciting. We'd arrived!

For dinner in the main dining room, I sat with Jean, Dilys, Avis, Tony and Paul. We were all very relaxed, had good conversation and plenty of laughter. It was an excellent meal - melon with port, pumpkin soup with ginger and honey, salmon, and strudel.

I walked outside round the boat, which had moved off at 8 pm, and saw some gulls and a tern, although not sure which varieties.

Antarctic Escape Day (5)

Thursday 22nd December 2005

I slept well but felt I could have slept forever. We'd been travelling the infamous Drake Passage overnight and I'd wondered whether I should take a sea-sickness dose, but as I'd never been affected by rough seas I'd decided against it - but we had been warned this could be very different. However, it was said to have been as quiet as it ever is, with calm seas, blue skies and hardly any wind: we were lucky, but not through it yet. I went downstairs to Reception and changed the splendid red complimentary parka jacket for a smaller one - having tried the original over the required layers, and found it uncomfortably bulky.

I enjoyed a good selection of fresh fruit (including pineapple) for breakfast and then went to hear the first Enrichment Lecture, 'Seabirds of the Southern Ocean', given by Patricia Silva, a charming Uruguayan lady, and an artist of some renown in addition to being a well-qualified experienced biologist. She spoke about the tube-noses, a group of birds which includes the Albatrosses and the Petrels. Their nostrils are in tubes on the upper hooked half of the beak: Petrels have one such, Albatrosses have two. She had some wonderful slides to illustrate her talk. She talked of the huge, long-lived Wandering Albatross, the Northern (black tip to the head) and Southern Giant Petrels: they have no natural predators (cats have been eradicated from Ascension Island). The Grey-headed Albatross has a tremendous flight path and can fly for days without stopping.

The fact that such long and arduous journeys are made prompts the question "Why?" Answer: (1) Food - krill in particular (2) Protection (back to no predators), and (3) Phylopatra - that I presume is something to do with home territory, where the family has always been for breeding etc. But there wasn't time for Patricia to finish or for any of us to ask questions because the siren went and Captain Moulds announced that there were whales all around the ship. Michael Schmid, the resident marine mammologist, said there were Sei and Fin Whales. The Sei Whales, fast swimmers, (which I can't honestly say I was convinced that I saw) left us quickly, but the Fin stayed around for some minutes, surfacing their huge bodies lugubriously and giving the occasional vertical blow. The conditions were just perfect to follow and to photo. The ship was said to be making good time.

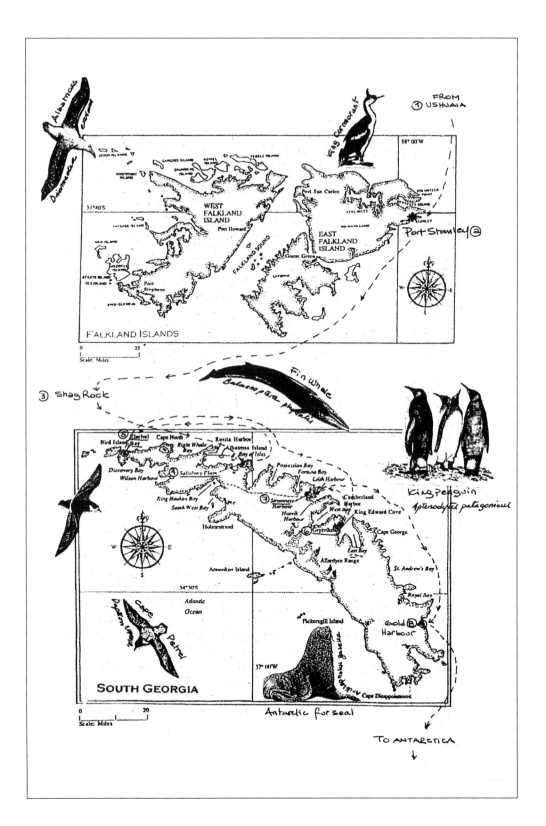

Albatross Diomedea exulans

Shag Cormorant

FROM ① USHUAIA

58° 00'W

51°40'S

WEST FALKLAND ISLAND

Port Howard

FALKLAND SOUND

Port San Carlos

EAST FALKLAND ISLAND

Goose Green

Port Stephens

Port Stanley ②

FALKLAND ISLANDS

0   25
Scale: Miles

Fin Whale
Balaenoptera physalus

③ Shag Rock

⑤ Elsehul Bay   Cape North   Rosita Harbor
Bird Island   Right Whale Bay   Albatross Island
Discovery Bay   ④ Salisbury Plain   Bay of Isles
Wilson Harbor   Possession Bay   Fortuna Bay   Leith Harbor
King Haakon Bay   ⑦ Stromness Harbour   Cumberland Harbor   West Cliff   King Edward Cove
South West Bay   Husvik Harbour   Grytviken   Cape George
Holmestrand   East Bay
Annenkov Island   Allardyce Range   St. Andrew's Bay
Royal Bay

54°30'S   Atlantic Ocean

Cape Petrel Daption capensis

57° 18'W   Pickersgill Island   Gold Harbour ⑥

Cape Disappointment

King Penguin
Aptenodytes patagonicus

SOUTH GEORGIA

0   20
Scale: Miles

Antarctic fur seal   Arctocephalus gazella

TO ANTARCTICA
↓

We were summoned to the lounge for Suzana's briefing on the use of the zodiacs, and Carol's modelling of the proper clothing and use of the life vests (a version of the life jacket for trips ashore). The sky fanned with light clouds. Dolphins were spotted in the distance by some (not me) and more whales, even further away. I realised I hadn't seen Dilys for a while and she had complained of feeling queasy: she was very sensibly lying down and coping OK.

I had a lunch of soup (the soups were really good), fresh fruit, cheese and an orange sweet. I went out on deck afterwards: I love the pretty little Cape Petrels (easily identified) of which there were plenty, weaving in and out over the ship's wake, together with Giant Petrels and Black-browed Albatross. There were some comparatively tiny birds, which one of the experts said were Wilson's Storm petrels.

The Expedition team gave "An Introduction to Port Stanley and the Falklands", each participant giving us the benefit of their particular expertise. The botany interested me in particular, not much of it really, but the tufted grass, which grows so slowly, is substantial enough to provide an environment for birds and insects, and even gives shelter for the seals to lurk behind.

I showered (how I missed my bath) and changed, ready for Captain's night. He introduced key members of the ship's staff, which was very international, and spoke like a professional. There seemed to be a great camaraderie between them. For dinner I sat with Jill, Richard, Robin, Libby, Jean, Avis and Betsy. Super company, super meal: lobster, strawberries, blackberries and cherries with excellent mint. And then to bed, at 11.30 pm.

Antarctic Escape Day (6)

Friday 23rd December 2005

I awoke 'Alongside Port Stanley' - so said the voice that came over the Tannoy at 7 am. I had breakfast with Melanie and heard about her extraordinary medical history. I had opted to go on the Long Island farm excursion and see the Falklands sheep. We bussed along reasonable roads for most of the way, with views of rocky bare terrain, by spectacular clumps of golden gorse and 'rivers' of stones, with a backdrop of low mountains. A small plantation of Alaska Pines was indicated, but the growth was so slow on this windy, unprotected island that such ventures were more likely to be a source of interest than of income.

The Watsons at the farm were very welcoming. Neil was a sixth generation islander and Glenda a fourth generation islander. The farm comprised 23000 acres and was run on traditional lines, the sheep being rounded up by Neil and family on Falklands-bred horses. We watched the cutting of peat (which, among other uses, was fuel for the Rayburn in the kitchen) and then went to see the splendid sheep. Neil explained that, over the years, Merino and Romney Marsh sheep had been introduced into the breeding stock. They looked good solid beasts, not that tall, and with a very soft, long-stapled fleece: not unlike Devon Longwools really. We watched a couple being

23 December 2005

FALKLAND SHEEP   East Falkland Island

sheared and then went into the kitchen for calorific super snacks, some of the sweet ones being served with generous helpings of clotted cream. Glenda talked of the trying period during the war in the early eighties when the children were very young. It must have been very difficult terrain to defend: long, wide sweeps of open bare countryside: no trees to hide behind. Neil had planted one Palm tree that had survived, and he took great pains to point it out. He demonstrated the saddling of his twenty-five-year-old horse, which was invaluable for his shepherding.

There was a stretch of water some distance away but we could identify Grey-billed Crested Ducks, Upland Geese and a Night Heron. Neil revealed that sheep farming was not what it once was, but together with their tourist input, they made a living. The main source of Falklands' income these days came from fishing. The 200-mile radius round the island was well policed, and Mullet was caught in inland waters. The Watsons came over like 'real' farmers anywhere: hard working, genuine people, who loved the traditional way of life on the land. Some oil exploration is going on.

Back in the town, Dilys and I visited Christ Church Cathedral – it was one of those places of worship that almost spoke of the loving care it received. A very pleasant gentleman, a comparatively recent resident on the island, showed us round. Outside we studied the enormous whalebone arch, made of the jawbones of two Blue Whales.

We felt hungry and, after all the wonderful exotic food we'd enjoyed, fancied fish and chips, which we ate in the Globe Tavern. They went down well, to the accompaniment of an extraordinary Rock video! We returned, as directed, to the Jetty Visitor Centre where a tender collected us for the Explorer, which had changed position in order to refuel from the supply ship.

Supper was taken with Bryn and Ann, Tom, Dilys, Doreen and Liz (mother and daughter) - we had crab, pork, and ice cream. Chantal played superbly again in the Shackleton Lounge. Anything she didn't know, she could sight read at the drop of a hat. What a talent, and she always looked so lovely.

Antarctic Escape Day (7)

Saturday 24th December 2005 - Christmas Eve

Dilys called at 8 am. She was really feeling herself again: I wasn't up. I went back to bed till 9 am. Drake Passage was still amazingly calm, sun shining, and blue skies. I had a quick breakfast and went along to Tim Baughman's "The Imperial Trans-Antarctic Expedition". What a man. He was Professor of History at the University of Central Oklahoma but that does not tell you of his talent as a storyteller. The only visual aid he used was himself, and he took us with Shackleton, somehow making Shackleton's passion and enthusiasm his own and transmitting it to us. One of the most brilliant presentations I've ever heard. He had me (and many others) in tears.

I tried, unsuccessfully, to send e-mails to the family - and that nearly had me in tears as well.

After a restorative cappuccino, I attended the second lecture of the day, "Plate tectonics and continental drift: How Antarctica came to the South Pole", given by geologist Henry Pollack, Professor of Geophysics at the University of Michigan. He had lots of illustrations of the changes in the world map, seabed pictures, eruptions etc. and explained how the earth's crust moved about the globe, carrying continents to new locations over millions of years. Earthquakes and volcanoes were the visible signs of this process. I marvelled how anyone came to understand all these phenomena, which happened so slowly and so long ago. I found it mind-boggling but very interesting.

I went outside on the Verandah Deck to clear my head. I walked around and talked to David and Kay (lovely Irish accent), a pleasant couple who had recently retired to Cambridge. I was joined by Tony, whom I did not recognize at first in his disguise of a hat. I went into lunch almost reluctantly, in the Verandah Restaurant, and sat with Ron and Betty. We had an excellent roast lamb (almost as good as Heronslake - with a more interesting sauce!) Robin came and talked to us. We covered the Argentine, the

23 December 2005

EXPLORER II's LOVELY PIANIST - CHANTAL

Falklands War and other topics of great import, all in fifteen minutes. He accused me of 'stirring it', which was quite untrue.

At 2.15 pm I was sitting out on deck in the sun again, with Jean and Avis; it was unbelievably hot, and I took off my jacket.

At 3 pm marine biologist Michael Schmid gave his "Furry Divers in icy waters - Seals of the Southern Ocean". I was looking forward to the Fur Seals and Elephant Seals in South Georgia at the very least. It was hard to imagine that Elephant Seals weighing up to 5 tons could dive so deeply. An Hourglass Dolphin (Porpoise?) was seen from the deck and I got a good view, even if I wasn't sure what it was! At last I managed to send an e-mail, successfully, to Wendy and co, assisted by Jill, Tom and Angela. I got the bill for this exercise - and another sent for New Year, together with scripts - under the cabin door, but in fact the e-mails never reached them.

At 5 pm there was a mandatory briefing by Suzana on the International Association of Antarctic Touring Organisations (IAATO) explaining the guidelines for going ashore, and behaviour in South Georgia and Antarctica. Lot of lectures - that's what you get for being at sea all day.

6.30 pm saw me at dinner with Bryn, Ann, Dilys, Tony, John and Paul: a festive affair with the crew singing Christmas carols during our dessert. (Ann didn't feel too well and departed to her cabin.) The Captain, Officers and Expedition staff then served the crew their Christmas dinner in the Verandah restaurant. Chantal played carols and old songs in the Shackleton Bar and most of us sang our hearts out.

It was a memorable Christmas Eve. I stayed up late with a few, drank Baileys and put the world to rights. It was probably a mistake because watches went on an hour.

Antarctic Escape Day (8)

Sunday 25th December 2005 - Christmas Day

I awoke slowly and made it to Chris Hill's talk "Tales from Bird Island: my experiences on South Georgia whilst working with the British Antarctic Survey." Chris was a Scottish bio-geographer, amongst other things, and he seemed very happy to have his girlfriend Fiona with him on this trip. His main work on Bird Island was with the Wandering Albatross and in his talk he combined the interesting research data with a background of the lifestyle of living in such unusual circumstances for so long.

At 10.30 am I went to the cinema to take part in a Christmas service put together by Jean Darlow: readings, prayers, carols - played by Chantal, with a solo by a lovely young girl who was doing a degree in music and having lessons at the Royal College. It was just right for the morning, somehow, and I was glad Jean had had the courage and experience to put it into practice. At 11 am (no peace for the wicked) it was "Penguins of the Falkland Islands and South Georgia", by Patricia Silva. It was to be Rockhoppers in the Falklands and Macaronis in South Georgia, and we could also expect to see King

Penguins, Gentoos, Chinstraps and Adelies. Patricia was great: her accent and her requests to the audience for correction to her English and her pronunciation added to the enjoyment and the humour.

We went on deck for a while, when whales were spotted - first by Jill, and then announced by the Captain: we had a good view of two of them: they seemed enormous. They were Southern Right Whales, named thus by the whalers because they floated conveniently on the water after they'd been killed, thus making them easier to cut up than some. (This exciting sighting cancelled the 'recap and briefing'!). At 5 pm Peter Zika talked on "Polar Plants - adaptation to life in the cold." Peter was a botanist at the University of Washington and his illustrated talk dealt with slow adaptation and growth, symbiosis and interactions with animals.

Christmas night's dinner was enjoyed with Richard, Jill, Ray, yet another Jean, Peggy and Peter. And, no, I didn't have the turkey. I had the lobster again – I can't get that at home! It was the most unusual Christmas I've ever had or am ever likely to have. I'd loved it.

Antarctic Escape Day (9)

Monday 26th December 2005 - Boxing Day

I got up at the 6.15 am early morning call, ready for going ashore at Salisbury Plain on the north coast of South Georgia, between two glaciers in the Bay of Isles. We were warned that it was colder, with overcast skies, and that the landing would be rough. I layered up and had trouble with the life-vest for some unknown reason. We then waited for the zodiac and had a bumpy run to the shore and a distinctly wet landing.

We had this incredible amble along the shore to the 'rookery' (I'd never heard that term for anything but 'rooks' before). Our path was surrounded by Fur seals, young ones romping in and out of the surf, tiny dark babies whining for their mothers, and grand aggressive males guarding their harems and their territory from intruders such as ourselves. Naturalist staff fended them off as we walked by. The Elephant seals were large and laid back and one outsized male gave a noisy, very smelly, disapproving belch from behind a large clump of tussock grass.

The place was positively crowded with King Penguins: there were said to be around 80,000 in the colony, the first real study having been made in the early 20th century by an American ornithologist, Robert Cushman Murphy, who named one of the Bay of Isles glaciers 'Grace', after his new wife. Maybe this honour was instead of a honeymoon!

Most of us just stood and listened to and watched the penguins. Some of the adults fed their chicks, others shuffled around with their precious egg tucked away under the brood pouch. Their smart markings and stately bearing somehow gave the impression of class, even if they were all living cheek by jowl in the biggest commune ever. The chicks were all woolly and cuddly, looking as if they were wearing brown fur coats. One or two looked comical with just a thick fur necklace left to shed. We kept to the edge of the colony but some of them approached us inquisitively, putting their heads on one side, probing and making matching sounds.

A dead Fur seal was being devoured by a Giant Petrel. This was a photographer's paradise, even for an amateur, and I couldn't believe that halfway along the beach my digital started registering 'card full'. I desperately deleted some of the less good pictures as we walked along, and then the battery packed up. I had thought to bring my 'ordinary' little camera which I managed to extract from an inside pocket. This was a once-in-a- lifetime opportunity not to be missed. It was very cold and we were glad of a hot drink after the rough ride back.

I removed some of the layers, sorted the cameras (the 'ordinary' one now needed a fresh battery as well) and then went up on deck, where I listened to Tony's life history, including the sad recent loss of his wife. The Explorer II moved on, the wind was very cold now, but this didn't interfere with an impressive seal-leaping display or the delight at seeing more icebergs: one of which looked for all the world like a marquee with an entrance at one end.

After a lunch of soup, fruit and cheese, I had a brief kip while we left the Bay of Isles and went north again as far as Elsehul, a bay near the north-west tip of the island and opposite Bird Island, where Chris had worked. Here we had a long zodiac tour and saw seals, Light-mantled Sooty Albatross, Grey-headed Albatross, a community of Black-browed Albatross nesting along the cliffs, Antarctic Terns, Snowy Sheathbills and Elephant Seals of all sizes. It was rough but great, and I felt that this was what it should be like really in this part of the world, even if it was a bit uncomfortable. The crew at the gangway did a wonderful job getting everyone in and out of the zodiacs safely. They inspired confidence.

It was 6.45 pm by the time we got back so it was quick change in time for briefing. Chris illustrated the Fur seal behaviour by using Mike and JJ and some of the youngsters, who all rose to the occasion with their acting skills.

Supper - with Robin, Tony, Betsy, Angela, Avis and Jean – involved delicious Sea Bass.

Antarctic Escape Day (10)

Tuesday 27th December 2005

I had a 7.00 am call (my room was too hot: I couldn't find how to bring down my temperature, apart from sleeping in the altogether). We had anchored at Grytviken in the shelter and stunning beauty of Cumberland Bay, halfway down the north east side of the island. Grytviken itself had the appearance of a rusting, abandoned whaling station, which was just what it was. In 1904 a Norwegian Captain Carl Larsen had set up the first whaling station in South Georgia, incorporated in Buenos Aires but run by Norwegian whalers. Many other companies moved into the area as whale stocks diminished in other parts of the world, but the shore-based whaling stations

27 December 2005
**Sir Ernest Shackleton's ship 'Endurance' beset in the Weddell Sea
(Scott Polar Research Institute picture)**

were gradually phased out in the 1920s when they were replaced by factory whaling ships and pelagic (open ocean) whaling. The last whaling station in South Georgia closed in 1965.

At 8.00 am we were being zodiac-ed to shore and, after an easy landing, our first stop was at the graveside of Sir Ernest Shackleton, where Tim Baughman led us in a toast to "The Boss". Shackleton had died aboard his "Quest" in January 1922, just six years after his heroic rescue of the "Endurance" crew. A humbling moment.

The church was an attractive, well-preserved building, built in 1913 and restored in the 1990s, full of memorabilia including a handsome bust of Carl Larsen. The museum was in the old manager's quarters, beyond the rusting buildings and machinery. The exhibits reminded us once again of the basic lifestyle of the hard-working whalers. The building also included a shop where I bought some wonderful bird photograph post cards, (just in case the cameras failed) and a couple of tea towels. Green mosses and lichens made spaces of colour between the patches of snow, and I was surprised by clumps of dandelions that, together with other plants, were a legacy from the whaling industry.

By the time we were returning, a couple of the younger guests were arriving to be married in the church. They said it had been less complicated to organise than a wedding in the UK. The island's lady Registrar officiated in the private ceremony and then the bride, in a lovely wedding dress and silver long coat with fur collar and matching hat, and her new husband, were whisked back to Explorer II in a balloon-decorated zodiac. The sun shone from the bluest of skies. Nevertheless it was cold and we were glad of the hot drinks on offer when we boarded.

Shortly after our return there was a 'man overboard' exercise for the crew. The rescuing of the headless dummy seemed somewhat protracted: moral - don't fall overboard. I sat on the verandah for a while and talked to Peter (a retired dentist) and Jan (a nurse) who had become fed up with the health service (here we are again!) and had opened a series of nursing/care homes for people with psychiatric problems, which were fulfilling a need and making them a living. They planned to retire soon and their sons were to take over the business: what a positive story.

I had lunch in the verandah bar with Jim (camera man), Dilys and Jean. I talked to Tom afterwards. He had a weird, stumping gait which I suspected resulted from some kind of spinal injury, but it didn't stop him from having a go, and succeeding, at any physical test which presented itself on this trip; a man of substance. It seemed he had recently been left on his own and there were times when he just sat and looked sad and didn't want to talk. He brought out my maternal instincts and I would have liked to have given him a hug - but of course I didn't. I just felt rather helpless.

By mid-afternoon we had sailed further north, to the old Stromness whaling station in Stromness Bay. Here some of the fitter travellers hiked up to see the famous waterfall down which Shackleton and his men slid at the end of their 16-month ordeal of a journey over the pack ice. I opted for the zodiac tour: I knew my limitations. This was a good trip with a chance to view the whole area of breathtaking scenery, as well as

27 December 2005

**King Penguins in front of abandoned vessels
'ALBATROSS' and 'DIAS' - aground at Grytviken Whaling Station**

(photographer unknown)

to identify Pintail Ducks, Antarctic Terns, and Giant Petrels. Reindeer were visible on the hillside (legacy from those imported for meat by the whalers) and the beach was littered with Fur Seals, a couple of blond ones (not albino, we were told) stood out conspicuously among the rest.

It started to snow - what big flakes - and by the time we were climbing out of the zodiac, my face felt totally detached. I should have invested in a Balaclava.

I dined with Dilys, Eve, Lisa, Elspeth and Mike and we had a particularly entertaining time. Robin came over and told us we were the noisiest table!

We retired to bed early as we had been told of the very early start in the morning. The passengers were divided into "my" Endurance group (a red dot on the credit-card-like boarding pass), and the Discovery group (a green dot). Each group comprised about half the passengers and the groups alternated their disembarkation times. The green dots were first, at 3.30 am in the morning at Gold Harbour, and the red dots would be called at 5.30 am - early enough!

Antarctic Escape Day (11)

Wednesday 28th December 2005

No-one (not even me) could sleep through the wake-up calls. Suzana did them, with the first "good morning" in a husky low sexy voice, followed by a higher-pitched warning that the green (today) group would be disembarking into the zodiacs at the specified time. I lay awake until it was time for the red group to get up.

It was cold, and snowing those very large flakes, but it was still possible to appreciate the beauty of Gold Harbour on the east coast, near the south of the island. The beach had a backdrop of huge mountains and the harbour had Bertrab Glacier at its head.

Walking along the beach was just a fantastic experience. Great Elephant Seals were heaped together emitting loud explosive noises, and a couple of them were sparring in preparation for the adult real thing. The light-grey baby Elephant Seals were scattered everywhere, regarding us with their big, dark, liquid eyes, and nuzzling up if we stood still. Two of the human children bonded with a group of babies: lovely to watch and something those fortunate youngsters will remember for ever.

Scavenging Snowy Sheathbills tripped nimbly about, between young penguins being fed and a Giant Albatross that was hacking away at a half-eaten seal carcass.

The King Penguin colony was crowded with the brown, woolly-coated chicks whistling softly for their parents' attention and creating, with the parents' harsher calls and the noises from the seals, an absolute cacophony that I shall never forget. We'd been prepared for the smell but once we'd landed I had hardly noticed it. (It didn't seem nearly as powerful as that emitted from a small colony of Galapagos Penguins, but then it was warm there). The King Penguins had the stance of executives near to

King Penguin Family
GOLD HARBOUR   SOUTH GEORGIA

the few Gentoos. A lonely Chinstrap looked singularly out of place. So many photo opportunities and no obvious camera problems that morning.

I enjoyed a late, light breakfast with David, Kay and Libby.

Mid-morning Henry Pollack was lecturing in the main lounge on "The Antarctic Treaty: an international governance success story". I felt sleepy and opted to watch it on the screen in my room. Consequently I dozed off and to my shame missed some of it, but what I did hear seemed to indicate an impressive and increasing cooperation between many countries.

In the afternoon, Marco Favero, the Assistant Expedition Leader, an Argentinian marine biologist with eighteen summer Antarctic expeditions under his belt - amongst other things - gave his presentation "Albatross - we have a problem! A look at the long line fishing and the problems it creates". All the seabirds, but especially the Albatross, (the Snowy Sheathbill is the only landbird in the vicinity) are naturally attracted to the fishing gear and the fish it catches and Marco gave us alarming statisics as to the number of birds killed in this manner. Research was looking into recyclable Bait-Setting Capsules (BSC) as a possible solutiion.

At 5 pm the 're-cap' included a puppet dialogue between an Elephant Seal and a Fur Seal, and then a penguin dummy piece by Carol, a superb naturalist and one-time vet to boot.

I had a supper/dinner with Jill and Richard, Pascale (the very lively French lady with a wonderful accent) and her husband Chris, and Libby. And later I sat in the bar drinking Baileys and talking to a slightly happier Tom, the bridal couple, and Bryn. Watches were being put back an hour tonight, so there was no sense of urgency.

Antarctic Escape Day (12)

Thursday 29th December 2005

Today was an 'at sea' day so there were lectures.

The first was by the charming Patricia, artist, photographer, as well as everything else, and author of 'Birds in Tuxedos - the Life of Penguins'. She had wonderful pictures. She told us that The Emperor and Adelie lived only in the Antarctic, that they had short, flat wings but could 'fly' under water and that they had a good sense of smell. They were bi-colour: with distinguishing marks on the head, and laid one egg.

The Pygoscelis family was brush-tailed, laid two eggs of different sizes, and included Chinstrap, Adelie and Gentoo. Eudyptes were the crested penguins, such as the Rockhopper and Macaroni. Aptenodytes were large and impressive, such as the King and Emperor Penguins that carried the single egg. I got a bit carried away with Patricia's unique delivery and her pictures, and failed to take enough notes but there's plenty to read in Tony Soper's 'Antarctica, a Guide to the Wildlife'.

I went up on deck and had a chat with Fiona, Chris's girlfriend. She was working in research in Cambridge so I guessed they didn't see much of each other. Rumour had had it that they were the couple to be married on South Georgia.

Tim Baughman took the stage again for his "The last expedition of Edward Wilson and Captain Scott". With his usual compelling style, he named all the members of that expedition, talked of their personalities, what they contributed, their strengths, their weaknesses, but what came over most powerfully was their unselfishness and tolerance, and their ability to work as a team, making allowances for their differences when it was needed. At the time of typing this, I had already ordered the book he recommended, 'Pilgrims of the Ice', which told this story. Yet again there were few dry eyes in the lounge by the time he'd finished.

After I'd had lunch, I took a walk round the deck, spotted some birds including prions (with help) and then went to the cinema in time for a showing of 'March of the Penguins' - well-timed. These were the Emperor Penguins (which we would not be seeing). I thought the photography was superb and the commentary OK. What a hard life these birds have: only the toughest survive, and as the Antarctic gets warmer and the ice less, one wonders whether nature will provide some way of adapting.

At 5 pm Karen von Juterzenka, a German biologist with an impressive list of related posts and experience, gave "Arctic - Antarctic: a comparison: if Polar Bear meets Penguin what would they say?" She reckoned they'd probably compare the marine habitat of the north and south Polar regions. The Arctic was surrounded by land masses, whereas the boundary of the Antarctic was defined by the Antarctic Convergence. She talked of the transporter shelf, sea ice, glacier ice, and the survival of sea cucumbers, brittle stars, gigantic isopods and the all-important krill. Polar Bears would not survive in the Antarctic because of the continental drift. They lived on pack ice that disappeared in the Antarctic summer. The Arctic Tern had the best of both Poles and flew all the way down to the Antarctic. I found Karen a bit difficult to follow at times because of her very strong accent.

Afterwards I had a cappuccino and talked to Tony. We went out on deck again to view some huge icebergs; one was like a great stage, another was tall and thin and strangely waisted.

At 7 pm we returned to the lounge for the "Liars' Club", with a team made up of four of the expedition team when they indulged in a 'Call my Bluff' exercise, which was very clever and great fun.

Supper was with Bryn and Ann, Jean, another Tom - an ex-marine, naturalist, ace zodiac driver and member of an expedition team, and Russ who was excellent entertainment. Was there anything he hadn't done?

And so to bed, at 11 pm.

Antarctic Escape Day (13)

Friday 30th December 2005

The Scotia Sea had continued calm during the night but the Explorer II had had to backtrack for a while to avoid thick ice floes, so we had lost some time. I mused about the judgement and expert decisions having to be made by the Captain and crew at all hours of the day and night: it was easy to take it all for granted. A blanket of fog surrounded the ship and the world seemed suddenly very small - just as far as the eye could see.

Henry Pollack started the day with his "Geology of Antarctica - A blanket of ice wih a few surprises beneath". His bald head was shining under the lights of the lounge until they were extinguished ready for his slides. He talked of there being no north or south to Antarctica, just the older east (where coal had been found) and the younger, narrower west, which included the Continental Shelf and veins of copper. These were separated by the Transantarctic Mountains, and the South Pole (10,000 ft.) was to the left (west) of centre. The sea ice doubled the size of Antarctica. It was around 3' thick and the weight of ice had depressed the crust of the earth.

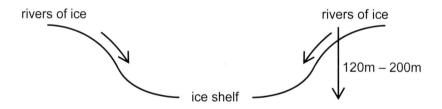

"Fragments" broke off, for example, 40' across by 20' down, and this was only the 'tip of the iceberg'. The Larsen Shelf lay to the east of the Peninsula. The ice shelf was added to each year, forming striations not unlike those in a tree. Rocks could be rafted by the sea, indicating the presence of a continent somewhere nearby.

Vostok, the Russian research station in East Antarctica, was specialising in devising drilling techniques to look for mineral deposits, and to reach the lake under the ice shelf, which may harbour ancient life (possibly bacteria) of 15 - 20 million years ago. The method must be without contamination: a sort of plunge method, where only the central core will be analysed.

During his talk Henry Pollack reminded us that the sun goes 'round' rather than 'up and down', and he described the seasonal growth and shrinkage of the sea ice, the huge pile of ice on the continent itself, and the slow flow of the continental ice to the sea.

At mid-morning, Michael Schmid lectured again, this time on "Whales of the Southern Ocean". He told us that these mammals had a gestation period varying from 10 to 16 months and were born feet first. They could communicate over amazing distances, and he compared these ultrasonic skills to those of bats. Although they were mammals, they were totally adapted to life in the sea, being a hairless fish shape covered with insulating blubber, with a nose on top of the head, with forefeet as paddles, and the tail becoming a horizontal fluke.

He talked of the Southern Right Whale with its V-shaped blow. It never came into land and seemed to avoid ships – possibly as a species it had some memory of whaling when many thousands were killed. They were easy to process at sea because (unlike others) they did not sink, which is how they came by their name. They could be identified individually by barnacle patterns on the head. Research in open waters was done in sailing ships. International Whale Conservation was founded only 20 years ago. Harpoons were very bad news for whales - 175,000 were killed in South Georgia.

The whales' value was in (1) the blubber, (2) the fat from cooking the meat, (3) the whale meat for animals, (4) the teeth as souvenirs, and (5) whalebone for corsets.

Several whale species travel south to feed in the Antarctic summer. The baleen or whalebone whales (Blue, Fin, Right, Humpback and Minke) feed on Krill and plankton, filtering through a series of baleen plates, whereas toothed whales (Sperm, Orcas, Dolphins and Beaked) are predators.

Orca - "overgrown dolphin' - patrol the beaches in groups: go for flippers: 'spy hops'.

The Fin Whale head is strangely dark on the left side and light on the right.

Peale's and Commerson's (Hourglass) Dolphins – these are common species in Falkland waters, north of the Convergence.

The Blue Whale is the largest.

The Humpback Whale (Michael Schmid called these 'buggers' and said it as if part of ordinary conversation) – has a small fin on a raised hump, made to look bigger by arching of the back, spectacular breaching, a long flipper, swims on the side, a bushy blow.

The Minke Whale – the fin surfaces with the blow, smallest of whales. Doesn't show fluke when it dives.

On reading this through, it seems like a series of disjointed facts but many of the points did help identification when out on the freezing deck.

A final gem - "dolphins are always whales: whales are not always dolphins".

After lunch I went on deck for a while but it was still pretty foggy so I went to the library and enjoyed reading Jerri Nielsen's 'Ice Bound', the moving story of her battle for survival with breast cancer when isolated at the South Pole.

The afternoon lecture (we were on another day at sea so there were extra talks) was by Peter Zika, the Washington naturalist - "Island Biogeography". He said that such biogeography was affected by the size of the island, the temperature, the rainfall, its vertical relief, access, isolation etc, and was also related to the movement of animals: the Antarctic wolf had walked from the Falklands to South America before the land masses were separated. Because of its extreme isolation the Antarctic had only two native plants, whereas Madagascar, because of its warm temperatures, oceanic currents etc, had 10,000 endogenous species.

Another relevant factor involved was the adaptation to environment - the salt and pepper moth became darker in industrial areas so as to increase camouflage when settling on deposit on trees. It has now become lighter again in order to match the cleaner bark of the non-industrial era. Hawaiian Honeycreepers have adapted to conditions in different islands, in the same way as did Darwin's Finches in the Galapogos Islands.

Additionally, flowers and plants can co-evolve to their mutual advantage, for example: 'curved beaks' <--> 'curved flowers'.

Other examples of evolving species:

    Flightless birds - on an island north of Madagascar
                the Dodo
                a flightless wren on Stephen Island, between the north and south
                Islands of New Zealand: a perching bird, with no predators, and
                carried by the wind.
    Some moths have also become flightless for the same reasons.

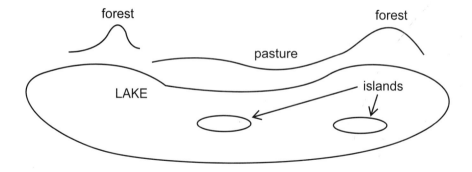

Biological islands

That evening I bought a light-weight black skirt and a hair scarf for the New Year's Eve reception on the morrow. The wool version had had a good innings.

Suzana talked about tomorrow and explained the zig-zag route the ship had been forced to take during the night because of the ice flows around it. At one stage it had sailed into a cul-de-sac and altogether had lost four hours.

We had a distant view of Elephant Island but, because of the delay, there had not been time to land. Sad.

I had supper with Elspeth and Mike, Dilys, Kevin (a Yorkshire coach driver with a warming North country accent) and his wife Elaine, a local government officer.

Antarctic Escape Day (14)

Saturday 31st December 2005

I gave a wry smile as I read the quote heading the day's Expedition Notes, from Harry Darlington, chief pilot on Finn Ronne's 1946 Antarctic Research Expedition: 'It's just that there are some things women don't do. They don't become Pope or President or go down to the Antarctic" … !

I awoke at 6.30 am and got up and had a glass of milk and a couple of croissants with Tony and Paul. We had arrived at Half Moon Island, which lies at the entrance to Half Moon Bay on the eastern side of Livingston Island, home of the Chinstraps, who greeted us as we stepped ashore at the civilised time of 9.30 am. They staggered round about and observed us from hillocks and sheer cliffs, noisy and many of them nesting. A few Skuas circled above, awaiting a breakfast opportunity and smart Antarctic Terns flew back and forth. We saw some brown, fluffy Kelp Gull chicks running around on the rocks. The walk was pebbled, with plenty of guano and patches of slippery snow. I took my time and enjoyed the views of the blue-streaked ice of Livingston Island across the bay. An enormous Grey Elephant Seal basked on a patch of snow near the water's edge.

The orange-painted Argentine station, Camara, where Marco and his wife Patricia had worked as researchers, was over to the southwest of the island. Weddell Seals slept on the snow near the shore.

It got foggier and foggier while we there and I didn't envy the lovely lady zodiac driver as she sussed the way back to the Explorer II. I had lunch with Kevin and Elaine and then we had a briefing from Suzana.

During the mid-afternoon, the ship was expertly steered through the narrow, treacherous Neptune's Bellows of Deception Island, at the southern end of the South Shetland Islands. It was known as Deception Island because many early navigators sailed right past the well-concealed entrance. It was discovered by American and British sealers in the 1820's. A series of volcanic eruptions in the 1960's destroyed bases located there.

There was to be an opportunity here to 'swim' in the waters heated by the geothermal Springs. I wondered whether I dared, but put on my bathing costume under everything else, just in case I could pluck up the courage. I did it! The water was hardly warm, in fact it was positively freezing as I got in, all my special clothes lying in a heap on the beach, but the volcanic ash underneath was comfortably warm and I soon discovered that the trick was to lie flat and make the best of the ash. Libby joined me but we didn't stay in for long.

The worst part of this mad exercise was getting dressed again in cold temperatures and putting all the layers on over a wet costume. I couldn't decide whether the exhilaration was mental or physical.

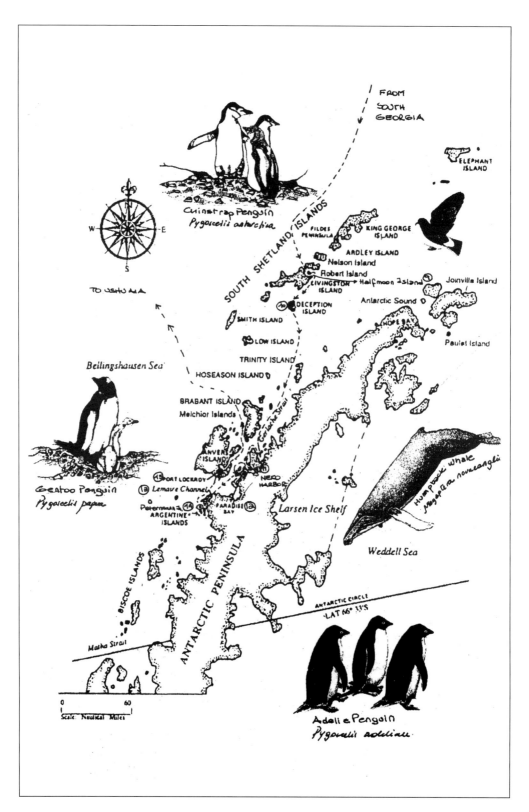

FROM SOUTH GEORGIA

ELEPHANT ISLAND

Chinstrap Penguin
Pygoscelis antarctica

SOUTH SHETLAND ISLANDS

FILDES PENINSULA

KING GEORGE ISLAND

ARDLEY ISLAND

Nelson Island

Robert Island

LIVINGSTON ISLAND

Halfmoon Island

Joinville Island

Antarctic Sound

TO USHUAIA

DECEPTION ISLAND

SMITH ISLAND

HOPE BAY

Pavlet Island

LOW ISLAND

Bellingshausen Sea

TRINITY ISLAND

HOSEASON ISLAND

BRABANT ISLAND

Melchior Islands

ANVERS ISLAND

PORT LOCKROY

NEKO HARBOR

Lemaire Channel

Gentoo Penguin
Pygoscelis papua

Petermann Is.

PARADISE BAY

ARGENTINE ISLANDS

Larsen Ice Shelf

Humpback Whale
Megaptera novaeangliae

BISCOE ISLANDS

Weddell Sea

ANTARCTIC PENINSULA

ANTARCTIC CIRCLE
LAT 66° 33'S

Matha Strait

0   60
Scale: Nautical Miles

Adélie Penguin
Pygoscelis adeliae

232

I sent a New Year e-mail to the family (which, like the first one, never reached them.)

After a much-needed hot shower and change, I dined with Libby and Dilys and enjoyed the wonderful lobster once again. There was a special New Year's Eve atmosphere, with party hats and poppers and a liberal supply of red wine.

After dinner the Filipino crew and staff put on their New Year's Eve Crew Show in the main lounge. It was just wonderful: so much talent. A couple of the vocalists were as good as professionals: the young waitress who sang "Don't cry for me Argentina" made everyone cry. Humour was provided by five of the men who did a girlie dance in drag: they were hilarious. The traditional Filipino dances were graceful and polished. Altogether it was a memorable and unique entertainment, all presented by the charming Cruise Director, Jannie Cloete, who supervised our disembarking and re-embarking with patience and good humour every time we went ashore.

Just before midnight, seven-year old Iain Gallagher, the youngest explorer, did the count down to the New Year from the Captain's bridge. We all hugged and rejoiced, and the staff brought in '2006' all made in ice, and penguins made from pumpkins. The Explorer II quartette played enthusiastically and most of us had a dance. They (the band) must have been delighted for although they played in the main lounge every night after dinner, they didn't normally get many takers: we tended to retire to bed ready for an early start or listened to Chantal playing the piano in the Shackleton bar. Shame, because they were good.

I retired to bed, sleepy but cosy and contented, at 1.30 am. What a day!

Antarctic Escape Day (15)

Sunday 1st January 2006 - New Year's Day

The 7th continent here we come!

We had sailed through the Gerlache Strait, which separates the Palmer Archipelago from the Antarctic Peninsula. It was named after the commander of the Belgian Antarctic Expedition of 1898.

During breakfast we dropped anchor at Neko Harbour, (named after a floating whaling factory) on the eastern shore of Andvord Bay on the west coast of the Antarctic Peninsula. The red dot group (mine) was not going ashore until 10.30 am, which suited me well, for the scenery was just so breathtakingly beautiful and peaceful that I enjoyed staying on deck and committing it to memory.

We landed on a pebble beach and walked along and watched the smart little white-bonneted Gentoos busying themselves in their colony, some carrying stones for their nest, one getting into trouble for stealing a pebble from a neighbour's nest. A lonely Chinstrap wandered aimlessly between his cousins, and a half-grown Elephant Seal chilled out on the snow. There was also a Weddell Seal, and plenty of Kelp Gulls and Skuas. A wind got up and drove the brash ice near our landing site, so Suzana changed the place for embarking on the zodiacs. This little episode gave some of us an inkling of how unpredictable and fickle can be the conditions: we needed experts like Suzana.

The spectacular glacier at the head of the bay was monitored by such experts for 'calving', as it is known to be very active. We heard several pieces booming down while we were there. Icebergs of all sizes were visible from every vantage point.

I had lunch with Chris, Cynthia and Stefan. After that we left Neko Harbour and went further south to Paradise Bay, arriving mid-afternoon and stopping near the bright-orange, abandoned, Argentine station Almirante Brown. The Captain chose not to anchor because of the icebergs and a steady wind, and just drifted while some of us had a zodiac tour. The water reflected the blue of the sky dissected by the snow peaks. This was the most beautiful vista I had ever seen.

The charming Costa Rican, JJ, our guide and driver, did us proud. In and out round icebergs, ice floats, past a cliffside Blue-eyed Shag colony, past rocks coloured by green and rich brown lichen and, in one part, coloured by a wide seam of turquoise-green copper, all under feathery white clouds racing overhead. It was all so grand and dramatic that I felt small and irrelevant. Good to be humbled sometimes.

The wind got up and the water became very choppy so that we were quite wet from spray. This was a long zodiac tour and the only time I felt really cold. It started to rain and my face froze after just a few minutes. However did those early explorers survive? When we got back to the Explorer II, I could hardly grip the rail to climb up the steps my hands were so cold, in spite of two pairs of gloves. The welcome drink of hot raspberry tea was just what we needed.

I warmed up and changed in the cabin and then went for the briefing - when Suzana warned us that weather conditions might necessitate a change of route.

There was to have been a special barbecue dinner on the verandah but it got so cold and windy that we came inside to the verandah dining room, shed our Parkas and ate the delicious meal in comfort - with Dilys, Jean, Avril, Angela and the hairdresser. Robin joined us and demonstrated his Explorer 'film' on his amazing camera. I wasn't too keen on the picture of me that had been taken when singing carols on Christmas Eve, but the shots of the Crew Show were great. Dan Dan, the star of the drag scene, was waiting on us, but he suddenly saw himself and flung himself down on the settee and cried excitedly "It's me, it's me!" I took a photo of his excited face.

We had lots of enjoyable after-dinner chatter and then went out to view the Lemaire Channel, which evidently could be so beautiful that it was also known as 'Kodak Alley', but the fog increased and it became obvious that there would not be many photo opportunities tonight.

PARADISE

We are anchored here in Paradise
That is to say the Bay
So appropriately labelled
On such a glorious day
The white stretches for ever
Over mountains, into creeks
Meeting clear blue Heavens
Pierced by jagged peaks

It's breathtaking and beautiful
Almost unbelievable
Unless you've really seen it
A vista inconceivable
The peace is awe-inspiring
Yet this majesty can hide
Death for the uninformed
Who take a risky stride
too far

For neath the bold blue cracks
A deep crevasse can take
And drop you to a world
Whence you'll never wake
So I'm content to sit
In a zodiac and wonder
At such unique creation
Which blows my mind asunder
and wets my face
This experience alone
Makes me glad I came
With this new dimension added
Life will never be the same!

1st January 2006

A "calving" iceberg NEKO HARBOUR

We passed more icebergs, beautiful and bizarre, one of the latter very suggestive and anatomically correct. I was on my own but two men stood further down the deck. One of them said, "Just look at that". The other rejoined, "Those were the days!"

I smiled and retired to bed quite early in view of the early start.

Antarctic Escape Day (16)

Monday 2nd January 2006

This was as far south as we would get. I got up at 4.30 am for an early zodiac trip to Petermann Island which lay just below the Lemaire Channel. It was cold, grey, and overcast and I was stiff.

We disembarked onto a large boulder. It had snowed a lot in the night and walking was very difficult. I managed to fall over once (a soft landing) and nearly fall over several times. Never mind, it amused the Adelie Penguins' "rookery", where they sat nesting and chuntering to each other. Some of the young chicks were just visible every now and then, as parents shifted about or gave them a brief feed. A smaller number of

Gentoos were scattered among them. An Antarctic Shag, nesting nearby, appeared almost to swallow its youngster as the latter's head and neck disappeared down its mother's throat. We stood and watched for some time, fascinated by the whole scene. The pebble-stealing technique was in evidence once again. The walking seemed even harder on the return journey.

Back on the ship, I suddenly felt very hungry, and enjoyed a rare indulgence in a fried breakfast of potato, beans, bacon and tomato. I sat with Betsy, Jan, Chris and a younger lady who had done all the longer walk options. Then I went to the cabin and had a brief kip, afterwards going to the library to study the map, as it had just been announced that we would not be returning through the Lemaire Channel as planned, because of the ice. There had been news from another ship, the Marco Polo, that she had only just got through. Now we were to use a longer route, the "French Passage".

I'd just settled down in the library to write my diary when "Humpback Whale" sighting was announced. I rushed back to the cabin to get the Parka and the camera. I could see several of them near to the ship, blowing bushes of foam and showing their flukes, but the camera registered "memory full" which surprised me as I knew I'd taken only around 130 shots: it was only later that I discovered that the '276' on the memory card referred to MBs and not the number of photographs. I re-visited the cabin for the back-up camera and thought I might have got a couple of shots.

It was now 11 am (was it really still the same morning?). Henry Pollack gave us an unscheduled lecture on the Ozone Layer, mainly about the ozone hole over the Antarctic, the causes, consequences, and 'remediations' (horrible word).

The atmosphere is 79% Nitrogen, 20% Oxygen, and the remaining 1% is made up of Carbon Dioxide, Argon, Ozone, and water vapour.

'Dobson' units are the measurement of ozone concentration. These measured 330 in 1957 but are now below 200. There are seasonal effects - lower in summer and higher in winter. The Antarctic summer hole (October - November) starts earlier, lasts longer, and finishes later, and is observed over a wider depletion area.

Chlorine monoxide – this is a factor in ozone depletion, as are:

Chloro Fluoro Carbons (CFCs) which come from ammonia-powered refrigerators - these are not to be manufactured any more; CFCs are inert, insoluble, non-inflammable - they enter the atmosphere from propellants of sprays (banned 1970).

CFCs are very heavy but can, nonetheless, reach the stratosphere. There is more chlorine in the ocean than in CFCs. Volcanoes are a source of Antarctic str. Chlorine.

CFCs have a food chain effect:

Phyto-plankton - loss of ozone - affected by ultra-violet light - grows deeper. Lichen - Krills

A smaller hole exists in the northern hemisphere, where the ocean has a more uniform temperature.

CFCs are broken up by the sun: solar energy and atmospheric ice crystals produce a fertile environment for this to take place.

CFCs plus oxygen give chlorine.
CFC production is down but there is still destruction of the ozone layer because CFCs linger in the environment: there is much leakage from abandoned and redundant equipment, and from chlorine coming from carbons.

Photocopying machines produce ozone but not enough to make any difference – they do not produce sufficient quantity to be statistically detectable.

I enjoyed a light lunch (I'd had a fried breakfast) with Avril and Jean. Jean had 'found' John Smith, an acquaintance of a medical colleague, Ben Armstrong, in Torrington and even now that I'd met this charming man face to face, I still experienced difficulty in distinguishing him from two others of similar age and hair quality!

I had another brief nap but was on deck in time to see us reach Port Lockroy, with its sunny bay, calm waters, and blue skies - a second 'Paradise'. It was explained to us that Port Lockroy (Base A) was established in 1944 by the British to report on enemy activity and provide weather reports during the Second World War. It had continued as a scientific base under the British Antarctic Survey until they relocated elsewhere in 1958. It was renovated by UK Antarctic Heritage Trust in 1994, and was now an historic site and monument. The three staff who maintained the base during the summer also investigated the visitor disturbance to the breeding Gentoo Penguins. Mercifully, it appears we have had no effect, which I could well believe when I saw all the birds with their young, nesting and waddling about right under our noses.

Lovely Patricia was our zodiac driver today and after we'd had our fill of the Gentoos, seen the museum and shopped (I bought some cards, and history and wildlife charts of the island) we were taken on a zodiac tour round the fantastic icebergs, shoreline seals, shags, and skua - on top of a memorial stone to a lost ship, while she regaled us with real live stories of adventure, survival and some foolishness. One of the latter was of a private yachtsman who had had no knowledge or experience of the Antarctic, but who sailed his boat into Port Lockroy and took his guests and crew climbing a nearby glacier. He died in a crevasse but the other five in the party survived.

She told us that small ships and crew were still not required to have any training, permission, or licence to enter these waters. We travelled back through equally stupendous scenery.

I changed and repaired to Shackleton's Bar to read, and to watch our progress through the Neumayer Channel, with Chantal playing the grand piano (chained - the piano, of course, not Chantal). Robin and Dilys and another couple joined me. I had dinner with Robin, Dilys and John - with very good veal, which I had not had for years.

Afterwards I sat in the bar listening to Chantal, and talking to Jim, Tony and John. JJ - our Costa Rican guide and driver - joined Chantal and showed us yet another of his talents as he sang a couple of songs in a melodious tenor voice.

Bed was at 12.30 am … there would be no early call.

We were now leaving behind the magic of Antarctica.

Antarctic Escape Day (17)

Tuesday 3rd January 2006

The first day of crossing Drake Passage started grey but calm. Chris Hill gave his "Parallels in Navigation - how birds and men find their way":

He compared the Vikings with Ravens, and told of an exercise when Macaroni Penguins were taken miles away from their territory in a rucksack, so that they couldn't see or hear what was going on, and yet they still had no difficulty in finding their way back.

Arctic Terns do their regular annual trip of 12,000 miles, Sooty Shearwaters 9,000 miles. A Manx Shearwater was taken to Boston from a Welsh barn but flew the 2500 miles back without any difficulty. 11,000 Starlings were taken from Norway to Switzerland, and the adults navigated back.

How do they do it, especially over the sea where there are no land masses for identification? Storm Petrels may have an olfactory landscape. They may use such navigation aids as the sun, the Great Bear, the Pole Star and Cassiopeia. Man certainly used these and then got into the latitude idea and comparison of magnetic fields. John Harrison (a carpenter) explored the longitude phenomenon with special clocks he made (without pendulums). Polynesian migration routes coincided with bird migration routes.

Over coffee we were observers as the crew went through their emergency drill, with a life-jacketed foreman in charge of each collection point.

Later in the morning Henry Pollack gave his "Earth's Changing Climate - What's in store for the future?" lecture:

(1) Earth is warming. From temperatures taken at fixed meteorological stations, from ships taking surface sea temperatures, and from work done at the University of East Anglia Climate Research Centre, all agree that from the 1960s to the present day there has been a 1°F (= approx 0.6°C) rise. The consequences of this temperature rise show ice melting, glaciers diminishing all the time, sea ice getting less – with sea levels rising, snow disappearing from the top of Kilimanjaro, more summer melting of Greenland ice, etc, so that the mean growing season has increased by 10 to 14 days.

(2) Causes:

(a) Not lack of sun spots (which causes 'little ice age') and not the increase in volcanic eruptions, as more ash produces more cooling.

(b) Greenhouse gases: we know ozone blocks out ultraviolet, and that earth radiates infra-red, so that the earth's atmosphere acts like a blanket and prevents the earth from becoming an ice house.

Are we changing the "greenhouse"? Carbon dioxide parts have gone up from 350 per million in 1959 to 380 per million in 2005, although seasonal variation reflects the role of vegetation. The burning of fossil-based fuels increases carbon dioxide levels. These levels may be changing anyway but we are speeding up the process by using fossil fuels.

(3) Consequences :

(a) plants: grow faster and bigger with increased carbon dioxide but the nutrients are distributed more thinly;

(b) a one-metre rise in sea level could wipe out Florida.

(c) excessive heat means that there are more heat-related deaths

(d) the fishing industry is diminished, as in Alaska

(e) an increase in growth of Sugar Maple in USA and Canada

(f) large prairie fires

(g) large-scale population shifts

(4) Greenhouse gases have the same effect as CFCs.

(5) Carbon dioxide and temperature are both going up.

(6) Methane is increasing but not by as much as is carbon dioxide. Methane is increased by ice fields, and by bovine flatulence.

After all this information, we needed lunch.

I ate with Jean, Avis and Angela and then had a walk round the deck. It was foggy and getting quite rough.

I went back to the cabin to have a read and saw on the screen that we had now cruised 3059 miles and the depth of the water was 3520 metres.

At 5 pm, Russ Manning, a former British Antarctic Survey reseach base commander, gave his "Twenty years of living and working in Antarctica" talk, describing a year of people working in various bases. His slides and accounts of hairy situations made a fascinating presentation. If I were in a life-threatening situation, I sense that his would be the practical help I'd go for. An amazing man. What detail, what endurance.

I showered and changed and went to the Captain's cocktail party. He made another entertaining speech, thanked everyone, and emphasised how lucky we had been to be able to make every scheduled landing. And so said all of us.

The farewell dinner was enjoyed in the company of Bryn and Ann, the other Bryn and Julie, Tom, Chris and Pascale. We had a great fun conversation time and then retired into the lounge for music. And so to bed, at 11.45 pm.

This had been something of an 'indoor' day, with plenty of food for thought, as well as nutrition.

I couldn't believe that tomorrow would be the last day.

Antarctic Escape Day (18)

Wednesday 4th January 2006

This was our to be last day aboard Explorer II. We were reminded of this sad fact (as if we needed to be) by the comprehensive disembarkation briefing from the Cruise Director, Jannie.

It was made memorable by another superb lecture from Tim Baughman on "Roald Amundsen - The Explorer". He described Amundsen, a Norwegian, as the most successful polar explorer of the early twentieth century, being the first to go through the Northwest Passage and the first person to reach the South Pole. He described him also as, sadly, probably the unhappiest.

In 1897 he had joined the Belgian expedition aboard the 'Belgica', with the American physician and explorer F A Cook. They were the first to winter in the Antarctic and, somehow, brought the crew through severe attacks of scurvy. An island in the vicinity was named after a man who fell overboard during Amundsen's watch.

In 1906 he made plans for conquering the Northwest Passage in the 'Gjoa', with a crew of six, sailing secretly to avoid creditors. It was a three-year expedition and the news was mismanaged by the press: " … too old to survive three years, etc".

Preparations were made to go to the North Pole, but it was then discovered that the American, Robert E Peary, had reached the North Pole in 1909. Preparations continued but these were secretly being made for the South Pole instead. Amundsen sailed from the Madeira Islands to the Ross Sea and set up a base 60 miles nearer the Pole than Scott. He completed the journey by dog sledge with four companions. As far as the Press was concerned, his glory was tainted by the fact that a disappointed Scott had died during his return journey; that someone involved in his own expedition had committed suicide; and that the love of his life did not leave her husband (a legal executive) as he had anticipated she would.

He then went on to start another six-year expedition to the North Pole in 1918, but things went wrong, so he abandoned it after three years and he tried to do it by air instead. Eventually he succeeded with Umberto Nobile of Italy. He was lost over the Arctic Seas during an attempt to rescue Nobile, who had crashed in the area. What a saga of achievement and disaster.

We all felt somewhat sad and humbled by this heroic tale and it was discussed with feeling over a hearty lunch with Tony, Avis, Jean, Dorothy and Angela.

I packed my main luggage in a never-to-be-opened way, hoping that I'd managed to put all I'd need for the overnight Buenos Aires stay in the hand luggage. I hate packing! I was taking home the red Parka and the neat little rucksack, and leaving behind a couple of shirts and the new boots, which were not that comfortable: they were cheap and had been bought in a hurry, so had served their emergency purpose.

Sightings of a Southern Right Whale and four Fin Whales engendered some last-minute excitement and photos, and then most of us partook of a 'chocolate to die for' tea.

Expedition Leader Suzana led the 'Expedition Overview', when we saw slides of the trip's features, and a preview of the second half of a DVD prepared by Sascha.

There had been raffles for the 'Save the Albatross Campaign' (a special expedition sea chart) and for the Explorer II Welfare Fund (one of Patricia's ink drawings) and the winning tickets were drawn. Then it was the last dinner and the last drink as we sat listening to Chantal's delightful music.

Finally, having said I didn't want a video, I changed my mind and fell for one.

Antarctic Escape Day (19)

Thursday 5th January 2006

I got up at 6.30 am. The luggage had already gone (at 2 am) from outside the room.

Breakfast was on the verandah – just beautiful: I felt quite emotional at seeing 'green' again. Ushuaia was looking warm and inviting. Some of the Expedition Team were greeting others, who were to join or replace them on the next scheduled Antarctic cruise, which was due to start at 8 pm that day.

We left on a bus at 8.15 am and were taken to the Tierra del Fuego National Park where we just stood and enjoyed idyllic scenes of water, mountains, soft reflections, Upland Geese, Southern Beech Woods, and interesting flora such as the Stick-Tight flower - which looked a bit like a Thrift and had leaves like a Silverweed - and the cheery Cabbage Daisy. I thought I spotted a Condor and got all excited but the experts said it was a Black-breasted Buzzard Eagle: amazing wingspan. A strange island is Tierra del Fuego, wedged between the Argentine and Chile, and with the Atlantic to the east and the Pacific to the west. I found that the green vegetation everywhere gave me a sense of relief and luxury.

We were driven to an Ushuaian restaurant for lunch, where we waited ages for the meal. The first course was a shellfish soup, thin but with plenty of prawn-like bits floating about which some couldn't face: I thought it was quite good. The main course was some kind of white fish enveloped in semi-cooked batter, which left a lot to be desired - but the company was good! We were then taken straight to the airport to fly back to Buenos Aires, where I had a light supper at the Meia Hotel with Jill, Richard, Dilys and Libby.

I had trouble with my room (key) ticket - it just would not open the door (on the eighth floor). Reception put it through some machine and then it was OK, but I stupidly left it inside (in the light socket) while I put out my luggage for early collection, the door closed and I had to re-visit reception.

Antarctic Escape Day (20)

Friday 6th January 2006

At breakfast we said our farewells and exchanged addresses, etc. Dilys gave me her card and there it was – she was an 'OBE' - for her work with the TouchTrust which she had founded: an amazing little lady. Some of our group were leaving on an earlier flight so it was important to communicate now.

Avis, Jean and I thought we'd walk to the eco-reserve (as it was not Monday, when it's closed!). We found our way over the wide busy roads, along the docks, crossed a bridge at the far end and then back along the other side. It seemed much further than when I had been with Dilys on December 19th.

We were greeted at the reserve by a very helpful man, who gave us a plan and asked us to sign the visitors' book. We walked until well into the afternoon: wonderful flora, many small brightly-coloured birds I couldn't identify (it would have helped if I'd remembered my binoculars, but dear Avis did lend me hers), but I did recognize a Night Heron, the now familiar Upland Geese, a Greater Spotted Woodpecker and a few Green Parakeets. An obliging Coypu crossed our path. The walk was longer than we had anticipated and I knew my legs had had enough. Jean went ahead to see how near we were to the waters of Rio de la Plata - it was not far so we soldiered on.

It seemed a good idea to have a late lunch where Dilys and I had had such excellent pizzas, but we couldn't find the way across the water, and I knew we hadn't walked the full length of the docks again: then it dawned! The bridge we had used was up - apparently damaged from the look of things. We couldn't face the long slog and eventually persuaded the only cab driver who wasn't having a siesta, to take us to the restaurant.

We ordered a different pizza each and shared: it was delicious. I ordered a half bottle of wine, which I thought was white but it turned out to be red. A strong-bodied little girl came begging and playing her accordion. Jean found some coins and the girl took them, played eight notes and moved on. I remembered that the last time I'd eaten there, a young man had come begging for money towards a drug-rehabilitation unit for teenagers. The management here was obviously tolerant and sympathetic. The waiter was charming, saying he'd charge us two euros for feeding the pigeons!

A middle-aged couple on the next table, with a younger lady, started chatting and I made the unforgivable mistake of thinking that they were Americans (probably worse than mistaking a Scotsman for an Irishman) and they pointed out, good-humouredly, that they were Australians. They were doing an Antarctic cruise later in the month. Then they were going to the UK where one of their sons was to marry an English girl. Another son had already settled for an Irish bride.

Back at the hotel, we washed and changed, said more good-byes, and checked that the luggage had been brought down.

There was then a protracted period of what I can only describe as airport chaos: long disorganised queues, no order of boarding, and everybody pushing. When we eventually took off, there was the same indifference from the staff, and the food was of a similar quality. My legs started to swell in a way they'd never done before, which was partly my own fault because I hadn't put on the support stockings as I normally did. Some time during the flight we moved into …

Saturday 7th January 2006

and my legs became more uncomfortable while we stood in yet another long queue at Madrid where - in spite of having hours of time, in theory, for the connection - we were still waiting at the check-in when the flight time had passed. Bryn and Ann took over my hand luggage. I was struggling and when we were eventually given sanction and allowed to board, Liz, and then Robin, carried my hand luggage. By this time I had sorted out my support stockings but too late, too late I feared. Bryn and Ann never did get the plane, as their seats had been double-booked: evidently not that uncommon. I spoke to Bryn a couple of days later and he said they'd been put on a flight two hours later, business class, given 500 euros in compensation and bottles of wine to take home. Not a very pleasant experience, nonetheless.

Robin was a star and looked after this disabled geriatric at Heathrow, where I was overjoyed (as no doubt was Robin) to see Lydia of the Shuttle Service waiting for me. She helped me while I pushed the wheely luggage and then her husband Bill, who was waiting outside, came to our aid.

They were travellers themselves and wanted to know all about the Antarctic trip, which was on their agenda for some time in the future. I loved talking of every aspect. Their latest project was the refurbishing of a boat they had bought in Australia, where they had family. They invited me to join them on this vessel for the fireworks in Sydney Harbour next New Year!

We made good time home, and I was glad to be back at base. My dream was a really hot bath and bed - but there was a note on the table to the effect that there was no water and no heating. So I put on the electric blanket and went to bed in all my grime.

I survived the Sunday (8th January) with the water the Heywoods had kindly left for me. My legs returned to their normal size, and I unpacked, with memories that will last for ever. Much of the Christmas mail was still to be opened and I did that in a leisurely fashion in the afternoon.

I rang the family and it was good to hear news of their Christmasses. This was when I learned that they had not had my e-mails. I felt sad about that for I did think so much about them and, yes, I confess I did miss them over the Christmas period.

The trip had been the most exciting holiday I'd ever taken. Hearing what happened to the weather, and therefore the changes of programme that overtook the cruise that followed ours, we had indeed been incredibly fortunate. Suzana said it was all to do with offering eggs to the gods – well, whatever it was, it worked a treat.

Corollary

Just a week later I had an emergency admission to hospital for a gynae blip. I had little time to pack my things, but I made a point of taking my holiday diary to write up properly, my photographs which had arrived that morning – to put them in order, and a copy of Jerri Nielsen's "Ice Bound" – which I'd read from the ship's library hurriedly, because there was so little time. I left behind my glaucoma eyedrops, my slippers and my dressing gown!

I was grateful I hadn't been taken ill in the Antarctic, and the possibility gave me a tiny window of understanding of the extraordinary strength of Jerri, who had been isolated at the South Pole as an expedition's doctor and had treated herself for breast cancer.

I've already had correspondence from several of the Antarctic travellers, including photographs of the mad bathing spree from Libby.

AFTER ALL

After just a week at home, I had a "woman's" bleed
Bright red and quite substantial, should I ignore or heed?
Training can make things difficult, must not be seen to panic
Keep quite calm, don't get wide eyed and manic

So to tell it as it happened, (I'd guessed I'd be admitted)
Made arrangements for the Labrador, with friends who were committed
To his care and spoiling
A neighbour'd feed the guinea fowl, another watch the sheep
And feed them extra ewe nuts on shrinking winter keep

The consultant was quite charming, but overtly pessimistic
In my mind I planned a future with complexion altruistic
To ease the passage for the children with an ailing mother
Dividing goods and chattels twixt each sister and each brother

We went through routine blood tests, then the anaesthesia
For a spell in theatre with complete blessed amnesia
Then back onto the ward in a bay of four sick ladies
Three into their eighties, at night a world of Hades
With minds detached and roving

One patient wanted pillows adjusted every minute
Another help to sort her locker and bring out all that's in it
The third was fit and spry, walked tall with supple joint
But her brain was out of gear and she kept making her point
"I don't want to be here!"

I came home and waited for results and diagnosis
A salutary interval for cerebral osmosis
The news was good, I'm grateful and somewhat humbled too
I've got away with life again: there's still so much to do!

February 2007

INDIAN OCEAN

with **NOBLE CALEDONIA**

MS Island Sky
Indian Ocean Odyssey
11-28 February 2007

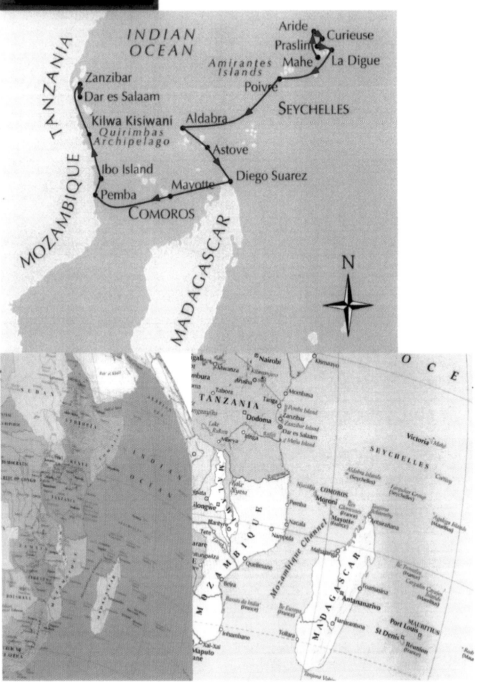

We have traveled to mere specks on the map in the wake of Arab traders, pirates, and merchants of old.

And in doing so, each speck has grown into a place with its own story to tell.

We have strolled with ancient tortoises, danced with manta rays, and been touched by the magic of fairy terns.

Thus, our own experiences will be woven into the island stories.

And when someone asks, "So how was your trip?"

Oh, the stories we will tell...

❧

SHIP'S OFFICERS	EXPEDITION TEAM
Captain Nick Hope-Inglis *England*	**Expedition Leader** Conrad Combrink *South Africa*
Chief Engineer Henrik Aspevik *Norway*	**Assistant Expedition Leader** Oliver Bühler *South Africa*
Chief Officer Konstantinos Dosios *Greece*	**Marine Biologist/Snorkel Master** Robin Aiello *Australia*
Safety Officer Arturo Defensor *Phillipines*	**Naturalists** Simon Cook *Wales*
Hotel Manager Jos Coppers *Belgium*	**Naturalists** Magnus Forsberg *Sweden*
Executive Chef Harm Roebel *Germany*	**Staff Assistant** Emma Hansen *South Africa*
Maitre D' Ozer Akbiyik *Turkey*	
Chief Purser Noe Salazar *Hunduras*	

On behalf of all aboard the *MV Island Sky*, we would like to
THANK YOU
for sailing with us!

INDIAN OCEAN
Island Odyssey

Sunday 11th February 2007

I felt I was almost prepared for this Indian Ocean holiday, so I even went to church on the morning of the day of departure. I was the only alto in the choir at that moment and had an extra obligation as Bishop 'Bob' of Crediton was honouring us with his presence. Ben, the choirmaster, was particularly keen that we should put on a 'good show'. The Ecce Panis Angelorum and a motet went better than average and, as I shook hands with the Bishop after service, he said how much he had enjoyed the music and that the choir sounded stronger than eight voices!

Back home again, I tied green thread round some heavy branches to identify them for my occasional gardener to saw off while I was away. I put more ostentatious wide green straps round my luggage to make it more easily identifiable.

The Labrador dog, Chester, had gone to friends in nearby Beaford; the sheep, a month off lambing, were with a farmer friend at Moortown; and a kind neighbour would feed the guinea fowl as she walked through the drive with her dog each morning. Her daughter was going to live in the house for part of my absence, which was always reassuring in the winter months. The organisation for absence was almost like having a family again, except that the animals did not have to come with me. Wendy, the eldest of the family, thoughtfully rang me just before I left.

For the last few years, since I've reached three score years and ten, I've given up driving to Heathrow, or taking a bus, or even the train. I have used the Shuttle Service, which has suited me well. However, after numerous fruitless calls, I heard on the grapevine that they had gone out of business, which surprised me for they had always seemed very businesslike. After exploring various possibilities unsuccessfully, I rang the local taxi service who accepted the job and David arrived promptly at 1.30 pm. This was the beginning of adventure number 14.

A couple of weeks earlier I'd wondered about the wisdom of taking my annual 'fix' on my own. The truth is that my right hip was giving me more than irritation, and having had my left hip replaced 14 years earlier, before all these New Year excursions, I knew the signs. I thought about those wobbly steps before getting into the zodiacs …

David was a very pleasant, retired Midlands gentleman who had moved to Devon to help with the family taxi business. We covered a wealth of topics during what was an easy trip, from birth, to community, through drugs and health and safety overkill, to death. I enjoyed the conversation: I hope he did.

I arrived unusually early and sat people watching for a while. I was reassured to see other (elderly) people sporting 'Noble Caledonian' labels. We were redirected from check-in 01 to 65 - 69. The luggage was checked and I opted for a window seat and then wished I'd said an aisle seat: after all it would be dark and window seats give less access to the prescribed walks, the loo, and the overhead luggage. As we went through the screening, we were required to remove our shoes. One of my laces was well knotted and I held up the queue.

Once I was in the departure lounge I found a seat that gave a good view of Gate information – "MK065 for the Seychelles - PLEASE WAIT" - so I did. It was then that I met Judy and Ann, friends travelling together from Farnham, and I enjoyed their company as we sat for an extra hour and a half before the plane's late take-off.

The plane was about two thirds full, and I had a double seat over which to spread myself. I indulged in a gin and ginger ale, which livened up the boring, overpacked meal. We put our watches on four hours and I settled down about 3.30 am, new time. I slept little. There was a very talkative couple in front. I tried lying down but the seat was not long enough. I leaned forward on to the meal tray and had a few dozes like this, and others sitting upright. The window seat did afford me a wonderful view of the dawn: I welcomed the sun and took off my warm clothes before breakfast.

ARRIVAL

Monday 12th February 2007

We had arrived at the airport at Mahe, Seychelles. We filled in embarkation cards and went through security reasonably quickly. It was hot! We were met and taken to the Plantation Club for a light lunch, where I sat with Ann, Judy, and two other ladies of fairly senior years. They were sisters, Angela and Rosalie, both retired GPs from Liverpool, and the eldest, Angela, had qualified there three years after me. It's a small world and getting smaller.

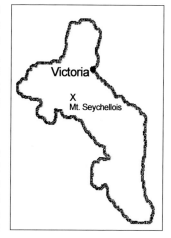

We were then taken on a tour of the capital, Victoria. We were all feeling hot and tired and probably not in the most receptive frames of mind, but we took in the capital's version of Big Ben, Civic Building, the library and then had a refreshing walk in the Botanical Gardens. There were some unidentifiable (to me) beautiful and very colourful flowers and trees, interspersed with the occasional recognisable Bougainvillea and Hibiscus. There was a tree that resembled a huge Shrimp plant, and magnificent Coconut Palms stood tall and stately. Land Turtles came obligingly into view, as did an acrobatic little Stick Insect. Marylese was our pleasant Mason's guide.

On the bird list, we ticked a Magpie Robin, a stunning White-tailed Tropic bird, Fruit Bats (I know they're not birds but they do fly), a Grey Heron, a Fairy Tern, and Swiftlets. Then it was back to the Plantation Club for a cup of tea, and to be collected, with our luggage, and taken aboard the MS Island Sky. I was in Cabin 257, with portholes, which was on Deck 2, the same floor as the restaurant. I registered and got my key card - Reception was one floor up, on the same floor as the lounge. I decided that those bits of basic information would suffice for the moment.

We'd hardly identified our cabins before a call came over the Tannoy, that we were all to listen for the emergency signal and go to our particular assembly points with a lifejacket for mandatory safety and lifeboat drill. I had a selection of no less than four lifejackets in my (double) cabin, two red and two black. I selected a red one, only to be sent back to 257 to fetch a black one. I hadn't read the instructions on the back of the door, had I!? I then seemed to be more stupid than most at putting the thing on properly. The black one was for the everyday zodiac rides, hence very important that we learned how to use it. The staff all had the red ones, which we would be required to use in a real abandoning of the ship in an emergency. A bit scary … This was followed by a zodiac briefing and instructions on how to get in and out of those little rubber boats, allowing for rough waters.

I went back and unpacked and washed. A screw came out of my specs and was forever lost; there was nowhere to recharge the camera batteries but Reception later obliged. Once sorted, I took a proper look at the cabin that was quite luxurious. The large wardrobe would have taken most of the clothes I possessed.

I went to the lounge for the briefing about what was to happen on the morrow at Aride and Curieuse: it sounded wonderful. I approached the dining room and was directed to a table with a quiet lady called Christine, whose husband was not feeling too well: he was unhappy, she said, because he couldn't get the information he wanted on his laptop. There were two couples also - John and another Christine, and a much-travelled couple, Peter and Heather, who took five holidays like this a year.

They asked me how many I had taken, and I said "just the one", and that I loved the community and the place where I lived for the rest of the year. They looked as if I'd rebuked them in some way but I truly hadn't meant to sound disapproving. I must watch my tone of voice.

The meal was quite delicious, plenty of fresh vegetables, selection of meat dishes, wide variety of super fish (including lobster) and temptingly presented sweets and fresh fruit. It was good. The conversation improved as the meal progressed: maybe the wine helped. I was not sorry to turn in at 10.30 pm.

ARIDE and CURIEUSE

Tuesday 13th February 2007

The Island Sky had arrived at Aride, and the scout boat had been launched, before I awoke after a good night's sleep. The sun was shining, the sea was calm and the sky was blue and filled with birds. This entire granite island was a nature reserve, mainly for nesting sea birds, whose population had thrived since the eradication of rats. It was in order to keep this state of affairs, that local restrictions prevented any but the local tenders from ferrying people to and from Aride. Hence the embarking and disembarking exercises were slower than we were to find, subsequently, with the Island Sky's zodiacs and their drivers. The island had been bought by Christopher Cadbury, President of the Royal Society for Nature Conservation, in 1973, "and is leased to the Nature Conservation Trust".

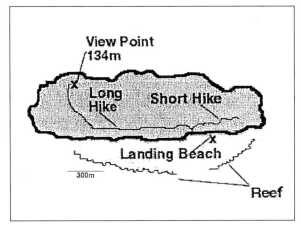

I opted for the short walk and we had a really excellent guide, Ben, who was resident on the island for a while, together with a selection of students doing PhD's on such subjects as Sunbirds, the Seychelles Fody and the Magpie Robin. Since the island had become a nature reserve, the Coconut Palms had been replaced by proper native species, which already looked incredibly well established. It was very hot even though we were in the forest.

We saw Fairy Terns with single, nestless, eggs balanced on small branches. They appeared so vulnerable but must have been more secure than they looked. Lesser Noddies occupied untidy nests, and a charming, White-tailed Tropicbird sat motionless, conveniently just below eye level. I liked the alternative name for the Seychelles Blue Pigeon, the "Pigeon d'Olande" (Holland) because of its red forecrown and wattles, pale grey breast and nape, and the dark blue plumage of the rest of its body - which succession of colours resembled that of the Dutch flag.

13 February 2007

We saw lots of lizards, and many Hermit Crabs in shells of different sizes and colours. Spooky Horned Ghost Crabs moved weirdly about a short stretch of shore, among piles of sand, which reminded me of molehills. The island was just so full of interest wherever we looked. I could have spent ages there, just sitting and looking and listening. A PhD girl was doing one of her three-times-a-day Magpie Robins' nest checks.

We visited the shop, where I bought John Bowler's 'Wildlife of Seychelles' book, a bird chart, and a soft little Turtle that I couldn't resist. I had lunch with Judy and Ann, and a chatty couple called Margaret and Jim.

We had been divided into 3 main groups - 1, 2, and 3! I was in Group 3, so expected to wait a while to be called for the zodiac. It gave me plenty of time to get on my lifejacket in a proper manner. I chatted to Ben and the Aride PhD people who had come aboard for lunch: they were delighted to talk about their work and obviously loved this slot of their studies.

I got away with Group 2, earlier than expected, when the call came "room for one more: anyone on their own?" It does occasionally have its advantages. The water was quite choppy and there was a lovely cooling breeze as we landed on the white sandy beach of Curieuse. More than half a dozen huge Aldabran Tortoises were gathered on the grassy lawn near the picnic benches. The upper surface of the shells of a couple of the males came to the tops of my thighs when they stood up, and they all responded to a tickle under the chin.

White-Tailed Tropic Bird - ARIDE

We swam and snorkelled: it was very pleasant although there were few fish. I loved the stunning rock formations, that reminded me of Zimbabwe's kopjes, and I remembered that both were part of that huge land mass millions of years ago.

I felt very relaxed, as did Judy and Ann I suspected, for we exchanged life stories. Judy had lost her husband who had died at 53 with Alzheimer's, poor things. Ann had divorced years ago but had 'two wonderful daughters'. More recently she had unexpectedly survived an extraordinary medical history. We lingered in the sunshine and were on the last zodiac going back to 'Island Sky'.

It had been a lovely afternoon and I was glad I'd gone, having wondered whether I should when I heard an announcement "… you need to be very sure footed" - but then, when I saw some apparently less-abled bodies joining the queue to board, I had to have a go.

I got showered and changed and went into the lounge to write my diary. There was no-one else about and I wondered whether I was supposed to be somewhere else. A lovely girl labelled 'Anna' was tidying the tables and she got me a gin and ginger ale. I guessed she was Filipino and asked about her life on board. She liked the work and would finish this contract in April. She will then see her husband again in August, when he will have finished his contract in Miami. She looked young and beautiful and I was surprised to learn that she had a son of 10. Her mother looked after him a few miles north of Manila. She seemed surprised to hear that I'd visited the Philippines, and asked me what I thought. I said I could see that many people had to struggle to survive, but the parts I'd seen were very beautiful, many of them unspoiled. "Yes", she said, "I could never live anywhere else".

I joined everyone else for the Captain Nick Hope-Inglis' "Welcome on Board Cocktail" and then made my way to the dining room, where I sat with those retired Liverpool GP sisters, Angela and Rosalie, and Christopher the retired urologist and his wife Janette, both ex-Guy's Hospital. We had a lot of fun, not all of it medical, and I retired to bed just after 10.30 pm.

13 February 2007
Strange Rock Vegetation
CURIEUSE

255

PRASLIN and LAS DIGUE

Wednesday 14th February 2007

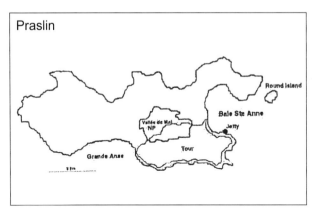

We were anchored off Praslin, the second largest island of the Seychelles, when I heard the 7 am wake-up call. I was scheduled to be in the second group off, but there were delays owing to a much larger cruise boat (1000 passengers) using the local tenders to ferry their people ashore: some of the staff seemed surprised it was there.

Once on land we were taken by small buses, with Mason's Travels' local guides, for a morning tour of the famous World Heritage Site, the Vallee de Mai, also known as 'The Original Garden of Eden'. Its claim to fame was the fact that it was the only place in the world where the Coco de Mer grew wild. These Palms grew tall and proud and produced the largest nut in the vegetable kingdom, which could weigh up to 35kgms: it could take a year to germinate and produce the first leaf; the trunk did not develop for about 15 years and maturity could take anything from 20 - 40 years. They may live for 400 years.

This factual introduction was given while we were in motion, but then we arrived and took a long walk. It was hot and tiring with lots of stone steps and other more casual rocks to negotiate, but the trees gave some glorious shade. As well as studying the tree's suggestive gametes, the female for all the world resembling the human female pelvis, and the male a very large long powerful organ, we were very fortunate to see and hear the endangered Black Parrot. Common Mynas, Seychelles Bulbuls, and Seychelles Turtle Doves were also identified. Startlingly Green Geckos lapped hungrily at the male catkins of the Coco de Mer, and a shining lizard, the Seychelles Skink, jerked its way over the stones.

We then headed for the Cote d'Or Beach for an hour's free time. I could have lingered longer but it was back to the Island Sky in time for lunch.

By 1 pm, we were lining up to reboard the tenders for La Digue, the fourth largest of the granite islands, named after the ship that carried Marion du Fresne for the island's first recorded discovery in 1768. Once ashore, we were met by oxcarts, which transported us in relaxed fashion to the L'Union Estate with its old Creole House, and a demonstration as to how they collected the husks and squeezed the coconuts to make the oil. Some of us enjoyed a welcome drink of coconut 'milk'. Our oxcart driver was a handsome young man called Sylvester, with the most impressive Rastafarian-type hair-do. He was pleasant and humorous and seemed to enjoy the chit chat. Other oxcarts and many cycles passed us as we drove along at a leisurely pace. Our handsome ox/zebu had a girl's name, Lily I think, although it was manifestly male. Sylvester explained that they are always called after a female ancestor, to state the genetic link. Only the males 'work': "the females just have babies", he explained.

We were dropped off and took a short walk to a white soft sandy beach with stunning massive worn granite boulders – and I had more kopje flashbacks. I joined some of the others for a heavenly swim, wriggling into my costume as modestly as I could, and was reminded of the old Northam Burrows days at home, although there the temperature was seldom as comfortable.

It was time to walk back to the oxcart, and en route I fell for some locally made earrings, as I am inclined to do, and put these little treasures carefully away.

14 February 2007
The Ubiquitous Tortoise   LA DIGUE

On board, Conrad, our expedition leader, read us a story from 'When Lion Could Fly', a collection of tales from Africa. It smacked a little of Aesop, and I made a mental note to try and get the book. Then there was briefing for the morrow and a recap by Simon, the bird man, highlighting how very fortunate we had been to see the Black Parrot, and the Seychelles Black Flycatcher, which I didn't see! Robin gave a brief dissertation on the marine mollusc called 'Chiton', which had iron-coated teeth for grazing on rocks.

After a shower and change it was time for dinner, which I ate in the company of Janet and Paul and we had another chapter of life-history swapping. Paul had retired comparatively early from life as a lawyer/banker to work for nine years for the Surrey Wildlife Trust. I thought he was very keen and clued up. He had recently retired 'properly'. Janet had done a degree in chemistry and worked in two schools with senior students. Having accepted that they would not have any children after years of waiting, they had adopted a son and then, in that inexplicable way it happens, they produced one of their own. One spoke at Spring Harvest (an interdenominational Christian Conference organisation) – I can't remember what else he did - and the other one worked for the Prince's Trust. Anyway, they were such easy company to be with, and I felt I'd known them for ever. I bought the bottle of wine. Janet and John joined us, as their friends had not appeared, but then they did arrive so they all moved to another table where there were four places. It had been a super and very full day. I went to bed early again, at 10.30 pm.

Postscript: Praslin was originally called Ile de Palmes (very apt) by Lazare Picault in 1744, but the ubiquitous Marion du Fresne renamed it after the French minister of Marine Affairs in 1768.

Poivre - Amirantes Group - Seychelles

POIVRE

Thursday 15th February 2007

I awoke at 7.15 am and enjoyed another fresh fruit breakfast. We were told that Island Sky had never before been to Poivre, the largest atoll of the Amirantes group (which included South Island - joined to Poivre by a man-made causeway at low tide - and Florentin), so this was real expedition stuff. We were anchored off-shore and then transported in the zodiacs for a rather rough and long crossing, via a narrow channel through the reef, to a small landing area. Group 3 was taking its rotating turn of being last this morning, so I had time to just look at the water, the sky and the island: a civilised start, at 9.30 am.

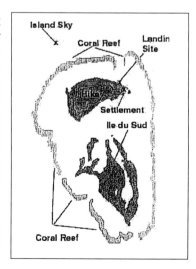

The Reef flats gave easy viewing of a Crab Plover, which I thought was an Egret until corrected. It had much longer legs than the other Plovers. We left our life jackets near some elegant but crumbling buildings, which spoke volumes about the former trading posts and settlements involved in coconuts, green sea snail, tortoisehell and cotton. Now there were plans for building a five-star island resort with lots of beach bungalows, etc. The island was called after the appropriately named Pierre Poivre, former governor of Mauritius (1763 - 1772), who introduced spices to the Seychelles.

This island looked different from the others: no prominent rocks and with just a gentle curve of land above the water. It reminded me of the Maldives. I was in bird-man Simon's group. We walked some distance over what was being prepared as a new airplane landing runway. We marvelled at positively huge Palm Spiders, had good sightings of Grey Heron, Striated Green Heron, more Crab Plovers, Whimbrels, and Lesser Noddies, amongst others. The vegetation was varied and much of it indigenous. Mangroves flourished in the sea water, Casuarina Trees and Sea Lettuce had their individual survival structures. Nature is a genius at adaptation.

At this stage I was not adapting too well. I was uncomfortably hot in spite of having drunk volumes and my hip was objecting, so I followed Judy and Ann back into the shade of the trees en route to the landing beach. I stopped and took photographs and then lost sight of them. Thinking I knew the way, I must have taken a wrong turn but eventually spotted Christopher and Janette in the dim distance. It seemed a long way. I caught them up while Christopher was assembling some of his complicated camera gear to take yet another perfect picture of a large Hermit Crab, and it transpired that they were 'walking round the island ' but were not exactly sure where we were. We made towards the shore, scrambling over felled and fallen trees (me on all fours!) and were reassured to spot the Island Sky within zodiac distance. The beach was beautiful but full of uneven coral. We had been told that the last pick up would be at 2 pm so we thought we had plenty of time.

Suddenly we saw Robin coming towards us. "Are there three of you?" she enquired. Everyone else had gone back. The seas had got rougher so people had been advised to zodiac earlier. She was very kind and didn't rebuke us at all, saying such things as "Sometimes you need to get away from the crowd". I don't remember us confessing that we were sort of lost. The crossing was the roughest to date, managed so well by Robin and Emma. I got really drenched.

I changed and then had a good lunch, with the enjoyable company of Paul and Janet. Snorkelling had been planned for the afternoon but the experts deemed the sea to be too rough. I found myself being almost relieved: I was really tired after the morning's unscheduled adventure and was happy to recline in a shady corner on Deck 6, write my diary, and read about the Seychelles. I suspect I may have had just a little doze.

Robin gave an incredible lecture on Sharks in the late afternoon. Her presentation was excellent - wonderful pictures, and her usual compelling descriptions and accounts of personal encounters. Was there anywhere she had not been …

At 7 pm I went, as invited, to Cabin 336 to have a G and T with Angela and Rosalie. Christopher and Janette, my erstwhile trekking companions, joined us for dinner in the dining room. And afterwards, to bed, at 10.30 pm.

AT SEA !

Friday 16th February 2007

I had something of a colonic disturbance during the night: surely I couldn't be sea-sick? We'd been drifting all night. I had the usual breakfast of fresh luxury fruit, and sat with another Jean (younger and larger than me) and her husband Graham. As many others did, I wandered about on deck and was rewarded with the flash of a sight of a Red-footed Booby catching a flying fish. The latter made me think of large dragon-flies as they propelled themselves several feet, skimming in apparent flight, just above the water, but not always fast enough to avoid predators. We were hoping to spot the odd whale or dolphin but none obliged.

Robin had a stomach upset (so I wasn't the only one) so, sadly, she was unable to give her scheduled lecture on "What's that? An Introduction to Marine Invertebrates", but Simon stepped in and gave a well-informed lecture on the seabirds, some of which we had seen, and whetting our appetite for those we hoped to see. He started off with a photo of the extinct Great Auk and information about fossil findings, and followed on with features about Puffins, Penguins of different varieties such as Emperor, Adele and Gentou, Skuas, Frigates' inability to walk and their lack of feather oil which prevents them from landing on the ocean, Albatross, Shearwaters who cannot walk so that if they land on a ship's rail they have to 'fall off', Prions with their 'sunglasses' of dark patches round the eyes, Gannets with their 'pecking distance' culture, Tropicbirds, and Skimmers.

I lunched on the Lido deck with Angela and Rosalie. Angela was quite recently widowed. Her husband had died after suffering Dementia for some years. She talked of him very lovingly: he had evidently been very supportive and had encouraged her to set up in what was to become a successful General Practice on her own. At present she had concerns about the health of her daughter-in-law. Dear Rosalie had been married to a vet and he had taken up a research post in South Africa, which sounded very exciting but, sadly, the marriage had not worked out, so she had come back to the UK, and worked and brought up her family on her own. Comparatively recently, an old admiring acquaintance had sought her out and they had been happily married for, I think, about 9 years.

The afternoon lecture, while we were at sea, was given by Magnus, on the vexed question of Global Warming. He went through the usual introductory historical facts, El Niño, the bleaching of the coral, 1960s' pictures from space showing the world as a 'blue continent' with 70% water, the incredible rise of recorded carbon dioxide in the half century from 1955 - 2005, no doubt related to industrialisation, the associated transportation, the use of oil and increase in 'greenhouse' gases such as carbon dioxide, nitrous oxide and methane. He talked of the fossil evidence and clues to previous rises in carbon dioxide levels in the Antarctic, how the raising of carbon dioxide produces a rise in temperature, the current visible evidence of the retreat of the glaciers and the collapse of the ice shelf. It seems that temperature change has more impact than the melting of the icebergs, and a rise in sea temperature is associated with more hurricanes. The east coast of Russia is now ice free. The Penguins have noticed and some are moving, to try to regain the conditions they are used to.

Inevitably it was all a bit depressing. We know it has all happened before but not with such speed, and there is unlikely to be time for the world's population to adapt. Magnus' parting shot was for us all to use long life light bulbs! For some reason, maybe because I was really overwhelmed by the Global Warming forecast, but the only other feature of the day scribbled in my diary related to 'Waffles on Deck' at 4 pm!

Angela and Rosalie and I ate dinner with Sarah and Ted, a genteel elderly (that is, even more elderly than us) couple from Surrey.

ALDABRA

Saturday 17th February 2007

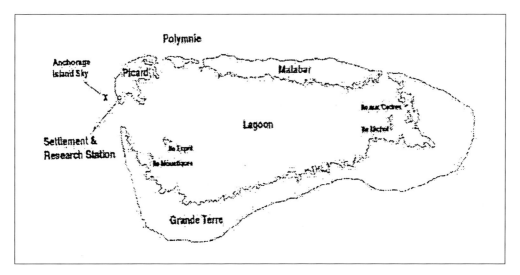

We were anchored off Aldabra and, just after sunrise, following a 6 am call, 'experienced snorkellers' (like myself [?] and Angela) were taken through the Main Passage by Emma and Robin and dropped off from the zodiacs into the world's largest lagoon. The current was so strong that we just floated quite speedily and effortlessly on the surface: it was more like flying. I found it impossible to halt my progress in order to take a second look at anything. The fish were spectacular, the turquoise and green Parrotfish were so large - over 2 ft - that at first I thought they must be something else, likewise the yellow and blue plate-sized Angelfish: an abundance of silvery fish of all sizes slithered about in between the contrasting colours. I had a fleeting view of a moderate-sized Turtle. There was some evidence of the coral bleaching events of 1998 and 2000 but there was also a wealth of colourful healthy colonies. Every now and then, I raised my head to make sure I hadn't been taken too far away from the rest and was rewarded with the sight of Frigate Birds, Red-footed Boobies, and White-tailed Tropicbirds flying overhead. On one of these position checks, I saw Grey Herons standing on the limestone banks of the lagoon. This was one of those experiences that I was sure I would never forget. It was all so rapid and exciting that I more or less gave up trying to master the underwater camera.

This was all over by 9 am. I dried and changed and had breakfast in the restaurant, the Lido deck being closed. I ate with Janet and John and we compared Barrier Reef scuba-diving experiences. Another snorkelling session was scheduled for after breakfast and I thought I'd give it a miss but Angela said "You can'd do that: you'll regret it!" and of course she was right. This time it was from the zodiacs anchored near the ship where there was little or no current and good visibiity, but not as exciting as earlier. The anchor was 'stuck' on 'my' zodiac so we had to transfer to another, where the sides were so hot they burned our bottoms! The water had become very choppy and getting off the zodiac for the Island Sky was the most difficult manoeuvre I'd yet experienced, but I did exactly as directed. Uppermost in my mind was the thought that I must not fall!

Then it was off with the wet and on with the dry again, and to the lounge where Aldabra products were on sale. I bought a well-identified black T-shirt and received a free 2006 calendar to go with it. The calendar photographs were just wonderful whatever the year, and some will feature in my completed diary. All the monies collected from these sales goes back into research and the preservation of the island. I lunched with Janet and Jim and another very pleasant older couple, who had just moved house, down-sizing, "as everyone should do as they get older", he declared. I said nothing.

We had to wait awhile for the tide to be just right before we headed off on the zodiac tour of the lagoon. Once we were through the channel's rushing tide, it was surprisingly calm so that we could see the sinister huge Black Rays, Eagle rays and Mullet Fish, gliding over the sandy bottom. The Mangroves were full of Frigate Birds and Red-footed Boobies, nesting so near to each other that it was strange to think how the Frigates, with their threatening one-and-a-half-metre wingspan, hassle the Boobies when they're carrying food in their beaks or even in their crops. Looking at them now, they presented a perfect diverse community relationship. The Malabar colony of Frigates is said to be the largest in the world and, because of their lifestyle, they are known as 'the Pirates of the Air' and are named after the type of sailboats, the 'frigates' that pirates used to use. We saw one group of Frigates mobbing a Fruit Bat that must have strayed away from home.

We moved gently up and down little passages between the Mangroves, just looking and listening. The birds have no natural land predators and don't often see people, hence they seemed completely unphased by our presence. I spotted a Crab Plover: I'm getting good at those. It was time to return to Island Sky. I'd not seen everyone so enthused and happy as they were that evening. The experience had been so very special, being able as we were just to see the birds, without binoculars or effort of any kind, in such idyllic surroundings.

There was discussion about the name Aldabra, which is thought to have come from an Arabic word meaning 'green'. A green light is said to be seen over the island sometimes - a reflection of light from the shallow green water of this very large lagoon. I looked and looked but I didn't see it.

I dined with Sarah and Ted again, and another senior couple to whom I never did put names, although I think the man might have been Bill.

ALDABRA ATOLL

Sunday 18th February 2007

A 6 am call - Group 3 were first off this morning. I had just coffee for breakfast, as the stomach still felt unsettled. We landed from the zodiacs on to Malabar Island. We felt very privileged when we heard that the Island Sky was the only cruise ship allowed to land its passengers. Lovely inquisitive Aldabra Rails came to meet us. The trail was not so lovely, over old coral and weathered limestone that was extremely rough and sharp. There were proud lumps and then deep pits and I was so glad that, for the first time, I'd taken my stick with me. As it was I managed to graze my legs on the coral, with pain and bleeding out of all proportion to the size of the scratches. I was embarrassed by the sympathy and concern.

Giant Aldabra tortoises wandered about and there was an impressive colourful Robber Crab clinging halfway up a tree. I didn't dare to look about too much: it was imperative that I looked where I was going. We managed to get back to the landing site for the zodiacs before the tides were too low to make it off the island. The water was coming out of the lagoon to meet the incoming tide. We were back by 9.30 am, very wet - again - and I washed and changed and had a coffee.

We sat and talked about the beauty of the Aldabra Atoll. There were some lovely cream flowers with elegant long stamens, maybe the Caper family: I'd picked one to press. The conversation was complemented by a glass of punch served on deck. I talked to one of the local guides, Catriona, who was based in South Africa, a very attractive articulate girl who was doing a bird study on the Aldabra Atoll. We were continually fascinated by watching the water rushing out of the lagoon. She pointed out a rescue boat nearby, ready to take serious emergencies some considerable distance for medical or surgical treatment. "Sometimes it's just not practical" she explained, "and we have to let them die … ".

Before lunch Guy Esperon (the Aldabron Station Manager) gave us a talk about his life as a ranger and research station manager. He told us that Aldabra had been given to humanity by UNESCO, as a World Heritage Site. They were now struggling to block a plan for a 5-star resort, as well as one for a floating resort in the centre of the lagoon. He touched on the Giant Tortoises, which were thought to have come to the island some 125,000 years ago, from either the Comoros or Madagascar. The research station needed a new photocopier, (I think) and he asked for some help. Subsequently a collecting box was placed at reception, where over $800 dollars was collected, and Noble Caledonia promised to match the fund for a high-class photocopier.

After lunch I sat outside until Group 3 was summoned to get into the zodiacs, the tide now being high enough to get over the reef and on to a sandy beach on the island of Picard. We had the 'King of Aldabra', Guy himself, as our guide. His knowledge and enthusiasm made it evident that his heart was in this place. We walked quite a way, seeing the mixture of station buildings, some of wood and colonial looking, others of corrugated iron, and I thought how hot that type must be.

He explained that they were steering in the direction of wind power, which he would dearly like to use instead of oil. Rails kept popping up and we saw more Giant Tortoises, as well as Whitebreasted Crows, Drongos and Sunbirds. It was a slow, easy walk to the lagoon where we saw Egrets, Herons and Turnstones and, after a satisfyingly long gaze around us, the zodiacs came to collect us there, on the calm side of Picard, as the winds had strengthened and the sea had become too rough to use the original landing site. Things change so quickly. How we need the experts!

On return I showered and washed my salty hair and then joined Angela and Rosalie in the lounge for the day's re-cap from Conrad. We ate dinner together and were joined by Jeff and Judith. Jeff had retired young after selling a computer business and had then been able to nurse his wife, who eventually died of her cancer three years ago. He was on holiday with his partner, Judith, a physiotherapist. They were good company.

Monday 19th February 2007

COSMOLEDO ATOLL

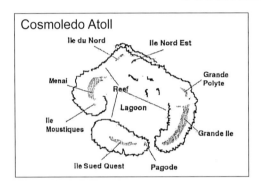

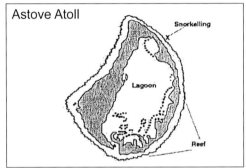

This morning's island visit had been added as an 'extra', to give us the chance to see its large and varied Booby population. We were called at 6 am before the sun had risen - maybe I could get used to these early mornngs? We were to have just 30 minutes ashore to minimize the disturbance to the seabirds. As we landed at Ile du Nord to the north west of the Atoll, we marvelled at the dense scattering of snail shells of various colours and sizes, and were positively amazed when we realised they were all on the move. The shells were, of course, all inhabited by Hermit Crabs. Evidently they had to find bigger premises (shells) every time they moulted. We just stood and took in this unusual picture. It was like a beautiful moving mosaic, and we walked very carefully so as not to tread on them as we went up the beach to see the Masked Boobies.

Masked Boobies were everywhere, chicks, fledglings, attentive adults, and some tucked away cosily on nests under the Octopus bushes all along the coastline. Further back, a few Brown Boobies and Red-footed Boobies sat higher up, some easily visible on the bare branches of a tree.

Frigate Birds swooped and soared about above us, occasionally hassling a Booby sufficiently to make it regurgitate its food – so that they were then able to catch the prize as it fell. Evidently the change of the Booby's call, when full of food, is recognized by the Frigate, which then homes in.

Simon pointed out a less obvious little bird, the Madagascar Cisticola, a somewhat insignificant LBJ (little brown job) until it opened its beak and made a distinctive clicking noise, almost like someone making a disapproving 'tut tut tut'.

It was very wet coming back and the cool soaking was welcome. I changed and had breakfast with Margaret, Christopher and Janette. The free morning that followed provided welcome time for reading and scribbling, and I joined Christopher and Janette again for lunch.

The plan for the afternoon, Island Sky having moved on to the Astove Atoll, further south, gave a choice of snorkelling from anchored zodiacs, or of swimming from the beach. I opted for the latter, having been so enchanted with the morning's beach experience. Conrad and Oliver went out in the scout boat but, with yet another change in the wind and sea conditions, they were unable to find a suitable landing site, even on the leeward side of the island. So the beach excursion was cancelled. Well, you win some, you lose some … I sat on deck and talked to Pam, whose husband Noel had signed up for the snorkelling. He and the other snorkellers had great tales to tell.

Dinner was with Pam and Noel, Margaret and Jim (who had had the misfortune to get his leg trapped between the zodiac and the Island Sky when boarding, and was now having to attend the Russian lady doctor every day), and Jeff and Judith. I sat next to Jim, who was the child of missionaries, and had been born in India.

Once again, it was a thoroughly excellent meal, with interesting company.

MADAGASCAR

Tuesday 20th February 2007

Diego Suarez - Madagascar

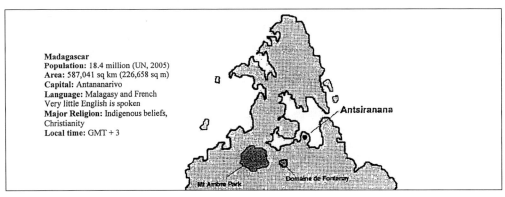

Madagascar
Population: 18.4 million (UN, 2005)
Area: 587,041 sq km (226,658 sq m)
Capital: Antananarivo
Language: Malagasy and French
Very little English is spoken
Major Religion: Indigenous beliefs, Christianity
Local time: GMT + 3

Antsiranana

Mt Ambre Park   Domaine de Fontenay

It was the inclusion of Madagascar in the cruise details that had originally attracted me to this holiday, for I'd had a wonderful three weeks on the island in 2003. When I studied it in more detail I found that we were to call in for just half a day but, by the time I'd realised this, I was hooked on the trip anyway.

During the night we had gone round the north of Madagascar, and in daylight we could see we were near the narrow entrance to the huge Baie du Courrier, in which Diego Suarez (Antsiranana) was situated. The pilot met the ship and guided it to a position alongside the harbour – luxury. We were all feeling wide-awake, after an extra hour's sleep following putting back our watches. I had fresh pineapple and mango for breakfast (I was going to miss this).

Then it was off by coaches to the Domaine de Fontenay, a colonial style estate in the foothills of the higher mountains. Our driver was a pleasant, communicative fellow with a fair bit of comprehensible English. I was lucky enough to get one of the single seats near the front, with a good view and a fair breeze.

It was a lovely drive through the flatlands of the valley up to the moist rainforest slopes of the mountains. I'd read about (and seen) areas of deforestation but the well-established native trees here were untouched. We had occasional unexpected stops as drivers spotted something of interest at the side of the road. The first was the weird and wonderful Oustalet's Chameleon with a prominent crest on its head, followed by other more colourful examples, such as the Panther Chameleon. Guides and drivers drew these to our attention from the coaches and on the forest walk. I doubt we'd have seen them otherwise, and yet they seemed so obvious. We were told about the Chameleon folklore: some of the Malagasy believed that they were their ancestors, others that in-laws must remove one caught in your hair, and yet others that the creatures represented evil.

The walk was very atmospheric, with the special sounds and smells particular to an unspoiled forest. There were Green Geckos, lizards, strange snails and long, shiny Giant Millipedes, fringed with orange legs. Some of the trees had exotic flowers. On the outward trek, we spotted a neat little nest containing three mottled pinkish-red eggs. On the return journey mum had come back: another of those LBJs sitting in the shade – perhaps some kind of warbler or sun bird?

The long-distance views from the occasional gaps in the foliage and trees by the side of the path were breathtaking. The first few spots of refreshing rain dripped through the overhead branches, but came to little. We were introduced by the owner of the estate to what is thought to be the world's oldest tortoise, a handsome monster of a beast, called Galileo and thought to be around 400 years old. I bought a couple of handmade raffia chameleons, said to have been made by local childen, and a bar of vanilla-scented soap at the attractive little shop.

Before we went back for lunch, we stopped off at the immaculately maintained Commonwealth War Cemetery. British forces became involved during the Second World War, in order to forestall possible Japanese seizure of the island, controlled by the French government in Vichy. It was a moving experience reading the headstones with familiar names like Cooke and Mather, and a range of ages from 19 to 44, and of course the grave of the 'unknown soldier'.

I ate lunch with Tom and Sheila, and Sarah and Ted. Then I grabbed one of the few lidos on deck and read, and watched the bay coastline as we sailed off for Mayotte. A special ice-cream tea, with the choice of every flavour you could think of, was served on the Lido deck. A senior Scottish gentleman joined me and asked an awful lot of questions. I said it was like an inquisition, and returned the compliment, during which I discovered he was a retired psychiatrist.

Robin did her lecture on "What's that? - An introduction to Marine Invertebates". As always, she was informative and entertaining. We heard about hard (tropical), and soft corals - "like a jellyfish upside down"; 95% of their nutrients came from the algae with which they had a symbiotic relationship, and only 5% from ingested food.

The sponges received the surrounding water (and food) through small holes, and got rid of the rubbish through larger holes. Some sponges were used cosmetically, but the loofah was a Cucumber plant, not a sponge.

Smooth-shelled snails lived in sand, and some cone-shelled varieties could kill a fish with a morphine-like substance. She told a great story about a young Octopus in a research centre, which could get one of its eight arms through the smallest hole for its 10-prawn supper, and which would not withdraw it until it had had the full 10. "They really can count!". I got a bit lost at that point, but there was some hilarious reference to an Octopus, I think - or perhaps it was a Cuttlefish - thrusting out an arm and depositing sperm behind its partner's nostril.

In the restaurant, for dinner I sat with Angela and Rosalie, and two retired gynaecologists and just one of their wives. The other had succumbed to what was becoming a prevalent chest infection. I wondered if it was being caused by the ship's air-conditioning .....

Wednesday 21st February 2007

MAYOTTE COMOROS

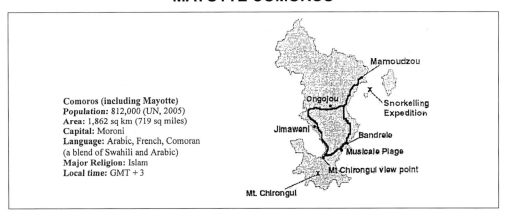

Comoros (including Mayotte)
Population: 812,000 (UN, 2005)
Area: 1,862 sq km (719 sq miles)
Capital: Moroni
Language: Arabic, French, Comoran
(a blend of Swahili and Arabic)
Major Religion: Islam
Local time: GMT + 3

We were still en route for Mayotte through the morning and, after breakfast, the multifaceted Robin gaves us an enlightening lecture on the Coelacanth, thought to have been extinct until a live specimen was found in a fishing trawler catch off East London, South Africa, in 1938. Once interested parties had been alerted, they and others kept a wary eye open for subsequent findings, which had come to light.

Fossils of the fish represented it as existing alive around 66 million years ago. The fish lived at depths of 650 ft to 3000 ft so that it, or its fossil, was unlikely to be found routinely, before the ability to dive to great depths had become possible. It was said to be a cousin to the species that ultimately evolved into amphibians, reptiles, birds and mammals. It had an egg like a grapefruit, and the young developed inside the mother, and at birth they were perfectly formed and mature. One female could produce between 5 and 25 young.

They had ears and DNA like frogs, and gill arches like jawbones that, due to a hinged skull, could open very wide to feed on large prey. They had very sharp teeth with which they grabbed and crushed, thick scales like armour, a swell bladder of oil, and intestines equipped with a spiral valve. The brain was small but the Coelacanth had a special electro-receptor at the end of its head for detecting electrical impulses coming from prey. It was described as a 'living fossil', and a 'prehistoric relic'.

Later in the morning we entered through the northern passage of the Mayotte lagoon and we cruised down to Mamoudzou. The pilot gave Island Sky the easiest clearance yet: he just stepped aboard and said "Ship's cleared!"

Mayotte is one of the four volcanic islands that make up the Comoros, but the only one that is a dependency of France. An influx of French investment has been used well, especially for education but it didn't feel very French. Our guide for the afternoon tour was a French lady, Maryline, who spoke excellent English and who was living in Mayotte with her husband, who was a civil servant on a 4-year teaching contract from the French government. She was enjoying the experience but wouldn't like to stay for ever: she missed 'decent clothes and decent food'. Well, she was French.

During our tour, Maryline told us how the Comoros chain of islands was formed by a 'hot spot'. Mayotte was the oldest volcano in the chain and had already started to subside, becoming an atoll. The newest island, Grand Comoro, was having volcanic activity at present and could 'blow' any day.

We visited the Ylang Ylang eco-museum at Jimawoni, where we identified the attractive Ylang Ylang flower on the trees outside, from which a traditional perfume is made. I bought two small bottles of the local Vanilla.

By a lucky chance, a small group of Maki de Mayotte Lemurs chose to visit a tree behind the centre. They obliged by accepting bits of banana and staying long enough for everyone to take pictures. I took several but something strange happened to my camera and I've kept just one poor example - but the memory is good.

We stopped at a viewpoint to take a look and a photo (better this time) of Mt Chirongui and the Bay of Boueni, and then later at a volcanic black sand beach, where stood the oldest Baobab Tree on the island: it was possibly 800 years old.

I sat with Jeff and Judith for the 6.15 briefing and recap, and then retired to Room 336 to enjoy a drink with Angela and Rosalie. I had dinner with them, and we were also joined by Clare and Bill. I thought how strange it was going to be when I would be eating on my own at home just a week from today.

Thursday 22nd February 2007

PEMBA MOZAMBIQUE - AFRICA

Pemba is the capital of Cabo Delgado province, which borders Tanzania to the north and the Indian Ocean to the east, but we were not arriving there until the afternoon. Hence there was a lecture slot in the morning, when Simon gave an entertaining lecture on marine cetaceans, "Finds, Flippers and Flukes'. Before that I had breakfast with Paul and Janet. The conversation turned to ME, I can't remember how. Janet had worked a lot with young people and seen the effects of this mystery condition.

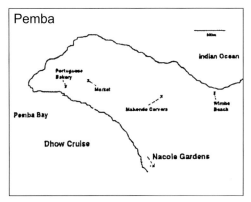

The lecture went over, amongst other things, the means of identifying some of these creatures by tail shape and movements, fin shape and movements, breeching, blow symmetry etc. I think I'd have to see many more of them before I felt confident.

We approached the Pemba pier just before 3 pm. The water in the surrounding bay was deep turqoise. The captain manoeuvred the boat deftly alongside the quay, in spite of there being another cargo ship already berthed. I was allocated to Town Tour bus No 2, with (another) Sylvester as our guide, in the company of Angela and Rosalie. We looked at examples of early 20th century Portuguese architecture and more basic local house construction techniques with a framework of bamboo, filled in with rocks and coral clumps and finally smeared with mud or cement on the outside to create a solid wall. There were stunning views en route, overlooking the bay of Pemba.

We stopped at Mbanguia Market where there was absolutely everything for sale: a true local market, not geared for the tourists. There were buckets, masses of fruit, electrical goods, brightly-coloured lengths of patterned material said to have come from Tanzania, paintings - and jewellery; yes, I bought some more earrings and shell necklaces, with birthday presents in mind.

We visited the Makonde carving cooperative and saw young boy learners, older boys finishing off small pieces and experienced adult professionals with amazing ebony sculptures. (I didn't spot any women apprentices.) There was everything from small snails to large elephants but the most impressive detailed pieces were tall, stylised members of the Makonde. Christopher bought a beautiful Springbok. The Makonde people are said to be fearless, indulge in tattoos and sharpening of the teeth, and are renowned for their initiation rituals with masks and dances. They all looked quiet and ordinary today! Our tour ended at the Dolphin café, which was right on the beach, where there was a choice of mango juice or a common Portuguese speciality of white rum, lemon juice and sugar - which I enjoyed whilst watching a local band playing exciting African music on the beach. We boarded the Island Sky at sunset, in time for the boat to depart at 8 pm.

It had been an action-packed four hours, and we had plenty to talk about over dinner with Angela, Rosalie, Noel and Pam, and Janet and Jonathon (John). Even so, we managed to stray into the medical arena when Janet told us of the long haul they had experienced caring for their daughter who had developed ME at the age of 10. At 28 she is now just about independent, able to work part-time, painting and teaching art, and has her own house. There is still so little we know about this condition. Jonathon was about to become chairman of the PCC: I could imagine he would fit the bill very well.

I went to bed just after 10 pm. The boat was rolling a little but I slept well.

22 February 2007
Colourful Market   PEMBA - MOZAMBIQUE

Friday 23rd February 2007

IBO ISLAND   MOZAMBIQUE

Island Sky had arrived early, at 6 am, off-shore at Ibo Island - before I was awake. We heard how the expedition team had had difficulty in finding a small channel through the sand and reef flats, leading into and out of the island. My Group 3 was called at 8.30 am for the 3-mile trip, a long wet boat ride in spite of the relatively calm seas. Ibo Island - in the Quirimbas Archipelago of Northern Mozambique, now Quirimbas National Park - was invaded by the Portuguese who, in the 1520s, drove out the Arab traders who had been around

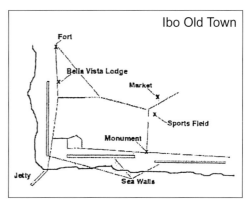

there since the 5th century. They were heavily involved in the trading of slaves, ivory, gold, iron and animal skins, having an important position in the shipping network running along the East African coast, and in moving commodities, from the interior of Mozambique, northwards to Zanzibar and beyond.

Later, in the 18th century, the island's trade links were bolstered by the French who, having been driven from Zanzibar by edict of the Sultan, took their slaves from Ibo to Mauritius and La Reunion. In the fullness of time, when the large trading vessels of the 19th century replaced the dhows and caravels, the harbour was too shallow, and business moved to the natural deep-water port of Pemba.

It was a long hot walk through the ruins of the old Portuguese settlement, and I was not sorry I'd been soaked on the way out. It was like strolling through a colonial ghost town. The elegant, crumbling buildings, some of them with little but a graceful façade, were pleading for restoration. It was all so sad. The three old forts took our attention and, at the Large Fort, deeper emotions were evoked at the sight of the 'Judgment Room' where Portuguese political prisoners were just left to die. Thousands of slaves were said to have been appallingly treated here. It all brought home the harsh realities of the slave trade. I was taken by surprise when a whole group of sparrows appeared, giving voice and pecking some seeds on the ground, as they do.

More cheerful encounters were experienced with the local population who all smiled and welcomed us. We saw some children in their classroom, (footwear all deposited on the ground outside) very neat and tidy, and full of enthusiasm. Later, others were just coming out of morning school: no doubt they had started very early before the day got too hot. They were anxious to talk to us, and some of them had quite a bit of English, which was being encouraged as a second official language after Portuguese. One boy agreed to show me his school book, which was a bit like a Janet and John publication, with a choice of picture answers to the questions at the head of each page. The books were not in English or Portuguese: possibly Swahili?   He said he was going to be President one day! Who knows?

A smiling young woman stood nursing her baby at the side of the path. The infant was well dressed in several layers of clothes (including a woollen knitted hat) but looked cool and comfortable in spite of the heat. I asked his age, imagining him to be a couple of months old, but he was just four weeks. "Well fed", I said. She laughed and put her hand under each bosom in turn, giving it a shake while holding the baby in her other arm. Obviously a good cow.

We went into the local hospital: maternity unit, 4 beds and no doctor: a young child was just having a drip put up. A few people sat waiting for attention. I would have liked to have known more about it but there was no-one to ask. I went into the church. The island people are mostly Muslim, described as 'gentle, religious and rural' and happy to live beside the minority of Catholic Christians. The Christian church had about it an air of poverty of cash but a wealth of loving care. I was fascinated by the collection of 'spare' icons in an unkempt little side chapel, presumably waiting their turn.

We all met back at Bellavista Lodge, a beautiful resting place, somehow incongruously well appointed after what we had seen on the island. It was newly refurbished, owned by one Fiona Record, who seemed very aware of the special nature of the island and its

23 February 2007
A Dance Presentation at BELLA VISTA LODGE

people, and presumably hoped to attract a wealthy, elite, non-intrusive clientele. In the meantime, we enjoyed a cool drink and a local African 'dance' presentation, although this was limited to very expressive body language from eight lovely, seated girls who sang to the young men's ensemble of drums and other instruments. It was charming and they all looked so happy.

The heat was unbearable and unlike other more far-sighted members of the party, I had not taken my bathing costume: even though we had been told there was a pool we could use. I've got this thing about travelling light. I asked Robin what she thought about going in fully clothed - shorts and T-shirt that is. "Just shower first", she advised. I did and then had a glorious dip. There were other opportunities at Bella Vista such as the Nsero face painting, a paste made from the Nsero Bush and applied with a brush made from the coconut tree. It was used traditionally by young girls of marriageable age (16), but also as a protection against the sun, and it was said to keep the skin soft and beautiful. Some of our ladies indulged and the effects were interesting.

There was also a chance to see the unique silver jewelry made on the island, originating with the Indians and the Arabs. It was an alternative to earning a living by fishing, and had (and still has) the traditional unpaid apprenticeship method of learning the skill. The results, all achieved by clever manipulation of the fine silver wire, are just so attractive: yes, I bought a pair of earrings. I then repaired to the balcony of the Lodge, a quiet, well-seated escape, with an unforgettable view, and took Janet and Jonathon's photo as requested. One or two others found their way upstairs also, and we just sat and looked - all except John Topp that is, who sat and slept.

It was time, after a very full morning, to head back to the beach for the zodiacs. I spotted a Yellow-billed Stork and what I can only describe as a toned-down European Roller en route. It was the wettest, longest, roughest ride yet. I did admire our drivers who had to concentrate like hell all the way. After a wash and change I had a pleasant lunch with Graham and the other (larger) Jean, and then as the ship sailed for Kilwa Kisiwani, I grabbed a lounger and took it down to Deck 3 and tried to remember everything for the diary.

Later in the afternoon, Robin gave her "Are the reefs really in danger?" lecture, citing in particular coral bleaching and the coral-eating Crown of Thorns Starfish (COTS), plus global warming, land development, certain agricultural processes and over-fishing in shallow waters. The reefs make an important contribution to the world's biodiversity, and production and research into medical products such as anti-AIDS and anti-cancer drugs. 10% of the world's coral reefs were said to be extinct, 30% in danger, 30% critical and 30% stable. Following natural disasters, the reef either takes much longer to recover or does not recover at all because of the concurrent damage being caused by man.

I had dinner with Angela and Rosalie (it was good to see her recovered after a migraine), Jeff and Judith, Christopher and Janette. Our watches went forward an hour. Help!

Saturday 24th February 2007

KILWA KISIWANI

Very few cruise ships had visited Kilwa Kisiwani on the coast of Tanzania, and it was the first time for Island Sky, so we felt very privileged. The famous ruins were visible from the boat but it took some time to collect together the (internal) local guides whom we were required to have. It was the turn of Group 3 to go ashore first and we got a super guide, with enthusiasm and a good command of English. In view of the famous Mosque ruins that we were to see, someone in the party presumed he was a Muslim but he overheard this comment and said vehemently, "My name is Paul. I am a Christian, like St Paul in the Bible."

Paul filled in some of the historical background, speaking of the Monsoons (from the Arabic word 'season'), the giving of access for the ships, and the agricultural prosperity, which had enabled the establishment of thriving urban areas. There had been trade in spices, ivory (it was a wonder there were any elephants left), ebony, gold, and, of course, slaves. By the 9th century the Muslims, with their adaptable dhows, were more or less in charge of the Indian Ocean, but in the 15th century they were challenged by the Chinese and then by the Portuguese (they really did seem to get everywhere). Their monopoly lasted for a century and a half until, in the late 16th century, the English and the Dutch came on the scene, establishing East India Companies, but by 1650, the Portuguese had again seized control.

Later, in the 18th century, Arab and French interests predominated - in the slave trade in particular. The first Europeans to show any interest in Tanganyika (as it was then called) in the 19th century were missionaries of the Church Missionary Society - Johann Ludwig Krapf and Johannes Rabmann (who reached Kilimanjaro in the late 1840s), followed by Jakob Erhardt and explorers Richard Burton and John Hanning Speke, the latter accompanied on a second trip by J A Grant, in an effort to explore the theory that the Nile rose in Lake Victoria.

Then came the well-known David Livingstone whose objective, when he set out in 1866, was to expose the horrors of the slave trade and, by opening up legitimate trade with the interior, to destroy the slave trade at its roots. The expeditions of Stanley and Cameron followed, but it was Livingstone's work and example that spurred on other missionary societies to take an interest in Africa in the 1860s. (Paul didn't tell us all this but his little snapshots prompted me to read it up later!)

We visited the Great Mosque with its domed chambers, monolithic pillars, and slabs for prayers. It still looked impressively powerful and solid in spite of being virtually in ruins. The small domed mosque looked neat and contained and, maybe because of its size, quite welcoming. The imposing Great House was believed to have been the house of the Imam, or even the Sultan. Then there were the impressive but crumbling tombs in the Malindi cemetery. Strong, studded doorways remained intact, inside the frames of falling stones. We saw the Mkutini Palace, which was built in a triangular shape, and the fort. We walked in between these Unesco World Heritage Site ancient buildings, along the network of local village paths, marvelling at the modern mud and thatch

24 February 2007

Indefatigable ROBIN and local guide PAUL   KILWA KISIWANI

dwellings. The proximity of the two was somehow incongruous, the one highlighting the qualities of the other.

An added bonus for the bird people were many interesting sightings: even I saw a Yellow-billed Kite, Sandpipers of some kind, a Scarlet-chested Sunbird and a Pin-tailed Whydah. Looking at Simon's official list after the holiday, I can't believe that the experts saw so many different species. They couldn't have looked properly at the ruins as well!

It was very hot and we walked for over 2 hours. Our legs were invaded by huge biting ants at one stage, and as I stamped my feet to dislodge them, I caused a dead thorny twig to leap up and seriously scratch my legs, just next to the coral wounds: the ants homed in on the bleeding blemishes immediately.

Paul had been an exceptional guide and I told him so. "Tell my boss" he urged, so I did.

I enjoyed lunch on deck with Paul and Janet, Angela, and Rosalie, and later went to the lounge to hear Magnus' lecture on spices and the importance of the Indian Ocean through the ages in the trading of the same. Cloves, Nutmeg (aphrodisiac?), Saffron,

Cinnamon, and the rest, had all had their moments of pre-eminence but of course every one had special qualities to offer, for those who knew how to use them. The French had been especially aware of their trading value, as they ploughed between East Africa, Mayotte and Madagascar.

Dinner that evening was preceded by the Captain's Farewell Cocktail Party. He made an amusing speech and this was followed by some words from our Expedition Director, Conrad Combrink, a South African whose dulcet tones had aroused us every morning. It was obvious from the way in which they ribbed and set each other up, that they got on exceptionally well - one of the reasons no doubt for the excellent atmosphere on board, and the apparent good relationship between all the staff. I talked to the young cruise pianist, Vladislav, whom I know I have not mentioned before; he was good, but played late into the night in the Club and, with the full programme on board, I needed my sleep. I was persuaded to have my picture taken with him. He would be playing on several more cruises and then going back to do various clubs around Europe.

I ate dinner with Robin, Justin and Rebecca (our young honeymoon couple), and Alistair/ John, a retired Appeal Court Judge, and his wife Glennis, an attractive, communicative lady who had struggled bravely with serious arthritis, in the heat and on the tricky walks. It was humbling to listen to: what was I complaining about?

We felt quite sad that the end of the holiday was looming, but there was still tomorrow ...

I went to bed at 10.30 pm.

Sunday 25th February 2007

ZANZIBAR ISLAND - TANZANIA

We docked at Zanzibar at 8 am. No more zodiac excitement now. Zanzibar was 53 miles long, 24 miles wide and about 22 miles off the African coast and, with Pemba, was probably once part of the African continent. Zanzibar + Pemba + mainland Tanganika = United republic of Tanzania (1964).

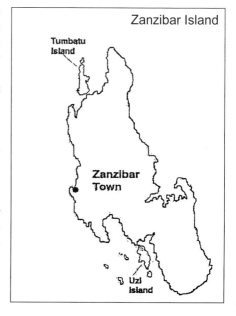

Buses took us off on the Stone Town excursion. We visited Livingstone House, once loaned by the Sultan Seyyid Majid to David Livingstone when he was preparing for his expedition to the mainland in 1866. We passed the Sultan's Palace and then visited the House of Wonders, which now contained, amongst other things, relics of early explorers - including Dr Livingstone's medicine chest; Gizenga Street, with plenty of souvenirs for sale, and sporting many impressive ornate doors; and Tippu Tip's

25 February 2007
SLAVE TRADE MEMORIAL   ZANZIBAR

house (his real name was Hamed bin Mohammed el-Marjebi) with its black and white marble steps and an incredibly beautiful carved Zanzibari door. Hamed bin Mohammed el-Marjebi was a slave-trader who always had red-rimmed eyes, resembling those of a small bird, locally known as tiptip (centropus superciliosus).

Near the old fort we walked round the impressive amphitheatre, and somewhere in that vicinity I spotted a large replica of the Girl Guide traditional badge set into a wall, presumably indicating early Guide headquarters. A sunken memorial to the suffering of the slaves, represented by five stone figures chained together, was beautiful and awful at the same time. This was near the cathedral, which was built on the original site of the slave markets. This was an impressive building, a mixture of Gothic and Arabic architecture in style. It was obviously loved and well cared for. There were beautifully painted Stations of the Cross, raised gleaming copper panels of Melchizedek and others, (whom sadly I did not identify), behind the altar, and colourful stained glass. The atmosphere was calm and peaceful and it was good to sit quietly for a few minutes. There was a strong association with Livingstone and I think I understood the guide to say that his hat was buried nearby. Adjacent to the church were the dark and gloomy slave chambers, where slaves were once housed.

A local Prayer that used to be displayed in the Zanzibar Museum

Please note: this has been reproduced exactly – spelling errors and all!

1. We ask you O our Lord the glorious, so give
   us from your great generocity, clearance in
   our all abouts.

2. And save us from bottlenecks and guide us for
   your generocity, O the one with access
   generocity and riches.

3. And for the great effort and glory that
   lengthened and proceeded its construction.

4. So we ask you O the Merciful to pass to
   those who did wrong among us, that repentance.

5. And give us from you, grace by your wealth
   in a gracious way, and blessing on us.

6. So in your gracious and protection which
   come before every and we have promised
   good dids.

7. And means of living in plenty in comfort
   and give us security and faith and give us
   good garment

8. For your limitless knowledge acceed your
   blessing and give us prosperity in agriculture
   with perpatual livestock.

9. And grow us abundance of grass so as
   to be fed by the livestock.

10. I have with me five people who cool hot
    stream water which burns skin instantly.

11. The Apostle (Muhammad) and Ally and
    their two sons (Hassan and Hussein) and Fatima.

12. So the Almighty God suffice them from
    every evil for he is all hearing, all knowing.

Today is the 16th of the Holy Month of Shaaban
Year 1276 (A.H. (1856 A.D.)

There was time to read a little more about the island before lunch. Today the economy depends on agriculture and fishing: cloves, coconuts, and local food crops such as rice, cassava, yams and tropical fruits flourish, and fish forms an essential part of the diet. But before the development of the eastern African mainland ports, it was the trade focus of the region, accessible to traders and colonists from Arabia, south Asia and the African mainland.

African immigrants were followed by Persians in the 10th century, but it was the entrepreneurial Arabs who became the island's aristocracy. The Portuguese (again) exerted their commercial dominance for a while in the 16th century, but the Omani Arabs were back on the scene by 1650. Turmoil and dynastic wars prompted the ruling sultan of Oman in 1832 to move his capital from Muscat to Zanzibar, which became central to the slave trade in the late 18th and early 19th centuries, with the rapid expansion of the demand for slaves for plantation work in North and South America.

In 1861 Zanzibar separated from Oman, then Great Britain and Germany divided most of Zanzibar's territory between them and in 1890 the British proclaimed a Protectorate over Zanzibar, the Sultan's authority was reduced and the slave trade curtailed. In 1963 the Sultanate regained its independence and became a member of the British Commonwealth.

In January 1964 the Sultanate was overthrown and a Republic established – thus the long-established Arab ruling class had been overthrown by Africans, who now made up the majority of the population. In April 1964 Zanzibar and Tanganyika signed an Act of Union to create Tanzania.

Phew! After all that history, I was ready for lunch.

The afternoon found some of us, devils for punishment, returning to the narrow streets to just wander on our own. Angela and Rosalie and I intended to locate a book shop recommended by Conrad, have a general browse around, and go up on to the balcony of Africa House for tea or a drink of some kind.

For the first time on this holiday, we found ourselves being waylaid by a would-be guide. We decided to let him take us to our destinations and at first he was pleasant and talked about his family, asking us about ours, as he led us along the narrow back streets with towering buildings on either side.

It soon became obvious that he had no idea of the whereabouts of the bookshop or Africa House, and so we gave him a tip and asked him to leave us. It was not going to be that easy. He became frankly abusive and a real nuisance but after we ordered him to be on his way, he shouted the ultimate of all abuses several times and backed off. In the event, we met some of the Island Sky party who had already found the bookshop but it had been closed. However, another shop came into view, selling a variety of things including books, and although I couldn't find 'When Lion Could Fly' I bought a substitute: 'Folktales from Africa'.

We climbed upstairs in Africa House and enjoyed a cool drink with another couple from the ship. The man had spent much of his time fishing from aft, having brought a grand selection of rods with him, and he registered some disappointment at his limited catch.

During the day I'd bought some spices, a book about an Arabian princess from Zanzibar, some 'elephant' earrings (no, not ivory) and - from a colourful market that the locals had set up near the ship - a couple of children's T-shirts and a bracelet. I'd gone mad! Well, it was nearly the last day.

Eventually I went back to the cabin and did the job nobody likes, I packed.

I had a memorable last night dinner with Angela and Rosalie (who else?), Jeff and Judith, and Christopher and Janette, who had all been special company over the whole trip.

We took repeated commemorative photographs and then retired to bed at the traditional 10.30 pm. It was the last night but then we were not going to have a bed on the morrow.

25 February 2007
LE GROUPE
Self, Jeff, Angela, Judy, Janette, Christopher, Rosalie

DAR-ES-SALAAM - TANZANIA

I managed to have my luggage outside the door by 7 am, and settle my account and collect my passport and the Island Sky photo CD by 8 am. After breakfast there was general disembarkation and most of us joined the morning tour of the city of Dar-es-Salaam.

The modern history of the place dates from 1857 when the Sultan of Zanzibar decided to turn the inland creek into a port and trading centre, the name meaning 'Haven of Peace'. When the port of Bagamoyo became impractical for the steamship services, Dar-es-Salaam came into its own, and in 1891 the German High Commissioner transferred the seat of his government there. In 1902 a floating dock became operational and its importance was further enhanced by the construction of the Central Railway to Lake Tanganyika. Now Dar es Salaam is the terminal of the new Tan-Zam Railway, connecting Zambia to Tanzania.

We got sightings of schools, and the impressive University Campus, with its many buildings and long list of available courses, set in vast areas of rolling lawns. We drove through the Mnazi Mmoja Park and saw the Uhuru Torch Monument, symbolising the Freedom Torch placed on the peak of Kilimanjaro in celebration of Tanzania's independence. On the opposite side there was the Republic Fountain, commemorating the founding of the Republic in 1962.

We then went to the Mwenge centre, where we could look again at ebony carvings and other Tanzanian handicrafts. (I bought wooden earrings - they're not all for me – honestly.)

The Village Museum was a ten-kilometre drive out and had a collection of authentically constructed houses of various tribes, with different architectural styles, and building materials ranging from sand, grass, and poles to mud and rock. They all looked substantial and attractive. The Tinga Tinga centre, where local painters displayed their special skills, was fascinating. Time was limited and I dearly wanted to buy one of the colourful examples of distorted animals. I loved one of Guinea Fowl (I think) but we were hustled on. There was a brief opportunity to look at crafts again later, but no-one stirred out of the bus. I said I'd like to look and two others followed suit. By sheer good fortune I ran down one of the Tinga Tinga Guinea Fowl oils on cloth and, after it had been dusted off, I parted with the five dollars needed to make it mine. At the time of writing, it's away being framed.

My favourite memory of Dar es Salaam is the all-too-brief visit to the National Museum. It combined Dr Leakey's finds from the Olduvai Gorge (including the skull of Nutcrackerman and other human fossils), the tracing of the stages of man's development over the last ten million years, references to Darwin's theory of evolution and the work of David Livingstone, a huge preserved specimen exhibit of the Fossil Fish, witchcraft paraphernalia, and a collection of traditional musical instruments from all over Tanzania - all my special interests under one roof – Magic!

Then it was down to earth back at the Holiday Inn, where there were supposed to be rooms in which to relax for the afternoon. It was all a muddle and I ended up dumping the luggage (which mercifully had all arrived from the Island Sky) in a room to be shared by Angela and Rosalie, and Chistopher and Janette. The lunch was OK – but not what we'd become used to - and then I sat outside, listened to some local male singers making a recording, had a swim in the pool after I'd managed to acquire a mattress to come back to, chatted to other swimmers and loungers, and took a picture of a noisy peacock high up in a tree.

Later on we took it in turns to use the shower and change, and assembled in the lounge for the advertised 'cocktails' for which we had to pay! The hot savouries were good and more-ish.

The coaches arrived at around 7 pm and we had a protracted ten-kilometre drive through very heavy traffic, to the airport. Here the heat was almost unbearable except for those who'd bagged one of the few places near a fan. I had a walk round the well-appointed airport shops and found 'When Lion Could Fly', so that was a bonus. The plane was 40 minutes late and we were served with a snack and a glass of orange en route for Nairobi, where we waited one hour and put back our watches 2 hours. This was going to be a long journey.

I was seated next to a man called John Topp, to whom I had not spoken throughout the cruise. I had heard him though! It was evident that he was very knowledgeable in the field of botany, and I'd been impressed by his apparent ability to classify some of the unusual-looking plants we had seen. He'd also sounded very dismissive and rather sarcastic on occasion. However, he turned out to be very pleasant company in a one-to-one situation and I had his life history – a spoiled only child and a 'permanent bachelor', he had wanted to work in films but his parents had steeered him into the navy, from which he had retired at 53. (I imagined him to be now in his early 60s.) He was a member of MENSA for whom he organised meetings up and down the country, and had an OBE for some plant research he'd done in New Zealand. Naturally I then shared some aspects of my life. A lady behind me, whom I suspected had been able to hear our conversation, said "Well, you've got more out of him than I ever did".

I did the mandatory walk, and at the front (first class) I discovered about ten of our party who had obviously paid over the top for the privilege. For some reason they were not the ones I would have expected. I didn't sleep much and felt I was succumbing to the Island Sky bug, as my nose dripped and my throat felt dry. We were aleady late for our connection at Zurich, where we had to go through all the routine checks again. The small size of my luggage was commented upon: this pleased me - some people take so much. I was amazed at their bulk, both main luggage and hand luggage, although there are now supposed to be these restrictions on size for the latter.

On a plane again, I was next to John Topp once more. Jeff and Paul and Janet sat behind so I had some chat with them during this last short component of the flight. The spaghetti supper at 1 am was welcome and tasty.

HEATHROW - LONDON!

It had been Tuesday for some hours of course, because we were late. We had missed our slot over Heathrow and had hovered and hovered … My ears popped, something which had never happened before - I'd got this cold. I was hoping I'd recognize Derek who'd shuttled me down. I'd hardly seen him full face: you don't when you're sitting next to someone. My luggage was one of the last to appear, but as I emerged from the 'Nothing to Declare' channel, there was a young man holding a board with my name on it. I was delighted. "They all said you were on your way … they seemed a friendly lot", he said. This was Kevin from Birmingham, Derek's son-in-law, who had been a partner in the business just since November and who loved Torrington. He preferred driving to working in a factory, as he had done previously. I really took to him as we drove back. He was very family minded (he had two young children) and liked doing the jobs for the elderly and disabled: "It's good for them to get out, and they're so appreciative". He had had several runs with foster children who lived some distance from their school and he talked about their problems. He'd been at the airport for nearly two hours because of our plane's delay, so he'd left home at 3 am. We stopped for a hot drink and he topped up his carbohydrates with a burger.

It was a good run, with little traffic, the house was all in order, and news of all the animals was good. I couldn't face the huge pile of mail just then, so had a snack, unpacked, left 'I'm home' messages on family answerphones, and went upstairs for a kip in my own lovely bed. I always love coming home and on this occasion the daffodils had welcomed me in full bloom – early by usual standards: it was that global warming again. I felt it was spring already.

It had been a really excellent experience. There had been not only the wonderful natural history of so many unspoiled places which I had had the privilege of visiting, but also the visits to historic buildings and the history of the places where they still stood – some of them likely to crumble into obscurity unless someone slapped a preservation or restoration order on them. I'd also experienced the reminders of the activity in the Indian Ocean, and the different races who had dominated the trading through the centuries and, perhaps even more, the reminders of people, slave traders, explorers, and missionaries. It would take me weeks to get my mind in order. I don't know how people go away on one expedition holiday after another: I couldn't absorb it all and hence I don't think I'd really be able to appreciate it.

The locals we'd met, especially the island folk, had been charming, natural, and had seemed pleased to see us. The 'boat people' I'd been with throughout the trip had been good company - from the unexpected Liverpool GP connections, through all the other retired medics, gynaecologists, urologist, paediatrician, psychiatrist, occupational health consultant – as one of them pointed out, we were short only of an anaesthetist! There were younger retired people who'd been bankers, sailors, sold a computer business and of course the honeymoon couple, still working. Others were definitely in their 80s, one or two with mobility problems, but they were game for everything and the helpful expedition staff took them under their wing. As one of them said, "You've got to admire them".

As always, there were a couple of overly-well-spoken travellers who projected their voices above everyone else's, and found fault with almost everything: why do they do that? One of these felt the material at the shoulder of my much-travelled ancient flimsy trouser suit, on a day when I was doing a cover-up because I was a little burnt, and said, "You've had this for some time!". "About 25 years" I replied. "Now what was the make?" she enquired. I honestly could not remember, whereupon she manoeuvred the back of my collar between her finger and thumb. "Oh yes, I remember – I had one the same, years ago but it wore out. Did you buy it in London?" "No, from a catalogue", I replied. She gave me a disparaging look and that was the end of the only conversation (if you could call it that) that I had with her.

And next year? Well, probably it will be to India, to see Helen and family and, while I'm in the subcontinent, to visit the Goan orphanage connection. A more immediate adventure (I hope) is to get my second hip done, and the sooner the better. I was lucky not to come to grief on this holiday, but I got away with the coral walk, not to mention climbing in and out of zodiacs!

INDIAN OCEAN IDYLL

I'm lying out reclining
In Indian Ocean sun
It's hot, it's quiet, it's wonderful
On "Island Sky" cruise run

We're doing Seychelles just now
And visit one each day
See Herons, Whimbrels, Ibis
Strung out across the bay

Clever crabs paraded
As Hermits, Horned Ghosts
I've heard and spotted that Black Parrot
One keen twitcher boasts

Coco de Mer Palms
With the double seed
The largest in the world
The Seychelles unique breed

Cut across it and you'll find
In a transverse section
It's like a woman's pelvis
With serious shell protection

Some islands have got rocks
Zimbabwe kopjes reminders
Once part of one land mass
But that's all well behind us

What an opportunity
Time to watch the birds
A Booby catching flying fish
An instinct without words

The lecturers and guides
With knowledge all-embracing
Their keenness is contagious
Sets the pulses racing

This morning it was sea birds
Shearwater, Skua, Skimmer
Tropic birds and Plovers
The Crab one, taller, slimmer

Ile du Nord is tiny
Unspoiled, undisturbed
Boobies, Masked, Redfooted
Watch us unperturbed

Hermit Crabs abound
We have to tread with care
Through meandering mosaics
In colours rich and rare

Tortoises exhibited
A life of quiet style
Moving slowly, lingering
Meeting Darwin's dial

They don't know how to hurry
And stir emotions fond
Creeping in the undergrowth
A prehistoric bond

The snorkelling is magic
Fish all colours, sizes, shapes
Large Rays bestowing shadows
With fins like curtain drapes

The whole island collection
Is wonderful, unique
But threatened on all sides
By Nature, so to speak

The water's rising daily
The Islands lie so low
In just a few more decades
They will all lie below
The sea which now surrounds them

We know from fossil findings
It's all happened before
But – man's misuse of the world
Brings it closer to the door

Oh listen to the Green ones
We could slow down the track
But now I'm feeling guilty
I've just flown there and back!

February 2007   VJT

286

FAMILY REVISITED

POOJA in PERSON   December 2007

INDIA

with **WEXAS INTERNATIONAL**

I N D I A   Christmas 2007

Friday 21st December 2007

I would be bound for India before the night was over! I went to bed really early, which was a waste of time. My body does not have the early night rhythm. I had made prophylactic farewell calls to the family so that they would not disturb this planned sleep. I suppose I dozed a little, on and off, but I was already wide awake when the telephone alarm went off for the pre-arranged call at 3 am.

Saturday 22nd December 2007 (already!)

The drive to Heathrow was not one I would choose to do any night, but the early morning of the 22nd found long stretches encompassed by a dense fog, which obscured landscapes and landmarks. Kevin had become very well informed on the local community in his four years here, working in the taxi business with his father-in-law and mother-in-law, a business which had been bought from the sale of the previous R and D set up. He talked in his friendly Birmingham tones as he drove, and in so doing I guess he had gleaned much from his passenger clients.

We arrived in plenty of time - to an overcrowded reception area at Terminal 4, where I was directed to wait in a heated marquee until there was room to go to the appropriate waiting queue. My heart sank when flights to Brussels and Geneva were cancelled, but the fog lifted and my 10.45 am flight to Mumbai was only an hour late in taking off. The preliminaries of obtaining one's own boarding pass from a designated machine, baggage drop-off, and a thorough hand luggage search, in separate queues, took three long, standing, hours, and took us well beyond the scheduled take-off time.

Once aboard, in my 41B middle of three seats, I felt mightily relieved to have made it this far. A young Indian gentleman, sitting on my left, slept really heavily for most of the flight, only waking to eat. Just before landing he talked, and told me of his work on a boat with thirteen other men, carrying supplies between oil rigs. This was his second long flight for the journey home, and he was hoping to get a connecting flight to the east coast of India, where he would be spending Christmas with his family. He was on a two-month break, after spending nine months at sea, and his employing company was paying the air fares. He talked of his family with excitement and affection.

On my right, a young Indian woman also slept very deeply and refused the vegetarian meal she had ordered. I was happy to be quiet and was quite sleepy myself but made a good in-road into the addictive "The Kite Runner". I was relieved to actually land in Mumbai, but a further ingredient was added to the waiting game when my green strap sashed luggage was nigh the last to arrive. I further delayed getting out of the airport by mislaying the landing document, which I'd filled out as soon as I'd boarded the plane. The tolerant, smiling, head-swivelling official (who, no doubt, was also tired of the day's waiting game) just asked to look at my passport and waved me on.

My heart leapt with joy to recognize the reassuring face of dear Mark, who took my luggage – the heaviest ever, but then everyone had remembered it was Christmas

– while I got off, literally lightly, with the hand luggage, which was crammed with most of my hot weather clothes.

The quiet, friendly driver, Mehesh, stowed away the luggage and put us both in the back. I suddenly felt wide awake and talked a lot, I know – at one juncture sending poor Mark to sleep. The traffic was amazing, so much, so large, so varied in speed, cargo and decoration – passing inside, outside, in between, even reversing out of one lane into another! This was the second four-hour drive of the day for which I would never want to take the wheel!

Sunday 23rd December 2007

We got to Pune about 6 am (12.30 am in the UK), where I was grateful for a cup of tea, a bed in Frazer's room, in the company of lots of woolly animals, and a deep six-hour sleep. I was vaguely aware of some bird calling outside, which in my sleepy state I decided was a Koel on the lake at home. At one point I dreamed the roof was falling in, but later was told that decorators were busy above, on the first floor.

Helen looked slim and fit, and the children had all changed and grown in the two years since I'd seen them. Frazer, now four and a half, had changed the most and, not surprisingly, didn't remember me. He'd seen his other Granny more recently and I suspect it was she that he'd been expecting. It took a while to get him on my side. Also, it seemed there was a surrogate baby-sitting Granny called Heather, who had found great favour with the children. I was going to have to work on this!

We ate lunch, enjoyed a building game, and then had a walk round the compound, meeting up with students who had stayed at the college over the vacation, and various members of staff, including Heather's pleasant husband, David.

After tea, I did the bedtime story and then unpacked the presents. Mark and Helen produced a bottle of Bombay Sapphire Gin, of which we partook, and I then sank happily into bed.

Monday 24th December 2007 - Christmas Eve

I slept like a top until 8.30 am, and then turned over and slept again until 9 o'clock! After a leisurely breakfast, we went to Victoria Park where the children enjoyed the slides and swings, along with other holidaying families of all shades and sizes, and the grown-ups studied the enormous surface roots of ancient trees, and the horizontal biggest Christmas tree of 150 feet, which had fallen down in 2005. Back at the car park, a lady with a small child begged for money. The car park attendant turned her away and then begged for himself: his patch, I suppose.

Mark drove us back through the nightmare traffic to a coffee shop and restaurant, belonging to a Muslim convert, associated with UBS (Union Biblical Seminary), and his American wife. Their infant, Sophie, added to the interest, and the super sandwiches and chocolate drinks went down a treat.

24 December 2007

Families at the Swings

UNION BIBLICAL SEMINARY COMPOUND

We had a walk round the campus in the afternoon, with frequent stops for chats, where everyone seemed to know everyone else. In spite of having been out for most of the day, Helen had organized a Christmas Eve supper party. The guest list comprised a remarkable family: Indian Jose - originally from Kerala, his American wife Sarah, who was still affected by a serious back injury from which she had made a partial recovery, their baby son Isaiah, and two handsome boys, Bemin and Benjamen whom Jose and Sarah had adopted after the boys' parents, (relatives of Jose) were killed in a road accident – plus an aunty and a niece, and Sarah's friend, Sosa.

The table was repositioned and a second table put up, and everyone was accommodated comfortably, with the children together at one end. We enjoyed a lovely meal and the younger ones helped with the washing up, which was great because Runjuna, Helen's faithful local help, was not coming in on the morrow.

There were lively games after supper, including an energetic "musical statues", and a dancing display by Sarah and Sosa. Everyone left quite early because of the baby. Mark and Helen restored the room to normal and I was actually allowed to dry a few plates. We settled down to a quiet Bombay Gin, while the morrow's presents were sorted – I was relieved to be able to hand everything over – and I had a reasonably early night.

At some time during the night the upstairs neighbours returned and moved furniture about, presumably restoring the flat to normal after the decorators.

Tuesday 25th December 2007 - Christmas Day

I awoke at 8.10 am to find Sarah, Callum and Frazer creeping into the room to see whether I was awake! The traditional present opening followed, with much excitement and trying out of battery-operated toys, including a noisy racetrack. I couldn't begin to understand how they worked.

I did some piano practice with Sarah: she's good and keen. We all attended service at 11.30 am at the Conference Centre, just across the road. I missed St Michael's bells. Students took part and the address was given by the Principal. We sang carols, some of them unfamiliar to me, but the words moved legibly down the screen. Then it was everyone up to the Basket Ball court for an open-air lunch of chicken, pork, vegetarian and perfect rice, plus wonderful pickles etc. We sat with a visiting Indian couple. It was so relaxing to just sit and eat and talk in the warmth of the outdoors, with pleasant shade from the large trees.

There followed entertainment by some of the visiting students, and then some games, including how many straws, and then rubber bands, competitors could put in their hair. I didn't volunteer! During these diversions, a would-be student, involved in a website business, commandeered Helen's attention, wanting to know about enrolment, and I could see she had difficulty in shaking him off after she'd furnished him with the information. As we walked back home down a dry, sandy bank, I managed to slip uncontrollably until grasped by Helen on one side and a miniscule little lady, a student call Aying (I think), on the other – what a powerful grip she had – so that I was saved from hitting the dust.

The house was full of the children's friends, playing with the Laings' new toys. Later, the Fox family, Americans, came for tea: Ruth, Frank, and their sons - two slim, older young men, and their well-covered, cheerful younger brother. Hetoni and Donhring also joined us but left early to prepare a meal for friends at their own home, after we'd all done justice to home-made cakes from the Laing and Fox households.

Wednesday 26th December 2007 - Boxing Day

No-one was on parade before 9 am, which suited me well. I did some piano playing with Sarah, and got back to "The Kite Runner" for a couple of chapters. Runjuna made puri, sort of puffed-up pieces of dough, which we all appreciated

After lunch we met up with Jose and Sarah and family and went to see "The Bee Movie", which was excellent and much enjoyed by children and adults alike, as we drank coke and munched popcorn. It was a hairy drive back home from the cinema.

As we walked over to Sosa's house for supper in the evening, we met Sarah, Jess, Simon and Tim – Australians, who were studying a variety of subjects at university, some of them doing two degree courses simultaneously (evidently this was quite usual in Australia). They were to provide projects for the children during the conference. The first impressions were great.

Sosa's mum, Annie, had prepared a lovely meal for us and it was interesting to listen to her husband, KV, talk about his early life in Kerala, where he was probably the only young man of his community to have had the privilege of an education. He had written a book, which was at the proof stage. Annie taught thirteen five-year–olds at an international school and she talked about her work and her way of disciplining the children. Their son, Richard, joined us later and gulped down his saved dinner.

Later, the families played 'hide and seek', using the 'transformer' (another of those unfathomable Christmas presents) as the object to be discovered in all sorts of clever hidey-holes.

We left about 9.30 pm and, after the children had been tucked up in bed, we settled down for the gin nightcap. I was thinking that I'd got Mark and Helen into bad ways – but they had bought the gin, ostensibly, for me! I found myself talking to Helen about South Mossley Hill Road, Liverpool, where I'd lived from birth until my teens, until after midnight.

Thursday 27th December 2007

Today's plan was to take the long drive to San Skruti to see the gardens there, and to be entertained. It was holiday time with heavy traffic, but Mark got us there safely – only to find that it was closed – so, for us, it was not to be holiday time there. Then we took the equally fascinating return journey, stopping at SRPF, a project owned by the State Registered Police Force. We enjoyed the excellent bird pictures along the entrance drive, and some of the real thing – including Mynas, House Crows, Bee-eaters, and Kingfishers of several kinds.

After coke and snacks, the family took a trip on the lake in the paddle boat and had a closer view of some of the bird life.

Then it was back to our favourite coffee shop for toasted chicken tikka sandwiches and Majorca coffee.

Sarah did her piano stint; the new piece was definitely coming on well. I sat outside behind the house for a while in the afternoon and, when I wasn't fixated on finishing "The Kite Runner", studied the House Crows. Later, Helen drew my attention to a Mongoose, cavorting about along the outside wall. Then … the pressure was off – I'd finished the book, the most compelling I'd read for years. Helen was going to read it now.

The evening World News shocked us with an account of the assassination of Benazir Bhutto in Pakistan.

Friday 28th December 2007

We had a lazy start to the day. Helen and I had planned a little shopping expedition and we picked up Scott (whose birthday it was) and his dad, en route for the town. We parked in an underground car park, beneath a store in which there were rows and rows of attractive Indian colourful cotton tops and trousers on display. I really fancied something in the style of Helen's Christmas Day black and red outfit, but the 'set pieces' all had very long, slim-fitting pull-ons, which then sort of wrinkled to accommodate the shorter legs. I eventually found a toning outfit, although I would be altering the voluminous trousers. I purchased a bottle of Bombay Sapphire so that the gin habit could be continued after I'd left! I also bought a selection of earrings for future birthday presents, etc.

We were well and truly hemmed in when we returned to the car park but, as the habit was here, everyone had left their keys with the attendant, who soon removed the blocking vehicles. Helen drove as one 'qui a l'habitude' in India and we stopped to pick up Katie, one of the Australians, as we entered the campus.

Mark had already started preparing the cold lunch by the time we got back.

We went over to the Conference Hall for introductions, and a series of games intended to help people to get to know each other. One such involved everyone having one half of a pair of well-known quotes or names. I had some Korean name but no-one recognized it or came up with the other half! There were also chopped-up cartoon strips from newspapers, but as they were from Indian publications, I wasn't very good at that either, but at least there was plenty of friendly conversation.

Supper was served in the Conference Hall, as meals would be while the conference lasted. The rice, daal and curry were more than palatable. I could have sworn the curry I ate was meat based, but it was vegetarian. Poppadoms and powerful lime pickle added life and interest. I came back to base and showered while no-one else was waiting.

Saturday 29th December 2007

I got up earlier – at 8 am – to be in the Conference Hall by 9 am to hear a talk by Theodore Srinivasgam, a former marine biologist but someone who had been involved in mission work for many years. I liked his practical approach. 'Healed' was not to be confused with 'saved'; you would not be much use to God if you worked until you dropped; you needed to know your limitations.

I didn't feel too well and blamed the lariam (an anti-malarial drug), so I went back to the house, sat outside, and did some sewing on children's clothes. Runjuna came and studied my needlework and my swollen ankles. She turned on the sprinkler, commenting "Grass green". "Like England", I volunteered. She nodded vigorously and smiled. I walked down to the Conference Hall later and sat outside. The meeting was still in progress, as evidenced by the steady voice of the speaker booming out from upstairs.

OTHERS' LIVES

I marvel at their commitment
Their lives are good and true
But I just don't feel able
To give as they all do

They understand the Scriptures
They read them every day
I enjoy the King James Bible
In a literary way

I can see there is a message
But I love the language too
Other versions just don't reach me
Read by no matter who

Is this a built in prejudice –
A mind that's closed too soon?
I feel safe in my life's cell
And don't ask for the moon

Contentment is a privilege
Has the comfort of a hug
But now I read this through
Is it a trifle smug?

The 'childminder' team was well occupied with the various age groups, Betty coping patiently and imaginatively with a group of four younger boys, including Frazer who was showing signs of rebellion. Eventually the awaited parents came down the outside staircase and families were reunited before going in for the Chinese-style chicken and rice. Diana, a doctor and the wife of the morning's speaker, and Katie, sat on our table, and then Peter joined us. He was another doctor, a Canadian, working in research into TB and AIDS, and with whom Mark hopes to do some walking and climbing in Nepal next spring.

Back at the house, Helen made coffee and tea for Scott, and Cynthia his mum, and a younger couple, Claire and Paul, who were working with HIV children on a two-year commitment. They had worked previously in London with refugees and asylum seekers: Claire's parents had worked in India and her father had become the Principal of All Nations Bible College. They threatened to visit me in the UK!

We had a good supper. I decided I would be doing more rice and daal when I got back home.

Afterwards, we went to see a film in the Conference Hall, "Chak De", which was all about an Indian girls' hockey team who eventually became world champions. It was excellent, with all sorts of underlying messages about community and team work. There were appropriately-timed, noisy reactions from the Australian, English and Indian factions in the audience.

Sunday 30th December 2007

It felt strange not to be at St Michael's. Cynthia and her pretty daughter Sophie came for breakfast, and to put their washing in Helen's machine.

The chorus words on the screen were lagging behind the musicians this morning. Theodore Srinivasgam continued his addresses related to the 2nd Epistle of Paul to Timothy. He talked about facing up to stress and persecution; that zeal and enthusiasm were not enough and that one should share tasks so as not to burn out. He then commented on bad stresses, which could come from the lifestyles of the surrounding community, and from being self-centred and money-based, factors which could lead to distress and depression.

He moved on to speak about stress in families, such as over-emphasis on the ministry, lack of communication and long absences. He talked of some of the causes of stress: cross-culture living, crises, grief, health problems and insecurity. He listed reactions, such as fright, fight, flight, depression and burn out; and suggested areas of practical preparation – social, spiritual, media, and legal. Finally, he stressed the need to teach people to read, pointing out that for non-literate people there were not only no opportunities to improve their lives, but also that illiterate people often didn't want to learn. Diana sat on the front row, signalling how he was progressing in the allotted time scale, but he didn't seem to take that much notice! Afterwards, when the address had ended, coffee followed, and then I sat in the campus garden and wrote a poem about the scenery.

SWITCH-OFF

I sit in a garden of alien trees
With long brown pods of seed
I want to take a full case home
Plant in pots and feed
To see it grow and flourish
In short English summer weather
Produce the fronded leaves
Light as any feather

I know it won't grow strong
Into a fruiting tree
But a short-lived-fledgling plant
Could stir the memory
Of sitting on a dusty seat
Near the Conference Hall
On the thirtieth of December
By a sheltering wall

I loved the peace and warmth
The buzz of study groups
The call of Common Crows
Kites' graceful loops and swoops
A Yellow Labrador walks up
And pushes for attention
He looks well fed and cared for
Unlike others I could mention

The Bougainvillea flourishes
In fulsome crimson glory
A Swallowtail or two
Fly their streamlined story
But now I'll have a walk
To take photos for me
Of flowers and birds and insects
Which others may not see

At lunch a tall lady ("eleven weeks pregnant", she announced), who worked with her husband in water engineering "in a very primitive area on the border of Uttar Pradesh", monopolised me with a detailed tale of woe about her mother coming to live in India and messing up her life. Maybe she was warning me on Helen's behalf! Her quiet, tolerant husband was permanently on the move in an effort to comfort and control their infant son. I had a briefer chat with Iris, a lovely Indian doctor, a widow probably in her late 50s, still working, to whom I promised to give my e-mail address.

Helen did the after-lunch coffee thing again and a collection of Indians accepted her invitation (including Iris). There was also Canadian Robyn, who was working as a staff nurse, funding her own PhD – which was based around the doctor-nurse relationship in working practice. She was a live wire and had everyone listening incredulously when she announced that she'd adopted: but the 'child' was a dog!

I returned to the family sewing and then Cynthia came with another load of washing and we tried to fathom out how to work the machine: it sounded OK. Runjuna was not here today, so I was allowed to wash and dry the dishes (oh, for hot water), and put out the washing, which always dries.

I talked to one Jeremy Biblett in the supper queue: he was reading Mark Tulley's latest book, which he announced had a chapter on psychosexual counselling: I'll have to get it. I then sat with Tiji and his Danish wife, Astrid, and their three fine sons at supper.

Then it was another film. This must be a record for me, three films in a week. "Evan Almighty" was about a modern-day reluctant Noah, with all the animals - and stroppy politicians. I sat next to Kathy, an Australian, who must be the original for Dame Edna Everage. She didn't sit still for a minute, her enthusiasm knowing no bounds, as demonstrated by her dramatic gesticulations during choruses. She was like an eccentric, well-rounded meatball, occasionally dropping off into a sleep of exhaustion, awakening seconds later to return to earnest scribbling on her notepad. She was a long-time Friend of Interserve, who had worked in the Interserve Hebron and Woodstock Schools and would be returning to Australia in January.

Callum and Sarah really enjoyed the film and lingered over the coffee afterwards, while I talked to another Australian, Heather, and to Nick, who introduced the topic of adapting to two sets of roots, one's original homeland and India.

Monday 31st December 2007

Cynthia came for breakfast when we were just surfacing.

Later I listened to Theodore Srinivasgam for the last time. He spoke on shaping up for the ministry, saying that missionaries were the scaffold by which people were given access to God. He said one must move on, hand things on, and delegate as Paul did to Timothy. He also commented on the fact that some missionaries stayed on and created their own empire, and that one should work simply to cover one's needs.

Then it was time for coffee, after which I wrote, walked, and collected seeds.

At lunch I sat with the pharmacist from Nottingham, and Mark and Frazer. I also talked to Fi and Eddy (the Indian 'fish man'), and started to make preparations for Goa tomorrow, planning to take a minimal amount of clothing.

It was New Year's Eve, so a concert had been laid on. The Scottish dancing had Mark, of course, as Master of Ceremonies and, in addition to Korean dancing and an Australian Waltzing Matilda number, and some sketches, Peter and his wife and daughters did a musical number, with singing and guitar.

I didn't stay for the service afterwards but went home with Helen, anticipating the overnight train journey to Goa tomorrow. I really regretted this later, when I heard that one of the Korean ladies, Gloria, who evidently had a beautiful, professionally trained voice, sang Cesar Franck's Panis Angelicus, accompanied by Peter. Callum and Sarah put me to shame, staying up to let in the New Year.

Tuesday 1st January 2008

Mark drove us, and the luggage, in his car to the Fox's house where Frank joined us and accompanied us to the station. Frank then took the car back to UBS. We were in good time, the train arrived punctually, and our booked bunks were easily identified in the full, busy train. Callum and Mark were allocated the top bunks, Sarah and Helen the middle ones, and Frazer and I had the bottom bunks.

The stand-up Indian loo was manageable (oh yes, my hip was fine!). Supper was served at 7.30 pm (instead of 8.30 pm, by special request from Mark) so that we were all settled by 9 pm and had a pretty good night's rest. Action stations started at 5 am and we arrived just after 6 am. The taxi had been pre-booked so there was no waiting around, and in about twenty minutes we were outside L'Amora Hotel in Banavali. There was no-one about but then a young man appeared and gave us a room in which to dump everything. We donned our bathing things and made for the beach and Anthy's. There was not a moment to waste!

Wednesday 2nd January 2008

The twenty-minute walk along the beach was bliss. It was still quite early, the loaded fishing nets were being hauled in and impressive waves broke along the shore. Anthy's (which also had accommodation) was the little restaurant that Helen and Mark always used for breakfast and lunch while staying in Banavali. It was open on all sides, but had both a roof to shelter from the sun, and loungers (free) that were available to clients. It also had pleasant, unhurrying staff, a loo and shower – plus an outside shower … and a few nearby coconut palms to add colour and atmosphere.

I was hungry and broke my usual habit in order to have a decent breakfast, selecting a fresh coconut and honey pancake. It was delicious and became my daily delight. An accompanying chocolate milk shake went down well.

A KIND OF CONTENTMENT

They were there on the station platform
A dark lanky man in check shirt
By a red, white and gold saried lady
They lay partnered close in the dirt

In front of the woman, two children
A girl of about two or three
And next to her a small boy
The mother's right hand on his knee

A loose-woven rug hid them partly
As all four slept quietly together
With a dog either side for comfort
Security, warmth or whatever

After a brief rest on a lounger I headed for the water, which was warm and comforting until a bigger-than-average wave knocked me over, and I had difficulty surfacing before the next one. The trick was to meet them standing sideways on, I discovered. I walked out far enough to be able to have a swim in the calmer waters beyond.

Coming out of the water was just as comfortable as going in – no chilling wind on a wet body. I sat and dried off in the sun and then got out the diary and did a bit of sketching with a biro … a lounger, the sea, a Coconut Palm, something I'd never done before in my life, but I enjoyed my amateur efforts.

We shared different choices of lunch at Anthy's: the prawn dish was particularly good. Then there was more swimming, watching birds and crabs, digging in the sand and seeing folk paragliding out over the water. It was idyllic.

We had been allocated Rooms 8 and 9 by the time we got back to L'Amora. En route I had managed to fall heavily (over nothing) but miraculously didn't seem to have done any serious damage other than bruising the right side of both knees. I really should learn to pick my feet up.

The rooms were pleasant and airy and supplied with an energetic overhead fan. I was to have one of the children in with me each night, and tonight was Callum's turn. Mark and Helen had the other two in with them. I showered (with hot water) and changed.

Dinner at L'Amora was great. The staff all knew the family and treated them like old friends. I had the mussels, which were presented in some amazing sauce that I'd never tasted before, but it was delicious. I wrote up my diary while the children were seen into bed and then Mark and Helen and I chatted in the restaurant over a glass of port wine and took off for bed at 10 pm. Callum slept quietly so far as I was aware and I slept well until 8 am.

Thursday 3rd January 2008

This morning Helen and I were to have a massage at a small establishment behind Anthy's so, after breakfast, I presented myself - only to find that there had been some confusion about the appointment time. At 12 noon the masseuse, Mary, arrived and I subjected myself to her attentions. She was small but powerful, worked on me for half an hour, and my neck and back had never felt anything like it. Ouch! But my neck was less stiff after her treatment. "We don't get arthritis in India. It is your climate in England". She studied my hip replacement scars. "If you'd had massage sooner, you wouldn't have needed those". Who knows?

I had a long swim and then helped Sarah and Callum with their castle building, and mused that two beach castles never look the same, even with the same architects! Back at Anthy's, a family of several generations had arrived and there was chatter about sun-block, Indian food, smoking (in which several of them were indulging) and some good-natured cross-cultural exchanges with the staff. This provided some entertainment over lunch.

BEACH PEOPLE

A Goan beach of contrasts
Dark-eyed beauties selling wares
In brightly-coloured saris
Usually in pairs
One with a small daughter
Impossible to resist
I bought amazing earrings
For birthdays on my list

Others spread out rugs
Patterned, heart-warming and bright
And small enough to manage
On a homeward flight
The vendors are so pleasant
Tho they barely scratch enough
They're patient, sometimes pleading
But survival's made them tough

Their body-covering garb
Contrasts powerfully with some men
Black-skinned with long exposure
The thonged lone fishermen
Other sun-baked people
Who work daily at their tan
As an unhurried option
Like one fat wrinkled man

I wondered if he lived here
Managed others in employ?
He rebuked some nearby youngsters
Quite hard on one small boy
There are women turning sunbeds
For some I make prediction
Of future rodent ulcers
From their every day addiction.

3 January 2008

A GOOD MORNING'S CATCH

Helen and I walked further along the beach to enquire about booking a trip to Old Goa on Saturday. I intended taking another, longer, ride to Assagao to visit Pooja, my special interest, in Rainbow House, one of the houses of the El Shaddai street child rescue centre. The taxi driver, Domingos, to whom we had already talked near L'Amora had at least heard of El Shaddai, which boded well.

After more swimming, and a bit of scribbling, it was time to walk back to L'Amora, shower and change and have supper at nearby Johnsons. A communal plate of chicken tandoori and other menu selections was very welcome. I washed mine down with a fresh lime soda sweet, which was so refreshing. I thought I'd try and make this at home. A vendor with battery-operated multi-coloured flashing candles was an understandable distraction and, after protracted negotiations with Helen, a price was agreed for a selected three (275 rupees). In a matter of minutes, one had ceased to function and Mark was dispatched along the front to change it.

There was ice cream to finish the meal, a few fireworks to watch, and then it was children's bedtime. Sarah would be with me tonight.

The adults had a chat, and the glass of port wine, and then retired just after 10.30 pm.

CASTLE RECALL

A false sense of security
The tide is going out
We'll build a castle that will last
For ever without doubt
Two fathers dig with vigour
Deep and broad and long
(It's for their sons – of course)
They sing a marching song

Their lads have little spades
And tamper at the edges
While dads complete the castle
With fancy crests and ledges
Then a moat is tempered
Ready for the flush
When the tide makes its U-turn
And fills it with a rush

They're concentrating well
Don't notice the conditions
"It's here, look out" the boys yell out
Full of premonitions
How this could mean the end
Of this architectural feat
The dads dig a deep pit –
A transient defeat

To deflect some of the waters
In the destructive tide
Which overflows the moat
And comes in from the side
The castle stands a while
Looking strong and indestructible
Then with foundations flooded
It collapses like a bubble

No doubt in years to come
They'll all remember this
But time will lend a gilding
As to who did all the building
And each will think it's his!

Friday 4th January 2008

We had an 8.30 am start and saw fishing nets being emptied of thousands of silver fish. The women were filling great baskets with them. It was a wonderful photo shot. I had a swim after Anthy's breakfast and then I did some more art work, drawing some of the hundreds of colourful shells.

Today we had rice, prawns and a chicken dish for lunch and then Helen and I went to the shop run by Domingos' wife, just off the beach, where we bought one or two possible presents. We saw the Korean family, friends of Mark and Helen, and the 'puppet man' gave the children an outsize sparkler for later. The shells were especially good at low tide today. I kept on collecting a few. Sarah and I each had our own special favourites. I was not sure exactly what I was going to do with them, but I reckoned I'd think of some way of including them in one of my school assembly talks —and others would grace the top of the soil around my houseplants. (I had just heard that it was snowing in Devon: hard to imagine from here …).

After another swim it was back for the shower and change. A handsome, large frog hopped about the room that Callum would be sharing with me tonight. I tried to ring Rainbow House but there was no reply from one number, and another, I was informed in clipped Indian tones, "does not exist". I phoned the El Shaddai office in the UK three times during the day but just got the answerphone. I would have so liked to see Pooja.

Over a L'Amora supper of various kebabs (Callum opted for shark!) Frazer amazed us by asking the difference between 'damage' and 'destroy'.

While the children were being settled into bed I walked down the road and bought some Alexander stone drop earrings that I'd looked at the night before. They appeared blue in the daylight and ruby-coloured in the electric light - and they were lovely.

After more adult chat and more port wine it was bed, at 10.15 pm.

Saturday 5th January 2008

Today we had a 7.30 am start in preparation for a trip to the Sahakari Spice Farm. Domingos collected us promptly for the 45-minute ride and we stopped for a snack breakfast on the way. We passed innumerable small, well-kept churches en route, and every now and then our driver crossed himself.

We were greeted with showers of petals and garlands of flowers, and our guide, Syd, had a degree in botany and was now studying for a PhD in the extraction of oil from plants. He was patient and pleasant and very knowledgeable about the plants, but knew little about birds, which seemed surprising when there was a wealth of twitchers' material in the high branches of many of the tall trees - such as a variety of Bee-eaters and Kingfishers, which Helen identified with her binoculars.

CREDIT AND DEBIT

To line a waiting nest
A House Crow shreds blue string
Steadying it with beak and claw
Then taking to the wing

Further down the beach
A Tern lies soaked and dead
With blue string meshed around its legs
And underneath its head

Is this fishing tackle
Or lazy throw-away?
Gave comfort for the House Crow -
The Tern its final day

Birds select their rubble
Adaptation they do well
But now we pierce too many holes
In nature's vulnerable shell

4 January 2008
WAITING FOR THE MORROW

But Syd was great on the spices, as one would expect. He showed us the Coffee Beans, the male containing two seeds and the female just one. The Peppers are the king of spices, he announced, and we looked at the green, unripe ones, then brilliant red ones, which are dried until they become white. The cases are then removed and the seeds are dried until they are black.

We handled Vanilla pods as they grew - the second most expensive spice, after Saffron. Vanilla's arrival in Goa had an interesting history and was introduced into Pondicherry by the French, who had probably got it from their Madagascar, which was the only place where the 'right' insects existed to do the pollination. Such insects being absent from Goa, the plant was pollinated by hand by groups of schoolchildren in the holidays! This same, more reliable, technique was now used in Madagascar. Having visited all these places, I enjoyed the unexpected connection.

We looked at Turmeric root, which I thought resembled root Ginger. The size of tiny Red Chillies belied their strength: we were told that they were 2400 times more powerful than your average Chilli! Green, unripe Cloves didn't look like Cloves, but would become brown as they ripened. Nutmeg, Cinnamon, and Alspice were all grown on this plantation, as were Betelnut Palms, Coconut Palms and Bananas, and fruits, including Papaya, Mango and Pineapple. A resident 'Tarzan' bound his feet together and shinned up one of the palms. This experience was offered to anyone brave enough to have a go, as did Callum, whose tree-climbing skills were well known on the campus, and he gave an impressive performance. Mark made the essential recording.

I was taken by surprise to come across Friesian Cows, sitting contentedly as they munched away in an open barn. They provided milk of course but their dung, together with the vegetable waste, provided compost - and a methane plant was attached to the dairy. Syd showed us a Cashew Liquor distillation unit during our tour.

Elephant dung also added to the compost, and Helen and the children (having come prepared, with their bathing costumes) opted for a shower in the river from the elephant's trunk as they huddled together on his back! They were really dowsed several times, Frazer almost hidden from view as he sheltered between Helen and Sarah. Helen had a well-deserved go on her own at the finish.

The buffet lunch, which followed, was in traditional village style, and good - with fresh fruit, including heaps of bananas, on offer afterwards, while a group of young women sang and danced just below the restaurant. The services of an Ayurvedic doctor, and masseurs, were available, but we'd done that. I bought some spiced honey, and then it was back to L'Amora to change for the beach. Mark helped me to send an e-mail to the UK El Shaddai office from an establishment opposite. We met the Koreans as we walked towards Anthy's, and Gloria told me that she was disappointed that she had not

5 January 2008
Lunch at SAHAKARI SPICE FARM - suitably adorned

been able to get hold of me to sing with her the previous evening. They were leaving today, but she said that she might come to see me if they came to the UK: I'd better start practising!

The beach was looking particularly inviting, with a very low tide, and hundreds of wonderful shells. We walked and swam and had a coffee: this was the life. A large dog, with a touch of the Great Dane, had taken over the Anthy territory and upset some of the regular canine population. It belonged to a resident in India, and his visiting earringed brother told us it was a French Muzzie called Basil and that his brother bred them. There was also a smaller dog, called Honey, attached to this party. These men were part of the large family gathering, some chain-smoking, and quite raucous.

Such gatherings fascinate me and I found myself musing that three of the men were probably brothers, and three of the middle-aged women also looked as if they could be related. An older, tanned, anorexic-looking organizing woman could have been the mother of them all. Two young children and a baby, other non-look-alike women, and two older men, completed the party. They were good customers – eating and knocking back the wine and beer. Mark labelled them 'the EastEnders'. Basil was played with enthusiastically by the children, and Frazer joined in the fun, getting scratched and a bit frightened in the process.

The Australian student helpers, Simon, Katie, Jess, Luke, and Tim, from UBS, arrived on the beach, much to the children's delight.

Finally, it was time for a shower and a change, and off to Johnson's for supper. I had a prawn-stuffed poppadum, which was different and very spicy. The restaurant was very full tonight with all sorts of ages, nationalities and dress. As we walked back to L'Amora a lonesome, aggressive Guinea Fowl made its presence heard and felt. I was reminded of home and the fact that the fox had seen off the last of mine just before I came away.

Sunday 6th January 2008

I slept until 8.30 am, as did Sarah. Helen was already out bird-watching. She joined us at Anthy's and, after a wonderful breakfast, I went for a walk along the beach and was approached by a lady and her young daughter selling jewellery. Anticipating the birthday present theme again, I quite fancied some of the very reasonably-priced necklaces and earrings, but I had left my money with the family kit at Anthy's and suggested they came back later. Then, I decided that I should buy now and hurried back to Anthy's, and then back to the other end of the beach where they had met me, but they were nowhere to be seen. I was getting plenty of exercise!

I did the swim with the children, who had already been in the water for ages, and followed it by some shell-spotting, and then we all had lunch at Anthy's: I knew that this idyllic life would come to an end soon, and I found – as I always do after more than two weeks away – that I was already thinking fondly about Heronslake.

RETAIL CHARM

These ladies are so thoughtful
"Would you like a chair?"
Says one, the while my daughter
Studies treasures there

They ask about the family
Work slowly, but not lazy
The lady with the shop
Has a girl called Daisy

Eventually the deal is done
Via a discount range
I know they flatter for return
But such charm makes a change

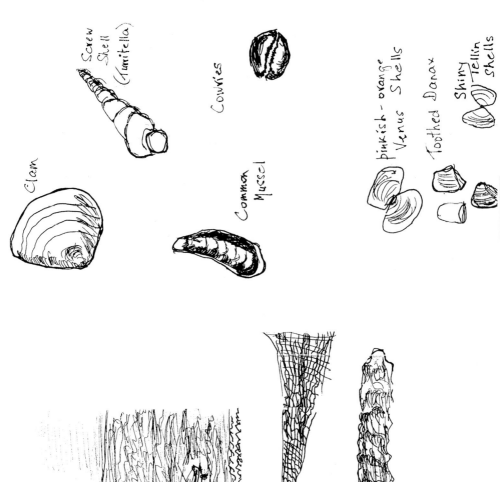

Clam

Screw Shell (Turritella)

Cowries

Common Mussel

pinkish - orange Venus Shells

Toothed Donax

Shiny Tellin shells

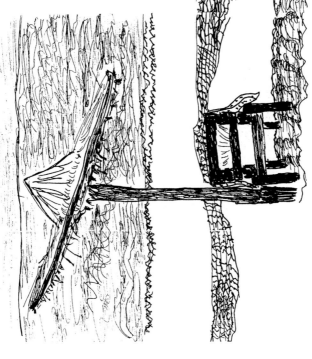

310

NAME AND SHAME

Shell collections left behind
Every single day
The tide drops where it will
Retreating on its way
To linger briefly at low tides
Ready for repeats
With more of shining Tellins
And rarer Venus treats

Toothed Danax looks so incomplete
Dainty, Asymmetrical
Near Cowries shells with open mouths
Both the halves identical
Pale Clams, larger, plentiful
Near Mussels, shaded, dark
And a circle of small blue shells
Round a loner, white and stark

They complete the day
      complete the life
On holiday for me
      shapes and colours
      gleams and sheens
Nature's seaside harmony

SHELLS OF THE SHALE

If only shells could tell their story
Of how they came to bide
Sitting on a beach
At the line of last low tide

They're gathered here and there
In groups of threes, fours, fives
Dainty, shaded, pink in pairs
Some joined like butterflies

Larger ones in cream and tan
With gentle sweeping shape
One pair angled and well-hinged
To give an empty gape

Now they're just adornments
To ignore, collect or please
But they've housed so many creatures
Right across the seas

Superfluous, discarded
Battered by the tide
A few provide new homes
Where Hermit Crabs can hide

Eventually all are ground
By the relentless sea
To finest grains of sand
Replaced by new shells, fresh and free

Helen and I went to book the taxi for Old Goa for tomorrow. Helen's Hindi is really impressive to me (although she is very modest about her linguistic skills) and she knows enough of the culture and language to strike a bargain and command respect. So the taxi was booked for Old Goa in the morning and, cashing in on Helen's expertise, it was also booked for my longer trip to Rainbow House, in Assagao, in the afternoon. I bought a couple of pendants that I'd viewed in the shop the day before, and also a necklace for Helen.

No sooner had we got back to our beach 'den' than the morning vendors reappeared, as did Callum, Sarah and Frazer. I bought my final collection, surprised but delighted that the boys also wanted necklaces. Sarah had earrings as well.

The Australians made an appearance about 5 pm and Callum, Sarah and Frazer went wild. I left the beach just after 6 pm in order to draw out money from the hotel safe, ready for the morrow, and also to take a shower. As I entered L'Amora I came across a wheelchair-bound man, whom I knew must be Claire's brother, Mark, about whom she had talked so much. She had said he would be coming to L'Amora. Sadly, Claire and Paul would not be arriving until after we'd left. Anyway, I went to talk to him, his full-time Polish carer, his beautiful fiancée (whom he had met through the internet), and her young son. He seemed a lovely guy.

The family was just returning when I went down to the dining room. The children had had high jinks with their Australians, swimming and doing cartwheels until the sun went down. I had a fresh lime and soda sweet with a gin (an excellent combination) while I waited.

Monday 7th January 2008

It was a 7.30 am start, with reliable Domingos as prompt as ever. As usual it was a lovely day and not too hot at this hour. We collected delicious hot cinnamon rolls for breakfast en route, and arrived in Old Goa at 10 am. A funeral was in progress at the Cathedral so we postponed going inside until later. We visited the Basilica of Bom Jesus church, where lay the casket containing the remains of St Francis Xavier. These sacred relics were taken in grand procession, to be displayed at Se Cathedral, once a year. We stood and looked respectfully at the beautiful casket, together with many other visitors. The front of the church was covered in scaffolding.

The altar of the Basilica of Bom Jesus church was quite stunningly beautiful, with ornate baroque-style woodwork. The Church of St Francis of Assisi was crowded with sightseers, but we were the only visitors in the neglected-looking little Church of St Catherine. We went back to the Cathedral and the funeral procession was just leaving, with many mourners and several trumpeters, which gave it the ambience of a celebration. Inside, the gold Cathedral altar was very impressive, but the organ was very small. There was a post-funeral sense of reverence as a steward removed the coffin supports on which the body had rested during the service. Finally, we saw the museum, where the inside was under serious repair.

7 January 2008
POOJA, at last!

The whole feeling and architecture of the place was very non-Indian, because of course it was Portuguese. Nevertheless, there were coachloads of Indians visiting the churches, many of them in garb that stated that they were not Christian. We had a drink by a small café, at the centre of acres of church-dotted grassland. I bought some cards to remind me of where I'd been – the camera was not working, but Mark supplied me with copies of some of his own excellent pictures.

The journey back was hot and sticky. We stopped at L'Amora for a wash and change and then proceeded to dear Anthy's, where I had my 'breakfast' fresh coconut and honey pancake for lunch. This afternoon I was hoping to get to Rainbow House and, as arranged, at 2.30 pm I met Domingos at the shop and saw his lovely little daughter Daisy. We picked up the Hindu Holy man just after we'd left base, his bizarre red and white attire complemented by the red band and paint on his face. We dropped him off at a well-built stone house, painted in similar colours. Domingos said what a good man he was. He had predicted that one day Domingos would have his own house (their current abode belongs to his mother-in-law) and that he would have a son next. Should his predictions become manifest, he would like to be paid with 2 kg of selected sweets! Domingos' own father had died of drink (which Domingos never touched) and his mother "is mad". He was one of eleven children, and he and two of his brothers looked after his mother financially.

He seemed happy to talk as we made the hot, two-hour journey to Rainbow House and he asked questions about my family, husband etc, and how old I was. I'd been relieved that at least he'd heard of El Shaddai and, what's more, that he'd taken the trouble to ring his sister, who lived not that far away from the orphanages, and check the directions. As we neared our destination she was standing at the roadside with her son and the 'mad' mother, who did seem a bit strange. Further instructions were given and on we went. Even so, it was difficult, partly because the relevant signs to the various houses that comprised the El Shaddai Trust were being repainted, and were at the blank stage. However, after one helpful roadside direction, I spotted "The House of Kathleen', which I knew was next door to 'Rainbow House'.

Millie, the locum lady in charge, had had notice from the UK office that I was hoping to get there and she welcomed me warmly. Seconds later, Pooja appeared. She was older than I had expected and it was to be her 13th birthday the next day. She was so easy to talk to. She had just got in from school: the uniform was a neat, check, waisted gymslip over a navy shirt. She told me about her schoolwork, which seemed to be going well. She'd got second grades in her exams, with which she had been a little disappointed and hoped to get firsts next time. She'd had a medal for running, of which she was justly proud. When asked about what she'd like to do with her life, she said she liked writing, would like to be a journalist and write stories, and also liked poetry.

She asked about my hip, which was thoughtful, and about my family. She had seen two of her sisters, who lived with 'an aunty' miles away, just once in the last year, but she didn't know where her brothers were. She had a lovely face and was very articulate, in excellent English. I asked whether I was allowed to give her a small present and she nodded vigorously. I handed over one of the necklace and bracelet sets I'd bought on the beach. I wondered about giving her money for her birthday. She said that would be OK and it would go into her personal fund, looked after by the staff. She seemed very

315

happy – and so was I. She showed me round the house, where the girls were doing the routine chores, and introduced me to her best friend. The dormitory had five three-tier bunks, which looked wider than average … they slept two to a bunk!

I was asked to sign the visitors' book, whereupon many other faces appeared, mostly of the younger girls. "What about 'fantastic'?" I asked Pooja. "Oh, yes, that'd be great. What else are you going to put?" I thought for a moment and then wrote 'Everyone here looks well and happy'. Pooja read it and then said, "That'll please them!"

I'd had just an hour and it was time to take the long drive back. I didn't want to leave but I was so glad I'd been. I'd seen this girl whom I'd corresponded with, and supported, for years. I'd talked with her and hugged her. Suddenly she was a very alive human being. She kept waving as I walked away from the shaded front porch and I responded. The camera had functioned for just one picture but it looked good. Domingos had been very patient but he was now anxious to go, and couldn't find his keys. He thought he'd left them in the porch where he had waited but, after much searching, he discovered them still in the outside of the car door.

It was a very hot journey back, with roadworks, plenty of traffic at the end of the day's work, and nobody giving way to anybody, not even to an ambulance with its siren going. At one stretch of the road, scrub was being burnt vigorously on either side, with sparks and bits of burning grass flying over and on to the passing traffic.

It was 7 pm when I got back. I paid Domingos, who had been very helpful, and who was one of the few courteous drivers on the road, and the family was just outward-bound for Johnsons. I had a welcome quick shower and change, and joined them, reviving myself with a fresh lime soda sweet with gin. It had been quite a day.

Tuesday 8th January 2008

This was Leaving Goa Day! I was up at 7.30 am and had my last special pancake at Anthy's. Then, there was a long swim with the family, and an enjoyable walk, when I couldn't resist the last few shells.

A very aggressive man came to take 'our' jewellery vendors off the beach. He confiscated their wares from under a lounger, when they were just selling to a couple of young women there, and he said he was going to take them to the police station to be fined. We asked why, when we enjoyed their presence and had been happy to do business with them. He said that they were not allowed to sell on this bit of the beach, which was under his jurisdiction. I imagined the bush telegraph between the beach vendors had not worked this morning and they'd appeared at the wrong moment. It seemed very unreasonable. They didn't upset anyone and it was much better than begging.

At the end of the morning it was back to L'Amora for a change and a shower, and for finishing the packing in an attempt to vacate the room by 12 noon. We were a bit late, but finished in time to have a good lunch and be ready for the pre-booked taxi to the station – no, not Domingos this time.

8 January 2008

Cartwheel Sunset - FAREWELL TO GOA

The reserved bunks on the train were scattered about for this journey, so negotiations were conducted with the staff and passengers to get a more convenient collection of sleeping facilities. We finished up with the children in three on one side (Frazer on the bottom), Helen and me on the twosome on the adjacent corridor, and Mark next door. I was grateful for the bottom bunk, for even if it did slope towards the floor, at the least the floor was not far away. During the evening, UNO, Nintendo, and snakes and ladders occupied the children, and then a couple of young Indian men played with them indulgently, as they sat on the top corridor bunk, allowing them to use their mobile phones to take their pictures, etc.

Supper came at 8.30 pm. I got two daals but I think this probably suited me better than the spicy alternative. Mark nobly made up the beds. Mine was in the glare of the corridor light and near the door to the loo, but I did get some sleep. Poor Sarah had earache so she was not very comfortable – those underwater somersaults, I suspect. I'd been deaf in one ear for a day.

At about 5 am everyone started stirring, and getting ready for Pune at 6 am.

Wednesday 9th January 2008

The faithful UBS taxi was waiting. It was a comfortable vehicle with a smallish boot for the luggage but with plenty of room for the people. The plan was home and into bed for a couple of hours, but the children were far too wide awake, and played that Nintendo again, and watched the TV. All was well at the house, and the flamboyant Angel Fish, and others in the addictive fish tank, had obviously been well fed and cared for, as arranged, in our absence.

I made the best of the climate and sat outside, scribbling and sketching. After a sandwich lunch, Sarah and I went on a botany expedition, flower book in hand. It was hardly the best time of the year for wild flowers, but we identified a tiny member of the Poinsettia family, a Coat Button, and a Touch-Me-Not, which did its Mimosa collapse as soon as we picked it. We also identified Babel, Banyan, Alder and Rudraksha trees.

Helen and I went to the UBS chapel, which was full for the evening service, many of the students having just returned from the Christmas vacation. A visiting man of some authority spoke, amongst other things, about the Basel Mission, which joined the Church of South India in 1958.

Thursday 10th January 2008

I had a slightly disturbed night due to gastric rumblings.

Sarah and Callum went off to school at 7.30 am, looking very smart in their school uniforms. At 8.45 am Helen and I went with Frazer, who was in his school uniform of yellow shirt and blue shorts and tie, to his school – "Bud and Bloom" – and then on to a 'stainless steel' shop to buy requisites for me to take back to Wendy. It was closed and a neighbour said it would be open "between 10 and 11".

Our timetable was being disrupted. Helen rang Ruth to bring forward our coffee appointment. We went to the Coffee Shop again and had a nice female chat, putting the world to rights in the process. Then we went back to the now-open 'stainless steel' shop, where we chose the tiffin boxes and beakers from an incredible range of goods.

We were tempted into a nearby craft shop that Helen had visited before, and yes, I bought yet more earrings. Then we went to pick up Frazer from his cosy little school, where several of the fourteen yellow and blue youngsters were doing some energetic kicking of a football. They all seemed very happy and the staff were pleasant and welcoming.

We were back at UBS in time for me to accompany Mark to get Callum and Frazer from their school on the campus. It was all very well ordered and disciplined. We spoke to the headmistress and were allowed to collect them from their respective classrooms. There were forty-eight in Sarah's class and thirty-something in Callum's, with 428 in the whole school. The numbers were expected to rise to 700 by the end of 2008. The education was very formal, with frequent compulsory tests, which meant there was plenty of homework. Here again the staff seemed very accommodating and happy to talk to us.

After a cold lunch, Mark did a great job on the computer and got me my Boarding Pass for the morrow. I enjoyed music practice with Sarah for the last time for a while, and then she joined Callum and Frazer in tackling the considerable amount of homework. I repaired outside to do my scribbling.

Heather (the popular surrogate 'Granny') and her husband David – both Australians – came for coffee at 4 pm. Heather was full of the exciting news that her second daughter, who already had four children, was expecting twins: she wondered whether there was an element of competition with number one daughter, who had five children. Heather is lovely, and so patient with the children, and I can see why they are so fond of her.

In the early evening Helen and I went, as promised, to visit a neighbour, Jessie, who apologised for Jacob's (her husband's) absence. She was a relaxed, articulate lady, who made us tea and talked of PhD's. There was a selection of children there, two of whom were hers.

I had expressed a desire to get hold of some handsome, large seed pods, all out of reach high up in the trees I couldn't name. With his climbing skills, Callum had offered to get some for me, and off we went. I was quite relieved when he dislodged some by throwing up sticks and stones. He decided to have some for himself and, when we got back, we planted his in pots in the garden. Mine were carefully packed away in my luggage.

At suppertime we had a barbecue, using secondhand charcoal, Runjuna's tray for collecting leaves, and the grill from the stove. Mark was in charge and served up steak, chicken and sausages. Helen made the sandwiches. Annie called with a letter for Naomi, a teacher and long-time friend of Helen's, who had visited her in India and had given me some educational material to bring out for Annie, who stayed for supper.

I did my Jack Russell bedtime story, and Frazer did David and Goliath.

Helen wrapped things for me to take back for the family, while we chatted and had our last communal Bombay Sapphire – here, anyway! I went to bed at 11 pm but found it difficult to sleep.

Friday 11th January 2008

I was up at 6.30 am, thanks to Helen. I managed to down some cornflakes and a cup of tea. The children were up shortly afterwards, for the early start of their school day. It was quite hard saying goodbye to them and I was comforted by the thought that it wouldn't be long before I saw them in the UK. Dear Callum made an impromptu farewell speech, and Frazer expressed disappointment that I was not staying on as a permanent member of the family. We'd become good friends eventually! Sarah was happy for me to take her mosaic fish art to put on my kitchen door. Of course, I would miss them. It had been a wonderful three weeks, with time to talk to Helen. Mark was very tolerant of our family conversations, and was always at the ready with cups of tea and coffee.

The taxi arrived at 7 am, which seemed very early and I anticipated a long wait at Mumbai. But, as Mark wisely said, "You never know what the traffic will be like". He was right, of course, and because the main road into Mumbai was closed for repairs, everyone was trying alternative routes. The traffic was horrendous as we jerked through villages, amongst other vehicles of all kinds but, in particular, hundreds of black and yellow rickshaws, with deviously skilled drivers, which reminded me of The Bee Movie stars. We passed roadside terraces of all kinds of businesses – shops, dentists, pharmacists, phone sales, marble works, florists, mouth-watering fruit and vegetables, and so on, all presumably making some sort of a living. It was hot and I began to get anxious about our slow progress – but it was so very interesting.

The journey had taken four and three quarter hours and, on arrival, my driver jumped out and commandeered a trolley, which I didn't really need with my wheely luggage. I paid him and then he asked for an English pound, to remember me by! I obliged, and thanked him.

Having already got my boarding pass, thanks to Mark, I was required to queue for only a short time, although a middle-aged man behind me complained that we had to queue at all when we "had all our documents". When our turn came, he very kindly lifted my luggage on to the scales, still grumbling. Security was thorough but efficient. My new hip gave a bleep but it was obviously so common these days that the girl just queried "Hip?" and accepted my affirmative answer.

I was in seat 29H but managed to find a slot for my small bag in overhead locker 28. The couple next to me had an amazing amount of 'hand' luggage. It transpired during the flight that they had been buying curtain material: for the whole house I should think. I couldn't decide about their accent - Tyneside or Scots? – but they volunteered the information that they were from the 'border country', which explained my problem.

The lunch included a hot-ish curry and rice, side salad, yoghurt, strange ground rice sweet, tasteless cheese and a small bottle of red wine. As I sallied to the loo afterwards, a young black chap spoke to me and said he'd seen me on the beach in Goa. I remembered his white girlfriend sitting next to him, and then recalled seeing them together. They'd been to a family wedding in Delhi, holidayed in Goa aftrerwards, and were now going back to their home in London.

I just could not sleep and was envious of my border country neighbours who slept soundly when they weren't eating. Within half an hour of the scheduled landing time, I got down my hand luggage and changed into my faithful, warm, home-coming outfit.

We were just 15 minutes late arriving at Heathrow, and my luggage came more quickly than at Mumbai on the outward journey. A young chap stepped in front of me at the vital moment and separated me from the green strap sashed masterpiece, so that I almost fell (again) in an effort to get hold of it. A fit young lady on my left came to the rescue.

I went through 'nothing to declare' without any trouble but Kevin was not to be seen, with or without a naming board. I waited a while and then made a phone call from an 'assistance' desk, where the lady was very obliging. Kevin's wife said that he had left in plenty of time and she would ring him. The lady at the desk said that I'd have to go to the floor above to be picked up because of repairs 'down below'. I wondered whether it was this that had created a problem. I got the lift and waited at the appropriate Terminal 4 - Exit 2 for nearly two hours.

I obliged a young man with long, fair hair, and took a requested photo of him, with two very attractive dark-skinned girls, with his mobile phone camera. I then asked if I could use the latter facility to make a call. At that very moment Kevin appeared, looking pale and anxious. Was I pleased to see him! The poor fellow had been stuck in floods on the M5 and literally been unable to move. To add to his dilemma, his mobile phone had gone on the blink. It had taken him 6 hours to drive from Torrington to Heathrow.

Once away from the traffic, we stopped for a snack, much needed for Kevin in particular, and then journeyed on, watching reports on the weather and the state of the roads. The floods seemed to have subsided, but somewhere in the region of Cirencester, we ran into heavy snow. It had obliterated the road markings, and covered all the visible vegetation, and was now coming horizontally at the windscreen, obscuring everything ahead. Several cars had already stopped but a few continued to drive like maniacs. Kevin was understandably anxious. I was prepared to spend the night in the car, but he drove on slowly for another ten minutes or so, and suddenly the snow stopped, the road was clear and there was no evidence of recent snow at the roadside – spooky!

We made Heronslake in the early hours. Kevin carried my luggage in, I paid him and thanked him. I dumped the luggage, had a hot drink, a hot bath, and went to bed with the electric blanket full on. It was so cold. I couldn't believe how hot and sticky I'd been, in spite of being scantily clad, less than twenty-four hours earlier. India being five and a half hours ahead, it would be breakfast time in Pune, so I'd been travelling for over 24 hours.

THE ROAD TO BOMBAY

The most-used road to Bombay
Was closed for heavy repair
No visible signs of diversions
Ils n'ont pas l'habitude there!
The taxi driver was skilled
In taking alternative ways
Through haphazard strings of villages
Slowly, with time to gaze
At men in freshly-ironed shirts
Emerging from shanty town hovels
With ladies bright-saried and jewelled
As in Bollywood films and novels.

One woman hung out the washing
On a murky boundary fence
Of irregular iron railings
Shading it well, and thence
With a broom of tight-tied sticks
She swept the dust that keeps
Settling in front of her shack
Inside the stack
Of surrounding throw-away heaps

A standstill later on
Gave a chance to view the shops
And businesses along the route
Marble for great table tops
Pharmacies by the dozen
And dental surgeries too
Phones by Vodafone, IDEA and Samsung
And a fruit shop all painted in blue
The florist's was gloriously colourful
I enjoy the manner of Asians
Stringing the flowers to welcome
And wear for special occasions

The driver's moving on again
He's smart, he doesn't make a fuss
But manoeuvres quietly in between
A TATA and a crowded bus
Rickshaws compete for spaces
Back, front, either side
They insinuate their bodies
For a fascinating ride
They shine in black and yellow
So I'm constantly reminded
Of the bees in that Bee Movie
Purposeful and single-minded

A flock of sheep is shepherded
How they must need some water
Undocked, short-fleeced, grey-headed
I guess they're going for slaughter
Beggars make a bee line
As we stop again
A frail-looking old lady
And two disabled men
Then a fraught young woman
Two children, one quite fat
The other nursed and tiny
In a crimson crocheted hat

Then a startling change
A transvestite in bright green
Glamorous, much-bejewelled
A kind of beggars' Queen!
And so the journey passes
Start, stop, start again
Not a drive that I could do
I paid the driver then
He asked for an English £
To remember me – and take a bet!
I've no need for reminders
That's a trip I'll not forget!

Saturday 12th January 2008

I died but only for three or four hours – sleep was elusive and, after lying awake for some time, I got up at 8 am, hoping that I'd sleep at night if I stayed awake during the day.

I unpacked and did the holiday washing, and rang the family and the neighbours who had been keeping an eye on the place, and spent the rest of the day drifting about doing minor chores. The house was warm with the heating on, but the sky was so grey and sad!

I went to bed early and had a better night's sleep.

Sunday 13th January 2008

I felt a surge of comfort as I got out of the car in Torrington Square and heard the bells of St Michael and All Angels. I'd had a wonderful three weeks, but this was where I belonged!